AFTER WRITING

Challenges in Contemporary Theology

Series Editors: Gareth Jones and Lewis Ayres
University of Birmingham and Trinity College, Dublin

The series will consist of carefully coordinated books which will engage traditional theological concerns with the main challenges to those concerns. Each book will be accessible to graduate students and good undergraduates as well as scholars. The intention of the series is to promote prospective, critical and contentious positions as well as synthetic summaries of the major positions. Volumes will cover fields that have not yet received sufficient theological discussion and will loosely group around the areas of philosophy; culture and media; ethics; and Christian self-definition.

Already Published
These Three are One: The Practice of Trinitarian Theology
David S. Cunningham

After Writing: On The Liturgical Consummation of Philosophy
Catherine Pickstock

Mystical Theology: The Integrity of Spirituality and Theology
Mark McIntosh

Engaging Scripture: A Model for Theological Interpretation
Stephen E. Fowl

Forthcoming
Torture and the Eucharist
William T. Cavanaugh

The Practice of Christian Doctrine
Lewis Ayres

Theology and Mass Communication
Robert Dodaro and John Paul Szura

Alien Sex
Gerard Loughlin

Critical Ecclesiology
Philip D. Kenneson

AFTER WRITING

On the Liturgical Consummation of Philosophy

Catherine Pickstock

BLACKWELL
Publishers

First published 1998
Reprinted 1998, 1999

Blackwell Publishers Ltd
108 Cowley Road
Oxford OX4 1JF, UK

Blackwell Publishers Inc
350 Main Street
Malden, Massachusetts 02148, USA

British Library Cataloguing in Publication Data
A CIP catalogue record for this book is available from the British Library

Library of Congress Cataloging in Publication Data
Pickstock, Catherine
After writing : on the liturgical consummation of philosophy /
Catherine Pickstock.
p. cm.
Includes bibliographical references and index.
ISBN 0–631–20671–X (hardback : alk. paper)
ISBN 0–631–20672–8 (pbk : alk. paper)
1. Language and languages—Religious aspects—Christianity.
2. Writing. 3. Plato. Phaedrus. 4. Derrida, Jacques. 5. Mass.
6. Lord's Supper (Liturgy). 7. Transubstantiation.
8. Postmodernism—Religious aspects—Christianity. I. Title.
BR115.I.25P53   1997   97–8844
190—dc21   CIP

Printed and bound in Great Britain
by MPG Books Ltd, Bodmin, Cornwall

This book is printed on acid-free paper

*For my mother, and
for Olga and Lilian*

How shall I sing that majesty
    Which angels do admire?
Let dust in dust and silence lie;
    Sing, sing, ye heavenly choir.
Thousands of thousands stand around
    Thy throne, O God most high;
Ten thousand times ten thousand sound
    Thy praise; but who am I?

Thy brightness unto them appears,
    Whilst I thy footsteps trace;
A sound of God comes to my ears,
    But they behold thy face.
They sing because thou art their Sun;
    Lord, send a beam on me;
For where heaven is but once begun
    There alleluyas be.

Enlighten with faith's light my heart,
    Inflame it with love's fire;
Then shall I sing and bear a part
    With that celestial choir.
I shall, I fear, be dark and cold,
    With all my fire and light;
Yet when thou dost accept their gold,
    Lord, treasure up my mite.

How great a being, Lord, is thine,
    Which doth all beings keep!
Thy knowledge is the only line
    To sound so vast a deep.
Thou art a sea without a shore,
    A sun without a sphere;
Thy time is now and evermore,
    Thy place is everywhere.

John Mason, *c.* 1645–94

CONTENTS

Acknowledgements   xi
Preface   xii

PART I: THE POLITY OF DEATH   1

1 Socrates Goes Outside the City: Writing and Exteriority 3

  1 Introduction   3
  2 The Plot of the *Phaedrus*   4
  3 The Trade of the Sophists   6
  4 Writing as Capital   7
  5 The Contagion of the Good   11
  6 Platonic versus Derridean Supplementation   20
  7 Plato's return to Myth   23
  8 *Erōs* and Exteriority   27
  9 The Socratic Gaze   32
  10 The Mediations of Egypt   33
  11 Intimations of Doxology   37

2 Spatialization: The Middle of Modernity   47

  1 The New Sophistry   47
  2 Peter Ramus   49
  3 The Cartesian City   57
  4 Reality Without Depth   61
  5 The Written Subject   70
  6 The City of Virtuosi   74
  7 The Theatrical City   81
  8 The Language of Modernity   88
    Nouns: a hardness as of cut stone   89
    Syntax: the contour against the void 95
    The warp of language   98

3 Signs of Death   101

1 The Necrophilia of Modernity   103
2 The Abyssal Gesture   106
3 Indications of Nothing   108
4 Postmodern Parsimony   110
5 A Dismal Sign   114

TRANSITION   119

'Can My Eating Slake Your Hunger?' On The Evacuation
Of Liturgy   121

1 Duns Scotus and the Priority of the Possible   121
  Univocity of Being   122
  The formal distinction   123
  The actual-possible   125
  The thinkable   129
  The eucharist and other possible miracles   131
  The haunted middle   134
2 The Decline of Liturgical Order   135
  Excursus on Scotist politics   135
  Kinship   140
  The economic realm   142
  The civic realm   146
  The juridical realm   149
  The political   152
  Eternal bonds   154
  The rupture of power and love   157
3 The Theological Body   158

PART II: THE SACRED POLIS   167

4 I Will Go Unto The Altar Of God:
  The Impossible Liturgy   169

1 Introduction   169
2 Spatialization and the Liturgy   170
3 The Impossibility of Liturgy   176
  A summary of the mediaeval Roman Rite   178
  The journey's name   180
  The problematic altar   183
  The time of purification   186
  The other offering   190
4 The Apostrophic Voice   192

5 The Permutability of Identity   198
   Divine identifications   203
   Borrowed names   208
6 Liturgical Satire   213
7 Liturgy as both Text and Voice   216

5 Seraphic Voices: The Space of Doxology   220

1 Introduction   220
2 '*Vesper in Ambiguo Est*': The Time of Liturgy   220
3 Christic Asyndeton   223
4 Liturgical Space   228
5 '*Dona Nobis Pacem*': The Liturgical Chronotope   233
6 The Gift of Citizenship   238
   The character of gift   240
   Giving the impossible gift   241
   The impossible return   246
   The gift of being   248

6 The Resurrection Of The Sign   253

1 Transubstantiation: Beyond Presence and Absence   253
2 Eucharistic Scepticism   256
3 Transubstantiation in Aquinas: a Defence   259
4 Transubstantiation as the Condition of Possibility for all Meaning 261
5 The Eucharistic Logos   264

Conclusion   267
Analytical Index   274

ACKNOWLEDGEMENTS

Parts of this essay have been read by the late Professor Gillian Rose, Professor John Clayton, Dr Paul Connerton, Mr Don Cupitt, Dr Eamon Duffy, Mr Timothy Jenkins, Dr Gerard Loughlin, Professor Nicholas Lash, Dr Alison Milbank, Dr Aidan Nichols O.P., Dr Robert Smith, Dr Janet Martin Soskice, and Dr Graham Ward. I am grateful to them for their manifold contributions. I would like in particular to thank the Right Reverend Professor Rowan Williams, and Professor David Ford, who examined this essay in its doctoral guise, for their support of my work, and their helpful advice. I wish to acknowledge gratitude for the friendship, love, and wisdom of my mother, and my dear friends Catherine and Edward Boland, Daphne Llewelyn, Dr Richard Buxton, Janette Gray R.S.M., Anne Dillon, and Dr Alex Walsham. To my father, I give thanks for a lifelong debate regarding theology, and, more recently, for discussions concerning the merits of Monotype Bembo. And for valuable assistance in proofreading, I thank Edward Boland and Dr Andrew Lenox-Conyngham. Thanks are also due to Dr Lewis Ayres, the co-editor of the series in which this book appears, and also to Alison Mudditt, Stephan Chambers, and Martin Davies of Blackwell Publishers. Above all, I thank my doctoral supervisor, Dr John Milbank, for his intellectual generosity and ceaseless encouragement.

I would like to thank the following for permission to reproduce material used in this essay: Fergus Kerr, O.P., for a version of chapter 4, section 2, originally published as "A Short Essay on the Reform of the Liturgy," in *New Blackfriars*, (February, 1997), 56–65; Paul Piccone, for an earlier draft of chapter 1, published as "How Plato Deconstructs Derrida," in *Telos*, (29.1, Spring 1996), 9–44; and the editors of *Modern Theology*, Gregory Jones and James Buckley, for permission to reprint in chapters 3 and 6 sections of my articles "Necrophilia: The Middle of Modernity" (12.4, October, 1996), and "Asyndeton: Syntax and Insanity" (10.4, October, 1994).

I wish to acknowledge various sources of financial assistance: the Clothworkers' Guild (Mary Datchelor Trust), the Mercers' Company, the Burney Studentship (Faculty of Divinity), and the Scholarship Fund of St Deiniol's Library. My thanks, above all, to the Master and Fellows of Emmanuel College for electing me into a Research Fellowship.

PREFACE

This essay completes and surpasses philosophy in the direction, not of nihilism, but of doxology. It shows how philosophy itself, in its Platonic guise, did not assume, as has been thought, a primacy of metaphysical presence, but rather, a primacy of liturgical theory and practice. This same primacy, it claims, was developed, and more consistently realized, in mediaeval Christendom. However, it will also be described how it was during this period that the destruction from within of a liturgical city and a doxologic, took place, culminating eventually in the restoration, during the early modern period and beyond, of those very Greek sophistic positions which the Platonic liturgical philosophy had initially refused. Through a detailed reading of Plato's *Phaedrus*, the mediaeval Roman Rite, and a discussion of the theology of the Eucharist, this essay points out the directions for the restoration of the liturgical order.

The essay falls within the new theological imperative of "radical orthodoxy." This imperative coincides with an increased presence of theology in the domain of public debate. The reason for this is that, on the one hand, postmodernism appears to have foreclosed the possibility of a benign, universal, rationalist humanism, while, on the other hand, it does not seem able to refute the suggestion that it is itself irredeemably nihilistic. Radical orthodoxy, however, has offered a third alternative: while conceding, with postmodernism, the indeterminacy of all our knowledge and experience of selfhood, it construes this shifting flux as a sign of our dependency on a transcendent source which "gives" all reality as a mystery, rather than as adducing our suspension over the void.

This new, more widely disseminated theology insists that the secular postmodern is only the logical outcome of the rationalism of modernity, and in no sense its inversion. And whereas the postmodern indulges in "playful" recuperation of the premodern cultural inheritance, radical orthodoxy rediscovers certain premodern themes as once again viable, by showing how they were not so trammelled by a dogmatic "metaphysics" as both modernists and postmodernists have tended to assume.

The present essay seeks to develop further this enterprise. Its chosen ground is language. This is for two reasons. First, the various versions of the claim that "all is language" is clearly a crucial token of the postmodern. Secondly, one can identify a contradiction within postmodern approaches to language which, after all, permits the possibility of a theological intervention.

The contradiction shows itself in the differing stresses of Derrida as against those of Michel Foucault and Michel de Certeau. For Derrida, it is writing, and not speech, which most reveals language as such, and points to its temporality, indeterminacy, and dominance over the human subject. Foucault and de Certeau, by contrast, stress the growth, from the eleventh century onwards, of the sinister project of *mathēsis* or of "spatializing" knowledge, that is to say, of mapping all knowledge onto a manipulable grid. The chief instrument for this is writing of the kind which Derrida most celebrates. But despite its continuity with the modern, postmodern thinkers often seem to extol the arrival of an "information" culture in which computerized writing flows into an orgiastic excess, deranging our fixed subjectivity and embodied localities. One might well ask whether this culture is not merely a nihilistic extension of the modern *mathēsis*, predicated upon language as an instrument of control by a detached "spiritualized" human self. Does not this culture merely consummate the abolition of time by space?

In the face of this contradiction, I seek to show, first, against Derrida, that the modern, fixed, "metaphysical" interior subject is indeed more linked to writing than to speech. Secondly, I seek to surpass Foucault's wistful regret at the dominance of *mathēsis* to show the grounds on which it can really be challenged.

To the first end, I tackle Derrida's perhaps most crucial engagement: that with Plato's *Phaedrus*, in which he argues that Plato's suspicion of writing establishes the metaphysical, logocentric "presence of self" of philosophy. I seek to demonstrate that, to the contrary, Plato favours orality because of its temporality, open-endedness, and link with physical embodiment. Such a reading offers an instance of the entire recasting of the premodern referred to above.

To the second end, I explain how, for several reasons, Plato considered that orality involved not merely a recognition of our temporality, but also an assumption of the mainly *doxological* character of language. That is to say, language exists primarily, and in the end only has meaning as, the praise of the divine. I show how it is this reference to the transcendent which *alone* allows one to keep space and time in a balanced interplay, avoiding either a spatial degeneration into a dominated presence, or a temporal degeneration into a flux without pause and therefore any real embodiment. (Although I also show how the latter is an extreme moment of the former).

The argument against Derrida is continued by an interpretation of the modern programme of *mathēsis* as, in effect, a realization of the ambition of the sophists, not, as Derrida would imply, of "Platonic metaphysics." The argument with Foucault is similarly extended by showing how he omitted to explain that spatialization came about primarily through the late-mediaeval and early-modern loss of the primacy of the doxological and liturgical within every realm of culture. It is not simply that space came to obliterate time; it is rather that this became necessary because space now had *to substitute for* eternity. Thus, spatialization constitutes a bizarre kind of immanentist ritual, or "anti-ritual," without any ultimate justification except its subordination to the State. As soon as subjects and objects are located within an undying space, they are also paradoxically robbed of life, and of any genuine bodily content. From the outset, *mathēsis* was really an arbitrary ordering of nothing, a nihilistic project in the merely formal interests of control itself. I show how this control was at first explicit, operating through politics, theatre, and science in the baroque epoch. Later it became explicit, operating through the self-control of the individual subject, and through ordinary language itself, whose grammar, as I show in detail, became gradually permeated by spatializing assumptions. Hence, in the nineteenth and twentieth centuries, language has finally become the very opposite of liturgy, although on my construal this means that it must cease to make sense.

As a concomitant of this degeneration, I show how the same spatialization leads to a sundering of life from death, involving an attempt to shore up life against death which paradoxically results in a universal sacrifice to death. This same metaphysical gesture is seen to be perpetuated in postmodern thought, and I describe how an immanentist duality of life and death dominates Derrida's theory of the sign in *Speech and Phenomena*.

All the above occupies the first part of the essay, "*The Polity of Death*." Before going on to articulate the liturgical alternative, I first expound, in the section entitled "*Transition*," how the early-modern shift to the dominance of space, writing, empty subjectivity, and necrophilia was pre-enabled by transformations in late-mediaeval theology, ecclesial, and social practice itself, and, more specifically, within its construal and practice of liturgy and the Eucharist. Before the dominance of sophistic writing could return, the liturgical city had first to forget and misrepresent itself. Our assumptions regarding the liturgical remain so affected by this disaster, that it has to be renarrated if the liturgical imperative is to be fully heeded.

In the second part of the essay, "*The Sacred Polis,*" I show how liturgical language operated in the high Middle Ages, in a period when Christianity had extended and perfected the Platonic doxological account of meaning. I achieve this through a detailed reading of the Roman Rite. Throughout this analysis, I focus on four dichotomies which will have already emerged in part I. These are: (1) language regarded primarily as written, versus language regarded primarily as spoken; (2) a prioritization of space over time, versus a chronotope which resolves the opposition between space and time; (3) a construction of the real as given, versus its construction as gift; (4) the realization of an essentially empty subject (whether self-identical or discontinuous in postmodern fashion), versus an wholly unironical, liturgical subject which is coherent but not foreclosed. Developing these dichotomies, I show how, although liturgy is primarily an oral phenomenon, the Roman Rite achieves a balance between the oral and the written which surpasses the dichotomy in a way most adequate to the echoing of eternity in space and time. Similarly, I show that the space-time dichotomy is surpassed in the direction of regarding both as gift, and, furthermore, as the gift of peace. Finally, I demonstrate that the liturgical subject, although constituted through deferral and supplementation, is nonetheless a coherent and analogically repeated subject, unlike the subject of modernity and postmodernity alike.

All these characteristics of doxology, I argue, permit a co-primacy of sign and body, whereas Derrida's theory of the sign is really predicated upon the body's evacuation. However, the coincidence of sign and body is most manifest in the event of the Eucharist. Moreover, this event, by giving death as life, also overcomes the opposition of death to life, which is a token of modernity and postmodernity. This contrast of perspectives constitutes the fifth dichotomy of the essay.

Not only is the Eucharist invoked as an example of the coincidence of sign and body, death and life. It is also claimed that only a realistic construal of the event of the Eucharist allows us to ground a view of language which does not evacuate the body, and does not give way to necrophilia. Since such an evacuating and necrophiliac account of language also amounts to the claim that meaning is indeterminate and abyssal, my claims about the Eucharist also imply that it grounds meaningful language as such. Indeed, throughout the essay, I suggest that liturgical language is the only language that really makes sense. But the essay builds to a conclusion which asserts that the event of transubstantiation in the Eucharist is the condition of possibility for all human meaning.

PART ONE

THE POLITY OF DEATH

In the struggle for time, state and art must destroy each other, since the state wishes to stop the flow of time, while art would drift in it.

Franz Rosenzweig, *The Star of Redemption*

Chapter One

SOCRATES GOES
OUTSIDE THE CITY:
WRITING AND
EXTERIORITY

1 INTRODUCTION

In the first Part of this essay, I trace the emergence of the unliturgical world, the lineaments of whose struggle to quell the agonies of obsolescence and desire can be seen in the lateral consolations of universalized strongholds, cities whose citizens are regulated either visibly via military force or written contract, or invisibly, via the dissemination of unquestioned assumptions regarding the nature of reality and the human subject. In such immanentist cities, the ideal course involves the eradication of the unknown, the choreography of "spontaneity," and the anticipation of all eventualities via a textual calculus of the "real." These unholy cities which claim clarity and knowledge as their secure foundations, conceal a nihilistic aspect which is the inevitable outcome of a separation of ontology from theology.

In this opening chapter, it will be shown that in Plato's depiction of the ruses of sophistry in the *Phaedrus* (a middle to late dialogue), he critically identifies the incipient structures of the immanentist city, and shows them to have sinister implications for a construal of language and the subject. In particular, I will argue that the sophistic protocols of division and manipulation can be seen to inaugurate a spatial reality without depth, in which a contractualized construction of subjectivity is substituted for genuine civic life grounded upon public, liturgical enactments of citizenship. For Plato, this critique centres upon the nihilistic implications for epistemology and ontology of the sophistic instrumentalization of language, both in their construal of rhetoric, and in their denigration of oral modes of discourse.

This reading of Plato's indictment of sophistry runs counter to that of Jacques Derrida who argues, in "Plato's Pharmacy," that Socrates' critique of writing in the *Phaedrus* implicitly advocates a metaphysical suppression of temporality, supplementarity, and difference in favour of self-presence, organlessness, and interior tranquillity.[1] Once this suppression is deconstructed, according to Derrida, his entire case collapses, revealing a still more radical sophistry. However, it will be shown that Socrates' preference for spoken rather than written language is not a defence of "metaphysical presence" but the *reverse*, an attack on presence. His critique of writing and rhetoric does not presuppose a preference for a supra-linguistic philosophical logos, independent of time and place, but, to the contrary, it is precisely such a preference which Socrates associates with a *sophistic* vision of a purely commercial reality. As heir to this vision, Derrida's insistence on the transcendental *writtenness* of language is revealed to be, after all, a rationalistic gesture which suppresses embodiment and temporality. Is Derrida, therefore, after all, a metaphysician, who does not attain to any genuine account of *différance*?

Instead of the notion that orality is a mask for "presence," it will be shown that orality is primarily linked to an account of the subject as doxological. For in the *Phaedrus* and other Platonic dialogues there are clear indications that the measure of good ethical practice is as much, or more, determined by its orientation towards liturgical praise of the divine as by the ideal of rational contemplation. By drawing attention to these indications, it can be shown, against Derrida, that for Plato, transcendence is not upheld by the notion of an unambiguous "present" truth.

2 THE PLOT OF THE PHAEDRUS

In the *Phaedrus*, the interlocutors, Socrates and Phaedrus, take a walk outside the city walls, along the banks of the river Ilissus. Phaedrus leads his

---

[1] Jacques Derrida, "Plato's Pharmacy," in *idem*, *Dissemination*, tr. Barbara Johnson, (London: Athlone Press, 1981), 63–171. All references to Plato's *Phaedrus*, tr. Harold North Fowler, (Massachusetts: Harvard University Press, 1990), appear in parentheses in the text. A detailing of the historical context and chronological relationship between the *Phaedrus* and Plato's other dialogues is provided in C. J. Rowe's edition of the *Phaedrus*, (Warminster: Arris & Phillips Ltd, 1986), 11–15; see also Thomas M. Robinson, "The Relative Dating of the *Timaeus* and *Phaedrus*," in ed. Livio Rossetti, *Understanding the* Phaedrus: *Proceedings of the II Symposium Platonicum*, (Sankt Augustin: Academia Verlag, 1992), Volume I, 23-30.

companion to a shady arbour where he reads aloud the script of a speech by Lysias which advocates a contractualizing of erotic partnerships for the avoidance of the difficulties – especially the transience – usually experienced in conventional relationships. Socrates is then persuaded against his will (and real opinions) to deliver a rival anti-erotic speech in which he opposes hedonistic pleasure to the good, and explains that these are paralleled by two conflicting principles in the soul: one, the natural desire which aims at pleasure, and the other (*doxa*), which aims for what is best (237d–e). The "non-lover" of Socrates' speech makes no attempt to reconcile these two principles, arguing that pleasure tempts us towards that which is not in our best interests. Thus through the mask of the non-lover, Socrates evokes a "love" of domination which reduces the beloved to the status of an object. Such a stance, while designed to guard against the non-lover's personal suffering, would inevitably cause the (objectified) beloved *a great deal* of suffering. Socrates then abruptly breaks off his speech in horror at his own attack on the higher *erōs*, and utters a recantation, or mythic hymn to Love, in which he contends that the philosophic life is rooted in the "divine" madness of *erōs*, as opposed to purely "mortal" and parsimonious modes of self-control (256e). He enumerates examples of prophetic and religious madness, and then further supports his contention by means both of a myth of the soul, and a theoretical description of philosophic love. In his myth, the immortal souls of both men and gods are likened to a winged chariot pulled by two horses and driven by a charioteer (246a). In divine souls, both horses are well-behaved, but in a human soul, one is good, and the other, lustful (246a–b). Socrates' declared intention in telling the myth is to reconcile erotic passion with the philosophic quest for the good, and at the close of the speech, he describes exemplary philosophic lovers, and the benefits to both lover and beloved reciprocally bestowed via the mediation of erotic beauty. He asserts that both lovers gain a good greater than that attained by either human moderation or divine madness (256b).

Socrates goes on to offer a sustained critique of the methods of "sophistry" in all its guises, including the theory and practice of rhetoricians who give no thought to the soul of their interlocutor, nor the pursuit of truth, and the practices of demythologizers and other practitioners who are concerned only with superficial matters rather than substantive content. He also supplies a myth to illustrate the dangers of displacing speech by writing, as inimical to the philosophic exercise of memory of the good, and the practice of dialectic. The critique of writing is therefore closely linked with an assault upon the sophists, especially the implications for epistemology and ontology of the sophistic instrumentalization of language, through manipulative rhetoric and denigration of the spoken word.[2]

3 THE TRADE OF THE SOPHISTS

Derrida argues that Socrates' critique of writing in the *Phaedrus* implicitly advocates a metaphysical suppression of temporality, supplementarity, and difference in favour of self-presence, organlessness, and interior tranquillity which, for Derrida, are aligned with capital and the king, to the exclusion of all forms of illegitimacy or secondariness. However, it is precisely a sophistic suppression of genuine difference in favour of commercial and manipulative interests – through the instrumentalization of language – which Socrates attacks for being inimical to the practice of dialectical differentiation. For both rhetoric and writing can be characterized by their assimilability to any cause and usefulness in any situation: a kind of saturation of difference which, Socrates implies, reduces to the closure of difference or sheer indifference.[3] It is therefore sophistry and not Socrates which is to be aligned with capital and a suppression of difference.

This alignment is nonetheless part of a subtly drawn and often ambiguous dualism which plays upon the ease with which the components of one category may be mistaken for those of the other, underlining the parodic relation between sophistry and true dialectic. For example, when Phaedrus – a character with whom we align the wavering allegiances of the market – selects the leafy arbour along the banks of the Ilissus and draws his interlocutor's attention to its *pneuma metrion* and soft grass, and speculates on the mythical resonances of the place, his apparent appreciation of specific spatial and mythic differentiations is after all no more than the recognition of a trading opportunity. His intention is to solicit the maximum quantity of speech from Socrates, and when subtle manipulations of ideal circumstances fail to induce his companion to yield this linguistic commodity, Phaedrus is willing to opt for explicit bribery and threats of violence (e.g. 237a). His commercial interest thus instrumentalizes companionship and linguistic interchange alike. Accordingly, his enthusiasm for Lysias' speech is not caused by the fact that what he said was worth saying, but that one could not have said *more* on the topic

---

[2] See further Deborah Tarn Steiner, *The Tyrant's Writ: Myths and Images of Writing in Ancient Greece,* (Princeton: Princeton University Press, 1994), 212–16.

[3] Pierre Rodrigo notes that rhetoric's assimilability to any cause ("*nomadisme*") is continuous with a kind of "*immobilisme,*" in *idem,* "*Dialectique Autochtone et Rhetorique Nomade dans le* Phèdre *de Platon,*" in Rossetti, *op. cit., Understanding the* Phaedrus, 269–74.

than Lysias has said (234e–235b), and the same enthusiasm is instantly transferred to Socrates, when he promises to deliver a speech containing not better, but *more* points than Lysias (235d–236b).[4]

Thus the sophistic consciousness is positioned in relation to the object as capital, of which it sees nothing but infinite variations of an equivalent measure. Such instrumentalized "seeing" is presented as a parodic version of the philosophic gaze, which is compared with that of the possessed poet who sees the events of the past as though he were present at their inception, and that of the lover who on seeing his beloved, recognizes in his beauty a flicker of the good. Whilst the sophistic assessment is fastened to oscillations of value and opinion, and remains entirely alien from its object, the philosophic gaze, in its exercise of *Mnēmē* (recollection), is a penetrative, essential recognition which links the seer to the seen without abolishing the distance of the "object" from the "subject." In this way, the Socratic "object" acquires a transcendent quality before which the philosopher abases himself. Through preserving doxological "distance" in this fashion, the totalizing relation of sophistic subject to object is surpassed.

4 WRITING AS CAPITAL

Now, given this explicit association of sophistry with market values in the *Phaedrus*, it seems curious that Derrida should so insistently align Socratic orality with *capital* and a metaphysics of presence.[5] In his essay, Derrida places much emphasis on the metaphor of *tokos* (interest) used by Socrates in the *Republic* to describe the *ekgonos* (offspring) instead of speaking directly of the good in itself, and Derrida associates this filial metaphor with financial capital and good or goods, in spite of the persistent alignment of writing and "capital" in the *Phaedrus*. In attaching the notion of capital to the good, Derrida is obliged to stress the nature of the good as both an original source and a permanent absence. Yet whilst Plato does *not* construe the good as a non-negotiable radical absence (as will be explained), is not writing itself capital's

---

[4] On Phaedrus' role as "impresario" and commodifier of companionship see G. R. F. Ferrari, *Listening to the Cicadas: A Study of Plato's* Phaedrus, (Cambridge: Cambridge University Press, 1987), 4–9 and *passim*.

[5] Ronna Burger detects in the *Phaedrus* a connection between the love of money and the act of writing. However, I would question her parallel collocation of orality with an equivalent ideal exchange within the soul. I argue below that Socrates' preference for orality over writing is part of an overall critique of the banausic. See Ronna Burger, *Plato's* Phaedrus: *A Defense of a Philosophic Art of Writing*, (Alabama: Alabama University Press, 1980), 28–30.

set of promissory notes, or mere abstract tokens of postponed value? Indeed, Derrida himself defines writing as just such postponed fulfilment, and because for him this postponement is never consummated, it remains tantamount to the emptiness and objectivity of death.[6] His own construal of writing as empty seems therefore very close to that of the sophists and rhetoricians for whom it functions as a mere tool.

Both Derrida and the sophists paradoxically hypostasize writing so that it becomes an ideal science which, like Lysias' scroll, both mystified and appropriated beneath Phaedrus' cloak, can be transferred equivalently to any place, and is unaltered by the passage of time. Phaedrus' concealment of Lysias' scroll beneath his cloak is emblematic of this mystification of the written word as supreme locus of science. It is an act of fetishization realizing a "metaphysics of presence," for the text is at once mysteriously absent and yet explicitly appropriated, as Socrates deftly underlines by his use of the language of ownership and materiality: "Yes, my dear, when you have first shown me what you have (echō) in (en) your left hand, under (hupo) your cloak. For I expect you have the actual discourse (ton logon auton)" (228d–e). Socrates' unexpected preference for a *reading* of this text rather than a duplicitous oral reproduction is continuous with his understanding of the implications of its fetishization, for Phaedrus' proffered *simulated* orality would engage a fully metaphysical obsession with a lost original – as if a speech could be sundered from its real occasion and its written recording permitted its *identical* reproduction. By contrast, an honest reading, confessing its secondariness, would constitute a new and different performance in itself.[7] But for Phaedrus' sophistic consciousness, an origin is enclosed in the past, and despite its absence and irretrievability, is representative of an ideal. Thus, the ideal of Lysias' speech is something Phaedrus wishes to keep for himself and to capitalize on in order to impress others. To this end, the text has various advantages: it is portable, can be possessed and hidden, and it offers a means by which the products of lived time can be spread out in lateral form and kept as an investment for the future. Phaedrus' treatment of the text is therefore predicated on a negative view of time, for by placing such value on the inert spatiality of the written word, he

[6] On the metaphor of *tokos* see Plato, *Republic*, tr. Paul Shovey in eds Edith Hamilton and Huntington Cairns, *The Collected Dialogues*, (Princeton, New Jersey: Princeton University Press, 1961), 506e. Derrida, *op.cit.*, "Plato's Pharmacy," 81–4. On this structural configuration see Rémi Brague, "*En marge de* La pharmacie de Platon *de J. Derrida*," *Revue Philosophique de Louvain*, 71 (1973), 271–77. On the perpetual postponement of the Derridean sign, see Derrida, "Tympan," in *idem*, *Margins of Philosophy*, tr. Alan Bass, (Chicago: Chicago University Press, 1982), ix–xxix; see also chapter 3 below.
[7] Ferrari, *op. cit.*, *Listening to the Cicadas*, 208–9.

seems anxiously to anticipate his own position in the past. In the *Phaedrus*, reliance on the written word is seen as representing an immanentist attempt to *circumvent* temporality and contingency and to spatialize time by gathering up the present moment with a view to offering it to an anonymous posterity, not for the sake of interpersonal benefit through time, but as a means to ensure lasting reputation, a reflexive "gift" which does not freely inhabit time, but seeks to reclaim identically the anterior moment of donation, thus transposing time into a spatial domain (257d–258c).[8]

In keeping with this fetishization of origins, Phaedrus' epistemological concern focuses on the excavation of verifiable facts or unchanging units of knowledge, the dangers of which are implicated for Socrates in his discussion of the practice of demythologization. Whilst Socrates is content to attribute mythic origins to a vague *akoē*, Phaedrus repeatedly asks for precise verification of details regarding whether a particular myth is rooted in fact (228a, 229b–c, 230a), and seems bewildered by Socrates' notion of the relative status of facticity as an epistemological product subordinate to that of knowledge of the self (229e). Phaedrus expresses his sophistic allegiances when he impugns the value of the myth of Thamus and Theuth: "you can easily make up stories" (275b), a scorn which Socrates identifies as a reflex of a modern "wisdom" concerned only with matters of pedigree and empirical fact, unlike the ancient wisdom exemplified by the people of Dodona who were prepared to take heed of the prophetic utterances of oak trees and rocks (275b–c).[9] Phaedrus' thirst for discrete, unchanging, and circumscribable facts is not motivated by a desire to disseminate truth allied to love of the good, but is pursued as an auto-erotic pastime, since the accumulation of empirical and therefore ideal objects of knowledge contrives the same immanentist security as the risk-free arraignment of "erotic" partners advocated in Socrates' *an*erotic speech. Phaedrus' appropriation and concealment of the text embodies this auto-erotic, self-returning rebound, but it also displays two aspects of the commodification of language.

[8] Burger likens the cyclical structure of Lysias' speech to the epitaph on the tombstone of Midas the Phrygian (274d). See Burger, *op. cit.*, *Plato's* Phaedrus, 8–29. The tombstone is the perfect image of the paradigm of sophistic writing because it points to the desired short-cut to immortality sought in the activity of writing. The clausal interchangeability of the epitaph is mirrored by its own unselectivity of recipients, hinting at writing's paradoxical mobility and closure.

[9] Ferrari, *op. cit.*, *Listening to the Cicadas*, 9–12; see also Bruce Gottfried, "Pan, the Cicadas, and Plato's Use of Myth in the *Phaedrus*," in ed. Gerald A. Press, *Plato's Dialogues: New Studies and Interpretations*, (Maryland: Rowman & Littlefield Publishers, Inc., 1993), 179–96.

First, Phaedrus is disposed to treat words as capital, as Socrates reveals in his ironic underestimation of the full extent of his companion's interests regarding the scroll. He detects that Phaedrus had wished to appropriate the text and consume it "from early morning" until he "grew tired," employing the verb *paralambanō* to convey connotations of seizure, occupation, and force, to his action of borrowing the text. This all-too-accurate caricature of his companion follows immediately on from Phaedrus' apparent denial of commercial interest – his claim that he would prefer to have the mnemonic skill to deliver Lysias' speech unaided than have a good sum of money (228a), to which Socrates exclaims, "O Phaedrus! If I don't know Phaedrus, I have forgotten myself." This irony institutes a link between Phaedrus' appropriation of the text and capital, a link which is repeatedly confirmed. Oblivious to Socrates' discomfort under the veil, he is concerned only for the production of speech and nothing else: "Only speak, and in other matters suit yourself" (237a). In this promotion of discourse over passion, Phaedrus is participating in the drainage of *erōs* depicted by Lysias' non-lover who reduces his "beloved" to the status of a prostitute in the interests of "*poly pleiōn elpis*" – a much better expectation (232e) of finding numerous and longer-lasting friendships by advocating relationships in the absence of *erōs*. Such a reasonable arrangement would be free from all the jealousies and resentments of traditional relationships, as well as other risks such as quarrelling and gossip (231e–232c).[10] By ironic parallel, the written nature of Lysias' speech means that it cannot be addressed to any particular boy, and so is exposed to the same absence of intimate and mutual interest as the non-lover's stratagem itself. Writing is thus structurally parallel to capital as the absence of the higher *erōs*, and as the standardization of exchange, just as the Lysian non-lover offers the homogenization and rationalization of human interaction, promoting transactions employed for purposes of a surfeit of advantages, preservation, and accumulation.

The second aspect of the commodification of language lies in Phaedrus' concealment of the text beneath his cloak. In this action, Phaedrus enacts capital's *fear of itself*, and this is echoed in Socrates' travesty of the sophistic condemnation of *erōs* in his first speech, when his "non-lover" is depicted deliberately debasing his beloved in order to guard against his loss, making the object of his desire less desirable, thus substituting the violence of ownership for *erōs* (239a–b, 239e, 240a). Might this suggest concomitantly that Derrida's own insistence upon absence and the postponement of value is precisely capital's fear of itself, or the fear of losing its recuperability through investment in any specific desire or intrinsic value?

---

[10] Ferrari, *op. cit.*, *Listening to the Cicadas*, 88–95.

5 The Contagion of the Good

In seeking to align both the Socratic good and orality with capital – in contrast, as we have seen, to the evidence – Derrida simply does not *consider* the Platonic alternative that instead of being at once radical absence *and* original presence, the good might be an inaccessible and inexhaustible plenitude.[11] This conception explains Socrates' demur at speaking directly of the good, preferring instead an economy of figures and traces. His withdrawal from such direct speaking of the good is neither a matter of capital's fear of itself nor a metaphysical construal of the good as an unapproachable and therefore fetishized ideal. It is rather that the good cannot be *circumscribed* in the manner of ordinary, empirical data, and is not accessible to technical knowing, but instead must be allowed to arise in and through the excess of supplementary figures which successively illuminate its nature. Derrida's approximation of the good to capital betrays a reading of the forms as scientific postulations verifiable by the immediacy of facts – as ontic rather than ontological – whereas, in this dialogue, Socrates is concerned to expose the dangerous dishonesty of such an epistemology. Certainly Derrida links the good not only with an ontic objectivity or "presence," but also with the quality of *absence* and perpetually withdrawing, abstract value. Yet *this* explanation of Socrates' reluctance to speak directly of the good overlooks its *transcendent* nature, which makes immanent propositions concerning its content impossible. Such transcendence is not coterminous with a fictitious enshrouded interiority, nor even retreating esoteric absence, as can be seen from Plato's icon of the sun in the *Republic*, by which he illustrates the ecstatic nature of the good.[12] As the source of all light, the sun is more diffi-cult to see than anything else, but it is a *beneficent* mystery which lets things be seen in their true nature, while itself remaining but obliquely visible. As well as letting things be seen, the sun *gives* things to be seen, for although it is beyond being,[13] it is the ground of all being(s). This

---

[11] T. G. Rosenmeyer underlines the *non-accumulative* structure of Socratic dialectical wisdom, and uses its *distributive* dynamic to explain Socrates' employment of the adjective *kalos* in his Prayer to Pan (279b–c), where one might have expected either *sophos* or *philosophos*. The use of *kalos* in this context expresses the generative, ecstatic, and non-containable nature of the philosophic "gold." Rosenmeyer writes that "(i)f they had no beauty, the products of the philosophic mind would remain hoards, buried in the house of learning." See *idem*, "Plato's Prayer to Pan (*Phaedrus* 279b8–c3)," *Hermes*, 90 (1962), 34–44.

[12] *Republic*, 507a–509c.

[13] *Ibid.*, 509b.

epekeina tēs ousias receives an immanentist definition from Derrida who insists on its con-tinuity with radical absence.[14] But the good is precisely "beyond" the distinction of presence and absence. Its transcendence does not signify emptiness, nor that Derridean postponement which reduces absence to objectivity, since the sun which shines light onto beings is present in the gifts of insight, truth, and beauty. The fact that it cannot be grasped by a *mathēma* and is unsayable does not identify it with absence. Rather, its mode of "presence" is articulated through the gifts which it bestows, the beyond-being which, as difference, gives things to be, and which (in Derridean terminology) *disseminates*. This contrasts with the *différance* of Derrida, which is assimilated in turn to his notion of writing. And it contrasts also with a perpetual postponement of an impossible giving and a radical disjunction of giver and gift.

The way in which the good surpasses the distinction between presence and absence is confirmed by Plato's designation of it by the feminine *idea* as opposed to the neuter *eidos*. Both grammatical forms were more or less interchangeable in the Greek of Plato's time, and yet he never refers to the good in the neuter form, whilst he uses that form for the other ideas. The neuter *eidos* suggests more specifically reference to an object and can be translated as a (visible) "appearance," whilst the feminine *idea* suggests something closer to a "looking toward the good" than an objective visibility.[15] As beyond being, the good is also beyond appearance, beyond objectification, beyond "capital." Indeed, in the *Phaedrus*, Plato portrays the transcendence of the good, its beyond presence-and-absence, as a kind of *contagion*, for its plenitude spills over into immanence, in such a way that the good is revealed in the beauty of physical particulars. The philosopher who, by the process of dialectic, has regained knowledge of the good, is wont to glimpse its transcendence in the mundane order, and is thus given to revere all physicality according to its participation in this spiritual sun. Concomitantly, Socrates is unwilling to speak directly not only of the form of the good, but even of anything at all, since *nothing* is outside the good's contagion. In all his speech concerning every reality he prefers to communicate via the openness of figures, the reserve of irony, or through the doxological mode of encomium. His reluctance to verify by fact the truth of a myth, to isolate the origin of a legend, or to speak directly of the soul, hold open this arrival of transcendence within immanence. And the excess of the good affects the philosopher himself

[14] Derrida, *op. cit.*, "Plato's Pharmacy," 168.
[15] Hans-Georg Gadamer, *The Idea of the Good in Platonic-Aristotelian Philosophy*, tr. P. Christopher Smith, (New Haven: Yale University Press, 1986), 27–8.

who is, by means of his communion through memory, initiated perpetually into the divine order (249c–d).

This excessiveness underlines the radicalization of our sense of time suggested by Socratic dialectic, for the good subsists within an anteriority which is *eternal* (247e). Thus, recollection of the good is not simply, even in Plato, an "aesthetic" or retrospective repetition (to use Søren Kierkegaard's terminology), meaning a mere identical re-attainment of something rooted in "the past," which cancels out all that has happened since.[16] Rather, the eternal transcendence of the good which causes a kind of overflowing into physicality keeps us within the movement of time, since the philosophic access to the good arises *not* as something subjectively *a priori*, but rather in and through the forward-moving existence of what is given to be by the good. Such temporality does not compromise that knowledge, but rather constitutes its condition of possibility for us: the good arrives through time, and therefore time is not merely a ladder of access which can be kicked away, its job performed. For the philosopher makes no attempt to fetishize the present, to stem the flow of time, nor to forego the necessary narrative through time of his striving toward the good. Instead by embracing his human narrative, he comes gradually to know himself, a knowledge coterminous with that of the realities towards which he strives. To this end, he inquires into every detail of the world, at once remote from and yet supremely incorporated within, his physical environment. The soul's charioteer makes his journey to the forms by means of an acceptance of the world's contingency, obeying the strictures which at once limit and facilitate its advance.[17] For this reason Socratic desire, in the *Phaedrus*, does not lack its object in the ordinary sense of lack, but attains its goal in and through its act of desiring. Similarly, the sensible husbandman carefully engages time-honoured Demetrian agricultural practices of unhurried placement of components and respect for the seasons, in order to secure continuation of the generations (276b, 277a).

The depiction of life in time as the condition of possibility for knowledge of the good is echoed by the way in which the qualification of our memory of the eternal realities by forgetfulness is *not* a purely privative phenomenon, but itself discloses the nature of the good's transcendence. The good is always more, and so the philosopher can only experience it positively via the process of slipping away from it. We cannot grasp or appropriate the good, but it is

---

[16] See Søren Kierkegaard, *Repetition: A Venture in Experimenting Psychology by Constantin Constantius*, tr. Howards V. Hong and Edna H. Hong, (New Jersey: Princeton University Press, 1983), 131–2.

[17] Ferrari, *op. cit.*, *Listening to the Cicadas*, 232.

only a sophistic consciousness which would interpret this as a *compromise*. Derrida's invocation of the *chora* or matrix in the *Timaeus*, which receives and distributes the difference between form and appearance, and so between truth and nontruth, suggesting something prior to the distinction between truth and nontruth which is yet more fundamental, seems to overlook an alternative, if merely incipient account of time and physicality as being as equally "real" as the forms in the *Phaedrus*.[18] Although this dialogue does not explicitly construe temporality as the gift of the forms, or as that which enables us to participate in the good, Socrates' more positive reading of physicality suggests a link between the processes of coming-to-be in time with the lure of the good, and a concomitant overcoming of the duality itself. In the *Phaedrus*, the encounter with an actual lover in time plays a positive role in stimulating the memory of the Forms, whereas in the *Phaedo*, for example, finitude tends to be invoked more regularly as lacking in a true equality only to be found in the eternal realm. Concomitantly, the *Phaedrus* exalts the *erotic* pull of the soul towards the beautiful as an integral part of the soul's eternal essence: even the divine souls are drawn around the eternal circuit by the horses of passion.[19]

As well as demonstrating that Plato did *not* wish to drive a wedge between form and appearance, the strongly positive view of *methexis* (participation) in the *Phaedrus* frees him from the charge of otherworldliness and total withdrawal from physicality, for the philosophic ascent does not result in a "loss" of love for particular beautiful things, since the particular participates in beauty itself. Thus the philosopher is synonymous with the lover of beauty, as also with one of a musical or loving nature (248d). Although, as Socrates acknowledges, the philosopher separates himself from human interests, turning his attention toward the divine, and is often thought to be insane, it is precisely within the physical world that he recognizes a likeness to the realities, and then is "stricken with amazement and cannot control himself" (241a). Furthermore, because of the transcendence of the good, this resemblance is no mechanistic mimesis, but a *constitutive* representation of that in which it participates, which can only be truly participated in through a *sustaining* of its distance and otherness. Hence, the "deviation" via the physical form remains in a sense unsurpassable, and for this reason, when the philosopher sees a face or a form which is a good image of beauty, he immediately recognizes its divine quality and would willingly offer sacrifice to this image itself (251ab). It is the beauty of that which possesses form which

[18] Derrida, *op. cit.*, "Plato's Pharmacy," 160–1.
[19] See M. P. Burnyeat, "The Passion of Reason in Plato's *Phaedrus*," (unpublished).

functions as the image, in the world, of the good.[20] Its proportion, measure, and truth are therefore named in the *Philebus* as the structural components of the good which thus appears *as* the beautiful.[21] Although the good remains other from all being, including the other forms themselves, and is seen in distinction from all mere *onta*, yet it is within everything, and is seen in distinction from each single being only insofar as it shines out from within them. Thus, in the *Phaedrus*, the myth of *erōs* singles out beauty as the only idea which preserves something of the former lustrousness of an idea even after its entry into the physical order. Beauty is that which shines forth most of all, and inspires love in us (250d), provoking the lover to strive for what is above the passions. Since beauty "shines forth" (within the visible), the good's *dunamis* or potential is displayed in the beautiful (*ekphainesthai*). Hence, in the *Republic,* the good is characterized not as existing for itself, but "in that in which it exists and which it effects,"[22] in such a way that the *dunamis* of the good is to be found in the manifold of what the *dunamis* brings about. Therefore the image of the good in the beauty of physicality is not just an empty "version" or simulacrum. And so if the philosopher can be accused of neglecting "things below," like the insane bird (249d), it is not that he turns away from physicality itself (for that would deny him access to the good), but that he neglects a *mundane apprehension* of physicality as merely immanent or crudely separated from the whole, and all the concomitant proprieties of property, custom, and conventional status (252a). By contrast the contagion of the divine urges the philosopher from place to place, yearning to see the beautiful again.

It is rather *the sophist* who denies genuine apprehension of the physical world, as we see during the diversion along the Ilissus, when the discussion about the myth of Boreas (229b–230a) elicits a revelation from both characters of their negotiation of physicality.[23] Phaedrus exploits the purity of the water

---

[20] Zdravko Planinc, *Plato's Political Philosophy: Prudence in the Republic and the Laws,* (London: Gerald Duckworth, 1991), 19.

[21] *Philebus,* tr. R. Hackforth, *The Collected Dialogues,* 64e–65a; Gadamer, *The Idea of the Good,* 124–5.

[22] *Republic,* 477c–d, Gadamer, *op. cit., The Idea of the Good,* 116.

[23] It is unusual to find such detailed topographical attention in Plato's dialogues, with the exceptions of the *Protagoras, Phaedo,* and *Symposium.* But in these three dialogues, it is the expository device of a distinct narratorial voice which is responsible for the attention given to these details, whereas in the *Phaedrus,* the interlocutors themselves provide our access into the landscape, beguiling us into a Phaedran sense of the secondariness or auxiliary nature of these details as mere "background." See Ferrari, *op. cit., Listening to the Cicadas,* 2, and *passim.*; Drew H. Hyland, "The Place of Philosophy," in *idem, Finitude and Transcendence in the Platonic Dialogues,* (Albany: State University of New York Press, 1995), 13–33; R. E. Wycherley, "The Scene of Plato's *Phaidros,*" *Phoenix,* 17.2 (1963), 88–98.

associated with the Boreas myth so as to occasion the production of conversation, whilst for Socrates, this topographical story provides an opportunity to impugn demythologizers and to introduce his special reverence for ancient wisdom and *erōs*. Similarly, Phaedrus' manipulative choice of the shady arbour prompts Socrates' encomium in which he systematically catalogues every aspect of the scene, dividing the physical stimuli according to the various senses to which they appeal, and assigning to each its own superlative, such as "spreading and lofty," "very fragrant," "very cool" (230b). He examines the soil and notes that it is well watered by the spring, and fertile for the grass, as well as for the plane and agnus trees. He notes the sweet and cool quality of the water, and verifies this with his toes (230b). The winds he notes are moderate. He also scrutinizes the inhabitants of the domain, the cicadas, the presence of Achelous, and the local nymphs. The arbour thus enables him to demonstrate the technique of dialectic as, specifically, an art of *differentiation*. But it also reveals its definitively non-meretricious motivation, for Socrates' exhaustive panegyric is spontaneous and uncommissioned: "By Hera!" he exclaims, as if possessed from without by the intensity of his surroundings. Furthermore, his reaction is in full accordance with his description of the philosophic lover in his second speech who, when struck by the prospect of the beautiful boy, recognizing in him the beautiful itself, lets slip all regard for ordinary values and attachments in such a way that he seems insane (249c–e).[24]

The contagion of the good in the physical order transgresses mundane proprieties of space. This is reflected in Phaedrus' description of Socrates' reaction to the arbour as *atopic* (i.e. out of place, inappropriate), because according to his commercial sensibilities, the environment is mere background extension, so that Socrates' treatment of each tiny detail as significant seems strange, out of place, foreign, and insane.[25] However, for Socrates as also for the philosopher-lover, spontaneous adoration is inspired, via *erōs*, by the memory of the beautiful itself which now infiltrates every aspect of life, great and small, in such a way that the "ordinary" becomes the "extraordinary." Whilst Phaedrus has relied upon the physical particulars remaining secondary, as a mere backdrop, Socrates' holistic and harmonious understanding of interconnectedness disallows any such hierarchical demarcation of phenomena.

It can be seen therefore that a transcendent apprehension of physical space, whilst it might mundanely seem to deflect attention from particular differences within the earthly order, in fact appreciates them better, for it is

---

[24] Ferrari, *op. cit. Listening to the Cicadas*, 16–21.
[25] Ibid.; Rodrigo, *op.cit.*,"Dialectique Autochtone," 269.

constitutive of those differences and their genuine apprehension. This is primarily because such a philosophic gaze discloses the real beyond its foreclosed finite appearances. Socrates thus combines the physical with the *psuchical* and *erotic* so as to reunite distinctions of time and eternity, background and foreground, finite and transcendent. And he does this not in order to remove, but precisely to permit difference.

Contrary to Derrida, who regards dialectic as opposed to differentiation, Socrates' critique of sophistry suggests that without knowledge of the good, differentiation itself is impossible. Socratic differentiation is not a scientific method in our sense, since its "object" is not demonstrable in the manner of a proof. Rather, it seeks to achieve two things. First, it seeks to clarify the nature of things, such as speeches, and to differentiate between types in order to match them to appropriate souls (271a–d, 252d, 277b–c). Secondly, it seeks to disclose what is simultaneously *already known* (remembered) and yet unknowable (*in the sense of a totality*). The suggestion of antecedent familiarity would indeed appear adverse to the quest for novelty, if one is thinking in terms of scientific and empirical inquiry, especially since Socrates assimilates knowledge of the good, via recollection, with *self*-knowledge, which he explicitly contrasts with the empirical epistemology of sophistry (229e).

Nonetheless, for Socrates, it is only by means of the dialogic art of differentiation (dialectic) that it is possible to transcend the confusion of mere opinions and prejudices, and only the dialectician, who holds steadfastly to the good, is in a position to differentiate and to discern the true from the false. This in turn means that only a certain obscure *anticipation* of difference through *erōs*, and recognition of difference through recollection, permits us to assimilate any significant novelty, which is to say, anything that can "stand out" as novel at all. When Socrates has delivered his first speech, in which he denies the philosophic life, his *daimonion* compels him to retract what he has said, and in responding to this, he unveils, both literally and figuratively, the nature of the true dialectician, for he had covered his head in delivering his anti-erotic speech (257a), and only in his recantation is he once again himself. And only then, when he has recovered his true self, does he uncover, or reknow, the true distinctions, identifying *erōs* as a divine gift, and distinguishing between "good" and "bad" madness — a distinction that is essential if human beings are to have a true understanding of themselves and what they experience in love. Dialectical differentiation is quite other from sophistic classification because it is thus combined with *synopsis*, which sees things together as one and only thereby as different, and exhibiting novelty through time (266b). Both recognition as self-knowledge and recognition as knowledge of everything else are a matter of seeing together and separating out.[26] Thus, we only glimpse the differences of the finite in their orientation towards, and yet separation from, the transcendent realm.

This coincidence of synopsis and differentiation suggests something anticipating a non-identical or analogical repetition as a condition of possibility for knowledge, in contrast to the sophistic synecdochic epistemology which mistakes the particularity and identity of a given datum for the whole truth, and is thus associated with false separation (266a–b) and confusion. Such an anticipation is apparent in Socrates' enumeration of contrasts between contemporary technocrats who are careless of difference, and traditional dialecticians. He opposes the true practitioner of an art to the mere mechanical technician (268a), the poet to the rhapsode, the possessed Pythia to the rational art of augury (244c–d), the Hippocratic physician, who studies all bodily symptoms, to the cursory physician who sees only surface effects (268a–270d). Similarly, a distinction is drawn between the genuine orator who will consider all the reasons for the success of his various methods, and match particular speeches to the nature of the soul to which it is addressed, and the rhetorician who merely seeks to elicit instant effects irrespective of truth or suitability (267c–d). The sophistic component in each of these pairs can be allied with the Lysian non-lover and the non-lover of Socrates' first (*anerotic*) speech, who both exercise a contractualizing of *erōs*. This abuse is synonymous with a simultaneous excess of utility and excess of pleasure, reducible to one and the same pursuit of cheaper versions and short-cut routes to traditional goals. The suggestion is that when sophistic methodology is carried over into the moral sphere of everyday life, it becomes immoral or amoral, debased by such an art of guaranteeing success in the pursuit of pleasure.

The synecdochic consciousness of sophistry seeks, by accelerated methods, to derive ontology from subjective methodological procedure, so concluding to the particularity and atomistic nature of beings from the partiality and compartmentalized nature of its epistemology. According to this scheme, clarity is made synonymous with empirical certainty and fixity, both of which are to be found in the facility of writing (277d). This contrasts with divine

[26] See Rodrigo, *ibid.*, 273, on dialectic as the art of mediating between the same and the different. In contrast to rhetoric, dialectic goes beyond the opposition *nomadisme/immobilisme* as "*focalisé et fluide*," 270. Rosenmeyer notes the connection between dialectical classification and clarification with Socrates' invocation of the god Pan at the end of the dialogue; see *op. cit.*, "Plato's Prayer to Pan," 37 n. 1. On Socrates' enumeration of the contrast between those who falsely differentiate or synthesize, and those practitioners, physicians, and authentic orators who deploy dialectical method, see Ferrari, *op. cit.*, *Listening to the Cicadas*, 77–9.

clarity and eternity which, as transcendent, remain mysterious (e.g. 237a). It contrasts equally with the only means by which to obtain such clarity, dialectic, which, concomitantly, can only remain partial. Sophistic cartographies are thus unachievable and dishonest, since human life is always in the midst of things; the clarity of empiricist conclusions is an illusion fostered by the falsely isolated and inert nature of its artificial findings, just as the apparent fixity of the text, taken for the noumenal permanence of truth, is a mirage, since the text is exposed to many different arbitrary interpretations (275d–e) (contrasting to the open-ended yet consistent "writing on the soul" which continues forever (277a)). The genuine "fixity" parodied by the sophists can be attained only in the unshakeable conviction of a certain way of life, where clarity and steadfastness of personal conviction are found through philosophic dialogue and wariness of all claims to instant certitude. The word which is "written with intelligence in the mind of the learner" (276a) is written in the *memory*, and so Socratic truth emerges from the temporal trace of anamnesis, as "the living and breathing word of him who knows" (276a). There is no metaphysics of presence here, but rather an infinite series of speakers and traces of memory (259b, 274c, 275b). The mythic tradition thus passes from generation to generation, written, through memory, in the soul, whence it "spring(s) up in other minds . . . capable of continuing the process for ever" (277a). And the seriousness with which Socrates takes myth suggests that a *tradition* of recollection is not altogether indispensable for an individual act of remembering the eternal forms.

This account of mythic tradition is to be contrasted with the metaphysics of the book whose physical and moral mobility, absence of situation, author, and *erōs*, plus mobility of value, do not detract from, but rather enforce, its fundamental character as an objective presence abstracted from time. For its abstraction from time and place is readily fetishized as an absolute origin, and its mobility is commensurate with an unhinged freedom which ultimately cannot exceed a formalistic closure. As I shall discuss below, Derrida's emphasis on writing is a denial of the living and dying physical *body*.

Instead of the epistemology of the book, Socrates proposes the partial nature of all knowledge, and suggests that our only access to it is via specific physical performance. This means, concomitantly, via *language*, an aspect of the physical world to which we gain access through Plato's dialogue itself. Indeed, Socrates' teachings cannot be discovered by stripping-away language as a kind of frivolous elaboration of truth's essence (as a sophist might hope). In the dialogues, language itself is not an inessential "detour"[27] but is integral to the

---

[27] Derrida, *op. cit.*, "Plato's Pharmacy," 121.

realising of truth. Furthermore, the dialogic structure obfuscates any attempt to discover abstract principles or essences of knowledge, as well as attempts to construct a compendium-like understanding of Plato's or Socrates' "intentions;" its dramatic form discourages sophistry in our act of reading, and its forward-moving dialogic dynamic removes any grounds for the expectation of an anterior essence. It would seem, then, that *genuine* intellectual clarity is obtainable only when that which is to be "known" is allowed to remain open and mysterious: an attitude synonymous with a kind of reverence.

6 PLATONIC VERSUS DERRIDEAN SUPPLEMENTATION

Given this suggestion of a more positive account of physicality and time in the *Phaedrus*, one could argue that Socrates' account of *erōs* and orality is assimilable to a theory of supplementation, and that the Derridean colonization of supplementation by writing is tantamount to a metaphysics of presence.

As I have described, the philosopher-lover remains steadfastly guided by his vision of the good, which is nonetheless *beyond being*. For this reason, his journey through life is simultaneously *erotic* and *hermeneutical*. It is erotic because it lies in the power of *erōs* to interpret and transport "human things to the gods and divine things to men; entreaties and sacrifices from below, and ordinances and requitals from above."[28] Thus it acts as a kind of angelic mediation between mortal and immortal. The philosophic life is, secondly, *hermeneutical* because it involves the perpetual discernment of divine mediation through physicality, "deposited" and emanating there because of *erōs*. The erotic *methexis* of mortal and immortal is not a physical or direct mingling (*Theos de anthropō ou mignutai*)[29] but, via the mediation of *erōs*, the human and the divine supplement one another (*sumpleroō*),[30] a fact which Plato makes no attempt to conceal. The philosopher's communion with memory not only nourishes the wings of his own soul and those of his beloved, but also "causes God to be divine" (*pros hoisper theos on theios estin*, 249c). This can be linked with the notion of *dunamis* in the *Sophist*, which is the idea that the definition of real being is the capacity of something to affect something else, or, concomitantly, to be affected, to however small a degree.[31] Participation in the

---

[28] *Symposium*, tr. Michael Joyce, *The Collected Dialogues*, 202e.

[29] *Ibid.*, 203a.

[30] *Ibid.*, 202e.

[31] *Sophist*, tr. F. M. Cornford, *The Collected Dialogues*, 247d–e.

divine (and it is unclear in Plato to what extent the divine is to be assimilated with the good), approaches a mutually constitutive supplementation facilitated by the relational overflowing of *erōs*. In the end, of course, the form of the good does *not* need to be supplemented by us, but this is because it *is* good as a self-supplementing reality which permits us a certain privileged position in advance. It is this self-supplementing power to affect (*dunamis*) which Derrida overlooks, since he assumes that the good is a simple objective presence *opposed* to supplementation. This of course makes the good available to a Cartesian measuring gaze, and misconstrues Socratic recollection as establishing equally Cartesian "foundations." Yet even in the *Republic*, it is only under the light of the good that one is able to see the other forms, and if they require this supplementation of ideal light in order to reveal themselves, then *all* the forms must be wholly unlike the objects of empirical science. And again, supplementation is reciprocal. To regard a table, one must have a broader idea of what a table is, even though one is only *reminded* of this broader idea by the empirical, particular table, since the idea is *not* something one possesses *a priori*.[32] Thus, knowledge is *an act of judgement* which hovers somewhere between the particular and the ideal, offered by the mediation of *erōs*, which disallows any isolation of a privileged epistemological foundation or starting-point.

Despite this implicit epistemology of supplementary traces, Derrida argues that "what Plato dreams of is a memory with no sign. That is, with no 'supplement,' "[33] whereas this is to overlook Socrates' erotic and hermeneutic understanding of the philosopher-lover's striving towards the good as commensurate with the act of knowledge. Whilst signs, both natural and conventional, are the essential and only route, via the trace of memory, to the good, it is the *sophists* for whom the supplementation effected by language is regarded as a secondary form, or mere vehicle for exchange and transaction. The rhetors commodify language, just as Phaedrus threatens violence in order to gain a quantity of words (236c). Furthermore, it could be argued that it is Derrida, and not Socrates, who suppresses the link between language and physicality, for in aligning writing with parricide or the absence of the father, and orality with a metaphysics of presence, he subtly denies the fact that language of any kind requires *bodily* presence. In attempting to distinguish his own position from that of Plato, Derrida argues that language needs no speaker, since it is more fundamentally a trace of a speaker who was never

[32] See Jean-Louis Chrétien, *L'Inoubliable et L'Inespéré*, (Paris: Desclée de Brouwer, 1991), 20.
[33] Derrida, *op. cit.*, "Plato's Pharmacy," 109.

present to begin with. However, the Platonic doctrine of recollection perhaps states the same thing in other terms, and yet in such a way as (*unlike* Derrida) to allow the physicality and communality of all language. For, in the *Phaedrus*, there is no account of a self-present autonomous speaker outside the series of traces represented by external (divine, human, physical) inspiration, or an anterior *akoē* (or orally received myth or tradition). In the *Ion*, Socrates explains to his interlocutor that his speaking well on Homer is not a skill of his own but a divine gift impelling him like a magnet, the "stone of Heraclea," which "does not simply attract the iron rings, just by themselves; it also imparts to the rings a force enabling them to do the same thing as the stone itself . . . to attract another ring, so that sometimes a chain is formed, quite a long one, of iron rings, suspended from one another. For all of them, however, their power depends upon that loadstone. Just so the Muse. She first makes men inspired, and then through these inspired ones others share in the enthusiasm, and a chain is formed."[34] By contrast, Derrida's written model suggests no people at all, only a word which comes from nowhere, an autonomous word which conceals or violently eradicates its origins and dictates to its "author," rendering him entirely passive before a disembodied and (spiritual?) power.

Derrida claims that the reason why Socrates apparently considers the supplement dangerous is that "(i)ts slidings slip it out of the alternative presence/absence."[35] However, it is precisely a movement beyond the alternative of presence and absence (which Derrida *cannot* really think, except as an aporetic undecideability) which is made possible by the transcendence of the good. For Socrates, there can be no absolute experience of either presence or absence since, first, the good always exceeds the object which manifests it physically and can never be grasped in an absolute presence; and since, secondly, on account of the excessiveness of transcendence, the good is always overflowing into that subject which, via *erōs*, strives to participate in it. A complete absence would suggest two discrete realms – the Forms and physicality – which for Plato would be an absurdity. Concomitantly, for Socrates, dissemination is not a "risk" as Derrida describes it,[36] but rather is natural to the contagion and excess of the good itself.

However, this excessiveness is not continuous with an unstructured saturation, and because of the magnitude of the good, dissemination must be carefully channelled. Therefore one must prepare carefully before being exposed to its manifestation. This is important with respect to the debate regarding writing

---

[34] *Ion*, tr. Lane Cooper, *The Collected Dialogues*, 533d–e.

[35] Derrida, *op. cit.*, "Plato's Pharmacy," 109.

[36] *Ibid.*, 149.

and orality, for whilst I would not quarrel with Derrida's argument that writing is more "democratic," there are several qualifications which must be added.[37] First, it is easily possible for *writing* to be used as an esoteric investment of bureaucratic control, and as such it does not provide an unquestionable democracy. And secondly, Derrida does not deal with the question of the availability of texts, of censorship or quality, plus the fact that one must first learn to read, nor the question of different languages and exclusive codes. Whereas by contrast the manipulative potential of the text is recognized in the *Phaedrus* by its hiddenness beneath the cloak, by Phaedrus' use of it to seduce his companion outside the city walls, and by explicit comments regarding the methods of irresponsible rhetors. In a similar fashion, Derrida does not negotiate Plato's concern with the way in which writing's potential saturation of availability cannot be *channelled* and disallows differentiation of what is "best" for a particular person at a particular time (275d, 276a–b). (Although our exercise of *phronēsis* is here guided by traditional grammars of differentiation and dissemination, analogous to those guiding agriculture (260a–b)). Thus, it is not differentiation or dissemination which Socrates considers dangerous – indeed, it is an *aim* of the philosopher-lover to communicate his vision of the good to his beloved – but *arbitrary* or undifferentiating "dissemination." For the latter, like the merely written text, undermines itself, and cancels its own message, in its incapacity to respond to the unexpected.

7 PLATO'S RETURN TO MYTH

Derrida's fixation with writing is responsible also for a simplistic construal of Socrates' rewriting of myth, which he attributes to an outright hostility to the mythic estrangement from the origin, arguing that, for Socrates, this estrangement is inimical to knowledge. He insists that both he and Socrates would agree to a structural similarity between writing and myth, and that for this reason, Socrates must give myth a "send off"[38] in order to assert his prioritization of self-knowledge. In this characterization, Derrida ignores the positive involvement of myth in the *Phaedrus* and the fact that it is its structural similarity with *orality* and not writing which can be seen in its multiple and

[37] *Ibid.*, 144–5. Although writing could promote equal justice, it has been argued that fifth-century Greek historians and dramatists portrayed writing as an essential tool of tyrants, who not only issue written decrees but also "inscribe" human bodies with brands and cut up land with compasses and rules. For a discussion of the despotic implications of writing, see Steiner, *op. cit., The Tyrant's Writ*, 127–85.
[38] Derrida, *op. cit.*, "Plato's Pharmacy," 68–9.

unassignable origins, the mysterious *akoē*. In fact, Socrates' quarrel is not with mythic epistemology, but with those who seek to render artificially univocal its origins and meaning, or to locate its origin in singular facticity. It is the sophistic act of demythologization which Socrates wishes to "send off."

With regard to this point, Derrida notes that Socrates' accusation that writing repeats the same over and over without knowing, given authority by reference to Ammon's words, is itself contained within a repetition-without-knowledge, for when Socrates introduces the myth, he expresses reserve as to its veracity: "I can tell something I have heard of the ancients; but whether it is true, they only know" (274c). Derrida writes, "One thus begins by repeating without knowing through a myth – the definition of writing: which is to repeat without knowing."[39] There would seem to be a structural parallel here, certainly, but I would suggest that it is a *parodic* parallel. It is true that as a construct of language, Socrates' myth has met with a similar fate through oral transmission as Lysias' speech through written transmission, in that belated recipients of each can no longer testify to its exact source. And there is some truth in the point that Socrates' retelling of the myth participates in the very process that the myth narrates, that is, a repetition without knowledge. However, the knowledge involved in each case is wholly different. The knowledge absent from Socrates' myth is that of its origin in fact, but this is precisely the kind of knowledge which he wishes to dismiss (229e). Furthermore, this absence of knowledge is constrained by Socrates' *awareness* of the lack of his knowledge, whereas the lack from which writing suffers is the absence of the possibility of knowledge of any kind, even of an awareness of ignorance.[40]

By assigning the origins of writing to a legend, Socrates suggests that the oral mythic tradition, with all its chains of supplementation, alteration, and arrival from without, can expose what writing is, in such a way that in a sense writing is transcendentally *oral*, rather than speech being transcendentally written, as for Derrida. And the first option is more plausible, since Derrida's emphasis on the commerce of absence and death with writing causes him irresponsibly to discount the way in which all language presupposes an engagement with living bodies. Even an apparently disembodied text is written and read by a living body, and, as Socrates stresses, is structured like one (264b–c). There is no case for arguing that Socrates aspires to a "simple, organless voice."[41] This phrase, derived from the *psilois logois* of the *Symposium*, refers to language unadorned by the manipulative devices of

[39] *Ibid.*, 75.
[40] Ferrari, *op. cit.*, *Listening to the Cicadas*, 216–17.
[41] Derrida, *op. cit.*, "Plato's Pharmacy," 188, referring to the *Symposium*, 215d.

rhetoric, and does not refer to an interior, abstract, or disembodied word.

If one must characterize language as either written or spoken, I would suggest that *spoken* would be the most apt designation, since this would include all that Derrida would wish to stress in terms of an infinite series of traces, but at the same time, would allow for the inclusion of living bodies at every stage. It is precisely his *care* for these living bodies, for time, and for exteriority, which dictates Plato's preference for the oral word. His construal of orality does *not* conceal its supplementarity nor favour an interior-anterior purity, whilst Derrida's written supplement is fissured by its disembodied, autonomous arrival and by the way in which its sign is empty, and reducible to the objectivity of death, a condition tantamount to the *closure* of the series. It would seem that Socrates' intimations of an orally-construed language allow a greater ecstatic dimension into his philosophy than Derrida seems willing to admit, and that there is an incipient account here of supplementation as the origin and possibility of language itself; this, together with a thematizing of the transcendent contagion of the good, and the repetition implicitly involved in any act of philosophic recognition.

The crux of Socrates' preference for orality over writing has to do with his interpretation of memory. However, memory is in turn crucially linked to myth and it is this which Derrida overlooks, thereby totally misconstruing Socrates' attitude to the mnemonic. As well as comprising a simulacrum of wisdom, being bandied about without regard for dialectic propriety, the written word will produce forgetfulness in the minds of those who learn to use it. It is an aid to reminding (*hupomnēseōs*) and not to memory (*mnēmēs*, 275a), the latter referring to philosophic recollection, coterminous with self-knowledge and Socratic ontology. In Plato's configuration of writing as a false memory, obfuscating access to the good, deceiving those who learn to use it, and his concomitant prioritization of the oral mnemonic, Derrida finds a metaphysical repetition, a return to the past by the individual in order to possess that anterior moment as if it were present. However, Socrates' account of possession from without, first, by the Muses, as in the myth of the cicadas, and, secondly, by the beloved, in Socrates' speech about philosophic love, and thirdly, by beauty in the physical world, contributes a degree of forward-moving *mediation* which frees him from this charge. Socrates' interest in place – the arbour, the gods of the locality, the statues, the cicadas etc. – means that what is recollected is not sought by a retrospective repetition, (for there is no question of recalling the *experience* of the pre-existent soul) but a non-identical repetition in the inhabited present. This is not a retreat into an inviolable self, but rather an opening of the self to receive the mediation of the transcendent in and through the immanent.

Despite Derrida's characterization of Socratic *zōon* as interior and tranquil, the breath of orality does not remain internal but penetrates bodies, and "escapes." It is not a fetishized, inviolable "life," but one which enters death. Derrida's structural assimilation of the *logos*, presence, and *zōon*[42] urges a characterization of orality as a manipulative device, but he thereby overlooks the possibility that it is *writing*, with its mobility of interest, ability to fasten itself to any situation, absence of particularity, and endurance through time, which is to be associated with a denial of physicality and death. Its deferred nature lends itself to concealment which enables it to be manipulative, particularly given the tangibility and assumed authority of the text and its untested power.

These qualities are concealed and repeated by Derrida's own text which conveniently edits the Egyptian mythology concerning the god Theuth in order to sustain the all-important structural assimilation of capital, orality, the king etc. Theuth is in fact as much linked in Egyptian mythology with *orality*, *non*-violence, and *protection* of the patriarch, as he is with writing and all the other attributes Derrida assigns to him. And here his escape-clause is rather weak: "No doubt the god Thoth (*sic*) had several different faces, belonged to several eras, lived in several homes."[43] Plato's own portrait of Theuth is very narrow, determined by the demand of the particular context, but Derrida asserts "(d)oesn't he have the same place in Egyptian mythology? . . . (t)here too, Thoth is an engendered god. He often calls himself the son of the god-king, the sun-god, Ammon-Ra,"[44] stressing the uneasy subordination of Theuth as son, a secondary figure as amanuensis to Ammon-Ra and the other gods, a mere transmitter of messages and not their originator, representing the creative moment but not coinciding with it. "And when Thoth *is* concerned with the spoken rather than with the written word, which is rather seldom," insists Derrida, "he is never the absolute author or initiator of language."[45] And yet it is by no means the case that in Egyptian mythology Theuth was exclusively portrayed as an engendered deity. In the Turin Papyrus, for example, an inscription reads, "Hail O Lunar-Thoth who enlightenest the Duat in the necropolis! Hail to thee Lunar-Thoth, thou self-engendered, the unknown!"[46] In addition, Ammon and Theuth are frequently represented as

[42] *Ibid.*, 104 and *passim*.
[43] *Ibid.*, 86.
[44] *Ibid.*, 88.
[45] *Ibid.*, 88.
[46] Patrick Boylan, *The Hermes of Egypt: A Study of Some Aspects of Theological Thought in Ancient Egypt*, (Oxford: Oxford University Press, 1922), 63. E. A. Wallis Budge, *The Gods of the Egyptians or Studies in Egyptian Mythology*, (London: Methuen, 1904), 400.

reigning by a common government. In some inscriptions they are treated as two equal aspects of the same deity, and occasionally, Theuth is represented as the superior of the two: "Thoth, the great one, who created all things, the tongue and heart that knows everything which is within him," and in another inscription, Theuth is he "who came into being when naught existed, who of himself alone has wrought all that is. There is no other like unto him."[47] Derrida is also inclined to overestimate the hostility between the two gods, when in fact, Ammon-Ra is known to give praise to Theuth: "Hail to Thee, saith Re."[48] It is not in the least seldom that Theuth's epithets link him with orality – he was "splendid in speech," "the first to utter command," and would not only teach the words to be spoken but also the way to speak them.[49] And when Theuth is associated with writing, it is not a *deathly* writing, but is closely linked with life. In the Temple of Chons at Karnak, Theuth addresses the Pharaoh with these words: "I write for thee a mighty kingdom; I give thee life unending as king of Two Lands, and everlasting life in years of peace."[50] However, the letters which Theuth is supposed to have invented are magical, efficacious, and *liturgical*. He is said to have invented sacred speech, worship, and the language of the gods.[51]

In the case of the myth of Theuth, therefore, supplementation is *not* construed as peculiarly written; nor, concomitantly, does this myth necessarily inscribe an unavoidable conflict between oral presence and written deferral. On the contrary, its promotion of *liturgy* tends to integrate writing with orality.

8 ERŌS AND EXTERIORITY

The suggestion that time and physicality are *as real* as the forms, put forward in the *Sophist*, could be seen as anticipating a nihilistic gesture for which "non-being" is implicitly as real as being. However, in this section it will be shown how one can read Socrates' configuration of *erōs* in the *Phaedrus* as an

[47] Boylan, *The Hermes of Egypt*, 177 and 215 respectively.

[48] *Ibid.*, 215.

[49] *Ibid.*, 182, 214. Also, Budge, *The Gods of the Egyptians*, 408.

[50] Boylan, *The Hermes of Egypt*, 85.

[51] *Ibid.*, 92–101; Budge, *The Gods of the Egyptians*, 407, 414. Samuel Mercer, *The Religion of Ancient Egypt*, (London: Luzae and Co, 1949), 146; P. Larousse, *Mythologie Générale*, tr. Delano Ames, *Egyptian Mythology*, (London: Paul Hamlyn, 1965), 82; R. V. Lanzone, *Dizionario di Mitologia Egizia*, (Torino: Litografia fratelli Doyer, 1881–6), Volume V, 1264–83.

alternative ontology which overcomes the possibility of such nihilism.

In his discussion of the story of Oreithyia's death, which is introduced into the dialogue by Phaedrus (229b), who wishes to arouse in Socrates a mood for conversation, Derrida focuses on the violation of her life by the involvement of her playmate Pharmacea, underlining all the connotations of exteriority, slippage, and contamination inherent in that latter name. This reading enables him critically to maintain the notion of an interiority persisting in a state of monadic, virginal purity shattered by the penetration of Pharmacea: "Through her games, Pharmacia (sic) has dragged down to death a virginal purity and an unpenetrated interior."[52] However, Pharmacea had no involvement in Oreithyia's death whatsoever, but rather, it was "a blast of Boreas, the north wind (which) pushed her off the neighbouring rocks as she was playing with Pharmacea, and when she had died in this manner she was said to have been carried off by Boreas" (229c). Is it sufficient that Pharmacea was present as a playmate on the occasion of the Boreal blast to hold her accountable for Oreithyia's death? An alternative reading of interiority in Plato would be that it is open to the outside without any need for violation, since reception of the external is represented in the *Phaedrus* as ontologically constitutive, whereas Derrida characterizes Plato's view as being that the "perfection of a living being would consist in its having no relation at all with any outside."[53] Certainly, the dialectical "antidote" works by allowing a disease to work itself out without the intervention of drugs, which Derrida regards as tantamount to a refusal of external "supplementation."[54] However, to accuse this Socratic psuchic physics of privileging a tranquil interior is, in effect, to read Descartes back into Plato, for this example of the *pharmakos* (drug) represents not a preservation of a dualism, but simply a suspicion of sophistic short-cuts. The metaphorical connotation which the text suggests is clearly that of "quick fix" rather than "alien intrusion." It is true that dialectics is itself a kind of pharmakon,[55] precisely because it involves some confusion of exterior and interior, but where Derrida would argue that dialectics allows only a suspicious or *guarded* admission of exteriority, for Plato it provokes rather a *full* and *excessive ekstasis*. In a false ecstasy, for Plato, reason is simply displaced by violence, manipulation, and sophistic exteriority, whereas in dialectical ecstasy, *reason itself* is defined as displacement, as *atopic*. *Erōs* does not offer an ecstasy under wraps.

The *ekstasis* which takes place in Socrates' account of the philosopher-lover

[52] Derrida, *op. cit.*, "Plato's Pharmacy," 70.
[53] *Ibid.*, 101.
[54] *Ibid.*, 121.
[55] *Ibid.*, 124.

would suggest that, for Plato, *erōs* introduces an element of *constitutive* loss of self. There is no clinging to interiority here. Socrates shows that a delimited *erōs*, such as the hidden, auto-erotic, rationalized seductions of the Lysian non-lover, no longer qualifies as *erōs* at all, but sophistic manipulation. By contrast, the philosopher-lover of Socrates' second speech is neither delimited nor contained, but "can no longer control himself" (250a). *Erōs* "flows into him, and some, when he is filled, overflows outside" (255c).[56] This radicalization of the division between inside and outside reaches its optimum in the complex process of dialectical recognition, for when the philosopher-lover glimpses the good in the physical world, he receives *from without* what he recognizes *from within* his memory – that which at one time he had received *from a* transcendent *without*, at the time when his soul was in harmony with the good. Because the Socratic self is in this way constituted from without, knowledge of the self, Socrates' ultimate epistemological goal, is knowledge of what is "outside" the self, which is the good and its mediations.

In spite of this positive account of exteriority, Derrida argues that for Plato "(h)ealth and virtue . . . always proceed from within,"[57] and that he wishes to exclude that which lies without by hopelessly maintaining the boundary. In response to this, one could first restate the argument that, throughout the dialogue, the act of recognition is initially triggered from without by some

---

[56] This metaphor of *Erōs* as liquid enables us to discern a structure of oppositions and parodic assimilations in the dialogue. Phaedrus draws our attention to the purity of the Ilissus where it is supposed that Oreithyia once bathed. And this stream's purity means that it also represents for Socrates a means of escape from Phaedrus' threats (242a). Water is linked with purification, immortality, inspiration, and orality (243d, 251b), and is opposed to the sterility of the dry, as when the soul is deprived of the company of his beloved, his feathers grow dry, pricking the passages of their growth (251d). The interpersonal overflowing of *Erōs* (255c) contrasts with the auto-erotic concealment of Lysias' scroll beneath Phaedrus' cloak, in the same way that Demetrian agriculture is contrasted with the dry, overheated, licentious and abortive growth of seeds in the gardens of Adonis (276b–d), grown in noon-day heat, an analogy introduced to elucidate the differences between orality and writing. The unending cycle of interpersonal nourishment provided by Demetrian agriculture (277a) contrasts with the hopeless and wasteful frivolity of the garden of letters (276d), its rootlessness, hiddenness, and absence of the higher *Erōs*. The little pots of the Adonians, parodies of the vast earth, are carried about, portable like the text, and deposited high on rooftops, private, and transgressive spaces. The unripened gardens of Adonis represent the forcing of life into death, like Adonis into the cask, a harnessing and violent appropriation of the beautiful into the arid and inert timelessness of objecthood. See Marcel Detienne, *The Gardens of Adonis: Spices in Greek Mythology*, tr. J. Lloyd, (New Jersey: The Humanities Press, 1977), and R. B. Onians, *The Origins of European Thought about the Body, the Mind, the Soul, the World, Time, and Fate*, (Cambridge: Cambridge University Press, 1988).

[57] Derrida, *op. cit.*, "Plato's Pharmacy," 101–2.

element of the physical world (e.g. 251b), and that the telos of recognition is simultaneously and *ambiguously* internal and external – self-knowledge and memory of the good respectively, as Socrates explains. Thus when the philosopher-lovers "search within themselves" to find the nature of their god, they are successful, because they have been compelled to keep their eyes fixed upon the god, and as they reach and grasp him by memory they are inspired and receive from him character and habits, so far as it is possible for a man to have part in god" (253a). In this explanation, eternity seems more contemporaneous than the present moment, memory more prescient than fact, and the inside-outside dichotomy is dismantled. Furthermore, the distinction between active and passive is also disturbed, since the gaze of memory is a *passive* reception of what is remembered, and yet philosophic recognition requires an *act* of judgement of likeness, as well as an "*active*" yearning or desire to recognize.

Secondly, I would argue that Plato's relativization of boundaries is not simply an unidimensional levelling of inside and outside to an equal degree. He differentiates between the two realms, and yet explicitly seeks an harmonious commerce or exchange of properties between them: "O beloved Pan and all ye other gods of this place, grant to me that I be made beautiful in my soul within, and that all external possessions be in harmony with my inner man" (279b–c).[58] Whilst this celebration of *harmony* might seem to suggest an ideal of equality of priority between the interior and the exterior, at times Socrates seems to favour a supremacy of exteriority over interiority. When the philosopher-lover recognizes the good in his beloved, he reaches

---

[58] On the significance of this concluding prayer for the dialogue as a whole, see Rosenmeyer, *op. cit.*, "Plato's Prayer to Pan," 37–8; and Philippe Borgeaud, *The Cult of Pan in Ancient Greece*, tr. Kathleen Atlass and James Redfield, (Chicago and London: Chicago University Press, 1988), 59, 139. The centrality of questions to do with *logos* in this dialogue (dialogue versus oratory, written versus spoken discourse, the versatility of the *logos*, its seductive powers, its variable capacity for self-correction, the uneasy terms of its compact with truth) should obviate the need to ask whether the debate regarding speech and writing is merely an awkwardly appended epilogue (see, for example, Ferrari, *op. cit.*, *Listening to the Cicadas*, 204). A connection can be drawn between Socrates' invocation of the myth of Theuth, the inventor of writing who was, (to borrow Boylan's expression), the "Hermes of Egypt," and his conclusory invocation of the god Pan, who in Greek mythology is Hermes' son. It is precisely the positive manner in which Socrates invokes Pan which should indicate to us that we should not read his critique of Theuth as a final verdict upon divinities of mediation. Moreover, one may note that the relation of Pan to his father Hermes, in Greek mythology, is certainly not one of *filial aggression*, but, on the contrary, an extension of the paternal legacy into other realms. One might see a kind of non-identical repetition instanced here.

a state of *captivation* by him, characterized by self-forgetfulness. The soul is willing to surrender all freedom and become captive to the beloved (252a–b). The ultimate moment of self-knowledge is characterized therefore by self-loss and release (259bff). It follows that this "horizontal" transgression of inside and outside (the self and the beautiful other) parries with a "vertical" transgression (the self and god) in a chiasmus which throws open all boundaries.

Socrates maintains a suspicion of all violent or insidious exteriorities, those which, it would seem, merely affirm the division of interior and exterior. The modes of exteriority which are given a positive account are those which do not violate the boundary by force, but which inspire a willing opening of the inside to receive or commune harmonically with the outside, whether divine or earthly. This is seen in Socrates' honouring of all sources of inspiration: the cicadas, the nymphs, the statues, the physical environment, and the gods. He explains to Phaedrus that the divinities of the place are the cause of his speech, "and perhaps, too, the prophets of the Muses, who are singing above our heads (and) may have granted this boon to us by inspiration; at any rate, I possess no art of speaking" (262d). In his mythic hymn, Socrates attributes inspiration to Stesichorus who uttered an ancient palinode to atone for his blasphemy (244a). This example notably portrays *purification from without*, a *katharmos archaios* (243a), received from the exteriority of tradition and transmitted through language, another kind of exteriority. Other positive exteriorities include the *akoē* origins of myth, Socrates' *daimonion* responsible for his wise and moderate actions, and the inspiration for the content of his speech, filling him "through the ears from some alien stream" (235d).

Moreover, when he explains the beneficial effect of the divine madness for the philosopher, Socrates enumerates three further modes of erotic possession which render provisional the inside-outside dichotomy. First, the prophetic madness of the Pythia at Delphi which is said to have benefited the nation of Greece on many occasions (244a–d); secondly, the madness whereby officiants ritually purified ancient families of their ancestral crimes, which is another example of purification from without, and ensures that "diseases and the greatest troubles" be released by the entering-in of erotic madness (244d–e); and thirdly, the madness of the poet seized by the Muses when he is inspired to glorify the deeds of ancient heroes (245a–b). Such forms of erotic possession are portrayed as eudaemonistic, bringing happiness, release from ills of many kinds, and purification by means of captivation and penetration from without (244e).[59]

---

[59] See Ferrari, *op. cit.*, *Listening to the Cicadas*, 113–14; on possession from without by the god Pan and the nymphs (258c–d), see Borgeaud, *op. cit.*, *The Cult of Pan*, 104.

So contrary to Derrida's claim that Platonic metaphysics is to be found in a privileging of truth-as-presence, and of subjectivity as interiority, it seems that from the enumeration of the myriad stimuli in which the philosopher-lover is immersed, one should derive instead an account of the self as constituted by its opening to receive its environment, both physical and divine.

9 THE SOCRATIC GAZE

In keeping with this interpretation of the interior-exterior relationship in the *Phaedrus*, one can also modify Derrida's characterization of Platonism as promoting a purely *ocular* epistemology, by stressing that the Socratic gaze is an *erotic* gaze. Whilst it is the case that the faculty of vision is hailed as "the sharpest of the physical senses" (250d), and in his mythic hymn he prays not to be deprived of his sight (257a) because of its crucial role in the process of recognition of the good, and while the metaphor of knowledge as vision is dominant in the *Republic*, this philosophic gaze is not a gaze of mastery. It is supremely a *double* vision of empirical sight combined with *recognition* or *recollection* which, as I have described, hovers between activity and passivity, whereas the sophistic parodic counterpart is both secret and wholly active (228b), (a gaze which Socrates implies is subject to closure by his action of veiling himself when delivering his sophistic speech, 237a). The sophistic gaze seeks to master and appropriate its object, and is typical of one whose soul has forgotten the realities, for when such a soul beholds a manifestation of the beautiful, "he does not revere it . . . and is not afraid or ashamed to pursue pleasure in violation of nature" (251a). By contrast the erotic gaze is non-violent and reverential (251a). The charioteer of the soul "falls backward in reverence" when his memory is "*borne back (passive of pherō)* to the true nature of beauty" (254b). Significantly, this gaze does not arise from an autonomous subject, but via the ambiguous action/passion of recognition, becomes a gaze which receives into itself that which offers itself to be recognized. "(T)he effluence of beauty enters him through the eyes"(251b), from without to within (and not the reverse), so that that which is gazed upon does not remain external to the gazer, but forms, through its mediation of the good, a source of nourishment to his soul. The gazer "receives the particles (of beauty) which flow to it . . ." (251c) by means of a gaze which is neither outward-bound mastery nor totalizing (250d). In contrast to the manipulative assessing gaze of the sophist, the philosophic gaze is *subordinate* to that upon which it gazes, which is the good. The yoke under which truth serves is not the ocular gaze, but the good as the transcendent good.

A gaze of mastery, by definition, issues from a firm *topos*, a ground of strength and action, of bounded propriety and clearly delineated space. It also assumes a contained subject, which must therefore be a *written* subject, such as Lysias, whom, we are led to understand, is *not* a genuine subject because he does not exceed his contractual, metic, and mercantile (rather than citizen) status,[60] echoed in the containment of his language beneath the cloak. The erotic gaze, by contrast, issues from a mobile, nomadic, atopic space (251e), no "stronghold," but a ground which moves from place to place, neither pre-established nor owned, for determined solely by the path of the good. The soul which yearns to see the good does not act upon what it sees in a mode of strength, but rather, as we have seen, is "perplexed and maddened," hastening from place to place wherever it hopes to see the beautiful one (251d). Despite this explicit reference to the shifting ground of philosophy, Derrida insists that the "Socratic word does not wander, stays at home . . . ,"[61] secure in its autochthony. By "home," Derrida means the *polis*, the patriarchal site of capital and presence. I would concede that the Socratic word "stays at home," but its home is in the good, a "site" beyond boundaries which transfigures all emplotments. The philosopher does not wander or stray from the path guided by the good, but that path could lead anywhere – *it* "wanders."

The erotic gaze is therefore neither totalizing nor rationalizing, since its "object" cannot be seen once and for all. One glimpse alone does not satisfy, for the lover yearns all the more to see again, differently, in another place, anywhere. That which is seen by the erotic gaze is *received* (as happiness) by the lover in his act of passing it on (253c, 255c), for *erōs* is, by definition, an interpersonal flow, just as "an echo rebounds from smooth, hard surfaces and returns whence it came" (255c). The beloved "sees himself in his lover as in a mirror . . . and in his absence, like him, he is filled with yearning such as he inspires, and Love's image, requited love, dwells within him, but he calls it . . . friendship" (255d). The erotic gaze institutes an ontologically constitutive loss of self, a redemptive return of that which one loves above all but is willing to give away: the very antithesis of capital.

10 THE MEDIATIONS OF EGYPT

In the above, I have argued that it is a resistance to time, supplementarity, and difference in favour of self-presence, organlessness, and identity upon which

[60] See Ferrari, *ibid.*, 228–9.
[61] Derrida, *op. cit.*, "Plato's Pharmacy," 124.

Socrates focuses in his attack on sophistry, and that recollection and dialectic work by means of differentiation, an embracing of the human narrative, *methexis*, and the ecstatic movements of the higher *erōs*. It could perhaps be argued that Plato possibly lacks a sufficient account of difference in the sense of a constitutive alteration, or mutability (2247c–d). However, by fastening exclusively upon this aspect of difference, Derrida himself denies difference in another sense, for he has no account of physicality, bodies, choice, circumstance, historical difference, and of what might be "best" for a particular person at a particular time. Socrates' account of reverence for the good and the erotic gaze by contrast leave difference open to arrive, and his transgression of the inside-outside boundary does not mean that there is *no* distinction at all between those two extremities, since such a situation would release univocal indifference.[62] In fact, it is rather Derrida who is inclined towards indifference, by virtue of his account of the *violence* of *différance:* "This process of substitution, which thus functions as a pure play of traces or supplements . . . which would be judged 'mad' since it can go on infinitely . . . this unleashed chain is . . . not lacking in violence."[63] And in his ascription of violence to Plato, Derrida overlooks the fact that it is the violent methods of sophistry which are Plato's target, and that he moves beyond this in his account of *erōs*. Here again, Derrida is obliged misleadingly to edit the mythological configuration of the Egyptian inventor of writing. Theuth, as son, demi-god, and vassal, "frequently participates in plots, perfidious intrigues, conspiracies to usurp the throne," and in his capacity as the Moon-god, Theuth "supplies the place of Ra, supplementing him and supplanting him in his absence and essential disappearance."[64] In each of Theuth's apparent roles (writing as supplement to speech, son as usurper of the king/father, moon as supplanter of the sun), Derrida insists on seeing exactly the same structure at work: for him, "usurpation" is perforce violent, final, and inescapable. But this construal of language as fundamentally written is arbitrary, and disallows the play of traces permitted by the series of embodied speakers. And in any case, Theuth's offering of his inventions to the king was neither an act of usurpation, nor entirely unsuccessful.[65] Ammon, after all, was happy to receive some of the

---

[62] On the significance of Socrates' reverence to the god Pan in the *Phaedrus* as synonymous with an embracing of difference, loss, exteriority, the unknown, death, and doubles, see Borgeaud, *op. cit., The Cult of Pan*, 55, 60, 92, 94, 99, and *passim*. Borgeaud stresses the compatibility of such celebration of difference with a non-violent, pastoral disposition. See also, Plato, *Cratylus*, 408d; Rosenmeyer, *op. cit.*, "Plato's Prayer to Pan," 37.

[63] Derrida, *op.cit.*, "Plato's Pharmacy," 89.

[64] *Ibid.*, 89, 92–3.

[65] Theuth himself was a "reckoner of gifts," Boylan, *op. cit., The Hermes of Egypt*, 193.

other inventions (274d). Moreover, it is not at all certain that Theuth's role in Egyptian mythology is that of an usurper. His central task in the legends of Horus and Osiris is as a peaceful mediator, erring in favour of legitimate sons (Horus). He is configured as a physician who heals the wounds of friends and enemies alike, and is a provider of justice and equilibrium. He functions also *to protect* the King (as in the battle of Osiris and Set), beheading the King's enemies and cutting out their hearts, and defending the rights of legitimate offspring.[66] His chief structural associations in the *Book of the Dead* (in which he is configured as a dog-headed ape or baboon), are conciliation and peace. It is he, the linguistic mediator, "who ends the strife."[67] In addition, Derrida describes the usurpation of the Sun by the Moon as a *finality* undertaken in a mood of resentment and violence. However, Theuth (as the crescent-topped Ibis) travels as the King's companion in the solar barque.[68] The supplementation of the sun by the moon is *positive*, not violent, and is, above all, a *cycle*. Furthermore, Theuth took the place of Re not by violence, but by consent. In the *Book of the Heavenly Cow*, Re decrees, "thou shalt be in my place as my *locum tenens*."[69] In these three examples, the interplays between son and father, writing and speech, moon and sun are not violent or incompatible spatial oppositions but enact a kind of asymmetrical reciprocity, or non-identical repetition. Derrida's insistence on reading violence into these structures betrays after all an underlying metaphysical dependence on the dichotomies of inside and outside and presence and absence, which leads to an eradication of difference.

This is carried over into his views on language, despite his attempts to assimilate *différance* and the middle voice. The middle voice is a grammatical category known to ancient Indo-European languages which was employed to denote action of a verb which was neither active nor passive. There is some evidence to suggest that its use was not simply to cast an action as either reciprocal or reflexive, but to express the mediation of divine by human action. However in *Dissemination*, the Derridean "middle" serves to confirm

---

[66] *Ibid.*, 58–9. Also, M. A. Murray, *Ancient Egyptian Legends*, (London: John Murray, 1913). See especially "The Book of Thoth," 29–40, "Osiris," 41–51, and "The Scorpions of Isis," 52–5. I do not discount the attributes of Theuth located by Derrida, but I would wish to loosen the rigidity of his structural configuration of Theuth's subordination to Ra, hostility towards legitimate filial relations and exclusive linkage to the written word. Although the theology of the Egyptians was by no means a self-consistent system, the epithets which Derrida assigns to the god Theuth are neither exhaustive nor representative.

[67] Boylan, *ibid.*, 95.

[68] *Ibid.*, 82.

[69] *Ibid.*, 81.

the duality of active and passive, and is characterized by a violent *conflict* between these two terms,[70] and not, as with Platonic *erōs*, an outwitting of the duality. The curious autonomy which Derrida assigns to language suggests the substitution of space for a differential relation of time. He describes the chain of significations as systematic and independent of the intentions of the author: "The system (is) not primarily that of what someone *meant-to-say* [*un vouloir-dire*]. . . . These communications or corridors of meaning can sometimes be declared or clarified by Plato when he plays upon them 'voluntarily,' a word we put in quotation marks because what it designates . . . is only a mode of 'submission' to the necessities of a given 'language' . . . then again, in other cases Plato can *not* see the links, can leave them in the shadow or break them up. And yet these links go on working of themselves."[71] Derrida's qualification of the autonomous subject, via the removal of all elements of choice, intention, desire, and particularity from the speaker or writer, does not mean that *différance* is in the middle voice, for rather than mediating all divine via human action, it merely forces the speaker into a situation of double passivity, both unable to choose language (rather, chosen *by* it), and *unaware* of this passivity. This false middle is echoed by the written text, for according to its violent protocol, writing acts upon a speaker, erasing his *act* of speech, and thereby erasing the speaker himself. Unlike inspiration from the Muses, there is here no *knowing* invocation of the impersonal Derridean god: writing. Such writing acts automatically, without reference to place or time. It is a universalizer in a nihilistic mode. There is no subject. There are only objects, death(s).

There lurks a contradiction in all this. When Derrida insists on the evidence to link capital and the good in Plato's use of the word *tokos*, child, as summoning, unwittingly, all the connotations of *tokous*, interest, he shows the autonomy of language, its systematic "corridors of meaning" at work. This autonomy is Derrida's excuse for bringing into play the whole freight of the metaphor, regardless of context or particularity as we saw in the case of the deployment of *pharmakos* (drug). And in what domain does this freight enjoy its play? Does it matter that neither author nor reader appreciate these corridors? Such a *différance* is impersonal and empty. By allowing metaphoricity this absolute reign, Derrida *obfuscates* the possibility of difference, which

---

[70] Derrida, *op. cit.*, "Plato's Pharmacy," 127. For a survey of uses of the middle voice, see Jan Gonda, "Reflections on the Indo-European Medium," Part 1, *Lingua* IX (March 1960), 30–67, Part 2, *Lingua*, IX (June 1960), 175–93; see also chapters 3 and 6 below and *passim*.
[71] Derrida, *ibid.*, 95-6.

requires literality, at least to a degree. There has to be a limit on the urge of metaphor, for difference *demands* that things are more alike to some things than to others. Certain things become linked by particularities of place, time, or even a kind of destiny. Everything is not indifferently alike. Derrida would concede that there has to be literality to be any meaning at all, the literality or particularity of a repetition, and yet his characterization of *différance* seems intent on undermining all such determinateness. In this way, his assimilation of metaphor and literality leaves only indifference, for his metaphor abdicates its power of yoking, to the same degree that his particularity abdicates all its power of distinction.[72] He describes writing as fundamentally neutral, but this is to read its indifference as non-violent and pre-given. Whereas in truth its autonomy reduces difference by a violence which rules out neutrality, an insidious violence which parades beneath indifference. To insist on neutrality is to take sides.

11 INTIMATIONS OF DOXOLOGY

According to Derrida's deconstruction of the *Phaedrus*, it is the sophists who are wedded to language and mediation through rhetoric and writing, whilst Socrates stresses the realm of unmediated truth before or beyond language. This opposition is the means by which Derrida accounts for Plato's hostility to poetry, rhetoric, and (written) language in general. However, there are intimations in the dialogue of an alternative configuration, in which Socrates is not hostile to signs as such, and construes the true language as *doxological*, that is to say, as ultimately concerned with praise of the divine. According to this view, he attacks sophistry *not* on the grounds of its linguistic mediation of truth, but because of its undoxological motivation. To conclude this chapter, I shall now argue that the most pertinent Platonic distinction is that of non-doxology and doxology, and not, as Derrida argues, that between the absolute rule of language on one hand, and a supra-linguistic philosophical logos on the other.

Plato's indictment of poetry in the *Republic* does not appeal to contemporary readers for whom the symbolic yield of art is seen as a revelation of truth which no techniques of reason or theory could ever equal.[73] For Plato, however, it is under the dictum that the better the poetic rendering, the

---

[72] *Ibid.*, 105.

[73] *Republic*, 377d–398b; see Gadamer, "Plato and the Poets," in *idem, Dialogue and Dialectic: Eight Hermeneutic Studies on Plato*, tr. P. Christopher Smith, (New Haven: Yale University Press, 1980), 39–72, 39–40.

further one is from the truth, that he exiles Homer and the Attic dramatists from his ideal state. In the *Phaedrus*, the poet and other imitative artists occupy a low position in the hierarchy of souls, only two levels above the sophists, and three above tyrants (248e). The reason given for the condemnation of Homer is his quarrelsome depiction of the gods and heroes as not conforming to the true *paideia*, and for his fear-arousing depiction of Hades. Similarly, he exiles the playwrights for not displaying an exemplary ethos. Yet within the extremity of his reproval, which perhaps was never intended as an actual design, Plato makes a serious ethical point which is that a certain political ethos, harmonious enough to tolerate the incorporation of Homer and the Attic dramatists, no longer pertains, because the agonistic structures of sophistry have come to dominate and define ethics. In his interpretation of Plato's indictment of mimetic arts, in the essay "Plato and the Poets," Hans-Georg Gadamer argues that for Socrates the sophistic concern for superficial effects has complicated ethical principles to such an extreme degree that those principles no longer appear valid in and for themselves, and the goals they instil are but upheld negatively, as strictures guarding against mutual distrust. Such a fractured ethos cannot securely accommodate those works of art which do not unambiguously depict the true *paideia*, based upon a positive, substantive construal of principle, since any inculcation of virtue they may contain can readily be perverted.[74] For Gadamer, "the contemporary *morality and moral education* which had established itself upon the basis of the poetic formulations of the older morality . . . in adhering to aging moral forms, found itself defenceless against arbitrary perversions of those forms brought on by the spirit of sophism."[75] Thus it is within the *sophistic* framework that poetic mimesis portrays human existence not according to its real dimensions, but by the mere appearance or surface as displayed to the *hoi polloi* from a distance. Its consequent delivery of a mere simulacrum means that it can only mislead the journey towards self-knowledge which seeks an undivided self, possible only on the basis of a vision of the good. Furthermore, in the sophistic *polis*, the merely negative upholding of ethical principles has eroded any sense of normative roles or appropriate blending of different roles, and this ensures that a person who imitates another person, whether poetically or dramatically, is a *divided* self. If he does not ascribe to the harmonious ideal of *paideia* based upon shared principles, the imitator is at once himself and *not* himself. He is not even coincident with the person whom he imitates, since his art of mimesis can only cleave to the mundane exterior of its model. Forgetfulness-of-self,

---

[74] *Ibid.*, 39–40.
[75] *Ibid.*, 61 (Gadamer's emphasis).

whether by means of imitation or otherwise, is fulfilled in self-alienation, synonymous with the passions of the unruly horse whose behaviour hinders all attempts to be reunited with the good (251a). (Just as when the soul is filled with forgetfulness, it grows heavy, loses his wings, and falls away from the good, 248c.) Thus contemporary mimesis is inimical to dialectic because it is defined by its confusion of roles. Indeed, it is considered most successful when there results as *little* difference between things as possible (261e). The mimetic art as practised is also predicated on a necessary lack of commitment to steady goals. Accordingly, Socrates banishes all "mixed" men from the ideal state, all double and manifold men, preferring instead those who perform just one task, the one best suited to their soul.[76]

However, for Plato there is a kind of poetry which falls outside these criticisms. This is *liturgical poetry*, in particular hymns to the gods and songs in praise of what is good: "We can admit no poetry into our city save only hymns to the gods and praises of good men."[77] Although these forms engage in a certain amount of mimetic representation, such as the depiction of gods as interlocutors, a key characteristic of a song of praise or hymn is that it does *not* involve self-division. In an act of doxological expression, the one who gives praise, the object of praise, and all those who share in its expression, are supremely centred and non-ironic, for genuine avowal involves commitment to such a degree that nothing can be held back or veiled. Liturgy is therefore not a constative representation now and then of what is praise-worthy, but constitutes a whole way of life. To give praise to what is praise-worthy by definition involves participation in it, just as emulation (Socratic mimesis) of the transcendent good must perforce involve *methexis* in the good. In addition, emulation of the good involves steadfastness and commitment, for the vision of the good does not yield a codifiable rule of conduct, consisting in negative prohibitions and protections upheld discretely now and then, but rather forms the soul through an experience of transcendence. Likewise, Socratic politics does not institute a judicial system based on the weakness of the individual protected from others by formal contracts, but depends upon rising above an insistence upon the self seen as discrete and defenceless. Dialectic is not a "skill" one employs from time to time, but a way of being, or constancy in the choice of life one leads, which ensures strong individuals, and a polity based upon their rule. The philosopher who exercises his memory rightly is "always being initiated into perfect mysteries" (249c). Dialectics is, in this regard, supremely concerned with ethical and political practice (272a) in the

---

[76] *Republic*, 397c–e, 398a–b.
[77] *Ibid.*, 606e–607a.

state, and is not, as Derrida argues, a refusal of practicality. The blinding by the brightness of the sun which befalls the cave-dwellers in Plato's allegory teaches that one must learn to accommodate darkness as much as light. This applies to the life of the *polis*, for the good is the reason why there *is* a polity.[78]

The implication is that doxology as a mode of life constitutes the supreme ethic. First, it is ontologically constitutive of the person who gives praise, for in that act he becomes fully central to himself, at the very moment that he is fully committed to the object of his praise. In the *Laws*, it is the divine gift of the liturgical cycle with all the concomitant sustenance which the deities bring to these festivals, which distinguishes human beings from the wild animals which have no such gifts of order, rhythm, or harmony.[79] Is doxology therefore the gift of humanity itself, ordered through song and dance? The primal state of the philosopher-lover, which he remembers and strives to recoup, was indeed one of perpetual doxological expression: "at that former time they saw beauty shining in brightness, when, with a blessed company . . . they saw the blessed sight and vision and were initiated into that which is rightly called the most blessed of mysteries, which are celebrated in a state of perfection, when we were without experience of the evils which awaited us" (250b–c).

Secondly, Plato's indictment of the mimetic forms of art, taking base objects as their model, implies that liturgy is the highest form of language, that which both expresses and performs shared values of what is praiseworthy. It is precisely that positive Socratic mimesis which imitates the good and so is, by definition, doxological.[80] Concomitantly, Socrates' attack on mercantile sophism includes an attack on its perversion of language, with all the implications for epistemology, ethics, and ontology which that entails. The sophistic manipulation of language irrespective of truth is presented as a subversion of civic life, contrasting with Socrates' gift or sacrifice of language to the gods (Kecharismena, 273e) and insistence that the good discourse is one which is pleasing to the gods. His second *erōs*-filled speech is offered as a liturgy, a linguistic gift to the gods, indistinguishable from dissemination of the doxological ethic: "Pardon, I pray, my former words and accept these words with favour" (257a).

When the model of excellence is given a new efficacy, embodied in civic life, as described in the *Laws*, the city itself becomes the true drama, inhabited rather than represented, and the life of the philosopher-lover enacts the true poetry, for that which he utters is harmonious with his whole mode of living.

---

[78]   *Ibid.*, 503a, 517c–d.
[79]   *Laws*, tr. A. E. Taylor, *The Collected Dialogues*, 653d–654a.
[80]   *Republic*, 396c.

The Athenian explains that "we are ourselves authors of a tragedy, and that the finest and best we know how to make. In fact, our whole polity has been constructed as a dramatization of a noble and perfect life; that is what *we* hold to be in the truth the most real of tragedies. Thus you are poets, and we also are poets in the same style, . . . and that in the finest of all dramas one which indeed can be produced only by a code of true law."[81]

This drama of philosophic life is noble and serious, and yet it is expressed through celebration and singing, so that the city itself becomes a kind of music, embodying the twofold sense of the word *nomos* as both law and song.[82] Such festivity is seen by Derrida as a containment of *paidia* (play) which for him would ideally be instantiated as a kind of riot. He argues that because for Socrates *paidia* is combined with ethics and politics, it is downgraded to the "innocent innocuous category of fun, or amusement." And he offers two possibilities for Platonic play. Either it is nothing (*alogos* or *atopos*), or it is dialectical absence, for "(a)s soon as it comes into being and into language, play erases itself as such."[83] However, an alternative account of Platonic *paidia* would be that play is not secondarily "brought into" political life, but is *constitutive* of the *polis*, thus dismantling the distinction between what is serious and proprietous and what is playful. When asked by Phaedrus if he has leisure (*scholē*, 227b) to accompany him to hear Lysias' speech, Socrates replies, "What, don't you believe that I consider hearing your conversation with Lysias 'a greater thing even than business,' as Pindar says?" (227b). Socrates' "leisure" falls outside the distinction between work and play, and is characterized instead by a perpetual philosophic readiness. Whilst it is only by chance that Phaedrus is without sandals, Socrates is always barefooted, always at "leisure" (229a). And even though Phaedrus is at leisure (barefooted), he is still plying his trade. It is his business to seem at play, just as for the professional, leisure is a labour.[84] However, the emphasis for the philosopher is not on labour and its productiveness, but rather upon the fact that he is never more "at work" than when he is immersed in the everyday. The sophistic parody hinges upon the confusion of dialectical *differentiation* and sophistic *dividedness*. And Derrida mistakenly characterizes Socrates as separating work from play: "On the one hand, the serious (*spoudē*); on the other, the game (*paidia*) and the holiday (*hearté*)".[85] Whilst Socrates does differentiate between good and bad play, as between the guided play of children in the *Laws* leading to the full

[81] *Laws*, 817b.
[82] *Ibid.*, 664b–d and *passim*, and *Republic*, 401e.
[83] Derrida, *op. cit.*, "Plato's Pharmacy," 156.
[84] Ferrari, *op. cit.*, *Listening to the Cicadas*, 15.
[85] Derrida, *op. cit.*, "Plato's Pharmacy," 150.

paideia,[86] and the wasteful "play" of the Adonians, or the misuse of dialectic as for its own sake, he does not downgrade play by opposing it to the serious. Rather, he is anxious to show *paidia* to be central to *paideia*, for both are etymologically and structurally related.[87] According to this Socratic ennoblement of play as the true ethic, defined as doxology, music, and dance, he describes the course of the day's discussion as a game (*pepaisthō*, 278b), and when he comes to demonstrate how his speeches exemplify the method of dialectic, he explains that the whole discourse was all play (*paidiai pepaisthai*, 265d).

This subversion of ordinary proprieties is seen in the *Laws*, where human beings are depicted as god's toys, and are not to be taken too seriously. In reality, only God is worth taking seriously (and what is divine in man). The human being is at best God's plaything, and the life we try to attain should consist in a form of play which alone is pleasing to God.[88] This *paidia* is not mere "fun" but is characterized by liturgical festivals, sacrifice, song, and dance.[89] The Athenian explains that it is a common error to think that war is a serious work to be done for the sake of peace, whereas in fact war is not the most serious thing as it involves neither true play nor true education.

Socrates' indictment of the poets is therefore *not* a condemnation of poetry as such, but rather of the separation of language from doxology, of art from liturgy, resulting in a sophistic "virtual reality," or realm of mere fiction which is manipulable, ironic, and uninhabited. The rise of sophistic structures means that allegiance to praiseworthy standards can no longer be pledged in a binding expression of glorification of the divine. Before the liturgical ethic can once again become a possibility, these standards must be both reinforced and defended against the arguments and strategies of the new consciousness of dividedness inimical to the holistic structure of praise. What is hinted at here is that Plato's dialogues themselves occupy this intermediate, remedial stage, forming a discussion between the opposing sides, in an attempt to lead the sophists into finding again the shared allegiance to the good.[90] The dialogues

---

[86] *Laws*, 653d, 794a–797d, and *Republic*, 539b–c.

[87] *Laws*, 653a. See Werner Jaeger, *Paideia: The Ideals of Greek Culture*, tr. Gilbert Highet, (Oxford: Basil Blackwell, 1939), Volumes I and II.

[88] *Laws*, 644d–645b, 803b–3, 804b.

[89] *Laws*, 803d.

[90] On the status of the genre of dialogue, see Planinc, *op. cit.*, *Plato's Political Philosophy*, 14, Gadamer, *op. cit.*, "Plato and the Poets," 66, Leo Strauss, "On Plato's *Republic*," in *idem*, *The City and Man*, (Chicago: Chicago University Press, 1964), 50–138, 52–4; B. Darrell Jackson, "The Prayers of Socrates," in *Phronesis*, 16 (1971), 14–37; Rosenmeyer writes that "Plato uses dialogue because of its variety, which mirrors the variety of the cosmos" in *op. cit.*, "Plato's Prayer to Pan," 37 n. 3.

represent the dissemination of "theology" in a fragmented society, as intended to lead therapeutically towards the doxological life, not only through their content, but also their structure, for the dialogic form dislodges an empiricist epistemology which seeks discrete manoeuvres at a remove from an embedded ethical existence. The Platonic dialogue is therefore a kind of writing free from the dangers of writing, resisting singular attribution of author, genre, and medium. Is it Socrates or isn't it? Is it a tractate or a drama? Is it a text or not? Its resistance to any foundation reveals it to possess the flexibility of orality, together with its form as a "literary," or theological, rather than straightforwardly doxological, prayer.

This theological interim of dialogue is crucial since we are led through it *into* doxology, which for Plato is our principle human function and language's only possibility of restoration. There are significant implications of this for ontology, as is suggested in the opening words of the dialogue, "*(p)oi dē kai pothen?*," which suggest a link between place and identity, citizenship and belonging, of what belongs and what does not, and thus provide a reappraisal of the city itself. This twofold interrogative, "where are you going and where do you come from?" is posed to Socrates' companion in the middle of his journey, the mid-point between destination and origin, reversing the chronological order, by first asking for the end and then the origin of the journey. The second part of the question is taken up as the first by Phaedrus, indicating his own priority of lineage, "(f)rom Lysias . . . the son of Cephalus". He thus traces his genealogical "place" of belonging to someone who does not "belong" at all, who is not autochthonous, for Lysias has metic status, which means he is a non-citizen resident alien whose security of place is purely contractual, supremely divided, and veiled. As a metic, Lysias would have been obliged to register with a *prostastēs*, a citizen who would have represented him in the law courts and other public places. Although he would have had to pay a special *metoikion* tax, and was also liable to the taxes which befell citizens, paid at a higher rate, he would have been debarred from the performance of *leitourgiai*, public acts of citizenship performed in honour of the gods.[91] In tracing his lineage to Lysias, Phaedrus chooses a very uncertain topos. Even in the metic terrain outside the city walls, marked by the presence of the altar of Boreas whose myth centres on the very problem of belonging (for Boreas was a god from the North, a region held in antipathy by the Athenians because of its Thracian connections, who was rejected as an undesirable suitor to the autochthonous

---

[91] Leonard Whibley (ed.), *A Companion to Greek Studies,* (Cambridge: Cambridge University Press, 1916), 448, 495; and Louise Bruit Zaidman and Pauline Schmidt Pantel, *Religion in the Ancient Greek City,* tr. Paul Cartledge, (Cambridge: Cambridge University Press, 1992), 92–101.

Oreithyia),[92] Lysias' voice is unable to speak for itself. Phaedrus must still act as his spokesman, and has gone beyond the city wall precisely to revel in the results of his voice – to revel, that is, in Lysias' absence. His voice is thus a text, portable and mobile, and we are led to assimilate his fixity (on papyrus: his speech and his metic contract) and dividedness (his hiddenness and inability to represent his own voice), with the commercial way of life. It is no accident that Phaedrus is prone to treat others, besides Lysias, as texts, for this is his "way of life." Socrates hints at this when he describes the way in which he has been led randomly all over Attica (230e), and indeed, Phaedrus offers himself as no more than a text when he proposes to reproduce Lysias' speech in the manner of a mere rhapsode. This is confirmed when we learn that he and Lysias are lover and beloved (236b, 275b, 279b), for in Socrates' palinode, it is explained that lovers can be expected to seek those of similar character (252c–253c).

Despite Phaedrus' genealogical tracing to such a displaced figure as Lysias, it is he who emphasizes the strangeness and foreignness of Socrates, how *atopic* he seems, for it is as if he is at home everywhere. Socrates' close attention to the topos of the arbour makes him seem paradoxically *atopōtatos* (230c), the same word used to describe the insanity of the Delphic Pythia and the philosopher-lover. He announces that if he were to denude the Boreas myth of its mystery, he would not be *atopos* (extraordinary) at all (229c), for the demythologizers (*hoi sophoi*) are intent on deciphering the *atopiai* (strange beings, 229e), of the chimaera and gorgons. But Socrates speculates on his own likeness to Typhon who was just such an oddity, which means that, for Phaedrus, Socrates is the oddest of men, behaving like a stranger even though he so seldom goes beyond the city walls (230c), and even though he is known to be autochthonous.[93]

And Socrates would seem to be in agreement with Phaedrus that he is wont to favour the city, when he says that "the country places and the trees won't teach me anything, and the people in the city do" (230d). But is this in fact an example of Socratic irony? Later in the dialogue, when he glimpses the beautiful in his surroundings and has described the nomadic life of the philosopher-lover, he seems to advance an entirely new definition of the city as that which is within the soul and is lived out through steadfastness towards the good,[94] rather than that which is divided by a wall from the Corybantic

---

[92] Ferrari, *op. cit.*, *Listening to the Cicadas*, 3–13 and 284 n. 39.

[93] On the significance of *topos* and *atopos* in the *Phaedrus*, see Ferrari, *ibid.*, *Listening to the Cicadas*, 13; Rodrigo, *op. cit.*, "*Dialectique Autochtone*," 274 n. 11. The god Pan, whom Socrates has invoked as the source of a mediation of outer and inner beauty (279b–c; see n. 58 above), shares with him this same paradoxical combination of hybrid monstrosity or strangeness and autochthony; see Borgeaud, *op.cit.*, *The Cult of Pan*, 48, 206 n. 14 and *passim*.

[94] *Republic*, 537d.

countryside. By leaving the city walls behind, both literally and figuratively, Socrates has *not* become indifferent to place, in the manner of the Phaedran *mathēsis* which can operate anywhere, but rather sees places all the more intensely.

Lysias' discourses are described as *asteios* (227d), "of the city," refined, of outward appearances, urbane. This *textual* autochthony, paralleled by Lysias' contractual status, represents the most secure locus in Phaedrus' eyes, far more so than Socrates' curious and ecstatic position. But Socrates is proposing an altogether new ontology, for, by reversing the chronology in his opening question, there is a suggestion that a person's identity is defined and performed not only by his position in a particular place, but also by a kind of journeying, an "identity" which is always *in medias res*. At the point when Phaedrus announces Socrates' condition of displacement, the latter is in fact superlatively *within* his place, for as a philosopher-lover, his home is wherever the good leads him. Rather, it is Phaedrus who is the stranger, not only to the landscape, but also to himself.

The radical doxological identity here hinted at is beyond *both* mimetic realism and secular irony. The person who gives praise is not estranged, yet neither can he lay claim to a fixed or completed identity which would define a secular or contractual role.[95] Whilst the figure of Lysias, held securely in place by means of written contracts, is an identity supremely confused and under erasure, the Socratic subject finds itself in and through its liturgical role in the *polis*, and through inspiration from the beauty of his surroundings. This self-knowledge cannot be singularly attained, but represents a life's work and a way of being, as the subtitle of the *Phaedrus* indicates: "On the Beautiful, Ethical." Praise of the beautiful is the supreme ethic, the route to the transcendent good which does not circumvent situatedness and contingency, and remains open to difference and multiplicity.

The Socratic *polis* is therefore not bounded-off by physical walls, for walls represent the exclusion of possibilities. Rather, Socrates' boundaries are more akin to philosophic conditions or psuchical principles. He carries this *polis* within him (253a), establishing its domain wherever he goes by uttering invocations, thanksgivings, and petitions, treading the spiritual boundaries of

---

[95] See above, n. 93. Borgeaud notes the association of Panic festival, music, and dancing, with the release from political repression and the attainment of a non-coercive cohesion, or redeemed citizenship. In the gestures of Panic dance, writes Borgeaud, the individual discovers that his movements correspond with the cosmic order. The individual is thereby restored not only to himself, but to humanity as such. See *op. cit.*, *The Cult of Pan*, 139, 251 n. 111. "(P)anic dissolves the bonds of a little society characterized by a high degree of reinforcement and involution," 101.

his physical placement by noting the different aspects of the divine presence – Achelous, the nymphs, Pan, and the Muses. Socrates' refusal of the final temptation to flee the city offered to him in the *Crito* (and as he takes leave of his friends in the *Phaedo*), does not necessarily illustrate his fetishistic rootedness in the city – the traditional interpretation – but instead illustrates his dialectical steadfastness, his holding fast to what is good, and his sacral construal of the *polis*. It is rather the mercantile city which is driven to expel scapegoats in its urgent securing of identity through the perpetuation of the boundary between inside and outside, seen ultimately in the expulsion of the atopic Socrates, whilst Socrates' own radicalization of that boundary through the psuchical *polis* shows an advance beyond the need for scapegoats.[96]

Citizenship of the psuchic *polis* is achieved through steadfast commitment to the good, but this itself arrives in answer to prayer, as a divine gift (245a–b, 279b–c). It is therefore neither statutorily assigned nor pre-given. In the Socratic city *everyone* is a metic, secured neither by fact nor contract, but by perpetual renewal of a particular mode of life, dialectic in character, sustained through acts of liturgy, which thus ensure that subjectivity remains open and in the character of gift.

This radicalization of boundaries as a kind of ethical goal, characterized by music and sacrifice, is far from the tranquil interiorities and suspicions of difference and language described by Derrida. Such monadic qualities are in fact isolated by Socrates in his attack on sophism. They constitute an anticipation of the characteristics of immanentist modernity, and subvert political life, not because of their reliance on language as such, but rather on account of their separation of language *from itself*, or from its ultimate character as an expression of liturgy.

[96] See Borgeaud, *ibid.*, 71–2.

Chapter Two

SPATIALIZATION: THE MIDDLE OF MODERNITY

1 THE NEW SOPHISTRY

In the previous chapter, I argued that Derrida misrepresents one source of the metaphysical tradition, namely, Platonism. I have shown how he is mistaken in his characterization of Socratic dialectical knowledge as "domination" and as predicated upon the triumph of capital. To the contrary, Socrates critically identifies the link between *sophism* and both domination and capital. It has equally been shown that the Socratic preference for speech over writing is not a covertly necessary support for a metaphysics of presence, but rather its explicit rejection. And I have suggested that in presenting a new sophism, Derrida himself is exposed to all Socrates' criticisms. He is *himself* culpably "metaphysical" insofar as he celebrates sophistry and writing, just as his exaltation of the *nihil* is tantamount to an abasement before the perfect abstract and graspable object, within the context of a perverse but nonetheless perfected *mathēsis*. It is as a *metaphysician*, after all, that Derrida upholds knowledge as writing, domination, and capital, for his exaltation of absence and postponement turns out to be but the inevitably nihilistic conclusion of a rationalism indifferent to the specificities of human place, time, and desire. The perfectly present *is* that which will never arrive, as he himself dialectically affirms.[1] Thus he perfects, and does not refute, the Cartesian abstraction from embodiment. Not only, on the above reading, does it seem that the Derridean and entire postmodern assumption of a seamless line of development of a culpable "metaphysics" from Plato to Descartes is false; it *also* appears that

---

[1] Jacques Derrida, *Speech and Phenomena*, tr. David Allison, (Evanston: Northwestern University Press, 1973).

Derrida *remains within* a post-Cartesian set of assumptions whose ancestry lies in sophistry and not Platonic dialectics.

If the above conclusions are substantively correct, the entire postmodern historical and philosophical perspective is called drastically into question. No longer are we the legatees of a Western logocentrism, fixated upon presence, and a domineering gaze secured by myths of transcendence. Instead it appears that it is *just those very myths* which, in ancient Athens, first radically challenged the beginnings of a technocratic, manipulative, dogmatically rationalist, anti-erotic, anti-corporeal and homogenising society undergirded by secularity and pure immanence. And instead of celebrating our final escape from a malign Western past, we should mourn our departure from what was once one of the most central elements in Western tradition: philosophy itself, in its revisionist Socratic variant. Finally it appears that the modern/postmodern debate is empty shadow-boxing, since nihilism is but the most extreme expression of a humanist rationalism. It should therefore cease to surprize us that postmodernism offers no new and critical politics beyond the *impasse* of commercialism into which modernity has led us (see chapter 3 below). Instead we should consider seriously the Socratic notion that only a doxological *polis* and the acknowledgement of transcendence can ever liberate us from the sway of capital and linguistic debasement.

In this chapter, I examine the subsequent extension of the sophistic *mathēsis*. I contend that during the period of early modernity, with Ramism and later, Cartesianism, which were encouraged by the facility of printing and its identical repetitions, and by the breakdown of the traditional religious order, space becomes a pseudo-eternity which, unlike genuine eternity, is fully comprehensive to the human gaze, and yet supposedly secure from the ravages of time. Through a discussion of various manifestations of spatialization in modes of scientific practice, government, and in the field of baroque poetics, I show how the attempt to bypass the intervention of human temporality and subjectivity (which a liturgical knowledge and practice had embraced) via an apparently unmediated apprehension of "objective" and "given" facts was not an eccentric or marginal phenomenon. Then in the final section of this chapter, I argue that "sophistic" spatialization has become increasingly normative, even to the extent that it has infiltrated the very structures of our language, almost obliterating its original liturgical character.

In the instances of spatialization which I discuss in this chapter, it will be seen how technological progress in writing and other modes of mechanical operation provides us with an all too seductive *facility*. If one takes this facility for "the real," one is led to imagine that the ease and predictability of operations within a new artificial sphere exhibit our true, primary relationship to the world. This is what I call a "spatial illusion." However, "technology" is not itself the prime cause at work here, for the illusions which it can encourage are only *legitimized* by an increasing denial of genuine transcendence, understood as doxological reliance upon a donating source which one cannot command. Without eternity, space must be made absolute and the uncertainty of time's source and end be suppressed. Hence, "sophistic" immanentism is the ultimate foundation of these illusions. Whilst for Plato, the genre of the dialogue offered a remedial interlude necessary for the restoration of language as a medium of doxology, the structures of sophistry are now so boldly inscribed into our linguistic and social practices that a liturgical attitude toward reality becomes increasingly remote of access.

In seeking to expose the illusions of contemporary sophistry in this chapter, then, I trace the expansion of the unliturgical world.

2 PETER RAMUS

In the Epistle to the Reader at the beginning of the *Logike* (1574), Peter Ramus boasts that his "lytle booke" will bring "more profytt" to the reader than "all thy fower yeares studie in Plato or Aristotle."[2] As well as the great utility of his book, "the facilitie and easynes of the same is not a litle to be commended."[3] The reason given for its facility and easiness is that the *method*, or series of ordered steps which it propounds, is applicable to every art and science, and its emphasis on clarity and simplicity is thought to open every discipline to a condition of availability and accessibility. This is accentuated by Ramus' use of diagrams and charts which apparently occupy space in a timeless domain of abstract lines, whose ability to communicate information at a single glance seems to bypass the mediation of language itself.

In seeking to supplant Plato and (especially) Aristotle, Ramus subscribes to a tradition which itself borrowed many features from Aristotelian logic and rhetoric. Indeed, the tradition itself began with Aristotle's treatise on scientific demonstration in the *Posterior Analytics*, followed by Boethius' *On the Different Kinds of Topics*, and Peter of Spain's *De Locis*. This was succeeded by the development in the middle ages of "suppositional logic" which, by treating terms as substantives, registered the progressive visualization and

[2] Peter Ramus, *The Logike* (1574), (Leeds: The Scolar Press Ltd, 1966), 14; see Lisa Jardine, "Humanist Logic," in eds Charles B. Schmitt and Quentin Skinner, *The Cambridge History of Renaissance Philosophy*, (Cambridge: Cambridge University Press, 1988), 184–86.
[3] *Ibid.*, 14–15.

spatialization of thought.[4] Rudolph Agricola's complex "place logics" continued the process of epistemological tabulation, and was assisted in this by the
development of printing with which it was concurrent. Printing accelerated
the drive towards spatialization because its multiplication of identical images
and containment of data in abstract and apparently timeless formulations gave
encouragement to the notion of the "availability" of a quantified and
objectified knowledge. Furthermore, the appearance of knowledge in the
impersonal arena of a printed page, in contrast to the individual and erratic
scribal "hands" of the past, precipitated the notion of a pseudo-eternity of
"given" reality unaffected by the human being who enacts its representation.[5]

Ramus, as Walter J. Ong has argued, carried through all these tendencies
to a new extreme. He was an educational reformer reacting against scholastic
subtlety which was alleged to have lost contact with the everyday world. In
an attempt to make amends for Aristotelian and mediaeval obscurantism,
Ramus offered a universal *mathēsis*, or calculus of reality, by which a *topos* was
divided into two distinct compartments. The first, *invention*, was intended to
lay bare the irreducible components of a proposition, and the second,
judgement or *disposition*, was concerned with the proper use of these basic
components or arguments in the process of reasoning. The first stage of
invention entailed a division of the given topic by successive and ordered
stages, beginning with the most general and progressing towards the most
particular. This deductive reasoning from general principles to particularities
was to be adhered to regardless of the nature of the subject under scrutiny. The
first step was a brief definition in the most general terms, whose purpose was
to establish clearly the extent and limits of the subject. True definition, as
opposed to description, was to be as brief as possible, so as to allow the real

[4] Walter J. Ong, S.J., *Ramus and the Decay of Dialogue*, (Cambridge, Massachusetts: Harvard
University Press, 1983), 65–72.
[5] On Peter of Spain and Rudolph Agricola as precursors of Ramus, see Ong, *Ramus and
the Decay of Dialogue*, and *idem, Orality and Literacy, The Technologizing of the Word*, (London:
Routledge and Kegan Paul Ltd, 1982), chapters 3–5. On Boethius and Peter of Spain, see
Etienne Gilson, *History of Christian Philosophy in the Middle Ages*, (London: Sheed and Ward
Ltd, 1955), 97–106 and 319–23. On the development of printing, its acceleration of the
notion of method, and other epistemological effects, see Edgar Zilsel, "The Origins of
Gilbert's Scientific Method," *Journal of the History of Ideas* II (1941), 1–32; Elizabeth L.
Eisenstein, *The Printing Press as an Agent of Change, Communications and Cultural Transfor-
mations in Early-Modern Europe*, (Cambridge: Cambridge University Press, 1979), Volumes
1 and 2; Marshall McLuhan, *The Gutenberg Galaxy: The Making of Typographic Man*,
(London: Routledge and Kegan Paul Ltd, 1962), and *idem, Understanding Media: The
Extensions of Man*, (London: Routledge and Kegan Paul Ltd, 1964).

essence of the thing being examined to be made superlatively clear. For Ramus, this meant simple classification according to genus and form. The second stage, *judgement*, comprised a division of the subject according to its principal components, a method of arrangement known as *distribution*, which was carried out in several different ways, depending on the logical relationship between the parts and the whole. Wherever possible, this distribution was to be effected by means of a *dichotomy* which split the topic down the middle, leaving two further classes upon which the operation might be repeated. When one particular distribution was exhaustively accomplished, each of the classes so obtained was to be defined in turn and subdivided following the same routine. Thus, according to a fractal epistemology, each topic, belonging to any discipline, and every aspect pertaining to that topic, was seen as available to the same lateral grid of inquiry. Equally, this method presupposed that every subject is already and to the same degree "there," simply waiting to be mapped and divided, and excludes the temporal aspect of knowledge as an "event" which arrives. When the division had been carried out properly to the furthest possible degree, all the arguments appropriate to the examination of the subject were assumed to be clearly evident.[6]

The second stage, *judgement*, was itself divided into three classes: enunciation, syllogism, and *methodus*. The first, which was to be used when the truth of the matter was evident, consisted in linking one argument with another, for when truth was not in question, a mere juxtaposition of arguments was sufficient to command universal agreement. With respect to these self-evident axioms, Ramus introduced three rules. The first was the *law of verity*, by which all precepts in all arts and sciences must be true without exception. The second rule was that of *justice*, which held that each art must be contained within its own bounds, and withhold nothing appertaining to other arts: a rule, therefore, of homogeneity. The third, called the *document of wisdom*, legislated that everything be taught in accordance with its nature (i.e. that the general be taught generally, and the particular particularly).[7]

When a statement appeared to be of doubtful validity, its truth or falsehood was to be demonstrated by syllogism. Ramus details the bifurcated structure of syllogisms and lists their various types, each suited to a particular proposition (such as "symple," "affirmant," "generall," "speciall," and "proper" etc.).[8]

---

[6] Although, in an aside, Walter Ong writes that Ramus never really demonstrates this certainty, *op. cit.*, *Ramus and the Decay of Dialogue*, 176.

[7] Ramus, *op. cit.*, *The Logike*, 74. For an exposition of this aspect of the method, see the sections on Ramus in Kenneth D. McRae, "Ramist Tendencies in the Thought of Jean Bodin," *Journal of the History of Ideas*, XVI (1955), 306–23.

[8] Ong, *op. cit.*, *Ramus and the Decay of Dialogue*, 80.

The third procedure, *methodus*, a technique for arranging precepts in conven-
ient order, was to be activated when many precepts were under consideration
at the same time, so many that a single, synchronic glance was impossible.
According to the *methodus*, the simplest notions were to precede, the more
complex to come later, with the most general precepts such as definitions
always being placed first.

The significance with respect to my theme of spatialization of the features
of Ramism described above, are threefold, and relate to a "sophistic"
negotiation of temporality: first, its epistemological construal of reality;
secondly, closely linked with the first, its simplification of memory; and
thirdly, its pejoration of language.

The Ramist method has considerable implications for a construal of the
perception of reality, and can be seen to prefigure the Cartesian subordination
of reality to geometric *extensio*. Indeed, it is not quite right to claim, like
Stephen Toulmin in *Cosmopolis*, that the modern desire to establish absolute
rational certainty, focused upon method, and free from the supposed distor-
tions of cultural particularity, is traceable first to Descartes in the seventeenth
century against a background of "general crisis." For already, the successive
crises of the late Middle Ages and the Reformation had engendered a search
for methodological and pragmatic security, of which *humanism itself* (as
Toulmin ignores) sometimes partook, especially when it sought to establish
a readily usable and universally accessible "place logic." This quest reached its
culmination with the work of Ramus.[9]

The philosophical emphasis of the Ramist method is upon formal arrangement rather than content or depth, and although spatial configurations are by
no means devoid of usefulness or profundity,[10] in the case of the Ramist
cartographies, their purpose is purely regulative and designed for the reader's
convenience. This "convenience" has a sinister aspect, for by adopting the
stance of methodizer, the pedagogue obfuscates the confusions of reality,
generating an apparently objective ontology, from a secretly subjective
method. This subterfuge depends entirely upon a new distinction from, and
elevation above, the flow of reality on the part of the subject, which alone
permits reality apparently to render itself in terms of discrete definition,
distribution, clarity, and distinctness. A new cultural fear that without such

[9] Stephen Toulmin, *Cosmopolis: The Hidden Agenda of Modernity*, (Chicago: University of
Chicago press, 1990); see also the chapter entitled *Transition* below.
[10] See, for example, Frances A. Yates, *The Art of Memory*, (London: Pimlico, 1992), 230–
1, on the stimulation of the imagination by the frescoed and sculptured images in churches,
such as the Fresco of The Wisdom of Thomas Aquinas by Andrea da Firenze, *ibid.*, plate
2.

imposition-disguised-as-mere-reading reality is ineluctably chaotic, is here scarcely concealed.

There is also a suggestion in this configuration of method as distinct from the myriad complications of reality it observes and configures, that the appearance of disorder is *merely* real whilst the method and the mind which deploys it are *supra-real*. The mind is posited as a superior cipher or mirror whose systematic operation discloses a hidden regularity.[11] Furthermore, the categories, both those inherited and those devised by Ramus, assume a supra-linguistic status which bypasses all contingency, as though ordained prior to language to deliver the clear and distinct essence of reality as it really is, rather than as it merely seems, by means of a direct and yet exalted access. According to such a scheme, the Ramist charts map the divisions and subdivisions of a particular proposition in a fashion which resembles exalted mnemonic devices (where memory is defined as local recall) for the storage and re-use of data, and yet what was once a mere art of memory now serves as a method for understanding, and the logic of this method in turn usurps the place of an ontology. Thus ease of comprehension and ease of communication are compounded with the neutral delivery of a reality whose authentic mark is taken to be such instant simplicity.[12]

The second implication for epistemology of the rise of Ramist method pertains to the status of the *mathēsis* it delivers. Previously, knowledge had been associated with mythical and iconographic figures such as statues and allegorical illustrations, regarded as derived from a transcendent and constantly arriving source.[13] The "reading" of these devices was as much part of the narrative of that arrival as the artefacts themselves, and was by no means dependent upon a singularly attestable "content." By contrast, the printed words of Ramist "reading" were connected to one another by lines in simplified binary patterns forming dichotomized charts of methodized noetic material, designed precisely to foreclose any such open-ended interpretation. Furthermore, the exhaustive dichotomization of Ramist method is a system which carries a totalizing danger. In Socratic terms, Ramism continues in the tradition of sophistic demythologization, construing knowledge as consisting in discrete items "contained" as objects in distinct and homogeneous *topoi*. Unlike the *topoi* of Aristotle, these are specifically *textual*, and, encouraged by

---

[11] On the mind as a mirror, see Richard Rorty, *Philosophy and the Mirror of Nature*, (Oxford: Basil Blackwell, 1980).

[12] See Ong, *op. cit., Ramus and the Decay of Dialogue*, 280, and Paolo Rossi, *Clavis Universalis: Arti Mnemoniche E Logica Combinatoria Da Lullo a Leibniz*, (Milan: Riccardo Ricciardi Editove, 1960), 140, cited in Yates, *op. cit., The Art of Memory*, 229.

[13] Yates, *op. cit., The Art of Memory*, 230–1.

the model of the manoeuvrable type of the printing press, seem infinitely transferable. Indeed, its apparently universal applicability[14] suggests that Ramism treated everything as equivalent in its availability to the *mathēsis*, which apprehended reality as an undifferentiated *given*.

According to this scheme, memory becomes a matter of simple retrieval of objects, merely a kind of stocktaking or enumeration, thus vastly reducing the reach of memory presumed by the traditional mnemonic treatises of earlier rhetorics. For when things are "available" in such a way, epistemological activity becomes purely speculative, and memory is simply a matter of repeating the "glance," rather than an act which testifies to the temporality of knowledge and which facilitates the judgement of analogy between instances, ensuring the continuity of the knowing subject.

The final consideration of the implications of Ramist method pertains to its pejoration of language, in particular as regards its denigration of rhetoric to mere *elocutio*, which can be shown to be related to its encouragement, as described by Walter Ong, of the demise of dialogue and its commensurate exaltation of mathematics and constativity.

The chief goal of Ramist dialectic, namely pedagogic clarity, problematized the tension between the traditional categories of dialectic and rhetoric, in such a way that the classical notion of dialectic as dialogue, and the Scholastic art of disputation (according to which, both dialectic *and* rhetoric had their own respective categories of *invention* and *judgement*), were conflated into a monologic art which simply retained the name of dialectic.[15] But it is specifically a *textual* monologue which further reduces dialectic to the condition of a sophistic rhetoric,[16] that is, a rhetoric which

---

[14] These "rules appertaining to the matter of every art" declare "the methode and forme to be observed in all artes and sciences"; "No farther seeke but in this booke thy self doe exercise," Ramus, *op. cit.*, *The Logike*, 7, 2. On Aristotelian *topoi* as predicated on the spoken word, see Giorgio Agamben, *Language and Death: The Place of Negativity*, tr. Karen E. Pinkus and Michael Hardt, (Minneapolis: University of Minnesota Press, 1991), 33.

[15] In spite of this textualization of both dialectic and rhetoric, Ramus claims (emptily) that his "Dialecticke otherwise called Logicke, is an arte which teachethe to dispute well," *The Logike*, 17.

[16] Walter Ong compares this textual rhetoric with Aristotelian logic which, although essentially diagrammatic, could not be reduced entirely to spatiality because it derives from aural-type analogies rather than visual. This residue of the auditory, though not made explicit by Aristotle, is inseparable from his thinking because the categories are conceived as *parts of enunciations*. Thus human knowledge for Aristotle exists, in the full sense, only in the enunciation, that is, in the saying of something about something, the uttering of a statement, the expression of a judgement, and the union of a subject and predicate.

makes no appeal beyond itself to the variable but always ethical circumstances of civic life, or that offers modes of praise and honour as the
traditional rhetorics sought to do. By thus removing the dynamic poles
of traditional dialectic, and the reality of sound, Ramus concomitantly
displaced rhetoric itself, encouraging its relegation to the now innocuous category of *elocutio*, which, in a context where the textual is now
normative, has less to do with the structures of oral delivery than with
spatially construed ornamentation.[17] This further accentuates the separation
of reality from the noetic categories, for this new casting of rhetoric
simply involves the ornate utterance of preconstituted truths. Moreover,
for Ramus, the notion of *elocutio* was doubly textual, for, in encouraging brevity, clarity, and schematization, he preferred above all, not
language, but the use of spatial diagrams. And as regards language
itself, he advocated the use of "plain style." This did not mean a "low
style," but rather, a synthesis of the three former styles of *elocutio*, high,
medium, and low, which emerges as an expository, cerebral, and analytic
style, highly depersonalized, and as close to mathematics as language
can be.[18] It is ironic that a system which rejected the obscurantism of
Scholasticism by seeking to assimilate "common parlance" should result in
a voiceless style which presaged the Cartesian attempt to "get outside"

Concomitantly, the *topoi* of ancient rhetoric were seen as fontal sources of arguments, with
such open-ended places as *relatio* and *similitudo*. With Agricola and Ramus, however, the
topoi are presented as headings, or as entries in a classificatory finding-system to a static and
given resource of information which admits of no development. This shift towards
knowledge as exhaustively contained in "places" was reflected in the structure of printed
books, for example, as regards the introduction at this time of the *index locorum*. On the
Agricolan and Ramist conceptual closure of *topoi* see Ong, *op. cit.*, *Ramus and the Decay of
Dialogue*, 104–12, and on the further implications of the format of printed books, *ibid.*, 311–
15.

[17] John Milbank, *The Religious Dimension in the Thought of Giambattista Vico 1668–1744*,
Volume I, *The Early Metaphysics*, (Lampeter and New York: Edwin Mellen Press, 1991),
278–80.

[18] Whilst it is true that Aristotle's philosophy of nature was also committed to the
unambiguous language of science, with much emphasis upon comparison and exhaustive
definition (not similitude), there remain fundamental differences between Aristotle's
philosophy and that of the new science. For Aristotle, the phenomena of nature are
not homogeneous, but are governed by different kinds of causes and principles. Science
cannot be any more uniform than its subject matter. The translation of methods from one
science to another leads to category-mistakes (or *metabasis*). For the new science, however,
such *metabasis* no longer presented a problem because it tended to view all being as

subjectivity and language altogether, and to find the pure, unmediated *mathēsis*.[19]

Such attempts to rid language *of itself* were encouraged by post-Gutenberg communications, for the effect of printing was to reinforce the dominance of a linear structure of "given" arguments apprehended at a glance on the surveyable page. Agricolan place logics and Ramist diagrams encouraged a sense of discourse as something which could be manipulated, as it were, from without, as an object. With this new development, the spatial notion of "structure" or architecture came to be applied to language. And the shift is reflected in changes of syntax and punctuation. For example, whereas formerly, syntax had been time-bound and aggregative in structure, and punctuation such as colons and commas had functioned to indicate pauses or emphases relating to oral delivery, with the progressive introduction of spatial models, syntax and punctuation now became more abstract and logic-bound.[20]

The attempt to find a logical and voiceless discourse also bears witness to the rise of a constative construal of language as a disinterested reporter of things, constituted not in opposition to the mind, but, paradoxically, *in opposition to language itself*– since it assumes that the naturalness and immediacy of its "language" permits a conflation of language and reality. Over against ordinary language and its local prejudices stands a pristine realm of diagrams and abstractions. But this involves a contradiction: Ramism's mathematical conventions *are* still mediated, and its lines are still metaphors. The reason why this did not seem to compromise his system was perhaps that the abstract and silent formulations of its charts *shared a kind of invisibility* with the transcendent, and so borrowed from its authority and eternity. But in their new immanent context, authority and eternity were translated (imperceptibly) into their mundane counterparts, pedagogy and permanence.

In the following three sections, I will consider several aspects of Descartes' philosophy which reflect the continuing programme of spatialization and confirm the above diagnosis. First, I will examine the implications for my theme

homogeneous. See Amos Funkenstein, *Theology and the Scientific Imagination from the Middle Ages to the Seventeenth Century*, (Princeton, New Jersey: Princeton University Press, 1986), 35–7.

[19] "Abolyshe all tautologies and vayne repetitions, and so thus muche being done, thou shalt comprehende the rest into a litle rome," Ramus, *op. cit., The Logike*, 12. See also Walter Ong, *op. cit., Ramus and the Decay of Dialogue*, 212–13, 283–4.

[20] Manfred Görlach, *Introduction to Early Modern English*, (Cambridge: Cambridge University Press, 1991), 101–2, 122–8; see also Ong, *op. cit., Ramus and the Decay of Dialogue*, 128.

of his ideas on the construction of the ideal city, showing how his account of subjectivity depends upon a prior *parody* of the Platonic sacred *polis* which involves, primarily, a spatialization of the city, avoided by Plato. Then, in section four, entitled *"Reality Without Depth,"* I will show how the Cartesian fulfillment of ontology in epistemology inaugurates an immanentist construal of reality as the "given," and how this gives rise to the possibility of an object; I discuss the implications of this for a theory of language and knowledge. Finally, in section five, *"The Written Subject,"* I consider how the spatialization of the city and the immanentization of being together assume the dominance of a new, non-liturgical subject.

3 The Cartesian City

Whilst it is generally considered that Descartes' ontology begins with the subject and what the subject knows, I argue in this section that his theory of the subject depends upon prior moves in, first, "politico-architectonics," and, secondly, ontology. In the first case, the city is defined as purely spatial, and, in the second, being is defined as immanent. Only because the city is now spatialized and being is now transparently graspable, is the city then construed as contained within the individual, and *esse* as first opened up by the *Cogito*.

First, therefore, the Cartesian city. The character of this city best emerges through a contrast with that of Plato. In the *Phaedrus*, the Socratic account of *erōs* and the contagion of the good contributes to a transfiguration of civic space, according to which the sacred polis is established wherever the philosopher-lover perceives the good. Although this means that for Plato the *polis* is instantiated in a certain sense *within* the philosopher-lover, it is not thereby "containable" in the manner of ordinary spatial appropriation, but is characterized by the ecstatic and interpersonal contagion of transcendent goodness. And in accordance with the good, the whole polity of the city is constructed as a dramatization of the noble and perfect life,[21] as outlined in the *Laws* and the *Republic*, where citizenship is sustained not by written contracts but through communal acts of liturgy, which ensure that subjectivity is both open and interpersonally constituted.

Whilst Plato compares the construction of the ideal city to the painter using a heavenly model,[22] for Descartes, the perfect city is primarily *written*, and

[21] Plato, *Laws*, 817b.

[22] "(A)nd will they distrust our statement that no city could ever be blessed unless its lineaments were traced by artists who used the heavenly model?" Plato, *Republic*, tr. Paul Shorey, *The Collected Dialogues*, VI, 500e.

wholly immanent. In Part II of his *Discourse on the Method*, Descartes employs analogies of architecture, city-planning, and governmental structure to describe his method for the composition and organization of knowledge. His main contention is that, in general, the singular and homogeneous is to be preferred to the multiple and diverse. In the various examples he cites, there is a suggestion also that this preference presupposes a substitution of the spatial for the temporal. He argues that buildings are "more attractive and better planned" when designed and built by a single architect than by various different craftsmen; that cities constructed by a single planner are better proportioned than those which have developed haphazardly; and that society is better governed by the laws of a single legislator than by laws which have arisen organically in response to changing circumstances. On analogy with the socially manifest priority of individually sustained consistency, the universal method in thought is devised by a man "shut up alone in a stove-heated room, where [he is] completely free to converse with [him]self about [his] own thoughts."[23] The science of many is never so closely approximated to the truth as the simple reasoning of a person led by himself alone, and a child is better guided by internal reason than by the conflicting pressures of his teachers and his own passions.[24]

The most important factor, for Descartes, in his new civic paradigm is *formal consistency*, rather than intrinsic embodiment of the good. In this fashion, he is precisely sophistic, for his model, detached both from mediations of the good and from particularity, draws significantly upon analogies of writing and draughtsmanship. These written analogies for the organization of knowledge constitute his assumed politico-architectonics: city-planning, legislation, architectural design. He cites the ideal example of Sparta, arguing that if that city-state "was at any time very flourishing, this was not because each of its laws in particular was good . . . but because they were devised by a single man and hence all tended to the same end."[25] Thus, he prefers the written, immanent, and homogeneous city, even when this might involve a kind of anarchy, for in the case of Sparta, Descartes concedes that some of Lycurgus' laws were nonetheless "very strange and even contrary to good morals."[26]

Hence we have already seen that the preference for a single legislator itself assumes the priority of formal consistency, or subjection to geometric, spatial

---

[23] René Descartes, *Discourse on the Method*, in tr. John Cottingham, Robert Stoothoff, Dugald Murdoch, *The Philosophical Writings of Descartes*, Volume I (Cambridge: Cambridge University Press, 1985), Part II, VI. 11.

[24] *Ibid.*, Part II, VI. 11–17.

[25] *Ibid.*, VI. 12.

[26] *Ibid.*, VI. 12.

rule over the incarnation of goodness. In the second place, it can also be seen that it is linked to the sketching out of a pure interiority. Descartes' choice of Sparta, as cited above, is significant not only because of the premium which it placed on formal order and the regulation of every detail of life, but also because Sparta is known to have been organised on military lines of warfare for the defence of its own absolute interior. Indeed, not only this feature, but also the stress on the single legislator as essential to the formal consistency of the city fulfill Jacques Derrida's characterization of metaphysics as the preservation of interiority, of reason as monadic self-presence, and of the city as a pristine enclosure which must resort to the expulsion of the impure.[27] For in the case of the Cartesian city, the impure is represented as that which bears traces of time, multiplicity, and difference, in the form of the emergent structures of ancient cities, organic legal systems, and philosophical and pedagogic traditions. To such instances of impurity, Descartes responds with a violent gesture of demolition. Regarding, for instance, the traditional philosophical opinions handed down to him from the past, he writes, "I could not do better than undertake to get rid of them, all at one go, in order to replace them afterwards with better ones,"[28] thereby re-enacting, in parodic form, Plato's banishment of poets and artists from the city. But whilst, for Plato, the pretext is that mimesis is inimical to a doxological mode of life, for Descartes, the axiom of singular authorship as the condition of possibility for clarity and distinctness dictates his indictment of resemblance in the *Regulae*, and of the traditions of philosophy in *The Discourse*.[29] At best, the multiple, different, and temporal can improvise as rudimentary halfway houses *en route* to the ideal structure. In Part Three of *The Discourse*, when Descartes describes his fourfold moral code, he explains that before starting to rebuild one's house, having demolished the previous one, it is necessary to provide oneself with a provisional home in which to live whilst the definitive edifice is under construction. Similarly, he explains, he has devised a provisional code by which to live until his universal method has been completed. In each case, this short-term structure belongs to the past, with its concomitant multiple authorship, and is reduced to a mere convenience or formality, simply bridging the way to its own demolition. The "laws and customs" of his society are not regarded as part of a living truth enacted by a whole community, but rather as exigential grids whose gradual diffusion and purely accidental

---

[27] See chapter 1 above, Section 6 "*Erōs and Exteriority*" and *passim*.
[28] Descartes, *op. cit., Discourse on the Method*, Part II, VI. 13–14.
[29] *Rules for the Direction of the Mind*, in Cottingham *et al. op. cit.*, *The Philosophical Writings of Descartes*, (Volume I), Rule One, X359–61.

moderation will prevent him from straying too far from the truth until his final attainment of the universal method.

Descartes' suggestion that the ideal method is produced in solitude, by "the simple reasoning which a man of good sense naturally makes," as opposed to the diverse books "compounded and amassed little by little from the opinions of many different persons,"[30] or by the child guided from birth by his reason alone, presupposes that certain knowledge (*scientia*) is self-producing, ahistorical, and extra-linguistic. Like the rhetorical methods of the sophists, and Ramist calculus, Descartes' formal arrangements present a lateral ideal whose autonomy refuses the mediations of tradition, myth or transcendence. Indeed, in the Cartesian method there is no equivalent to the Platonic Forms, except to the extent that for Descartes the Forms exist as a universalized textual system which acts as an identically repeated paradigm.[31]

From the above, it can be seen that Descartes' preference for a single legislator is explained in terms of this legislation's more reliable delivery of, first, formal consistency without respect for the good, and, secondly, a pure, inviolable interiority which depends upon absolutely surveyable bounds. The city is, by the first condition, entirely predictable because immunized against new arrivals in time, and, by the second, totalized in order to be defensible. This double circumstance amounts to spatialization, since time is neutralized, and all is ordered and surveyable without remainder, within absolute borders. Hence it can be seen that the preference for a single legislator only makes sense on the assumption that legislation is itself an operation of mere formal spatial arrangement. *Before* the *Cogito*, already in the *Regulae*, Descartes espoused the ideal of an entirely portable method, of an *ars* that is more reliable because precontained and foreordained in the single mind. Yet this mind cannot, surprisingly, merely be first invoked in relation to private science, but, instead, the metaphoric detour via civic construction – politico-architectonics – is required, to justify the priority of the single legislator in the field of public knowledge also. (For this reflection on politico-architectonics is what *first* occurred to Descartes when he was alone in the stove-heated room).[32] Why? Because knowledge is only ideally "single" if, at the outset, one's public ideal of *both* practice *and* theory is not of oral transmission through time, but of spatial, written arrangement. At the beginning, therefore, stands not the *Cogito*, but *mathēsis*, and before even *mathēsis*, stands the spatialized city. This

---

[30] Descartes, *op. cit.*, *Discourse on the Method*, Part II, VI. 12–13.

[31] Physicality is explicitly ruled out as a potential mediator of the truth. See *ibid.*, Part IV, VI. 37.

[32] *Ibid.*, Part II, VI. 11.

is precisely the portable, convertible, formalized, transferable, mercantile city which is the subject of Socrates' critique in the *Phaedrus*.

Just as this city requires, ideally, a single legislator, so also, inversely, such a legislator is able to stand alone because he pre-includes all the civic space inside himself.[33] It follows, then, that the city has now been drastically subordinated to the individual,[34] in a sense impossible for Plato, for although, in the *Republic*, reform begins with the individual, the individual is still formed through public education and dialogue, as a member of the philosophic community. And it follows also that this prior individual is itself internally mapped like a spatialized city: there will follow absolute divisions between mind and body newly conceived as "areas," and the mind itself conceived as the spatial traverse of an inevitable order of intuited deductions.

4 REALITY WITHOUT DEPTH

I shall now show how Descartes' spatialized politico-architectonics is comple-mented by an equally spatialized ontology which is the other precondition for his espousal of the *Cogito*. As between the two preconditions, one can assign no priority since, if, as I would claim, a spatialized ontology is without real, objective warrant, its secret motivation is the political imposition of a *mathēsis*. Yet, conversely, if "single legislation" is held by Descartes to produce not only order but also knowledge, then, before imposing spatial order by mere *fiat*, he must assume that his impositions of method genuinely disclose a spatialized reality.

There is some disagreement as to the chronology of Descartes' develop-ment of an ontology. Jean-Luc Marion contends that his ontology is to be found in his later work, the *Meditations on First Philosophy*, in which matter is defined as extension, and the physical world is reduced to the principles of extension, motion, and mechanical causes, whilst Jean-François Courtine argues that Descartes redefines ontology even before he arrives at his theory of the *Cogito*, in the stress in his earlier *Regulae* on clarity and distinctness as the most fundamental criteria for the existence of a thing.[35] This would suggest

[33] "My plan has never gone beyond trying to reform my own thoughts and construct them upon a foundation which is all my own," *ibid.*, VI. 14–15.
[34] *Ibid.*, VI. 16.
[35] Jean-Luc Marion, *Sur le Prisme Métaphysique de Descartes*, (Paris: P.U.F., 1986), 14–43; Jean-François Courtine, *Suarez et le système de la Métaphysique* (Paris: P.U.F., 1990), 485–95; John Milbank, *The Word Made Strange: Theology, Language, Culture*, (Oxford: Blackwell Publishers, 1996), 51 n. 16.

that Descartes follows in the tradition of Duns Scotus, for whom a being is that which is univocal and therefore graspable. (In the "*Transition*" between parts I and II of the present essay, the significance of this legacy will be elaborated). In thus objectifying being, Descartes transforms the determinations of reality into purely spatial classifications, as the "given" rather than the gift of a donor through which the transcendent is mediated. And in a sense, the disagreement between Marion and Courtine is purely formal since an ontology separated from theology is reducible to an epistemology, as I shall show in later sections of this chapter. In any case, Marion and Courtine agree in developing Etienne Gilson's analysis of Descartes, by pointing out that the turn to epistemology is pre-enabled by a radical reconstrual of ontology itself, inherited from later scholasticism. In line with their analyses, I shall now show, first of all, how this new ontology, which *naturally* fulfills itself as the primacy of epistemology, inaugurates a construal of reality as the spatial "given." I will go on to show how this objectification of reality turns the object into a sign, and how this gives rise to a contradiction in Descartes' theory of language. Finally, in section 4, I will discuss the way in which, for Descartes, secure being has become being for the *Cogito*. Such a single legislating subject, commanding both the city and being itself, is supremely a non-liturgical subject. Against Derrida, I shall show how writing, not orality, is the precondition for Cartesian subjectivity.

In the classical and early to high mediaeval periods, although truth had been regarded as unchanging, it had not been considered as graspable and available to an exact and unchanging *mathēsis*. It was thought that things "are" according to the way in which they are manifested, which can never be exhaustive. An apophatic reasoning gave play, therefore, to the mediations of memory, time, and tradition, as for Plato and Augustine. But, with Descartes' Scholastic antecedent, Duns Scotus, a new model of truth as transparently available and immanent began to emerge (see "*Transition*" below). Following Roger Bacon, Scotus and Ramon Lull developed the notion of an *a priori* experience of an object which is, by definition, above alteration, and univocally common to finite and infinite.[36] Accordingly, in Descartes' *Regulae*,

---

[36] On Roger Bacon, see Gilson, *op. cit.*, *History of Christian Philosophy in the Middle Ages*, 294–312; Umberto Eco, *The Search for the Perfect Language*, (Oxford: Basil Blackwell, 1995), 53–4; On Duns Scotus, see Amos Funkenstein, *op. cit.*, *Theology and the Scientific Imagination*, 26–7, 57–9; Gilson, *Jean Duns Scot: Introduction à ses positions fondamentales*, (Paris: Librairie Philosophiques, 1952); Alexandre Koyré, *From the Closed World to the Infinite Universe*, (Baltimore and London: The Johns Hopkins Press, 1952/1970), 124; John Milbank, *Theology and Social Theory: Beyond Secular Reason*, (Oxford: Blackwell Publishers, 1990), 301–2; *idem, The Word Made Strange*, 9, 44; On Ramon Lull, see Gilson, 350–3, Eco, 53–72, Yates, *op. cit.*, *The Art of Memory*, 175–96.

being is defined as that which is clear and distinct, available to absolute and certain intuitions, and "perfectly known and incapable of being doubted."[37] Existence becomes a "simple" or common notion, which, along with "unity" and "duration," is univocally common both to corporeal things and to spirits.[38] Absolute and certain intuitions of such entities form part of a *mathēsis* modelled on the abstract and timeless certainty of arithmetic and geometry.[39]

Descartes delimits the knowable by ruling that one should attend only to that which manifests itself clearly and distinctly, that is, "to those objects of which our minds seem capable of having certain and indubitable cognition."[40] This departure from the pre-Scotist notion of being as something with unknowable and unanalysable depth, inaugurates the "object" as a phenomenon. There arises, therefore, an epistemological circuit whereby knowledge is based entirely on objects, whose "being" does not exceed the extent to which they are known. Representation is now prior to ontology. Furthermore, the objects which are posited as knowable are basic and simple: "We must concentrate our mind's eye totally upon the most insignificant and easiest of matters."[41] By thus excluding the difficult and multiple, Descartes is able to reduce objects to items on a consistent and formal continuum of matter in such a way that all branches of knowledge become equally available, "since they are all of the same nature and consist simply in the putting together of self-evident facts."[42]

This determination of what is knowable, and therefore of what "is," according to a set of unchanging rules, apparent to the single mind, inverts the traditional movement from ontology to epistemology, yet nonetheless *assumes* an ontological redefinition of reality as the clear and distinct. It is this assumption which undergirds the new construal of *material* reality as *extensio*, an homogeneous quantity divided into degrees of motion and mechanical causes, and grasped fully in its "givenness." Concomitantly, the qualitative and hazy differences of colour or attribute are reduced to abstract spatial quantities, by analogy "with the extension of a body that has shape,"[43] so that in a gesture not unlike the fractal epistemology of Ramism, the *Regulae* is thereby able to

[37] "All knowledge [*scientia*] is certain and evident cognition," *Rules for the Direction of the Mind*, Rule Two, X362.
[38] *Ibid.*, Rule Twelve, X419–20.
[39] *Ibid.*, X364–5; Rule Four, X374–9.
[40] *Ibid.*, Rule Two, X362.
[41] *Ibid.*, Rule Nine, X400.
[42] *Ibid.*, Rule Thirteen, X428; Also, "We should note that comparisons are said to be simple and straightforward only when the thing sought and the initial data participate equally in a certain nature," Rule Fourteen, X440.
[43] *Ibid.*, X441.

bring all problems into conformity with an axiomatic system. Imperfect problems are reduced, as far as possible, to perfect ones. And then perfect problems are further reduced so that they become manifest to clear and distinct intuitions. Descartes' metamathematics of order and measure is therefore a general science with no reference to particular objects, for it both precedes and establishes all other knowledge of the world.[44]

This epistemological virtual reality (which is the remote heir of the Scotist "formal distinction" – see "*Transition*" below) therefore assumes a prior ontology which, by defining being as the unvarying, clear, and distinct, subordinates it to the measure of the knowing subject, and finally places its objectivity in doubt. But this new ontology is itself the logical outcome of an ontology prised away from theology. Descartes consummates a movement which separates being from its donating source by taking Being to be, first of all, not the divine *gift* of a participation in a plenitude of infinite actuality, but rather the mere inert *given* of a contentless "notion" of existence univocally common to the finite and the infinite. However, this prior movement requires a further movement in order for it to be secured against nihilistic nothingness. The immanent must be adequately grasped in its givenness, as fully known and transparent, and thereby secure from time and multiplicity which threaten self-identity. The given is guaranteed as never *not* present to us, since its objectified components "are all self-evident and never contain any falsity . . . for if we have the slightest grasp of it in our mind . . . it must follow that we have complete knowledge of it."[45]

And yet, in spite of this gesture to secure the object, there is, after all, something nihilistic about the Cartesian "given" which at once contradicts and fulfills the project of the universal mathematics, for, as I shall show, it is above all "nothing" which fulfills the criteria of clarity and distinctness, and which is superlatively consistent.[46] First, the reality to which his *mathēsis* refers does not exceed the "virtual." Secondly, the triumph of epistemology

[44] For example, in Rule Thirteen, when Descartes expands mathematics to deal with physical problems through an examination of the nature of magnets, like the logicians who presuppose the terms and matter of a syllogism, he proceeds by assuming that the question to be solved is perfectly understood, in such a way that the inferences are foreclosed in advance. In the case of the magnet, the knowledge of what is meant by the two words "magnet" and "nature" will determine the interpretation of the experiments. The reduction of the question to its basic elements thus replaces any superfluous considerations of the object. *Ibid.*, Rule Thirteen, X431.
[45] *Ibid.*, Rule Twelve, X420–1.
[46] In the next chapter, I argue that the postmodern preoccupation with death, and reduction of everything to the simple nature of "nothing," betray its metaphysics of presence.

denudes the given of its corporeality. And thirdly, the sceptical structure of the *Cogito* ensures that before anything ever quite attains the status of the absolute given, it evaporates, under the forces of doubt, into a disqualified nothingness.

First, the Cartesian "given" colonizes a peculiar liminal space of virtuality. Even when Descartes concedes that there is another mode of knowing in addition to intuition of simple natures, namely deduction, this second mode of knowing is ultimately reducible to the spatiality or virtuality of intuition. By deduction, he means "the inference of something as following necessarily from some other propositions which are known with certainty." This form of reasoning is still able to deliver absolute knowledge, "provided (its facts) are inferred from true and known principles through a continuous and uninterrupted movement of thought in which each individual proposition is clearly intuited."[47] Following this, in Rule Five, he ordains the systematic "ordering and arranging of the objects on which we must concentrate our mind's eye" according to reduction of the complex into the simple.[48] This structuration of objects does not reflect the order in which reality arrives for everyday, confused, passional perception, but subsists only within the abstract realm of mathematics, or else in the region where mathematics corresponds to reality, which is in physics. Although it is the case that in mathematics and physics things do indeed follow from one another in the orderly manner required by Descartes' method, he insists that this orderliness alone constitutes what is relevant of fundamental reality. So although he concedes, in Rule Twelve of the *Regulae*, in agreement with the traditional Scholastic trope, that the order in which one comes to know reality differs from the order in which it exists,[49] Descartes is concerned only with the former ideal epistemological reality, and also projects the order of knowing as a more fundamental order of being. Hence, for example, in Rule Twelve, he concedes that body, extension and shape are inseparable in being, though not in understanding, and yet proceeds to assert that bodies are really composed of such genuine "simple natures" whose mark is that they are always predicated univocally, and never analogically. The traditional trope is hereby undone. The given is no longer in excess of what can be known by means of method, for it is now commensurate with the structures conferred upon it by Descartes' rigid and ascetically drained kind of method.

Thus, the "given" is, in one sense, supremely corporeal, consisting in matter reduced to concrete *extensio*, and, in another sense, is denuded of that corporeality by being purely an epistemological projection. This apparent

---

[47] *Rules for the Direction of the Mind*, Rule Three, X369.

[48] *Ibid.*, Rule Five, X379.

[49] *Ibid.*, Rule Twelve, X418.

contradiction arises from the separation of ontology from theology, and the concomitant removal of concealed forces from physics. In Rule Fourteen, when Descartes invokes the question as to whether the extension of a thing is different from the body itself, he attacks the Platonic aporetic mathematics of the "point," whereby a point constitutes an *ideal* reality since it has no extension, and yet the moment it is actuated, acquires breadth and so ceases to be a point. By sustaining the *aporia* according to which number is an ideal or spiritual reality, Plato implies that the true reality of material things is spiritual, thus outwitting a simple dualism of idea and matter. But Descartes suppresses the *aporia* of the "point" by contending that geometric realities constitute entirely *material* realities, thus denying that number is to any degree ideal or spiritual.[50] In a similar fashion, Descartes (unlike Nicholas of Cusa before him and Pascal after him)[51] suppresses the *aporia* of the presence of the infinite in the finite, arguing that the extension of space and its microscopic division should rather be described as "indefinite." His pious excuse is that this reserves the term "infinite" for God who is alone without limit, whereas, he avers, macro- and microscopic extension may be subject to some limit of which we do not know. But this is to prevaricate: infinite extension and division are given with the fact of space – for how, for example, could space be limited except by further space? One might further defend Descartes by arguing that God's "simple" infinity is not simply the unending. However, this objection again seeks to avoid the *aporia*: if spatial, material things are infinite, then they seem to pass over into something "spiritual," for of space *as* infinite it does not, indeed, make sense (at least in terms of traditional mathematics) to ask, can infinity be halved etc.? This is an example of a "meaningless" question regarding the infinite which is mentioned by Descartes himself, in order to argue that such ineffability beyond question be reserved for God alone.[52] But this is an arbitrary restriction: infinity *does* paradoxically invade the finite and give rise to antinomic and irresolvable questions, like that of the reality of the "point." In both cases, Descartes rejects what the tradition had always (regarding the "point') and recently (regarding the great and small infinities of the universe) taken as "traces" of the spiritual in the material.

[50] *Ibid.*, Rule Fourteen, X444–5.

[51] "When we know better, we understand that, since nature has engraved her own image and that of her author on all things, they almost all share her double infinity." Pascal, *Pensées*, tr. A. J. Krailsheimer (London: Penguin Books, 1966), ¶ 199; see also ¶¶ 68, 201, 418; A. Koyré, *op. cit., From the Closed World.*

[52] *Principles of Philosophy*, in Cottingham *et al., op .cit., The Philosophical Writings of Descartes*, Volume I, VIII. A. 26–7; *Objections and Replies*, Volume II, *Author's Replies to the First Set of Objections*, VII. 113–14.

By thus secularizing or de-spiritualizing geometry and physics, disallowing the *aporias* of the "point" in its incorporeality and of finite extension in its infinity, he concomitantly drains extension or corporeality itself of all its force and power. This act of immanentizing matter is tantamount to its erasure. Paradoxically, to immanentize reality, or to insist on its exhaustive corporeality, is to turn it into an unmodified ideal, since the secular "given" of the universal method is purely formal, articulated only in abstract structures which do not coincide with any actual embodied reality. But what is an immanentized ideal except the *nihil*, something which vanishes the moment it is posited?

This nihilistic gesture of the "given" is reiterated when the implications of the *Cogito* for extended reality are considered. The two stages of this consideration are as follows. First, to think is to think *something*. Secondly, if the content of one's thoughts are to be doubted, all except the intransitive "I think," which supposedly cannot be doubted, then nothing one thinks will ever quite meet the criterion of the absolutely given, since only what is absolutely available to an intuition cannot be subject to doubt. So, the structure of the *Cogito* means that the givenness of the given evaporates. For the purposes of the *Cogito*, only the *ego* itself qualifies as "given," and the *ego* is not exactly an "item" for Descartes at all. As a pure formality which has nothing to do with what lies outside, the pre-legislated Cartesian city is contained within an interior which has no exterior, and the "given" is thus seen to be a *written* reality, self-consistent because empty, motionless in its superlative mobility.

We have seen how the Cartesian object is contradictory insofar as it is purportedly part of physical *extensio* and yet its materiality is seen to be reducible to immanentized ideality, equivalent to the *nihil*. This contradiction is embedded in the character of the object as *sign*. By being reduced to comply with mathematical criteria, the objects of Descartes' science acquire the symbolic value of corporeality as the incarnation of truth in a physical image. And yet this embodiment fulfills the requirements for the production of a pure, spiritual cognition in such a way that the extended realm is "eminently" present in the mind.[53] As ideal signs, Cartesian objects are above alteration, and are arbitrarily related in advance by a conventional system of order and hierarchy, in such a way that they instantiate a break with the natural order.[54] Descartes' rejection of spontaneous experience liberates reality from its perceptual limits, leading to the creation of a new manipulable *cosmos* on a theoretical plane. Its elements,

[53] Descartes, *Meditations on First Philosophy*, in Cottingham *et al., op. cit., Objections and Replies* Volume II, Third Meditation, VII. 453.

[54] Arithmetic and geometry alone "are concerned with an object so pure and simple that they make no assumptions that experience might render uncertain," Descartes, *op. cit., Rules for the Direction of the Mind*, Rule Two, X365.

because of their simplicity, abstraction, and reduction to the same transferable "substance," imply a freedom of permutation, like the exchangeable type of the printing press, suggesting that the language to which these signs belong is conceived on the lines of a visual (and typographic) analogy. Indeed, an intuition made on the basis of the Cartesian object leads to an assimilation of properties within a lateral chain of temporal metonymy always reduced in advance to prescribed synecdochic substitutions: the succession of necessitated intuitions, or explications of the primary intuition that merely masquerades as a process of "deduction." Thus, the universal *mathēsis* comprises isomorphic signs devoid of content, whose self-referential character of certitude replaces the referential character of experience, as expressed by the former principles of resemblance and difference.

With this idealization of the object as sign, it is curious that Descartes should explicitly undertake to emulate the practicality and worldliness of artisans and their ordinary crafts.[55] Similarly, he adopts an apparently Socratic position in rejecting the method of sophism on the grounds that an intuition cannot be made via empty ciphers of knowledge, and that an artificial memory encourages a lapse into mechanicalness, inimical to pure cognition.[56] For this reason, Descartes proposes an idealized *ars* which constitutes an anti-method method – a method supposedly without artifice – and yet which is in the end sophistic because of its wholly internalized, formalized, and immanent perspective. Again, like the sophists, (for all that he is a "rationalist" and they were "sceptics"), Descartes seeks an extra-linguistic philosophy in and through the instrumentalization and humiliation of language, simultaneously invoking and denying the sign. For whilst he turns the objects of his science purely and exhaustively into signs, he chooses algebra as a model for a *mathēsis* whose logical principles appear to extend beyond number, shape, and language.[57] Similarly, his emphasis on the importance of *acceleration* in deduction, and on fixed order, suggests a subordination of time to the spatiality of the immediate *punctum*, in an attempt to elude all the inherent problematics of both memory and representation.[58] His method, it seems, is offered as an alternative to eternity

---

[55] *Ibid.*, Rule Eight, X397 and Rule Ten, X404. Descartes immanentizes these crafts by characterizing them as autonomous and methodized, carried out without appeal to the transcendent.
[56] *Ibid.*, X405–6, and Rule Seven, X388.
[57] *Ibid.*, Rule Four, X377.
[58] On the importance of *order* in deductive enumeration ("so that memory is left with practically no role to play, and I seem to intuit the whole thing at once," *ibid.*, X388) see especially *ibid.*, Rule Seven; and on the merits of deductive *speed*, see *ibid.*, Rule Eleven,

and divine ineffability. Indeed, this space is even more idealized (or immanently spiritualized) than that of Ramus, since the Cartesian intuition is fully interiorized. It does not occupy the physical space of a map or chart whose scores are surveyed in inhabited time and space, but rather, the accelerated conflation of the first and last links in a deductive series approximates an emptying of visual space in order to obtain true intellection. Thus, physical space is replaced by a purely rational, homogenous substrate which houses not "things," but idealized figures or signs which, as interior, appear to "get outside" language itself. The interiorized "flattening-out" of this new intellection thus offers an immanentized version of the angelic vision for which diverse perspectives are unified into a single omniscient gaze.[59] But the Cartesian gaze is inward and reflexive, gazing only at its own projection of order and sign, as if in its own mirrored reflection.

This withdrawal of epistemology into an interior and reflexive "space," repeating the construal of the totalized and surveyable city as a metaphor for the individual, fulfills Derrida's characterization of metaphysics as self-identity and the separation of mind from the *extensio*, although Derrida sees Descartes' prioritization of the pure interior as consistent with the production of an idealized *speech* or orality: "We already have a foreboding that phonocentrism merges with the historical determination of the meaning of being in general *as presence*, with all the subdeterminations which depend on this general form and which organise within it their system and their historical sequence (presence of the thing to the sight as *eidos*, presence as substance/essence/ existence [*ousia*], temporal presence as point [*sigmè*] of the now or of the moment [*nun*], the self-presence of the cogito, consciousness, subjectivity)."[60] But in this characterization, he fails to recognize that, for Descartes, the pure interior is sustained through writing and not speech, as was seen above in my

---

X408–9. Because of the deficiences of memory, "I run over [the operations] again and again in my mind until I can pass from the first to the last so quickly that memory is left with practically no role to play, and I seem to be intuiting the whole thing at once," Rule Eleven, X409; see also Rule Three, X369–70.

[59] Dalia Judovitz, *Subjectivity and Representation in Descartes: The Origins of Modernity*, (Cambridge: Cambridge University Press, 1988), 71–2.

[60] Jacques Derrida, *Of Grammatology*, tr. Gayatri Chakravorty Spivak (Baltimore: The Johns Hopkins Press, 1976), 12; "But this violent liberation of speech is possible . . . only in the extent to which it keeps itself resolutely and consciously at the greatest possible proximity to the abuse that is the usage of speech – just close enough to *say* violence, to dialogue with itself as irreducible violence, and just far enough to *live* and live as speech": Derrida, "Cogito and the History of Madness," in tr. Alan Bass *Writing and Difference*, (London: Routledge and Kegan Paul, 1990), 31–78, 61.

demonstration of the textual and contractual status of the Cartesian city. And although Derrida might argue that Descartes' writing, as alphabetic, is still metaphysical since it is always already subordinate to speech, in fact, although he does refer to alphabetic writing,[61] Descartes' emphasis on both formal order and diagrammatic consistency suggest that his epistemological writing is closer to Derrida's supposedly non-metaphysical *hieroglyph* than to alphabetic script. Indeed, as well as the examples of knowledge as compared with architecture, building, and city-planning, he exalts the morphological arts of weaving, carpet-making, and embroidery as pictorial and structural analogies of ideal and interior intellection.[62] His interest in order and proportion, as well as totalizing and punctiliar cognition, imply a preference for the spatial pictogram rather than the seriality of alphabetic writing.[63]

5 THE WRITTEN SUBJECT

The logical outcome of an immanentist ontology where epistemology is paramount is, as we have seen, the reduction of being to the "object" whose existence does not exceed the extent to which it is known by the subject. Thus the subject assumes the status of that which confers existence upon reality. But we have also seen that the subject's realm of operation contains contradictory and nihilistic aspects. In this section I will show how the Cartesian subject finds it necessary to offer a gesture of security against the void, where the given is perpetually threatened by doubt, by substituting method for memory, estranging itself from all that is material, including time, place, and particularity, and like Lysias' endeavour to sustain his metic status in the *Phaedrus*, ordering itself through writing. This textualization of the subject in turn gives rise to an *aporia* which, because of its immanentist setting, can only be "resolved" through nihilism.

After introducing the notion of the universal mathematics in Rule Four of the *Regulae*, Descartes advances the concept of order as the means for guarding against the failures of memory, and, ultimately, displacing it altogether.[64] Although he views memory as one of the perfections of the human mind,[65] he confesses to having a weak memory. His attempt to counter this via the ideal spatiality of the instantaneous and thus self-identical intuition also

---

[61] Descartes, *op. cit., Rules for the Direction of the Mind*, Rule Ten, X404–5.
[62] *Ibid.*, X404.
[63] Descartes, *op. cit., Discourse on the Method*, Part II, VI. 20–1.
[64] Descartes, *op. cit., Rules for the Direction of the Mind*, Rule Four, X378–9.
[65] *Ibid.*, Rule Twelve, X441, *idem, Discourse on the Method*, Part I, VI. 2–3.

constitutes, as we have seen, an evacuation of his philosophical past, and, in particular, the arts of memory. Whilst Ramist method aimed at designing a simplification of education by providing new and better ways to memorize information, Descartes' enumeration functions not as a way of *conserving* memory, but of *abolishing* it altogether through its reduction to intuition. Although memory is necessary for the initial constitution of the concept of order, it is, by virtue of the order now established, dismissed.[66] Furthermore, and more radically, his system for the attainment of certitude (conceived as a *punctum*) challenges the prior significance of memory as a means which inseparably links knowledge, tradition, and the transcendent. Indeed, the system defies Plato and Augustine for whom the mind could only perceive "being" once it had recollected its own transcendent source, and would be unable to apprehend its object unless it was illumined by a source other than itself. Thus, for this intellectual legacy, memory was both ontologically and epistemologically necessary. Significantly, the icon of the sun in Plato, representing the transcendent bestowal of life and knowledge, becomes for Descartes the light of human reason itself.[67]

The elision of the role of memory for knowledge and ontology has sinister implications not only for the reduction of being to the object, but also for the constitution of the philosophical subject. As I argued in chapter 1, memory is crucial for self-continuity whilst allowing for variation, and so its replacement by formal, isomorphic structures transposes the subject's continuity-with-difference into self-identity and permanence, the prime criteria, that is, for the Cartesian object itself.[68] This is also implicit in the formulation of the philosophical subject in the *Discourse*, for the structure of the *Cogito*, as I discussed above, suggests that whilst all else evaporates into doubt, the *ego* alone remains indubitably "given." For all that, it cannot be given the positive quality of a real "item." And in consequence, in subjectivity, vacuity and

---

[66] The problem of memory continued to haunt the Cartesian text, since in the *Meditations on First Philosophy* he admits that only memory can separate the states of waking and sleep, and is essential to knowledge; Fifth Meditation, IX 69–70.

[67] On "the natural light of reason," see *op.cit., Rules for the Direction of the Mind*, Rule One, X361; Rule Three, X368; Rule Four, X371. In the *Discourse on the Method*, Descartes compares method with daylight: Part VI, VI. 71. See further Dalia Judovitz, "Vision, Representation, and Technology in Descartes," in ed. David Michael Levin, *Modernity and the Hegemony of Vision*, (Berkeley, Los Angeles and London: University of California Press, 1993), 63–86.

[68] In chapter 3, I will show how the self-identity of the object suggests that the superlative object is death itself, as conceived in modern Western, and postmodern thought. For this reason, there is a Cartesian element in postmodern "nihilism" of a Derridean kind.

objectivity once again coincide, for Descartes' subject is only indubitable *because* it has been emptied of its contents by its definition as pure thought, and by being differentiated from its specific modes of existence. The subject is the most certain thing there is because it is the superlative object, whose existence is a void and is thereby ideally unconstrained either by place or time.

Furthermore, the self-presence, autonomy, and lack of memory of this subject suggest that it is modelled on the text as a pure subjectivity, whose sole gesture is the act of writing itself. For subjectivity manifests itself in Descartes as the method which produces the ideal positioning of things according to their most identically repeatable characteristics. The mind which gathers itself in the (writing of) method is also an *ideal writing*, a collection of printed marks, divorced from circumstances, voice and body, occupying the achronic instant of the text, in which there is no passing, progression, or transference. Rather, the mind's writing localizes, or imprints, in the instant of intuition, outside duration, and therefore outside the act of writing too. The mind of the Cartesian subject is the purest possible text. In his deconstruction of the *Regulae*, Jean-Luc Nancy detects a supposedly hidden link between the subject and a pure interior writing when, adopting the "voice" of Descartes, he affirms that "I write while not writing in the instanteneity of the movement, describing each time different movements subordinated to the same instanteneity."[69] However, *contra* Nancy, it is not necessary to *deconstruct* the *Regulae* in order to show how the Cartesian subject depends on writing, and in particular, writing as interiority. Rather, this structure is manifest in the method itself. Writing is therefore not the opposite of Cartesian interiority, or, as Nancy insinuates, its *suppressed* condition of possibility, but is commensurate with it.

The radical solipsism of the Cartesian subject leads to an aporetic *mathēsis* and a contradiction within the subject itself. First, the universal *mathēsis* is identified as that which is supremely *private*. If the subject arrives at certain knowledge by deducing from its own existence, will this truth hold for others? How can a universal knowledge be deduced privately, in isolation from the world? Since the private *ego* is all that remains absolutely given, it alone qualifies as the warrant for the existence of truth. The *ego* thus acts as a textualized and immanentized version of the Platonic good, the sole ground for all knowledge and existence, but in privatized form. Although Descartes deems his method *universal*, he does concede in the *Discourse* that he would not necessarily advise anyone to imitate it.[70] Indeed, by definition, it could not be

---

[69] Jean-Luc Nancy, "*Dum Scribo*," tr. Ian McLeod, *The Oxford Literary Review*, 3.2 (1978), 6–21, 9.
[70] Descartes, *op. cit.*, *Discourse on the Method*, Part II, VI. 15.

imitated, since it is radically subjective. Is it therefore the formality and emptiness of the *mathēsis* which qualifies it as universal? Or is it universal because the individual is all there is, and so paradoxically the individual *is* the universal to the extent that there is nothing "beyond" the individual? The tension between universal and private amounts to the question as to which is truly prior and foundational, given that each is a necessary metaphor for the other: the supreme individual is he who surveys a universal totality, a "*cosmopolis*" (to use Toulmin's accurate term), while this cosmopolitan universe is in turn simply that which is surveyable by a single gaze.

This tension can only be resolved by reducing the subject to an interiorized written template which bears no traces of its physical situation, and so to the scalar flexibility of the object as death. The interior of such a subject, as we have seen, has no exterior; it can only open onto itself. This is confirmed in the *Discourse* when Descartes compares the unmethodic mind to a darkened underground cellar, evoking Plato's allegory of the cave. Whilst, for Plato, illumination involves *ascent* to the sun, for Descartes there is no such invocation of the transcendent. Instead, the cellar is illumined by a lateral and instantaneous gesture of opening windows upon the cellar to admit daylight.[71] The implications of this for a Cartesian theory of the subject and epistemology are twofold. First, daylight is a diffused and diluted version of the transcendent sun as it is figured in the *Republic*. The Cartesian sun is simply "there" without need of education or pilgrimage. And, secondly, to build windows in an underground cellar is an ambiguous act, since it is tantamount to opening windows onto the *inside*, an opening which confirms closure. A cellar is an inside with no outside, merely returning the inside to itself. Thus the image of the cellar repeats the construal of reason as monadically pure, deriving its evidence from its own self-reflection. This underground subject is surrounded by an exteriority which merely affirms its interiority. It is enshrined in *written* form in the sense that, like the textual sign, it is outside alteration, like death itself, emplotted. And it is emplotted in another sense: it resides in firm ground, as its own "ground," which is also the "ground" or warrant for the existence of all reality. Its ground is indeed so firm that it needs no Lysian contract of citizenship, because it is self-governing. Further, it is its own *everything*, its own universality, and so there is no authority (transcendent or otherwise) from which to borrow its own existence.

Thus, in the end, after Descartes, a spatialized written *polis*, a spatialized written being, and a spatialized written subject, cohere perfectly together, without priority or foundation, in a triadic mutual collusion, which sustains the

[71] *Ibid.*, Part VI, VI. 71.

"self-evidence" of the immanent, and its secular closure against the sun of the good only as a conspiracy; a conspiracy both cosmopolitan and esoterically concealed.

6 THE CITY OF VIRTUOSI

So far we have examined textualization and spatialization as exemplified in two influential writers of the early modern period. However, these processes were as much or more exemplified in social practice as in written theory. I shall now briefly enumerate ways in which this becomes apparent. In this section I will examine the polity of the experimental philosophers of the Royal Society in the Restoration period, showing how its monitored interiority, and dependency upon the production of knowledge as its condition of possibility inscribe it within the structure of the Cartesian city – which is to say, *cosmopolis*, politico-architectonics, and idealized interior *ars* – as described above. Furthermore, I argue that the properties of the Boylean "facts" are reducible to the Cartesian given, and presuppose a similar relationship between the knowing subject and extended reality. In section seven, "The Theatrical City," I shall show how the mechanisms of spatialization can be seen also in baroque modes of government, in particular with regard to the deployment of studied excess in civic life, and architectural and poetical trends.

In the social and epistemological practices of Robert Boyle's researches in pneumatics and his employment of the air-pump, as described in Steven Shapin and Simon Schaffer's *Leviathan and the Air-Pump*, the institutionalization of experimental practice and the scientific prioritization of the matter of fact as the basis for knowledge, became firmly established.[72] Boyle's experiments did not offer any systematic or metaphysical philosophy of knowledge. Rather he maintained that natural philosophy should be generated through practical experiment and that the foundations of such knowledge were to be constituted by experimentally produced matters of fact, which offered the highest degree of probabilistic assurance. Whereas, prior to the seventeenth century, probability had been associated with the incalculable, Boyle's practices in the seventeenth century bear witness to a more general attempt to quantify the uncertain.[73] To this end, Boyle proposed that matters of fact be constituted by

[72] Steven Shapin and Simon Schaffer, *Leviathan and the Air-Pump: Hobbes, Boyle, and the Experimental Life*, (Princeton, New Jersey: Princeton University Press, 1985).

[73] Ian Hacking, *The Emergence of Probability: A Philosophical Study of Early Ideas about Probability, Induction and Statistical Inference*, (Cambridge: Cambridge University Press, 1975). Shapin and Schaffer, *ibid.*, *Leviathan and the Air-Pump, passim.*

the aggregation of individuals' beliefs, which necessitated the establishment of regulations to enable members of an intellectual collective mutually to assure themselves and others that belief in an empirical experience was justified. The process of multiplication of the witnessing experience was crucial, and if it could be extended to many people (ideally to *all* people), then the result could be constituted as a matter of fact. The foundational item of experimental knowledge, and of what counted as knowledge as such, was therefore an artefact of *dissemination* as much as experiment. Shapin and Schaffer emphasize this social aspect of the knowledge produced, and enumerate three technologies which were developed for the production of matters of fact: a material technology, which involved the construction and operation of the air-pump; a literary technology, by means of which the phenomena produced by the pump were communicated to those who were not direct witnesses; and a social technology which incorporated the conventions experimental philosophers should use in dealing with each other and in considering knowledge-claims. The latter two technologies are of particular significance for my consideration of spatial models of the city because, on the one hand, the link between knowledge and number meant that the constitution of facts depended upon accessibility to as many witnesses as possible, and so to a certain degree it was necessary for the city of scientists to be *open*. And yet, on the other hand, it was important to regulate the interior workings of the scientific community in order to keep disputes to a minimum, and guarantee the social solidarity necessary for the production of knowledge. So the success of the scientific community depended upon its being constructed as an ideal city comprising individuals whose activities and discourse were not hermetically interior, but, at the same time, were regulated by laws of admission and behaviour similar to the textual city of Descartes, and his regulation of the mind.

This Boylean city operated strict border controls. The problem was that there existed a conflict between openness and closure which could only be negotiated by means of a scrupulous guarding of its boundary, and criteria for citizenship. The cause of the problem was that the multiplication of witness, necessary to indicate that testimony referred to a true state of affairs in *reality*, required the risk of opening the interior scientific space to an audience of outsiders. However, Boyle devised three ways of monitoring or minimizing this openness. First, direct witnesses within the laboratory were carefully selected, on the grounds that not everyone's testimony was of equal worth. The experiments were therefore performed "in the presence of an illustrious assembly of virtuosi,"[74]

---

[74] Robert Boyle, "The History of Fluidity and Firmness," (1661) in ed. Thomas Birch, *The Works of the Honourable Robert Boyle*, (London: J & F Rivington, 1772), I, 377–442, cited in Shapin and Schaffer, *op. cit.*, *Leviathan and the Air-Pump*, 58.

that is, fellow scientists all seeking the common goal of the production of matters of fact. A second way of obtaining multiple witnesses without threatening the purity of the experimental space was to facilitate the literal replication of experiments in other locations, and, a third, to report the experimental procedure in great detail so as to reproduce it in the reader's mind, a process which Shapin and Schaffer call "virtual witnessing." Whilst replication of an experiment was difficult and unreliable, virtual witness was potentially unlimited, and therefore the most powerful technology for producing matters of fact. It relied upon an establishment of trust that the things reported had actually happened, which was effected by means of the development of a literary style which contained circumstantial detail, mimetic illustrations, and even, for verisimilitude, notification of failed experiments. This literary style, although apparently very different from the abstract diagrams of Ramism and Cartesianism, is nevertheless reducible to the same attempt to capture reality "as it is," and to produce certain and universal knowledge of that reality in as clear and distinct a way as possible.

How did Boyle regulate the scientific community itself? The problem here was that the legitimacy of the facts produced relied upon the freedom of the collective. In order to safeguard the value of their facts, therefore, the experimentalists could not be *compelled* to give their assent to an item of knowledge, and so a certain amount of dispute and disagreement was unavoidable. However, in order to avoid the chaos of "private judgement," and any qualification of the absoluteness of the facts produced via the fragmentary effects of disagreement, it was important to *contain* such disputes. Indeed, a certain amount of stage-managed argument was desirable, since it suggested genuineness. Accordingly, Boyle produced exemplars of how disputes were to be conducted, between whom, and regarding what exactly was permitted to be questioned.[75] Most notably, he legislated against speech about entities which resisted attempts to be made sensible or mobilized into a matter of fact.[76]

---

[75] On the three Boylean technologies and the regulation of the experimental space see Shapin and Schaffer, *op. cit., Leviathan and the Air-Pump*, chapter 2 and *passim*.

[76] *Ibid.*, 337. A consideration of the historical context explains why the Boylean polity was so successful. Its regulation of human interaction, procedures of work, and degree of publicness place the city of virtuosi in the tradition of Cartesianism. Boyle's polity depended upon a delineated interior legislature laid down by a single master, although in Boyle's case, this was a constitutionally restricted master. The city was therefore not quite tyranny and not quite democracy, and it was stressed that the community was composed of free individuals, freely acting, and faithfully delivering what they witnessed. However, these freedoms were kept from dissolution into anarchy by being regulated and controlled, by agreement, from above. The crisis of the Restoration settlement made any proposals for a means of guaranteeing assent and collective harmony desirable, since the experience of war and the Republic had shown that disputes over knowledge produced civil strife. In this

Although the borders of the virtuosic city were safeguarded against unregu-
lated permutation by exterior forces, this does not mean that it had no significant
relation with the wider state in which it was situated. However, this relation was
regulated by the non-ecstatic strictures of banausic contract and thus amounted
to a token, virtualized exteriority, which in a sense redoubled to emphasize the
interiority of the scientific city after all, since the contractual relation relied upon
the maintenance of the duopoly of the two communities. As Jean-François
Lyotard argues, there is a symbiotic exchange between science (which advances
the profits of capitalism) and capitalism (which invests in science), due to a
common interest in an extension of the repertoire of power.[77] In this sense, the
state itself can be seen to comprise discrete satellite states-within-states, each
internally methodized, and whose inter-state relations are codified and mutually profitable. Such a lateral condition of political advancement is predicated
upon the virtue of *progress*, a sort of immanentized pilgrimage, not towards a
transcendent altar, but towards an ultimate and transfigured *self*, which, in
secular (nihilistic) parody of the liturgical journey, is an impossible goal.[78]

We have seen above how the virtuosic city was regulated and bounded, and
how, like its Cartesian counterpart, its legitimating principle was the production of knowledge. I shall now discuss the Boylean criteria for the establishment of knowledge, its properties, and implications for a theory of reality, the
knowing subject, and government of the city.

The first Boylean criterion for a fact of knowledge is that it should be
infinitely and identically *repeatable*, and replicable by anyone in any (suitable)
place.[79] The second is that a fact is constituted when its production is *directly
witnessed*, either physically or "virtually," so as to obtain an unmediated
apprehension necessary for the attainment of the status of reality. Accordingly,
knowledge was assumed to be available to *observation* by an authentic witness,
and as such, was *materially visible*.[80] The interpretation of the phenomenon
must finally be universally agreed by all witnesses.

These properties had implications for a construal of extended reality. The
Boylean programme apparently gestured towards a view of reality as divinely

---

context, the organization of the experimental scientists constituted an ideal polity which
showed itself to be practicably possible.

[77] Jean-François Lyotard, *The Postmodern Condition: A Report on Knowledge*, tr. Geoff
Bennington and Brian Massumi, (Manchester: Manchester University Press, 1984), 24–7
and *passim*. See Shapin and Schaffer, *op.cit.*, *Leviathan and the Air-Pump*, 339–40; Steven
Shapin, *The Scientific Revolution*, (Chicago and London: The University of Chicago Press,
1996), 123–35.

[78] See chapters 4 and 5 below.

[79] Shapin and Schaffer, *op. cit.*, *Leviathan and the Air-Pump*, 225–82 and *passim*.

[80] *Ibid.*, 337.

ordered, presenting the natural philosophers as priests of the universal temple of nature, who reported their results as verifying the presence of God working in and through material reality. In this way, it avoided the two extremes of materialist atheism on the one hand, and the unchecked "enthusiasm" of alchemists on the other.[81] However, this middle course was still tantamount to immanentism. Despite Boyle's voluntarism, by which he stressed God's sovereign ability to direct the world in any fashion He might choose, and not to be limited by any supposed "essence" of a personified "Nature,"[82] he nonetheless tended to interpret divine presence and divine causality as univocally comparable with finite presence and finite causality.[83] Hence, rejecting the received view that "Nature abhors a vacuum,"[84] Boyle regarded the *apparent presence* of a vacuum as evidence of the presence of a divine spirit in the world, something that could be made palpably manifest through experiment on the air-pump. For this reason Boyle and his followers saw Hobbes' espousal of a plenistic philosophy hostile to any vacuum as also ruling out any "spiritual" intervals within which God could operate. In a parallel fashion, they were happy to speak of a "spring" in the air, despite the fact that this was not to be attributed to any occult force in nature, and yet does not seem, as Hobbes repeatedly urged against them, to be accountable for in purely mechanistic terms. The implication was that the "spring," like the appearance of the vacuum, is a manifestation of that boundary where the hand of God impels the machine of the world.[85] In this fashion, Boyle rendered the transcendent empirically verifiable through the evidence of facts, and even as something quasi-embodied, and, in certain aspects, manipulable. For the universal transferability of such experiments suggested a deity which could be whimsically delivered, as in a conjuring trick, by anyone, anywhere, any number of times.[86]

It might seem that the Boylean protocol of the practical experiment presaged a return to the pre-Cartesian *event* for the delivery of knowledge, with all its concomitant emphasis on corporeality and time, such as was implicit in the allegorical "readings" of frescoes mentioned above. However, the "event" of the scientific experiment was, after all, reducible to spatiality, even though it appeared to inhabit time and to engage with corporeal

[81] *Ibid.*, 283–332.
[82] See Robert Boyle, *A Free Enquiry into the Vulgarly Received Notion of Nature*, ed. Edward B. Davis and Michael Hunter, (Cambridge: Cambridge University Press, 1996), 70–1.
[83] *Ibid.*, 106.
[84] *Ibid.*, 31 and *passim*.
[85] See Shapin and Schaffer, *op.cit.*, *Leviathan and the Air-Pump*, 109, 168, 206, 315, 330–1.
[86] *Ibid.*, chapter 2.

phenomena. The experimental procedure was emplotted into stages, thus *anticipating*, and thereby cancelling, the event's contingency, regulating responses divorced from genuine and spontaneous reaction, and reducing the phenomenon produced to a singularly interpreted and universally agreed "end result" which had none of the particular uniqueness of a genuine event, and concomitantly, none of its openness. This "event" was, after all, infinitely and identically replicable.

The revision of the notion of "event" involved a demythologization of reality as a repository for mobilized, unaltering, and discrete matters of fact, secreted there only to be extracted and deployed on behalf of secular power. It presupposed the reduction of space to a single, abstract medium, where its idealized components are made equivalent according to various permutations of measurable extension. This construal of space as self-identical was necessary for the project of a totalizing scientific knowledge of reality, based on exhuming its basic structures, and submitting phenomena to its all-encompassing calculus.

The matter of fact thus fulfills the criteria for the "given" as idealized and therefore permanent corporeality. Although the experimental philosophers stressed the bodily nature of absolute knowledge, by requiring it to be infinitely repeatable, they transmuted physicality into *ideality*: an idealized spatiality occupying a pseudo-transcendent position, which, like its Cartesian counterpart, bracketed any reference to an ontological cause or donor.[87] This gave rise to a contradiction, for although underived, the matter of fact was implicitly not only available to, but reliant upon, the human gaze for its existence, to the extent that it only qualified as given once it had been manifested and witnessed universally. Indeed, the experimental philosophers were not permitted to discuss what could not be mobilized into matter, and, like adherents of the *Regulae*, were to attend only to that which manifested itself clearly and distinctly. This seems to presuppose the same tautology as the Cartesian epistemology, for what qualifies as knowable is that which is objectively real, and yet the objectively real is defined as the knowable, or the clearly manifested. So, despite this hidden derivation from the scientific subject, the given attains the status of a transcendent, designated as unchanging, undergoing no modifications or loss, definitely "fixed" as an unquestioned foundation. In secular parody of divine omnipresence, it could be reproduced anywhere and by anyone, resulting in a "transcendent" which is at once familiarized (available) and mystified (indisputable). This latter quality

---

[87] K. L. Schmitz, "The Given and the Gift: Two Different Readings of the World," in ed. Jos Kocinski, *Philosophical Papers of the Cracow Conference*, (Lublin: Poland, 1980), 2–3.

was heightened by the involvement of the machine, the purpose-built *machina Boyleana*, or air-pump, one of the significant features of which was that it appeared to stand halfway between the status of a human artefact and natural reality itself. Its physical complexity, expense, and rarity, as well as the edifying effects of its display, caused the air-pump to become an emblem of power. The intractable means by which it transubstantiated invisible phenomena into visible substances, and its impersonal nature, intensified the unquestionability of the facts produced.[88]

The reality of the subject's axiomatic role in the production of knowledge was disguised by the natural philosophers' apparent emphasis upon natural reality, the centrality of the practical experiment, and the concentration on physical objects of knowledge. This disguise involved a series of redoublings. First, as we have seen in the case of Descartes, reality was *demythologized* as purely corporeal and immanent, so as to be drained of its force and power. Although Boyle and many other experimental philosophers *did* recognize force in matter (*contra* Descartes),[89] their identification of it as a direct presence of divine causality can be seen as a variant of the same Cartesian paradigm. For divine presence was thereby immanentized by being placed alongside other causalities, and advertized as empirically demonstrable,[90] while matter itself remained inert. Thus contained, the given fact was then *re*-mythologized as ideal, self-identical, and universal by a process of spiritualization which nonetheless kept matter entirely within bounds. This wholly innocuous ideality was exalted as the (manipulable) pseudo-transcendent of the virtuosic city, located outside time in the same way that death is beyond alteration, repeatable in renewed instances, and above all, unambiguously simple. So although Boyle explicitly stated his departure from abstruse metaphysics towards the practicality of experimentation and the physical witness of empirical results,[91] thus announcing an apparent departure from the Cartesian priority of the mind as supra-real, towards corporeal reality itself, as a constant

---

[88] See Shapin and Schaffer, *op.cit.*, *Leviathan and the Air-Pump*, 26–40. This immanentization of God echoes the way in which Descartes reduces God to an instrumental force which sustains matter in being. For Descartes, the *Cogito* will not explain our duration from moment to moment, so he invokes God to explain the continuity of duration through time. However, the idea that "I exist" remains, for Descartes, independent of God. See Descartes, *op. cit.*, *Meditations on First Philosophy*, Third Meditation, VII. 49–51.

[89] But see n. 85 above.

[90] Shapin and Schaffer, *op.cit.*, *Leviathan and the Air-Pump*, 205–7, 315–16, 340.

[91] "I take that which the doctor contends for, to be evincible in the rightest way of proceeding by a person of far less learning than he, without introducing any precarious principle": Boyle, *An Hydrostatical Discourse, occasioned by the Objections of the Learned Dr. Henry More* (1672) in ed. Thomas Birch, *op .cit.*, *The Works of the Honourable Robert Boyle*,

touchstone for truth objectively comprehensible,[92] this shift ultimately returns the subject to a position of priority, since it is the subject which first decides what qualifies as objectively real.

One may conclude that while the virtuosic city advertized its displacement towards physical nature, the subject remained in a position of mastery. However, this was not an altogether simple position, for the construal of the subject as "active" over against a "passive" *extensio* was underwritten by natural reality itself, as the guarantor of his mastery. The new epistemology, which permeated the new secular power, depended for its status upon an absolute fidelity to extended reality "as it is," as if in mock servility to nature, awaiting its own visible delivery.

Finally, although the virtuosic city claimed to be both immanent and free from tyrannical power, its government had a sinister aspect. For it involved a disguised projection of human power which operated not according to a consensus about its values and implications, but according to an unquestioned advancement of knowledge in the service of the promotion of hidden sovereignty. This structure of governance both presupposed and perpetuated a concentration of power at an absolute centre which was projected invisibly *through* the expansion of its repertoire, rather than visibly, as the overt legislator presented in Descartes' *Discourse*. Such authority cannot be questioned since it eludes detection. This betokens, therefore, a superlative absolutism which permeates invisibly the structures of the city, thereby gaining a hold which cannot be unravelled, isolated, or deposed. In the concluding section of this chapter, I shall show how the same configuration of power, predicated on spatiality, is inscribed into the apparently innocuous structures of twentieth-century language, thus continuing its untraceable infiltration of the city. However, before that, I will show how such a deflected absolutism, disguised by the carnival of knowledge for knowledge's sake, can be seen elsewhere in baroque society, notably in its deployment of the device of theatre.

7 THE THEATRICAL CITY

In this section, I will discuss the cynical aspect of baroque excess – its hypertrophied and semi-secularized ritual. In particular, I will consider its

---

III, 596–628, 596–8, cited by Shapin and Schaffer, *ibid.* On Boylean experimentation as breaking the bounds of privileged learning, see *ibid.*, 216–17.

[92] The ordering of human activity and multiplication of the witnessing experience were presented as ways to guarantee objectivity.

deployment as an expedient of societal containment in the form of a theatrical
"event" which works to accomplish the ruses of absolutism. This may be
described as "cynical" because, unlike the outline of the city's structure in
Descartes' *Discourse*, the true source of power works invisibly, appearing more
as a *subversion* of control, so gaining a double grip. In a consideration of the
various forms of baroque excess, and its implications for a construal of the city,
representation, and the subject, it will be seen that its carnivalesque abandon
was a flourish at the margins, beguiling the masses in a florid gesture which
pointed not to any real transcendence, but towards the king. Such excess,
remaining only at the margins, is tantamount to a reinforcement of *lack*, for
its subjects are kept enthralled, begging for more.

In his essay "*Espace et Langage*," Gérard Genette distinguishes between two
types of spatiality: first, the universal, primary space which has always informed
human practices on account of the experience of the human body, and
secondly, the radical and comprehensive rationalization of late modernity
which he calls "overspatialization."[93] In the case of the latter, it is not merely
that we speak of space, but that space becomes our language, space speaks itself.
Indeed, in the next and final section of this chapter I will discuss the way in
which the spatiality of late modernity not only speaks itself, but extends its
programme to speak *its speakers* as well. Genette explains that systematic
spatiality is experienced on every level, but that precisely *when* it was
inaugurated, or *why*, are difficult to discern. But it will be shown below that
the difficulty of discerning a cause of spatiality is integral to its project, and
indeed betrays its political aspect. The effect of eliding the origin of spatiality
or concealing its derivedness, instantiates an imposed mysteriousness, an
instituted Other, which commands power in and through its disguised and
dispersed effects.

There is a Cartesian aspect to such a negotiation of governmental control,
insofar as it implies a construal of subjects as a flattened-out extension or
"mass" available to regulation from above, (like the objects of the experimental philosophers) as well as in its prioritization of the single legislator. Genette
observes this implicit Cartesian structure, in another essay, "*L'or tombe sous le
fer*,"[94] where he comments on the mistaken belief that the beginning of the
seventeenth century was a time of deliquescence, when all aspects of artistic
life were characterized by fluidity, and a melting into volutes and tendrils, and
where an animation of space followed the models of living nature, in vegetable

[93] Gérard Genette, "*Espace et Langage*," in *idem, Figures*, (Paris: Editions du Seuil, 1966),
101–8.
[94] Genette, "*L'or tombe sous le fer*," in *ibid.*, 29–38.

tumescence and nebulous lines. The *topos* of movement in the baroque, he argues, with all its gestures of excess, which might seem to occlude the calm units of Ramist or Cartesian cartographies, was in fact not at all an embrace of difference and time, but rather an artificial and quantified, homogeneous colonization of neutral, abstract space. It was the *universality* of the apparent disorder, its systematic diffusion, which betray its chaos as strategic, studied, and fully contained. As Genette emphasizes, poetry of the French baroque could not be less fluid. As well as noting the prevalent use of organized, almost geometric duplets of air and water, water and fire, hot and cold, he also notes the abundant use of lapidary emblems which push off against one another, like baroque architectural folds, without inter-penetrating. Baroque nymphs stop adorning themselves with garlands of flowers, and take instead to wearing jewels. And the flowers they *do* wear bloom with a borrowed life, enduring unnaturally through every season. Stable substances are imposed upon liquid, so that water is variously described as gold, jasper, alabaster, and crystal, and the female body is described as ivory, marble, and silver, in such a way as to introduce the facticity of the substantial order into the contingency of things, forming antitheses to provide spatial symmetry. In this poetics of mineral and metal, words receive their value by virtue of their solid contrast, their folding against one another, in a way which seems to organize the flux, to (im)mobilize every difference and fasten it to its opposite. Thus, an alliance of lapidary words surmounts discordance, and makes contrasts secretly commune at a *hidden centre*, the pleat of a fold which divides in order to fasten together.[95]

It can therefore be seen that baroque excess resides in the interstices of Cartesian regulation of mind and matter, and represents a *beginning* of absolutist power which pretends to be a *vanishing* point, or abdication of power. What forms did this apparent abdication take? Although its forms were manifold, it can be seen chiefly in areas of artistic spectacle, such as fiestas, theatrical machinations involving lighting, fireworks, and other spectacular devices, diversions of violence such as Spanish bullfighting, forms of artistic representation and illusion like the devices of anamorphosis (see below) and *trompe l'oeil*, architectural excesses, interest in novelty of all kinds, particularly matters of invention and costume, and above all, monarchical display, such as processions, emblems, magical effects, and pageantry.[96]

---

[95] See Gilles Deleuze, *The Fold: Leibniz and the Baroque*, tr. Tom Conley, (London: Athlone Press, 1993), 3–4, 28ff.

[96] "The fact that kings are habitually seen in the company of guards, drums, officers and all the things which prompt automatic responses of respect and fear has the result that, when they are sometimes alone and unaccompanied, their features are enough to strike respect or fear into their subjects, because we make no mental distinction between their person and

In considering these forms of apparently uncontained excess, it will be argued first, that physical space is here ultimately reduced to a single substance; secondly, that the human subject, as manipulated from above, is implicitly included within this single substance, and is a fissured subject; and thirdly, that the central power, whether visible or invisible, colonizes a pseudo-transcendent realm which combines both the overt absolutism of the Cartesian legislator, and a covert absolutism of dispersed power. Above all, it will be seen that baroque excess disguises its true character as lack.

Baroque architectural space can be seen to repeat the structure of the Cartesian city whose interior has no exterior, and whose centre is both a universal and a *punctum*. Since the possibility of a single legislator requires totalization, while the totalized city collapses back into the gaze of the isolated individual, baroque architecture expresses precisely this coincidence of the whole with the singular. Thus, the exterior of a baroque building is characteristically not real, but a façade, an artificial outside. Whilst there have always been special, sanctified interior spaces such as the crypt, the cell, the sacristy, and the ecclesiastical space itself, such spaces were not "closed," for they were designated as open to the transcendent, and designed in order to emphasize this aspect.[97] By contrast, the baroque interior was invested in such a way as to affirm its own autonomous and self-gestating power. Its space was clear and self-identical: a pure and abstract arena. Like the Cartesian mind, its light was its own, the light of reason, which entered secretly through the *camera obscura*, via a play of mirrors, or through tilted orifices placed so high that it was impossible to see outside. Thus, the interior was illuminated without contamination, an inside with no outside, and yet universally repeated. And the decor of the prestigious surface of the baroque artificial

---

the retinue with which they are normally seen to be associated. And the world, which does not know that this is the effect of habit, believes it to derive from some natural force, hence such sayings as: "The character of divinity is stamped on his features.' " Blaise Pascal, *op.cit.*, *Pensées*, ¶ 25; see also ¶ 308. See further José Antonio Maravall, *Culture of the Baroque: Analysis of a Historical Structure*, tr. Terry Cochran, (Minneapolis: University of Minnesota Press, 1986); on baroque architecture see Deleuze, *op. cit.*, *The Fold*; Henri Lefebvre, *The Production of Space*, tr. Donald Nicholson-Smith, (Oxford: Blackwell Publishers, 1991), 232, 275; Jean Baudrillard, *Symbolic Exchange and Death*, tr. Iain Hamilton Grant, (London: Sage, 1993), 50–3; on the manipulative effects of monarchical display, Louis Marin, *Portrait of the King*, tr. Martha M. Houle, (Minneapolis: University of Minnesota Press, 1988); Eric Alliez, *Capital Times: Tales from the Conquest of Time*, tr. Georges Van Den Abbeele, (Minneapolis: University of Minnesota Press, 1996), 197–239, especially 215–16.

[97] Erwin Panofsky, *Gothic Architecture and Scholasticism*, (New York: Meridian, 1957 and London: Thames and Hudson, 1957).

exterior conformed to the same logic. It too expressed an eloquent, powerful, and fraudulent expansion of space, forcing that expansion to the limits, with dizzying undulating folds, and eruptions of palms and fronds. These turned material space into a locus of risible consecration, offering nature transformed by art into an apparently simpler or more fundamental nature, recreated in riotous combinations, which were secretly contained by being reduced to the single, rational, legible substance of stucco, a covertly meaningless infinitization of meaning.[98] Its recurrent valleys, labyrinth of spongy holes, and infinite repetition of the fold's duplicity appear both as an enthrallment of space, and as an effacement of delineated contour, or obfuscation of the straight line which a Cartesian subject might wish to draw. But its folds are *duplicitous*, for although they appear turbulent, they enact a subdivision of space, in such a way that it becomes *readable* and dichotomized. Furthermore, that riot of difference is no more than a simulacrum, a secret equivalence which returns the exterior to the hermetic interior which it both conceals and repeats – the fold appears to fold about a secret enclosure, but the true secret of the fold is its ruse of enclosure, whereby the pleating of a surface generates the illusion of a substantive interiority.

Such concealment of Cartesian order beneath a surface of apparent abandon redoubles upon itself to become again a kind of disorder, by virtue of its manipulative dynamic, effecting an objectification of the subject, which leaves only the space of the absolute king in the privileged position of power. This can be seen in the structure of artistic apprehension. The undulating folds of architectural surfaces, like the indistinct edges of the baroque artistic technique of anamorphosis (an oblique drawing or picture appearing regular from one point), are not a genuine release, but a tactical absence whose distorted projections provoke the onlooker's intervention,[99] so that he (passively) experiences the need to act upon the world within a channelled arena. The onlooker's desire (as lack) issues from a studied denial, but appears attracted by the lure of excess. This process extends the Cartesian programme so as to draw the subject into the domain of extended nature. Whereas, for Descartes, the regulations of the mind were presented as a possibility for other minds, notwithstanding the *aporia* of solipsism, with the theatrical city of absolutism

[98] See Maravall, *op. cit.*, *Culture of the Baroque*, 231–2; Lefebvre, *op. cit.*, *The Production of Space*, 275; Baudrillard, *op. cit.*, *Symbolic Exchange and Death*, 50–3; Deleuze, *op. cit.*, *The Fold*, 28ff.
[99] Maravall, *op. cit.*, *Culture of the Baroque*, 218; "The receivers of the baroque work, being surprized at finding it incomplete or so irregularly constructed, remained a few instants in suspense; then, feeling compelled to thrust themselves forward and take part in it, they ended up finding themselves more strongly affected by the work, held by it," *ibid.*, 220; see also 244–5.

the subject no longer possesses such abstracted possibilities for predictable initiative. Dazzled by the apparent release of difference offered by excess, he fails to notice its dissolution into the indifference of its universal and rationalized substance, the common measure of stucco, which underlies every gesture, for he is himself encompassed by that universal substance. Hence, what he takes to be an opening for his own participation is only a pre-structuring of his appointed position within a new *political mathēsis*. Whereas Descartes subsumed the city within the self-legislation of an isolated, but universalized individual, baroque political theatre subsumed the subject within the self-legislation of the lone arbitrary will at the centre of the sovereign state.

Therefore, the elided outline which the subject is urged to supply is ultimately that of the king, strategically positioned as a vanishing point, according to a geometry of absence. For the source of ultimate power must, like the sun, also be the source of vision,[100] and so must, by definition, be invisible, its absolute power being figured through the perfection of a self-inverting symmetry. For otherwise, he would be brought into the position of *seen object*, and this position is nothing but to be beneath the king's gaze, the beam of his eye, which is the source of representation. And so in a sense, absolute power can never be seen in itself, but only in its signs, which *coincide* with the power they disperse and perpetuate – perpetuate, because they offer forever deferred satisfaction. To the bedazzled subjects of the king, the excessive display seems transparent. They are caught off guard, in the myth of exchange where none exists, flattered by the display, gazing, but doubly gazed upon.[101]

The baroque subject is therefore denied genuine subjectivity, for when he thinks he intends an action, his advance is always already outstepped, his action already passive; but passive twice over, since he remains unaware of this inscription.[102] And the glossy impressions of monarchical display divide the subject from himself. By succumbing to the shimmering perform-ances of fabricated presence, the gloss of transcendence, whether perman-ently figured in an architectural façade, or in a fleeting gesture, his attention is momentarily immobilized or suspended by a glazed state of

[100] See Marin, *op. cit.*, *Portrait of the King*, 66–9, for a discussion of the significance of the icon of the sun for Louis XIV, the Sun-King, drawing upon Descartes' use of that image in Part Five of the *Discourse on the Method*.

[101] Marin, *ibid.*, 71–2.

[102] *Ibid.*, 71–5. This repeats the structure of carnival which, by momentarily upturning the established order, more firmly re-establishes it after all. See Maravall, *op. cit.*, *Culture of the Baroque*, chapter 9.

astonishment, precipitating a loss of all critical or historical continuity.[103]

What is the relationship between the absoluteness of the king's power and its representation in signs? The king's monuments, like tombs, configure his eternal power, and his excessive gestures are his "real presence,"[104] and although these representations are not the *same* as the power they configure, they are perhaps *better* than such identity, for they are *permanent effects* of presence, rather than absence and death. The permanence of the king's effects are a placing in reserve of absolute power in signs – which *is* absolute power precisely because it appears under the contradictory mode of the negation of power, since force seems neither to be exerted nor manifested: what could be more pacific than signs? This power is absolute by virtue of the apparent peace of its infinite significations.

The dispersal of absolute power into a plurality of signs, and the effects of these signs on the king's subjects, constitute the possibility for realizing the arbitrary, political version of self-legislation, in contrast to the Cartesian, privatized one. By ensuring the ultimate passivity of every "action" of the citizens of this city, the king envelops them in the unity of his field, so that they act only through or within his own already enacted action. As an absolute force, the king by definition annihilates all other forces, and so ultimately has no exterior, and is without possible comparison. The multiplicity of his signs, relayed and transmitted throughout the reality they produce, sparkles across the whole surface of the city, which is the king's stage, centralized at a point of non-existent form so as to elude objectification, but always ensuring that there is no corner which his signs do not reach, or where he is not absolute.

Through the universality of the monarchical apex, it can be seen that the triumph of the singular legislator, of rationalization and reason incarnate in a single king, enacts an immanent *re-mythologization* which reveals the *mythic* basis of the vaunted new objective reason, in a way that Ramism, Cartesianism, and the "New Science" could only disguise. First, in the case of Ramism and Cartesianism, as well as the experimental philosophers, its universality is an overall *pattern*, but this is now manifestly a mythic *ideal*, since only the unilateral summit ordains an intellectual geometry, even if, for its deluded subjects, it disperses its power within its interstices. And

---

[103] "Manifestations whose goals were to suspend and attract became general and frequent in the baroque," Maravall, *op. cit., Culture of the Baroque,* 242; see also chapter 2.

[104] Marin argues that the absolute rule of Louis XIV was deliberately projected in signs which echoed or parodically repeated those of Christ's body. See Marin, *op. cit., Portrait of the King,* 11–12; See below, chapter 6.

88 THE POLITY OF DEATH

this delusion is never to be counted upon forever. In the end, the arbitrary apex of absolutism, which, by definition, has no dealings with consent, relies upon the *myth* of divine right as its final court of appeal.[105] Later on, a purer immanentism emerges, and a purer blending of politics with *mathēsis*, in which the apex is reason itself. But even here, it seems, the mythical is always liable to return, whether in absolute terms, as in the case of Nazism, or dispersed into localized cults of stars and presidents. So, in conclusion, it can be seen that the *political staging* of the formalist reason of immanentist modernity, as sketched out by Ramus, Descartes, Boyle and the "New Science," already reveals a void at the heart of reason and enlightenment. The more one surrenders the localism and traditionalism of substantive content for the universality of a formalist method, the more this method is inevitably lacking and requires supplementation by mythology always more manifestly crude and arbitrary than anything enshrined in pre-rational antiquity.

8 THE LANGUAGE OF MODERNITY

To conclude this chapter I shall discuss the way in which the various manifestations of spatialization and textualization described above have become increasingly normative, in such a way that it is no longer possible *even to observe it as a distinct phenomenon, or speak of it as though it were external to our language.* This results in the most extreme immanentist re-mythicizing of reality, for the central point of power is now scattered by our own linguistic signs, disseminated in and through the locus of our creativity, where it takes root. Our signs carry this power invisibly, and so it transgresses mundane borders without our knowledge, colonizing every corner, in such a way that we unwittingly deploy the very thing which seeks to disempower us. Thus, we bespeak our own termination when we think we freely live; and when we imagine we advance an intention in words, that advance has already been out-worded, our command stopping short of our words' prewritten limit.

[105] See Sir Robert Filmer, *Patriarcha and Other Writings*, ed. Johann P. Sommerville, (Cambridge: Cambridge University Press, 1991); Ann M. Blair, *Restaging Jean Bodin: The "Universae naturae theatrum" (1596) in its Cultural Context*, (Doctoral Dissertation, Princeton University, 1990), 63–7; Julian H. Franklin, *Jean Bodin and the Rise of Absolutist Theory*, (Cambridge: Cambridge University Press, 1973); McRae, *op. cit.*, "Ramist Tendencies in the Thought of Jean Bodin"; Perry Anderson, *Lineages of the Absolute State*, (London: N.L.B., 1974), chapter 1.

In considering this spatialization of language, I shall discuss, first, the ascendancy of the noun in twentieth-century poetics and linguistic practice, and secondly, the implications of this for discourse structure, namely the inevitable substitution of complex by simple asyndetic syntax. I will show how these characteristics of contemporary language perpetuate the structures of spatialized and textualized power described in the previous sections of this chapter, and can be located in a more general prioritization of the constative over the performative.

Nouns: a hardness as of cut stone

In this section, it will be shown that the prioritization of the noun in modernist poetics and contemporary discourse is one aspect of the sinister deployment of the subject's own unwitting self-termination. For, by receiving its language of nouns – a nominal language in every sense – the subject receives from without that which it assumes to arise from its own internal creative autonomy. Caught off guard, the subject delivers its own sentence of termination.

The protocol of objectification as a means of perpetuating absolute power implicit in the theoretical, scientific, and aesthetic manifestations of spatialization in the seventeenth century continued and intensified beyond the baroque era. The rise of historical representation in the nineteenth century, accompanied by a succession of technical developments such as lithography, photography, and the daguerreotype, seemed to actualize a summoning of reality distilled from the flux of time, as a spatial given.[106] The nineteenth-century novel and the photograph share the same struggle towards immediacy and facticity guaranteed by an abundance of circumstantial detail (reminiscent of Boylean "virtual witnessing") which can be seen as part of a valorization of objects, via an apparent bypassing of the contaminating layers of subjectivity, equated

---

[106] Sections 1 and 2 of Part 8 of this chapter owe a great deal to the Sylvia Adamson's brilliant lecture course, "Poetry and Parts of Speech," in the Department of English, Cambridge University, which I attended in Michaelmas Term, 1992. For a discussion of the increasing importance and manipulative aspect attached to minute and arbitrary details from the rise of photographic techniques to today's concept of "live media coverage" for which the visibility and transparency of detail are seen as guarantees of veracity, see Paul Connerton, "Fabricating Histories," in eds Nicholas Boyle and Martin Swales, *Realism in European Literature: Essays in Honour of J. P. Sterne*, (Cambridge: Cambridge University Press, 1985), 158–68; Stephen Bann, *The Clothing of Clio: A Study of the Representation of History in Nineteenth Century Britain and France*, (Cambridge: Cambridge University Press, 1984), chapter 6.

with death and obscurity, according to an instantiation of the maxim that the "[t]his was so defeats the it's me."[107]

The ascendancy of the object is associated with the disintegration of the tripartite sign. This disintegration insinuated a direct relation of signifier to referent, at the expense of the signified which is the inescapable cultural and ritual mediation of "reality." Openness and spontaneity are the assumed guarantees of probity of this project, yet it in fact conceals its *own* ritualistic nature as a closed and controlled formulation. Taken to its extreme, the removal of the signified is itself another signified, one which disguises itself as immediacy, but is in fact the tyranny of scattered power at work in spatialization. Because the myriad impressions of concrete details cannot point beyond themselves, all such representation can do is project one object after another in a serial procession whose only cohesion, the linearity of succession and the sum of its quantity, is in any case evacuated by the annihilative order of obsolescence and desire as lack. This hidden signified of death, which equates freedom with chaos, orders through its disorder, manipulating from a point of secluded absence that which thinks itself to be free. Further, since there is after all nothing outside language, the act of representation has always already altered that which it represents, as a kind of secular *ekstasis* from interior to exterior, traced by the eye. Because of its secret derivation from the knowing subject, this is also an auto-erotic gaze, neither active, nor passive, but rather the Cartesian redoubling action of reflexivity, the pseudo-middle voice of modernity. And so the affirmation of the object rebounds secretly to applaud the subject.

Other attempts to magnify objecthood – even if in the paradoxical form of an attempt to liberate it from commodified equivalence following Bergson – were those of Imagism, Cubism, and Futurism.[108] In some cases, these

---

[107] Roland Barthes describes the photographic making-manifest to the spectator as the "having-been-there . . . the always stupefying evidence of this is how it was," in *idem, Image-Music-Text*, tr. Stephen Heath (London: Fontana, 1977), 44. For an account of the ascendancy of the noun and arbitrary detail used to obtain the "reality effect" see Barthes, *S/Z*, (Paris: Seuil, 1970) on Balzac's *Sarrasine*; Georg Lukács, *The Historical Novel*, (London: Merlin, 1962), 186–9 on Flaubert's *Salammbo*; for a discussion of the continuity of Joyce's *Ulysses* with the realist tradition already established by Balzac, Flaubert, and Zola, in the eruption of the everyday as represented by myriad unrelated objects, and testifying to the loss of the signified, see Henri Lefebvre, *Everyday Life in the Modern World*, tr. Sacha Rabinovitch (London: Allen Lane, 1971), 7–19.

[108] Henri Bergson wished to vindicate the role of art in the twentieth century, calling artists to free the will from its abdication of liberty, by attempting to pierce the veil between the subject and reality. See his *Time and Free Will*, tr. F. L. Pogson, (London: George Allen and Unwin Ltd, 1910). However, Bergson's formulation is predicated on a construal of reality

attempted to convert the object into an event, or else into a kind of subject, whilst in others the object was shattered or eliminated altogether.[109] The rhetoric of quiddity which informed Ezra Pound's Imagist poetics sought to deliver a precise rendering of the "thing," influenced by T. E. Hulme's plea for accuracy, precision, and definite rendering,[110] focusing on the object as a phenomenological effect produced by a dizzying and clotted succession of concrete nouns and noun phrases, and an elimination of verbs. The project of Imagism was to deliver the solid cleanliness of the concrete object, and accordingly the noun was exalted as the least conceptualized part of speech, most suited to a production in language of an epiphany of the real. However, there are at least two ways in which this project can be seen to conceal a Cartesian dualism of mind and extension which, after all, determines the object as *ideal*. First, the noun carries no markings of time or personal agency and so appears both permanent, unchanging, and given. Secondly, such dislocated quiddity is situated not in a diachronic, "lived" narrative, but rather in a non-discursive Cartesian cartography of spatial juxtaposition within a "closed field".[111]

Whilst Imagism's project sought implicitly to attenuate time in its phenomenology of nominal density,[112] Futurism's task was to *accelerate* apprehension to such a degree that the object could only be contemplated in retrospect, thus eliminating the fetishistic moment of presence.[113] Here

---

as given "out there," available to be committed only secondarily into language. In seeking to apprehend "pure reality" by construing it as comprising autonomous and unsignified entities, redeemed from the nothingness to which our standardized and ritual experience relegates them, the disguised signified of scattered space was enthroned, unwittingly reaffirming the spatialization he sought to undo. For a pure isolated "quality" is as much subject to the standardization-effect of spatialization as a measurable quantity.

[109] Frederic Jameson, *Marxism and Form: Twentieth Century Dialectical Theories of Literature*, (New Jersey: Princeton University Press, 1974), 410; Glenn Hughes, *Imagism and the Imagists*, (New York: Biblo and Tannen, 1972); Wylie Sypher, *Rococco to Cubism in Art and Literature*, (New York: Vintage Books, 1960), 324.

[110] Hughes, *op. cit.*, *Imagism and the Imagists*, 27.

[111] Hugh Kenner, "Art in a Closed World," *Virginia Quarterly Review*, 38 (1966), 600–5; William Carlos Williams, "The Poem as a Field of Action," (1948) in *Selected Essays* (New York: Random House, 1954), 280–91.

[112] On the political ambiguity of the Imagist project see David Hayman, *Re-Forming the Narrative: Toward a Mechanics of Modernist Fiction*, (Ithaca and London: Cornell University Press, 1987), 208.

[113] Andrew Hewitt, *Fascist Modernism: Aesthetics, Politics, and the Avant-Garde*, (Stanford, California: Stanford University Press, 1993), 109.

again one can detect a metaphysics of spatiality at work. Filippo Tommaso
Marinetti, the father of Futurism, and celebrator of speed and ontological
nostalgia, despised the adjective which he saw as impeding and decelerating
apprehension of the pure noun.[114] Like all the Futurists, he felt that the
redundantly decorative and supplementary adjective contaminates or shades
the brilliance of the noun, offering an artifice which distorts its essence even
as it would seem to clarify it. In a sense, therefore, the adjective was seen as
constituting a monopolizing moment in the system of simultaneous free
exchange of one noun against another,[115] a perturbation of spatial equivalence, so that we can read Marinetti's fear of the adjective as capital's fear of
itself, of its own desire to amass all in one place.[116] The object is not liberated
from the tyranny of equivalence after all, and, furthermore, to see the
adjective as mere precious adornment is to assume that there is a kind of
subjectless representation which is not itself already adornment, issued from
a subjectless subject which contains the constituents of the regulated interior
of the Cartesian intellect. Marinetti's attempt to undo a metaphysics of
presence and givenness by means of a metaphysics of absence or retrospection is, therefore, reducible to what he opposes.[117]

   The increased use of nominalizations, nouns derived from verbs, in
contemporary public discourse, is a further example of the ascendancy of
the object and the concomitant and paradoxical re-mythicization of reality.
But where the exaltation of nouns in modernist poetics had been part of
a self-conscious programme focusing on the object, the manipulation of
civic realities via the prolonged and repeated use of nominalizations in
certain contexts has a more sinister impact, for we are given the city's names
to repeat amongst ourselves, as more than appended nominations, since they
give rise to the nature of what they name. And yet we think we arrive *after*
the naming, and so our consciousness does not think to question what we
take as given. Although these words tend to involve public and official
discourse, and might seem to be of merely marginal importance, yet they
deliver to us, in linguistic form, the nature of our city, and our creative role
within that city. The language we are given to speak of "our" city speaks
the sentence of our own citizenship, and our words position us, therefore, at

[114] Filippo Tommaso Marinetti, in ed. R. W. Flint, *Selected Writings*, (New York: Farrar,
Straus, and Giroux, 1971), 66–8; Andrew Hewitt, *op.cit., Fascist Modernism*, 115–16.
[115] Hewitt, *ibid.*, 117.
[116] *Ibid.*, 118.
[117] Futurism's metaphysics of absence or retrospection anticipates the nihilism of
deconstruction in whose attempt to "lose" the object there lurks a concealed corollate of
covetousness which tries too hard to undo itself. See chapter 3 below.

the margins of ourselves, and write, from without, our unimportant liturgy.

What is a nominalization, and what are its semantic and philosophical properties? Nominalizations (such as "derailment," "allegation," "inflation," "recession") are characteristic of the formal and impersonal prose of media news reports, political speeches, and bureaucratic discourses. They are seen as essential components of "linguistic efficiency" due to their integration and condensation of several words – indeed whole clauses – into a single nominal unit, part of the economy of transformational grammar whereby one constituent of language can be substituted for another according to an equivalent and exigential exchange. For example, the nominalization "allegation" is a condensed transformational equivalent of the clausal "X has alleged against Y that Y has done A," and so, in pragmatic terms, the nominalization is ideally suited to discourse which places a premium on the transference of information in as economical a way as possible.[118]

Besides economy, the choice of a nominalization over its clausal equivalents has implications for a semantic organisation of reality. A nominalization elides grammatical voice, in such a way that the active or passive participants in a particular action are removed, leaving a reified, intransitive, and obscure *given* in their place.[119] Thus, when a politician speaks of "inflation," "privatization" or "recession," the lack of any explicit or implicit expression of personal role in the transitivity structure of the named phenomenon enables him to abdicate responsibility for all its subsequent effects. Moreover, the elision of agency included in the term encourages an unquestioning acceptance of the phenomenon as a mythicized authority, discontinuous with any human intervention, and so, implicitly, immovable. This, together with the nominalization's elision of modality, or indication of the speaker's view as to the phenomenon's desirability, provokes an attitude of uncritical obeisance before that which is

---

[118] Katie Wales, *Dictionary of Stylistics*, (London: Longman, 1989), 238; Douglas Biber, *Variation Across Speech and Writing*, (Cambridge: Cambridge University Press, 1988), 227; *idem.*, "Spoken and Written Textual Dimensions in English," *Language*, 62 (1986), 384–414; Rulon Wells, "Nominal and Verbal Style," in ed. Donald C. Freedman, *Linguistics and Literary Style*, (New York: Holt, Rinehart and Winston Inc., 1970), 297–306; Wallace L. Chafe, "Integration and Involvement in Speaking, Writing, and Oral Literature," in ed. Deborah Tannen, *Spoken and Written Language: Exploring Orality and Literacy*, (Norwood, New Jersey: Ablex, 1982), 33–44; Robert B. Lees, "The Grammar of the English Nominalizations," Part Two, *International Journal of American Linguistics*, 26.3 (1960), 5.

[119] George Orwell, "Politics and the English Language," in *idem*, *Collected Essays*, (London: Mercury Books, 1991), 80; Norman Fairclough, *Language and Power*, (Harlow: Longman, 1989), 51, 124; Norman Fowler, *Language in the News: Discourse and Ideology in the Press*, (London: Routledge, 1991), 79–80.

ultimately reducible to a political construct. In addition, this mythicization of the derived is supplemented by the elision of temporality inherent in the nominal form,[120] so that its constituent human activity acquires the status of a permanent object or reality which neither begins nor ends, and so, again, is beyond the reach of any human manoeuvre.

The nominalization's manifold elision of human involvement and temporality therefore has a double aspect. First, its non-ascribability conceals responsibility and commitment, covering the tracks of power; and secondly, it sustains an unquestioning attitude amongst those who receive the various names of the city. The power of modernity is the power to *disguise* itself. Furthermore, implicit in this grammatical congelation of human activity in terms of an object is its treatment as a standing reserve, equally available to abstract measurement, appropriation, and disappropriation.

The "availability" of the object presupposes a centralized power standing over against the object, and yet this systematic centrality has no exterior: its realm is *global*, and its universality, seen in the very structure of the nominalized form as a unilateral subsumption of the multiple and diverse under a single name, is self-perpetuating. This appropriation of reality by a single, abstract nominal form reduces the diverse to the condition of the personally absent spatial "mass" through which the system of power flows without leaving a trace. And furthermore the impossibility of isolating cause from effect, of ascribing agency or patient, or temporal location or aspect, played out in the recursive linguistic phenomena of derived nouns and concomitant signs, is the very system of power, dependent upon the impossibility of finding the first thread from which to unravel spatiality. Once established, the structure parades as given, a self-generating and unquestioned system which seems neutral – it passes unnoticed.

The system of spatiality is, however, not genuinely freewheeling, for it depends upon the perpetuation of certain assumptions in the construction of the citizen of the spatialized city. These are primarily the suppositions of possessive individualism and universal subordination to the laws of the market.[121] But there are other, less overt, assumptions which are disseminated invisibly through the signs we think we freely intend. For our language ordains our relationship with reality as consisting in certain seminal ritual gestures:

---

[120] Aristotle, *De Interpretatione*, in *Organon*, 2. 16. a. 19, and 3. 16. b. 6.

[121] C. B. MacPherson, *The Political Theory of Possessive Individualism: Hobbes to Locke*, (Oxford: Clarendon Press, 1962). See also, Paul Virilio, *Speed and Politics: An Essay on Dromology*, tr. Mark Polizzotti, (New York: Semiotext(e), 1986); Ulrich Beck, *Risk Society: Towards a New Modernity*, tr. Mark Ritter (London: Sage, 1992); Jean Baudrillard,

unlocking energy, ordering, measuring, storing, commanding.[122] These ontological tasks are our own measure, and we perform them automatically, without genuine "activity," already claimed by a certain mode of apprehending our role. Thus, in our seeking always to name, to concentrate in the name, to place and transfer through the name, we are ourselves included within that name, unwittingly ordering ourselves from within by that which we think we order from without. What is this nomination, but *carnival* naming?

Finally, the implications of this construction of the subject are not limited to the question of disempowerment. It functions also as the opposite of the apostrophic trope of personification which transcends spatiality by restoring to time and personhood that which is physically absent.[123] For nominalization conceals human and temporal reality under the guise of objecthood, removing the personal *from itself*. Thus, in the contemporary spatial city, the person is encountered not as a genuine subjectivity performed and renewed through public acts of citizenship, but as the *absence* of a person, on the fringes of self-annihilation. Like the spatial stratum itself, the citizen cannot be found, for its perpetuation is contemporary with its erasure.[124]

Syntax: the contour against the void

In this section, I shall discuss the syntactic category of asyndeton, and show it to be a trope of spatial modernity. I argue that it is a duplicitous trope in several ways, proclaiming but secretly reversing cohesion, affirming but secretly containing the subject, and denying but secretly establishing absolute power.

Asyndeton, syntax characterized by the absence of co-ordinating and subordinating conjunctions, has been identified as the logical syntactic

---

In the Shadow of the Silent Majorities, or, The End of the Social, and Other Essays, tr. Paul Foss et al. (New York: Semiotext(e), 1983); Michel de Certeau, *The Practice of Everyday Life*, tr. Steven Rendall, (Berkeley: University of California Press, 1984); George Lakoff and Mark Johnson, *Metaphors We Live By*, (Chicago: Chicago University Press 1980) whose "ontological metaphor" is parallel with nominalization.

[122] Martin Heidegger, "The Question Concerning Technology," in ed. David Farrell Krell, *Basic Writings*, (San Francisco: Harper, 1977), 287–317.

[123] James Paxson, *The Poetics of Personification*, (Cambridge: Cambridge University Press, 1994), 137–8 ; see below, chapter 4, "The Apostrophic Voice."

[124] The subject therefore has a demonic aspect, "whose only proof of existence comes to us from the abyss of which often the vertigo of existence pushes us towards suicide": Jean-Luc Marion, "*Le Mal en Personne*," in *idem, Prolegomenes à la Charité*, (Paris: E.L.A. La Difference, 1986), 12–42, 42.

development for a language whose verbs seem neutrally to serve the ascendant noun, noun phrase, or nominalization.[125] It is regarded as typically modern syntax, linked with the search for scientific clarity, and the unadorned, "simple" rendering of reality. Indeed, its cumulative, stichomythic swiftness and "curt" style seem to satisfy many of the epistemological and aesthetic demands discussed above. Like the apparently functional and neutral short-hand of the nominalization, asyndeton structures language in terms of a linear, informational sequence which, because of its lack of figural anaphoric repetitions, seems panoptically assimilable, subdivided into unilateral units which can be uniformly delivered to the reader. Its clauses, therefore, are equivalent to discrete nominal items, projected one after the other, in an accumulation of densities. Furthermore, its apparently "natural" aggregative structure is well suited to the new post-Romantic celebration of spontaneity, immediacy, and authorial delitescence, as against the apparently rationalizing interventions and concomitant closure of complex syntax.

It seems, then, that the triumph of asyndeton, both in modern poetics and ordinary discourse (both formal and everyday), is continuous with other efforts to deliver an unmediated and exact apprehension of "the real," free from any ritual and tyrannical ciphers of cultural organization. But, like nominalization, asyndeton both reflects and perpetuates the new, invisible tyranny of unquestioned assumptions regarding the nature of reality, repre-sentation, and subjectivity, which undercut its claim to neutral transparency.

Although asyndeton is presented as the ideal representational structure for bypassing mediation, and undoing the division between mind and matter, it is nevertheless predicated upon that very division. The absence of conjunc-tions in asyndetic syntax ensures the omission of all clausal relations and hierarchies, in favour of a serial juxtaposition cast in the genre of the catalogue or list. Thus the events narrated or objects described in asyndetic prose are necessarily presented as obtainable, scrutable, and given, but definitively *other* from the text as list. This syntax *appears* to efface itself, as well as the subject, by pointing away in a gesture of humility towards the objects arraigned elsewhere in reality, but in fact this humility secretly rebounds to affirm the act of representation. In its apparent extirpation of subjectivity in the objective and blind relay of the passive gaze, asyndeton disguises an epistemology which

[125] Morris W. Croll, "The Baroque Style in Prose," in ed. Stanley Fish, *Modern Essays in Criticism: Seventeenth Century Prose*, (Oxford: Oxford University Press, 1971), 26–52; Richard Foster Jones, "Science and English Prose Style, 1650–1675," in *ibid.*, 53–89; on the drift towards quantification in prose style, Julia Kristeva, "The Bounded Text," in ed. Leon Roudiez, *Desire in Language: A Semiotic Approach to Literature and Art*, (Oxford: Basil Blackwell, 1981), 36–63.

claims mastery over a reality which in fact derives from, and seeks to affirm, the supremacy of the knowing subject.

This apparent affirmation of the subject is a *carnival* affirmation, for it is always ultimately contained. This can be seen in several ways. First, the openness and spontaneity which appear to be offered by asyndetic structures are inscribed within a fundamental closure which secretly erases the subject's achievement. Reality itself, as objectified, and represented in unhierarchized and disjoined clauses, is rendered static and inert, beyond any possible manifestation of difference, a condition tantamount to closure or indifference, thinly disguised by the jagged display of its promiscuous juxtapositions.[126]

Secondly, in this manipulation of the subject, the ambiguity of the genre of the list is crucial. On the one hand, the list appears as a powerful organization of random phenomena. But on the other hand, this "order" slips constantly into chaos, for the list also represents a loss of stability, in its random assembly of unrelated elements.[127] And although the spatiality of juxtaposition and absence of connections communicate a consoling permanence and immobile density to the components of the catalogue, ultimately this unity is shattered by the inherent violence of linearity, or the perpetual outrunning of clauses, and also by its aleatory yokings. This hidden violence and disarray induce the reader to abandon the passive role of recipient, in order to engage in a private re-establishment of coherence.[128] Thus, the citizen of the spatial city experiences the need to control, but only as a palliative expedient, within the confines of private hermeneutic activity. Furthermore, the citizen unconsciously experiences its relation with reality as consisting in *control by force*.

The representation of reality as lying outside language in a consistency of serial objects, and of the subject as in charge of representation, combine in such a way as to perpetuate the structures necessary for a capitalist economy. For the model of asyndeton presupposes a dreamed-of object lurking behind every real (textual) object which the reader is urged to supply – as if to say, "there is an object that desire feels the lack of; hence the world does not contain each and every object that exists; there is at least one object missing, the one that desire feels the lack of; hence, there exists some other place that contains the key to desire (missing in this world)."[129] This lack resides at the heart of capitalist economy which organizes wants and needs amid an abundance of production, so that desire is secularized, and equated with the fear of not

---

[126] See Hayman, *op. cit.*, *Re-Forming the Narrative,* 149.

[127] *Ibid.*, 149, 206–7.

[128] *Ibid.*, 149.

[129] Clément Rosset, *Logique du Pire*, (Paris: Presses Universitaires de France, 1970), 37.

having one's needs satisfied.[130] The reader's gaze provokes an individualist endeavour of self-satisfaction within an arena of reduced, garish stimulus, via the supply of missing nutrients of cognition, casting the consummation of subjectivity as epistemological, in contrast to the interpersonal and *ontological* gaze of Socratic *erōs*.

The perpetual emptying of satisfaction by the reassertion of lack, the arraignment before the subject of permanent objects which nevertheless do not last, has a further significance. The work of citizenship, thus constructed as the search for the ultimate object to end all lack, is implicitly understood as the denial of death.[131] The linear temporal structure of spatiality, mirrored by asyndeton, both provokes the anxiety of obsolescence, and wields the promise of a panacea, the eternal object to end all desires.[132] Thus organized from without, the citizen becomes complicit in his own exile from the city, for in striving to end the agony of desire, he strives to become an object.

The warp of language

The ascendancy of nominal and asyndetic structures in contemporary linguistic practice bears witness to a more general triumph of scientific or constative epistemology[133] which assumes that reality comprises "essences" of fact, and that knowledge is ultimately an act of hermeneutic isolation of truth and falsehood. Concomitantly, language is banally advertized as the (paradoxically) ideal storage of the "real,"[134] with its facilities of nouns and lists, performing nothing of its own, but only re-entering the ideal realm it never leaves, of simulated chances and textualized desire.

The contemporary city is publicized in and through these simulations of myriad "events" and their analysis. Its various configurations of information

---

[130] Gilles Deleuze and Félix Guattari, *Anti-Oedipus, Capitalism and Schizophrenia*, tr. Robert Hurley *et al.*, (London: Athlone Press, 1984).

[131] See chapter 3 below.

[132] On the linear temporality of modernity and its negotiation of the past, see Connerton, *op. cit.*, *How Societies Remember*, 27; Paul de Man, "Literary History and Literary Modernity," *Daedalus*, 99.2 (1970), 384-404; E. Hobsbawm and T. Ranger (eds) *The Invention of Tradition*, (Cambridge: Cambridge University Press, 1983).

[133] Lyotard, *op. cit.*, *The Postmodern Condition*, 18-27; J. L. Austin, *How to Do Things With Words*, (Oxford: Clarendon Press, 1962).

[134] For an example of this instrumentalization of language, see H. P. Grice, "Logic and Conversation," in eds. P. Cole and J. L. Morgan, *Syntax and Semantics 3: Speech Acts*, (New York: Academic Press, 1975); C. E. Shannon and W. Weaver, *The Mathematical Theory of Communication*, (Illinois: University of Illinois Press, 1949).

– summit meetings, at-the-scene immediacy – yield a linguistic continuity of diurnal travail. Whereas in the baroque, the representation of the king produced this continuity consciously, today, it is conveyed through the warp of the fabric of sensory impressions produced and regulated by a market economy whose condition of possibility is, as we have seen, the impression of controlled chaos. The radical impoverishment of stimuli, with their endless variations on the theme of the "free offer" or the ultimate "choice," return the so-called "diversity" of the modern age to its Ramist and Cartesian origins of simplicity, clarity, distinctness.[135] In their time, these reductions operated politically through the omnipresent sign of the king, but today, the imprint of power on all public surfaces has its (untraceable) "origin" in that which is both everywhere and nowhere.

Whilst the principle difference between the seventeenth century and the twentieth is apparent in the decentralizing strategies which multiply a reduced number of effects, scattering a single domain, the overall pattern holds true. Our lives are determined by institutional models of language which contain the creative elements of our productions within the overriding order of the dominant "mode" of language, inherited from the schematic thinking of Descartes and intensified by the spatial allegories of modernity, in such a way that the effects of power accomplish its *actualization* when its subjects assume their height of autonomy, in their most innocuous everyday deployment of signs – signs whose permanence seems to separate them from the life they in fact hold in their grip.

Spatialization is therefore a *ritual* order which monitors the desires of the masses, achieving domination as much or more by the control of ideas about reality as by military forces and visible voted-in apexes. This ultimate, invisible force, deviously inherited from baroque absolutism, has no recourse to "consent," and passes unnoticed in the apparently harmless dissemination of signs, which we assume it is our task to command.

In this chapter, I have described a situation whose origins can be traced in Plato's depiction of the struggle of immanentism in his *Phaedrus*, but which became increasingly normative from the baroque era onwards. This struggle involves the turn to the self in an effort of security against the void, when, in a newly unilateral universe, that which is multiple, different, or fluctuating represents the abyssal reality of death, against which the mobilizing gesture of spatialization seems the only possible defence. I have also shown how the urgency of this gesture, and the fear which provokes it, are the condition of

[135] See further Tom Conley's introduction to Marin, *op. cit.*, *Portrait of the King*, "The King's Effects," vi–xvii; see also Baudrillard, *op. cit.*, *Symbolic Exchange and Death, passim.*

possibility for absolutist power, and that for its ultimate deployment, it is
necessary that the citizens of immanentism think themselves free to *choose*, out
of an array of several possible gestures, that which awards them the bonus of
self-advancement. I have further argued that the dizzying array of possibilities
are reducible to the *nihil*, and dazzle the subject so that he is in a state of
permanent suspension. Insofar as the phenomenon of spatialization has
become an organizing principle which orders the structures of our language
and the enactment of our relation with the city, it is a component of our
grammar. And its determination of the subject as superficially active and
fundamentally passive reveal it to be the dominant grammatical *voice* of
modernity, that is, in its negotiation of the attitudes of activity and passivity.
This "voice" is invisibly *written* into the grammar of our language and
behaviour in such a way that when we think we speak or act with all the
contingency of an open and temporal event, that contingency is choreo-
graphed in advance. There is no surprise: the indicative mood inscribes even
the unknown. The subsumption of activity within passivity, or the pendulum
between the two, suggests that this "voice" is a pseudo-middle, ordering our
relation with reality, and in a reflexive sense, with ourselves, because it refers
us to a reality which is wholly immanent, in which there can be only a shuttling
between action and passion, and no wholly Other "third" position.

In the next chapter, I will show how the apparently urgent avoidance of
death in spatial modernity results in a universal sacrifice to death, and how the
response of post-structuralist nihilism preserves and indeed intensifies the
same metaphysical gesture.

Chapter Three

SIGNS OF DEATH

In the previous chapter, I described the invisible dissemination of assumptions concerning what constitutes a genuine human action, and the status of the subject, via the cynical duplicity of language as the true locus of power. It was seen that the lure of desire as lack is a condition of possibility for absolutist power, for it provokes the subject to strive for the eradication of absence, by searching for the superlative acquisition to end all acquisitions. The disposition of the subject as yearning for the once-and-for-all termination of the agony of desire guarantees an unwitting collusion in its own objectification. Moreover, this termination of *erōs* coincides with the condition of the inert object, and therefore fulfills the criterion for death. Perversely, the lineaments of secular power are sustained by the provocation of necrophobia, the consolation of which is presented as the desire to cancel desire, whose sinister corollate – as I shall now show – is necrophilia itself.

This implicit necrophilia remains universally at the level of dissimulation. Indeed, there is an established consensus to the effect that modernity is predicated not on a love of death but only upon its evasion and eschewal. It is a common thread in the work of the twentieth-century historians of death (Edgar Morin, Henri Bremond, Pierre Chaunu, John McManners, Michel Vovelle, Philippe Ariès) that a shift in attitude has occurred, where a former cultural familiarity with death and its integration into life is replaced by a retreat from death in a double gesture of denial and mystification – although these writers account for that shift in different ways and situate it at different times, from the twelfth to the seventeenth and eighteenth centuries. In general, the main reasons offered by these writers for this retreat focus, to differing degrees of intensity, on, first, the drift towards immanentism, culminating in the triumph of reason in the Enlightenment, according to which, death is the last remaining scandal which refuses to be mastered; and, secondly, advances in medical science which mean that in the West, so-called "untimely" death or deadly epidemics occur less frequently, encouraging the synecdochal dream that mastery over disease presages an eventual triumph over death itself. And so contemporary historians appear to have shown that the apparent imminence of a scientific triumph over death finds expression in an evasion of the continuing reality of death. This necrophobia can be seen already in the increasing early-modern focus of attention not on the deceased person but upon his survivors and their display of piety in the erection of elaborate tombs and monuments. Although these displays appeared to be bestowed in the direction of death, such monuments in fact consecrated the disappearance of life by attesting to its perseverence, thus sheltering life from death. Later, this evasion of the dead and the dying is manifest in the extradition of the dead to a position at the margins of the city during the industrial era, the removal of the dying to the functional space of hospitals, in the discreet elimination of corpses, and in the domestication and beautification of death which has taken place from the Romantic period up until the present day American cult of "morticians" and "death parlours." From the funeral excesses of the baroque, the perfected technique of embalming, to the ghastly tableau of a corpse preserved in his favourite armchair reading the newspaper, these practices, which on the surface appear as fetishizations of death, nevertheless act as consolations which parade personal extinction as an illusion of art.[1] Indeed, the wax museum is a perfect example, conflating the fascination with the preserved corpse with aesthetic pleasure and recreation. The apparent paradox of simultaneous confidence and fear in the face of death is perhaps not so difficult to understand, for studies have shown (with one exception – F. Lebrun's study of the Anjar)[2] that an increased expectation of life leads to a concentration on the arts of the living, and that as the experience of the death of others becomes more remote, so death is mystified. Furthermore, however far medical science advances, death remains always a step ahead. Because of this, the contradictory coincidence of a conceptual exclusion of death and its "representational

---

[1] Philippe Ariès, *The Hour of Our Death*, tr. Helen Weaver, (London: Penguin, 1983), on the "North American variant," 596–601; G. Gorer, *Death, Grief, and Mourning in Contemporary Britain*, (London: Cresset Press, 1965); Michel Vovelle, *La Mort et L'Occident de 1300 à nos Jours*, (Paris: Gallimard, 1983); Jean Baudrillard, *Symbolic Exchange and Death*, tr. Iain Hamilton Grant, (London: Sage Publications, 1993), 125–94; Elisabeth Bronfen, *Over Her Dead Body: Death Feminity, and the Aesthetre*, (Manchester: Manchester University Press, 1992), 86–7, and *passim*.

[2] John McManners, "Death and the French Historians," in ed. Joachim Whaley, *Mirrors of Mortality: Studies in the Social History of Death*, (London: European Publications Ltd, 1981), 106–30.

ubiquity" have been understood as a natural consequence of contemporary ("modern") necrophobic attitudes.[3]

From these examples, it would seem that necrophobia is understood to be at work on all occasions where artifice replaces the horror of impermanent reality, that is, where time is elided in favour of space (the process of spatialization described in chapter 2). However, in the first section of this chapter I will explain how lurking beneath the surface of necrophobia, is a much more fundamental *necrophilia*.[4] And whereas necrophobia is linked by the historians to a banishing of the fact of death, I shall show that necrophilia is linked to an again more fundamental metaphysical separation of death from life. In the sections which follow I will then explain how necrophilia and a life/death dualism is explicitly articulated in recent "postmodern" and "Levinasian" philosophy, again concentrating on the work of Derrida. It now turns out that his theory of language as writing, not only sustains modern spatialization, but is also driven by the concomitant modern embrace of death.[5]

1   THE NECROPHILIA OF MODERNITY

The baroque expansion of a lateral universe and suppression of temporality described in the previous chapter served to produce an absolute theoretical boundary between life and death which eventually resulted in the physical extradition of the dead from the living. This boundary expressed and itself helped to constitute the entire post-baroque practice of epistemological representation. Its institution had several decisive preconditions. One could mention: the baroque claim to represent God as a mere being alongside other beings (an anthropomorphization which accompanies the formulation of liturgy as external worship, characterized by spectacle and enthrallment); the rise of centralized powers which construe human beings not as individual narratives but as a spatial accumulation of statistically equivalent reactions; and the methods of the experimental philosophers, isolating matters of fact from

---

[3]   On the link between the modern conceptual exclusion of death and its "representational ubiquity," see Bronfen, *op. cit.*, *Over Her Dead Body*, 88.

[4]   Whilst maintaining an overall definition of death as the terminus of a thing in time, I would like to distinguish a particular construction of death which results from the conceptual dislocation of life and death, peculiar to immanentist thought, both modern and postmodern.

[5]   In chapter 6 below, I argue that only the extraordinary relation of sign to reality at work in the eucharist inaugurates an alternative semiotic which releases language as such from the necrophiliac order.

phenomenal processes of becoming – in each case, such "management" involving the reification of the temporal and the construal of phenomena as spatially self-identical.[6] All these preconditions of the age of representation together established a hierarchized polarity between subject and object, where the extra-narrative subject is determined by its array of graspable, non-figural objects accumulated over against itself in space as a passive and inert resource. This accumulation was driven by an anxiety to cancel lack and to retain presence through identical repetition. But such apparently guaranteed possession interrupts the inevitable passage of life into death, and mistakes the passing away *which is life* for sheer deletion, so effecting a pseudo-eternity of mere spatial permanence which, unlike genuine eternity, is exhaustively available to the human gaze. Such pseudo-eternity is composed of things which are only preservable and manageable as finite, and therefore as "dead." On this basis it can be claimed that modernity less seeks to banish death, than to prise death and life apart in order to preserve life immune from death in pure sterility. For in seeking *only* life, in the form of a pseudo-eternal permanence, the "modern" gesture is secretly doomed to necrophilia, love of what has to die, can only die. In seeking only life, modernity gives life over to death, removing all traces of death only to find that life has vanished with it. And so there is a nihilistic logic to this necrophiliac gesture, this sacrificing of life to a living death so as to ensure that when death arrives to unmask life of its tinsel, he finds only the presence of absence, life reduced to the deathliness of equivalence.

Underlying the modern negotiation of death is the assumption that by reifying a quality, one obtains access to it in its true nature. However, this act of reification suppresses its real nature, which is to remain open. Hence if death and life are seen as discrete and opposed, then existence itself is turned into a closed object – which is to say, given over to death. And it is true that such a production of death can serve many interests. The invention of the baroque anguish of death permitted the fully fledged inauguration of the ethic of accumulation and sacrality of investment. New mercantilist operators in alliance with experimental philosophers were able to take advantage of the situation by advancing – or inventing – a risk, and then offering – or rather, marketing – the supposed "necessary" security to counter it.[7] The secret idea

---

[6] Michel Foucault, *The Order of Things: An Archaeology of the Human Sciences*, (London: Tavistock Publications, 1970), 46–77; Dominique Dubarle, *Dieu Avec L'Être: De Parmenide à Saint Thomas, Essai d'Ontologie Theologale*, (Paris: Beauchesne, 1986), 330–43; Louis Bouyer, *Life and Liturgy*, (London: Sheed and Ward, 1956), chapter 1; José Antonio Maravall, *Culture of the Baroque: Analysis of a Historical Structure*, tr. Terry Cochran, (Minneapolis: University of Minnesota Press, 1986); C. B. MacPherson, *The Political Theory of Possessive Individualism: Hobbes to Locke*, (Oxford: Clarendon Press, 1962); See also chapter 2 above.

behind this economy is that death is unnatural to life, and yet the protocol of such machinations, predicated on desire as lack, moves by means of the oscillation of supposedly natural life and supposedly unnatural death. For the murderous outrunning of the obsolete and derelict by innovation is a production of the very death it proposes to obfuscate. And I have argued above that the production of the anxiety of mutability is the condition of possibility for absolute power.

The necrophiliac pseudo-middle voice,[8] or grammar which inscribes the subject's activity within a fundamental passivity controlled from without by an immanentist power, refers our "actions" to a false transcendent which conceals and confirms the abyss. For this life as separated from death, which claims to take death hostage, is at once given over to death, according to a sacrificial logic which does not immolate just one host, but instead, everyone, through the notion of "life insurance at no cost."[9] This is the cynical ex-ecution of a non-eucharistic sacrifice, a fear of death which turns everything *into* death as due payment. The greatest misnomer of all, therefore, is the word "security" – financial, medical, legal, global – which is an industrial business surrounding life in cellophane, providing statistics which domesticate the unknown, and offering a life which lives only by the production of death through premature burial and ceaseless warding off. In a positive guise, security seems to offer something we suddenly realize we need, in such a way that we feel we are getting a good return for a very small renunciation. So, to posit death as opposite and unnatural to life, is to incite us to attempt to prolong our lives by certain sacrificial investments. This is of course not exclusive to capitalism, for state socialism also aimed for the exorcism of death through the being of the class and the schema of eternal accumulation of productive forces. In both cases, the sanctification of labour is predicated on human life as a positive value, which requires a denigration of, and therefore sacrifice to, death.

---

[7] Steven Shapin and Simon Schaffer, *Leviathan and the Air-Pump: Hobbes, Boyle, and the Experimental Life*, (Princeton, New Jersey: Princeton University Press, 1985), 339–41; Baudrillard, *op. cit.*, *Symbolic Exchange and Death*, 177–80.

[8] I am again using the term "middle voice" to denote the way in which God can act in and through a subject but without denying the subject its freedom, and to describe the way in which action under grace is neither active nor passive in voice. See Jan Gonda, "Reflections on the Indo-European Medium," Part 1, *Lingua*, IX (March 1960), 30–67, Part 2, *Lingua*, IX (June 1960), 173–95, and chapter 1 above. Where immanentist thinkers such as Heidegger and Derrida claim to appropriate this voice, I argue in this chapter that in fact their middle voice is reducible to a shuttling between action and passion, and therefore does not outwit this metaphysical duality.

[9] This advertizing slogan was commissioned by the Abbey National Building Society. See further Baudrillard, *op. cit.*, *Symbolic Exchange and Death*.

2 THE ABYSSAL GESTURE

It seems that in spite of its claims, the staging of reason does not result in an excess of life after all, nor in a successful management of the terrain of death. Although death's narrative is discreetly elided and removed to a space outside the *polis*, and although there are truly no places for death, that is because death has been universalized.

To the modern yoking of a refusal of death with identical repetition, postmodern thought has responded with a gesture towards the void. We have seen how modernity rallied the forces of identical repetition in order to refuse death's entry, and that the conclusion of this was an exhaustive mobilization of that which it sought to refuse. Postmodernism claims to propose a critique of both the refusal of death and identical repetition itself, but, as will be seen from what follows, in the work of Jacques Derrida especially, there are unacknowledged lapses into identical repetition which betray the truth that postmodern nihilism is not the "end" of modernity but abides in its middle, which is, of course, a pseudo-middle.

According to Derrida's deconstruction of Husserl in *Speech and Phenomena*, the identical, or ideal in Husserl's phenomenology is correlated with life, self-presence, and a kind of monadic interiority in which there can be a pure expression present to an inner perception which has not yet gone forth from itself into the world. All such "goings-forth" evacuate this life of self-presence in the worldliness and deathliness of mere "indications." This relation of language with death cannot be dissimulated, for, as Derrida says, "We know now that indication, which thus far includes practically the whole surface of language, is the process of death at work in signs. As soon as the other appears, indicative language – another name for the relation with death – can no longer be effaced."[10] Derrida shows that according to Husserl's distinction between

---

[10] Jacques Derrida, *Speech and Phenomena*, tr. David Allison, (Evanston: Northwestern University Press, 1973), 40. Derrida's linking of writing and death is anticipated in the work of Maurice Blanchot who described writing as a process of radical self-loss, as a dispersal without direction, a "breath around nothing" [*The Space of Literature*, tr. Ann Smock, (Lincoln: University of Nebraska Press, 1982), 145]. For Blanchot, death is something we are inscribed within but can never confront, an unreality which never "happens," and in this way, he introduces the question as to whether one can distinguish between an authentic and inauthentic death. This "death" is that which dissolves all human activity, and as such, can be seen as opposite and inimical to life, an absolute *end*, rather than something we pass through. However, for Blanchot, the one kind of death which can remain a "possibility" for us is *negation*: "That which produces meaning is the risk which rejects being" (155). He

"expression" and "indication," in the latter case one steps outside oneself into an actual, visible world involving other people and communication, and that such visibility is the death of self-presence and of all certainty. He then seeks to claim that this relationship to exteriority is in fact *primordial*, which means that the relationship to death is itself primordial. But in arguing this, Derrida leaves Husserl's association of life and self-presence firmly in place, even though he appears to move a step beyond it. His argument, in effect, runs as follows: (1) life is presence-to-self; (2) there is no presence-to-self; (3) there is only exteriority which is the opposite of presence-to-self; (4) therefore there "is" only death. This grim advance (or intellectual funeral procession) does not question whether life is to be correlated with monadic presence-to-self, nor whether life and death are not in fact *arbitrarily* opposed to one another, nor even whether death really *is* a stage which one can never exceed. Suppose, for example, that life were an encounter between living bodies which was not primarily a passage across the mortal abyss? Perhaps space, externality, and perception are not, after all, an inevitable void. An alternative phenomenology, such as that of Merleau-Ponty,[11] might be one in which the act of perception is not cast as a totalizing, strategic gaze, but is, reciprocally, to *be perceived* and thereby displaced from self-presence, according to an interpersonal life in which death is as much constitutive of our life as other from it. Or else, could it be that dying in time might lead not to the abyss but to a greater living towards eternity? Or that there might be a living which is also dying?

Derridean *différance*, in leaving the correlation of ideality or meaningfulness with presence in place, even as it claims presence as that which is perpetually postponed, and therefore never truly available, is itself dialectically identical with presence. For the vehicle of *différance*, the deathly formality of the sign, remains the same in its repeatedly pointing to something which never arrives. This renders both signification and repetition univocal, precisely because they point to the nothing of postponed presence. Or, to put this the other way round, the fact that any univocally representable object of knowledge is postponed, means that this merely formal-because-empty-identity which persists is that of

argues that the meaningless has priority over meaning because the condition of our producing meanings is that we might produce *other meanings*. However, in response to this nihilistic construal, one could question why a "new" meaning must be a negation – could it not alternatively be a positive surplus?

[11] Maurice Merleau-Ponty, "The Intertwining – The Chiasm," in ed. Claude Lefort, *The Visible and the Invisible*, tr. Alphonso Lingis, (Evanston: Northwestern University Press, 1968), 131–55.

the dissolution of identity, which is death. Here, the word "identity" is especially significant, because for Derrida, the identity of death, or that by which one might recognise death, would be the release of chaos, of a superlative difference dissolving into flows of unrecognition. But in response to this, it can be asserted that such unmediable difference is coincident with indifference, an absolute equivalence or common measure which eminently establishes identity, and *understands* or *mediates* each difference after all. For difference is here held to be at such optimum pitch that any growth or alteration it might undergo would be imperceptible. Since each difference is identically superlative, there persists only "closure," the "same sameness," only one thing after another in an ordered disjuncture. Moreover, the word "identity" refers not just to that by which we identify a thing, but also the remaining-identical of the thing. And here one can argue that the primacy of death in the postmodern order is one and the same with the hegemony of the homogeneous in modernity, for nothing is more identical than nothing is to nothing. Although postmodernity would deny the possibility of the identical repetition upon which modernity is predicated, it transpires that postmodernity is after all the condition of possibility, and the optimum consummation, of that identical repetition. The claim that there can be only death is identical with the claim that there can be only identical repetition.

3　Indications of Nothing

In league with this supremacy of the deathly identity of sameness, there lurks a triumph of the indicative mood, that is to say, the grammatical category whose commerce is in fact and constative knowledge. And this is curious because Derrida claims that his adherence to Being as time occludes a privileging of the indicative mood insofar as this adherence turns every being into non-being.[12]

In his essay entitled *Aporias*, a deconstruction of Heidegger's analytic of death in *Being and Time*, Derrida, following Blanchot, argues that death cannot be approached phenomenologically because it does not "appear," and so one cannot have a "more" or "less" authentic relationship with something that does not appear, which is to say, with the radically unknown and unknowable.[13] But does not Derrida here domesticate the unknown by defining it as

---

[12] Derrida, *op. cit.*, *Speech and Phenomena*, 70–4.
[13] Derrida, *Aporias*, tr. Thomas Dutoit, (Stanford: Stanford University Press, 1993), 78; Blanchot, *op. cit.*, *The Space of Literature*, 95.

"nothing," reducing it to the indicative degree zero of neutrality? In effect, he makes the fact that death is unknown equal to the fact that death is nothing: either, for Derrida, something appears, in which case it is *something*, or else it does not appear, in which case it is *nothing*.[14] And then this "unknowing" of that which remains as nothing, which is death, fulfills a requirement for the superlatively objective, for as "nothing," death is indifferent, inert, and cannot be affected from without. In fact, it would seem that secularized death is the best example of an object there is. And so with this gesture of unknowing, we are returned to the middle of modernity where the object is measured once again by its equivalence, univocity, and undifferentiated *stasis*, where it is self-identical and available to the knowing subject. Derrida has merely developed Husserl's equation of the signified – the merely indicated, and "second hand" as opposed to the "living phenomenon" – with death, by arguing that it is the *invisible* which is death. And since, for Derrida, all *visibility* is postponed, there is *only* invisibility and death.

This treatment of the invisible and unknown as nothing, presupposes an opposition between subject and object. That which lies beyond the subject's own territory – and Derrida is right insofar as he implies that there is an unknown which exceeds what is already known – is seen as negating the subject, for it is at once indifferent to, and threateningly over-against, the subject's domain. And he treats the way that the unknown appears to the subject, namely, as unknown, as constituting the exhaustive *content* of the unknown. Such a stance *maintains* the post-Cartesian movement from an indicative epistemology to ontology. But is it so unquestionable that the unknown is felt by us as an emptiness? Does it arrive as a neutral nothingness? Moreover, by understanding the "now" as really nothing, is not the flux of time itself reduced to a real, pure self-identity of nothing, according to a linear temporality of discrete present nothingnesses which occludes any figural anticipation of the unknown future? And again, might not the modalities of desire, hope, or faith be genuine instances of the unknown felt within the inhabited known, in the same way that commemoration of a past event is not merely an afterthought added on to the past, but involves the non-identically repeated sacrificial return of time as the proleptic condition of possibility for any present act of remembering? If one stands in relation to the unknown in an indicative mood, seeking to bring that region into the category of the known, even in a nihilistic fashion, one will not escape the domain of identical repetition. For by treating the unknown as nothing, it is placed within the category of that which does not change, which is complete, given, and,

[14] Derrida, *op. cit.*, *Speech and Phenomena*, 54–5 and *passim*.

absurdly, *known*. In this way, the sceptical postmodern subject still speaks in the face of what is present to it, even though what it announces is the flux of nothing. Indeed, to announce the flux at all is *to represent* reality, and so the postmodern subject is the modern subject, self-present, contemplative, and distinct from the flux it observes. Yet an alternative and feasible relation with the unknown would be to stand open to the surprize of what arrives, according to the non-totalizing gaze of faith. This *alone* would permit the unknown to remain itself, for otherwise one must engage in the diabolic transubstantiation of the open and the real into the discrete movements of closure whose interminable sameness never consoles as an oft-repeated lullaby, but rather invokes the despair of the terminal. Hence, after all, Derrida is profoundly right: this is what atheism means, when nothing is the same and the same is nothing.

4 POSTMODERN PARSIMONY

The triumph of the indicative mood in Derrida's negotiation of death is seen elsewhere in his synthesizing of Heidegger's irreplaceable "mineness" of death with Levinas' privileging of the death of the other, for which the "I" is responsible – even to the point of including itself within death.[15] What is the nature of these two approaches to death, and how, for Derrida, are they reducible to one and the same approach?

For Heidegger, a person's death is superlatively their own. Death is a task which can neither be delegated nor performed by proxy.[16] Levinas differentiates his own position from this by establishing a priority of the death of the other over one's own death, which allows one to relate to the other via an alterity which cannot be commanded in a mode of mastery.[17] According to Levinas, in order to relate to the other as other, that is, outside the mode of possession, it is necessary for that other to be "beyond being." Therefore the other is only accessible to me via the cancelling of my living being, for as long as I remain a living being, I can only confront the other as another being, and not, therefore, as genuinely other.

However, Derrida points out that Heidegger does indicate that one aspect

[15] Derrida, *op. cit.*, *Aporias*, 38–40.

[16] Heidegger, *Being and Time*, tr. John Macquarrie and Edward Robinson, (Oxford: Basil Blackwell, 1962), 281–4.

[17] Emmanuel Levinas, *Time and the Other*, in ed. Séan Hand, *The Levinas Reader*, tr. Richard A. Cohen, (Oxford: Basil Blackwell, 1978), 38–58.

of authentic being involves *mitsein* (*being with* the other). Since he defines subjectivity as being-towards-death, it follows that *mitsein* must equally presuppose being with the other who is, presumably, also towards-death. Although Heidegger does not develop this point, there is certainly something not unlike Levinas' position implicit in *mitsein*. In turn, Derrida explains, Levinas' own position must implicitly presuppose Heidegger's "mineness" of death, for in establishing ethical responsibility for the other even to the point of *one's own* death, as a kind of sacrificial hostage for the other, Levinas must assume that one's death is *one's own*, in order for it to be so offered. The establishment of the priority of the death of the other over one's own death can only take place once the priority of the originary and underivable mineness of dying is also established.[18]

It would seem that Derrida shares these morbid ethics of his predecessors: death alone guarantees our singularity, and as death is uniquely our own, it is the only thing we can offer. Indeed, for Derrida, death is the only example of the pure gift, for it is supremely unreturnable, supremely silent, and therefore the optimum moment of disappropriation.[19] Thus, the offering of our death for the other is seen as the ultimate ethical good, alone guaranteeing our responsibility for the other, although it is not clear that, for Derrida and Levinas, this ethic can be put into practice.

These three positions of the three authors, and their final synthesis, raise certain questions. First, is it so certain that one's death is the only thing which is one's own? Perhaps the particularity of our life, and the arrival of unique circumstances upon our subjectivity, circumstances which we perspectivally share with others, are our own as well? Secondly, Heidegger wrote that by facing up to one's own death, "one is liberated from one's lostness in those possibilities which may accidentally thrust themselves upon me,"[20] thus seeming to prioritize an *essence* of ourselves, according to a metaphysical distinction between substance and accident. It would also seem, from this quotation, that being resolute in the face of death is not a *disinterested* stance, as Heidegger claims, but rather a defiant strategy of security against the arrival of the unknown. And so, is its necrophiliac urge just a cover for an all too modern necrophobic desire to get to death before it gets to you?

A theological alternative, which will be developed in chapter 6 of this book, would be to assume that *nothing* is one's own, but rather that everything, life

---

[18] Derrida, *op. cit.*, *Aporias*, 38–40.
[19] Derrida, "Donner la Mort," eds Jean-Michel Rabaté and Michel Wetzel, *L'éthique du don: Jacques Derrida et la Pensée du Don*, (Paris: Métailié – Transition, 1992), 48–9.
[20] Heidegger, *op. cit.*, *Being and Time*, 308.

and death alike, arrive not as possessions but as gifts. As such, they cannot be owned without ceasing to be themselves, and so we can only receive such gifts in the very act of passing them on. The two movements of receiving and passing on are mutually constitutive and perhaps one could add that the act of receiving is indistinguishable from, or is itself, a counter-gift of return. Such circulation of gift is only possible in a theological order genuinely spoken in the middle voice, an wholly other mode which authentically outwits the shuttling between action and passion of the secular order. For according to a theological reading of the gift, to give is already to receive the return, which is the gift *to be able* to give. The "giving up" of the gift occurs in trust of a "return" with difference, but this return is not something we can earn, nor is it over against the moment of giving up. It is neither subject to any calculation, nor is it a giving-away in order for others to be grateful for the price one has paid. In contrast to Derrida, one can speak of a "return" indissociable from the act of giving, simultaneous with it, a condition of its possibility, and yet *not* reducible to an economic market exchange – not reducible because the return is not simply something one is hoping to receive later, but is something one is already receiving in giving. And insofar as one hopes for a continuous return in the future, one is looking to be surprized rather than for the return of a debt of an anticipated amount.[21]

If, as for Derrida, the hope for a return is not an ethical category, then *mutuality* or the enjoyment of shared society is not seen as the ultimate ethical goal, but is replaced by self-abasing sacrifice as unambiguous "loss," which, by definition, betokens a prior *ownership* of the thing lost. Perhaps in this light one could read the unilateral gift of nihilism as a kind of sinister disguise for a covetousness of life, which seeks to be rid of that which it too much desires.

The next question regarding the nihilistic gesture concerns Heidegger's construal of *Dasein* which, as only complete at the point of death, (i.e. when it is no longer there), betrays a desire for a totalized "thing" or given essence.[22] For although Heidegger is not so crude as to see death as a single and final event occurring uniquely after the detour of life, but as a conditioning of the whole of life, nevertheless, he does see it as a transcendental condition, conditioning that which is already conditioned, and alone making life's wholeness possible, even at the moment when it also brings forward that life's extinction. This making of death as decisive of life is rather like a pagan view of death as a

[21] Derrida, *Given Time: 1. Counterfeit Money*, 161; John Milbank, "Can a Gift be Given? Prolegomena to a Future Trinitarian Metaphysic," *Modern Theology*, 11.1 (1995), 119–61.
[22] Heidegger, *op. cit.*, *Being and Time*, 281.

gateway to fame, seeing life as a spatial catalogue of seized opportunities and heroic triumphs. Above all, such a reading presupposes that the totality is that which matters over all else – which would seem to involve a view of time as homogeneous and linear. Yet what of the excessive "now" which, though still incomplete and unconsummated, betokens some magnificent event yet to come, and makes that future event possible, and then exceeds its own consummation in magnificence even in spite – or perhaps because – of its liminal and inchoate status? The future from which death arrives, for Heidegger and Levinas, is after all an indicative future – one inscribed into the "now" of light and mastery, because it arrives over against us (as the given to which corresponds a merely false or illusory humility), without links to any figural past or present creative act.

The same non-excessiveness which characterizes these conceptions of time can also be seen in Heidegger's determination of death as that which alone discloses Being. He declared that "(t)he this-worldly ontological interpreta-tion of death takes precedence over any ontic other-worldly speculation," thus disguising the way in which any interpretation of death itself can never exceed speculation.[23] Heidegger claimed that his construal of being-towards-death decides nothing about the immortality of the soul which is, he considered, merely an ontic matter, not disclosing Being in any way at all. He thus sweepingly privileges death as that which, alone, is an ontological matter, since any merely living being whether mortal or immortal is by him confined to an ontic occlusion of Being itself. It is necessary for Heidegger to maintain this privilege if he is to argue that Being is time. And his argument enlists a deliberately spatial reading of eternity as simply the remaining in existence of a being, whereas one could think of immortal life in ontological terms, as the participation of a being in Being as such, regarding Being therefore as an eternal plenitude rather than as time, death, and nothingness. Such a plenitude would mean that reality could be approached in an optative mood of desire, hope, or faith, rather than Heidegger's cognitive preference for nothingness as the only disclosure of Being, which – since the "nothing" is the superlative object which can be known with security – remains an indicative reading.

Another question, addressed this time to Levinas, would be this: is it so unquestionable that one is brought into subjectivity only by means of the persecution of the ethical demands of the other? Why must real bodies be thus reduced to need or lack? Is subjectivity so negatively based, that we must evacuate ourselves completely in order to realize this moral imperative? One could argue that it is not the *demand* of the other, but the *gift* of the other which

[23]   *Ibid.*, 292.

introduces us to being – as for von Balthasar, for whom it is the mother's smile which inaugurates us, by bringing us into an intra-subjective communion.[24]

Lastly, one may question the argument that one can only relate to the other without mastery via death. If the otherness of the other arrives only through the potential death of the other (his vulnerability), and given that secular death is the ultimate object, it would seem that the other is after all reduced to an object, just as he in turn is bound to transmute his own "I" into an object as always passively available to the demands of a further other, in this way opening an infinite regress which postpones forever the living subject. Levinas' reading assumes further that: (1) "life" is unambiguously life, light, and action; and, (2) that, for the grasping subject, death is never "now." I would suggest instead, after Merleau-Ponty, that one cannot see a thing without being seen by it in a fashion that interrupts our mastery of a living other, without recourse to death. And also that death and life are not opposed in this way, since it is death's perpetual entry into life which constitutes our temporality and alone allows one to be a subject. Finally, remembering that, for Levinas, mystery is by definition that which is utterly unanticipated, he seems to occlude the possibility of mystery also within the apparently known. Is not a partially imparted mystery *more* mysterious than one which bears no traces in the known whatsoever?

5   A DISMAL SIGN

I have shown how the "nothing" of postmodern death is set within the indicative mood of metaphysics, and I have related this to ethics and practical reasoning. My task now is to show how the "nothing" is set in terms of knowledge in general, or, more specifically, for theoretical reasoning, as already invoked with respect to Derrida's privileging of the ideal over real bodies. In order to do this, I will consider Derrida's account of the sign, and why it is for him that the sign is more the written than the spoken sign.

In response to Husserl's logos as "total restitution,"[25] Derrida insists that there can be no dissimulation of absence or sign. The prerogative of Being disappears because he has identified Being with time, so that it is equally non-Being, just as the "now" immediately "is" not. In his characterization of the

---

[24] Hans Urs von Balthasar, *The Glory of the Lord: A Theological Aesthetics*, Volume V, *The Realm of Metaphysics in the Modern Age*, tr. Oliver Davies *et al.*, (Edinburgh: T&T Clark, 1991), 647.

[25] Derrida, *op. cit.*, *Speech and Phenomena*, 75.

sign as "written," he wishes to outwit the epoch of the technical mastery of objective being, which he associates with the metaphysical privileging of the spoken word. This privileging has for Derrida two aspects. First, the spoken sign fades the moment it is produced, thus seeming to cleave to ideality, or a realm of fixed original truth anterior to language. Secondly, the breath of orality is construed as ultimately tied to the presence of the speaker who claims in his self-identity to be able to guarantee his meaning. The oral sign, by seeming to favour a pure anterior truth, seems too much to cling to life. In contrast, the written sign is characterized by its ability to survive its author, and in fact would seem to be the author *of* that author.[26]

This association of orality with the metaphysical must, as was seen in chapter 1, be called into question. First, Derrida's characterization of speech as fading in favour of pure presence rests upon a *phenomenology* of speech (it *appears* to fade; it *appears* to be commanded by the subject, etc.) as compared with writing, even though it is claimed that phenomenology itself is disturbed by the primacy of writing and the trace, since the trace is more primordial than present appearing. Is it, then, that we need a phenomenology to show that we cannot have a phenomenology? But this contradiction is avoidable. For Derrida's phenomenological account of orality as fading towards ideality arbitrarily occludes an alternative phenomenology – namely, that speech is dying and living at once, in such a way that the recurrent dispossession of each syllable of the spoken word, rather than being related to the ontological disposal of the sign towards an anterior ideal, is in fact, as Augustine explained, the condition of possibility for there to be a sign at all. For it is only by means of the speaker's being reconciled to the ultimate "passing" of each spoken syllable that the word in its fullness can arrive, in such a way that its self-consuming character is paradoxically necessary for its fulfillment.[27] Such an account of the spoken word would also suggest that, contrary to Derrida, orality is supremely disposed *in favour* of supplementarity: this is to be seen not only in the ever-renewed utterance of individual words, but also in an individual word's making-way for subsequent words. One could argue that because, for Derrida, the meaning of the written sign is always postponed, and is therefore identified with death – that which one can never experience – in a certain way he makes meaning *complete*, just as the written text itself, in all its distance and assumed authority, would seem also to present knowledge as accomplished, and to impose a gulf between

---

[26] *Ibid.*, 77; on the ideality of voice, see also Giorgio Agamben, *Language and Death: The Place of Negativity*, tr. Karen E. Pinkus and Michael Hardt, (Minneapolis: University of Minnesota Press, 1991), 35, 39

[27] Augustine, *Confessions*, Book XI, Sections 26–7.

subjectivity and meaning. Derrida *disallows* any sense of meaning as non-ideality, as an inhabited, developing occurrence, but instead presents it as an absent ideal which does not permit even the slightest degree of participation. But if he really wished to allow for truth as a contingent event, he would have to concede that although time is always at once broken down and distended, yet also it does not merely comprise moments of pure illusion. Such an account would outwit the miserable choice between investing security *either* in the flux, *or* in discrete present moments, by restoring time as "the moving image of eternity." By the same token, one would no longer be trapped in the secular, immanent *aporia* of having to place all significance either in death (as with Heidegger, Levinas, and Derrida), or in the spatialized living play of mortal bodies (as with Merleau-Ponty and Luce Irigaray). Such a reading would also be able to relate the fading away of the sign in speech to the trace of time and memory rather than interpreting it as a lapse in favour of an ideal meaning. It is, indeed, one would have thought, only a metaphysical reading of orality which would refuse to associate fading-away with the trace, for one's only experience of what one has said is as the trace of memory, or else, as something one has forgotten. The fading-away of the sign is in fact supremely physical, and embodies ecstatic time in and through its fading-away. It can also be argued that the spoken word's physicality is such that it can be related to physical space, for although it does not occupy space in the manner of an extended thing, yet it is always spoken by physical bodies in particular places, and as such, is not external to things but can inter-penetrate them. Does not the written sign, by contrast, occupy an idealized space which is non-ecstatically present, and supremely decontextualized? Do not these characteristics suggest that a written meaning is somehow independent, or in excess, of events in time? And why, in his critique of orality, does Derrida wish to construe speech as that which most readily inclines towards the ideal when, according to the traditional (metaphysical) hierarchy of the senses, it is the *visual* and not the *acoustic* which is held to be the most immediate and proximal to reason?[28]

In the above, I have tried to show that Derrida's theory of the sign is

---

[28] In chapter 1 above I imply that in Derrida's application of his notion of the supplement to criticize what he sees as a metaphysical prioritization of the interior self-present subject (in his "Plato's Pharmacy") he reads Descartes back into Plato. First, in Socrates' account of oral wisdom, the origins of myth are held to be both multiple and unlocatable, and the demythologizing act of excavating anterior essences is condemned by Socrates as inimical to the constitutive openness of myth. Secondly, the oral performance does not derive from an interior subject in charge of his delivery but is portrayed as being received from without – in the handing down of myths, genealogies, and oral diction, and in the inspiration or possession from without by one's beloved, *erōs*, and Mnemosyne.

grounded in the false middle of modernity, in that it produces a pseudo-transcendent of studied absence acting as a hovering, mysterious source, towards which each sign would seem to gesture. Just as the indistinct edges and undulating folds of the baroque epoch did not constitute a genuinely medial release but rather a strategic absence which channelled peoples' action, and so concealed a cynical dualist order, violent by virtue of its hiddenness, so the postmodern release of difference appears to embrace the flux, but is, after all, at the very middle of modernity, for all the reasons I have outlined. Derrida likens the middle voice of *différance* to words such as *mouvance* and *resonance*, in whose "undecideability" he adduces the middle voice. However, his casting of signs into the apparent medium of *différance* repeats the totalitarian structures of language described in chapter 2, for *différance* does not exceed the contrast between active and passive. According to Derrida's construal of the sign, the subject actively intends a meaning, but is *acted upon* by the signs which always prevent that meaning's realized arrival. Therefore, the subject does not receive this retrospective action as a living gift but instead receives merely its own death, and the end of its capacity to receive at all. The apparently medial undecideability of *différance* is not attributable to a genuine mystery, but rather to a false intransitivity which suppresses both agency and object, and transposes a temporal event into the spatial domain of givenness where nothing ever happens except the illusion of something happening.[29]

In conclusion to the first part of this essay, it would seem that the problem for postmodern thought – for Derrida, as also for Heidegger, Blanchot, and Bataille – is that its appeals to death remain a mere gesture, without upshot, leaving us with only the modern technologist illusion after all. This gesture, whilst boasting its proximity to the "real," is tantamount to an ideal mythology by which we order our lives: a mythology which operates a double bind. For while the gesture claims to undo all tyrannically disseminated assumptions, it actually reinforces these assumptions with the same cynical secrecy as the baroque king. In the case of Bataille, for example, since the dereliction of death alone refuses a banal productivity, life cannot after all be released into an optimum experience of *jouissance* and excess, but is simply confirmed in its mere productiveness. But if all that is offered here is an unmasking of a

[29] Jacques Derrida, *Dissemination*, tr. Barbara Johnson, (London: Athlone Press, 1981), 251–2, and *idem*, *Margins of Philosophy*, tr. Alan Bass, (Chicago: Chicago University Press, 1982), 9; Jean-Luc Marion, *L'Idole et la Distance*, (Paris: Editions Grasset & Fasquelle, 1977), 271. On Heidegger's use of the category of the middle voice, John Llewelyn, *The Middle Voice of Ecological Consciousness*, (London: Macmillan, 1991), and Charles E. Scott, "The Middle Voice in *Being and Time*," ed. John C. Sallis *et al.*, *The Collegium Phaenomenologicum: The First Ten Years*, (Dortrecht: Kluwer Academic Publishers, 1988), 159–73.

humanly-constituted illusion (the postmodern version of our inevitable metaphysical transgression in seeking after essential *telai*, spoken of by Kant), then what one is permitted is a singularly futile control, a satanic control for control's sake, which is the complacent and impotent satisfaction of the nihilist philosopher.[30]

It has been shown in the first part of this essay how the systematic exaltation of writing over speech has ensured within Western history the spatial obliteration of time, which in seeking to secure an absolutely immune subjectivity, has instead denied any life to the human subject whatsoever. It has further been suggested that this project of textual spatialization is equally a suppression of eternity, since time can only be affirmed through the liturgical gesture which receives time from eternity as a gift and offers it back to eternity as a sacrifice. Hence the city which seeks to live only in spatial immanence is a *necropolis* defined by its refusal of liturgical life.

[30] By opposing productive work to erotic disintegration and violence, and concomitantly casting death as the only resistance to production, Bataille perpetuates the metaphysical duality of life as opposite to death. According to this duality, the primacy of the former as that which protects identity through reason is held as distinct from festivity, which Bataille defines as an absolute violence which returns everything to the flow of an impersonal continuum. (This theory of sacrifice as a purely nihilistic self-expenditure into the "community" of disinterested, universalized flows is based on an outdated anthropology which sees human sacrifice as the secret "original" essence of the "sacred," disconnected from any expression of "purpose," and hence, opposite to work and life: see John Milbank, "Stories of Sacrifice: From Wellhausen to Girard," *Theory, Culture & Society*, 12 (1995), 15–46). It could be argued that both alternatives, life as productivity, and death as the purposeless abandonment to the impersonal continuum, are reducible to the same (metaphysical) identical repetition. See Georges Bataille, *Theory of Religion*, tr. Robert Hurley (New York: Zone Books, 1992); *Eroticism*, tr. Mary Dalwood (New York: Marion Boyars, 1962); *The Tears of Eros*, tr. Peter Connor, (San Francisco: City Lights Books, 1990).

TRANSITION

TRANSITION

[A]nd will they distrust our statement that no city could ever be blessed unless its lineaments were traced by artists who used the heavenly model?

Plato, *Republic*, VI, 500e

"CAN MY EATING SLAKE YOUR HUNGER?" ON THE EVACUATION OF LITURGY

Before describing the liturgical alternative to the sophistic, modern, and postmodern refusal of liturgical life, it needs to be said that liturgical culture can itself be debased. Indeed, in this transitional chapter, I will go further to show how it was corruptions of the theological intelligence and liturgical culture in the late Middle Ages which themselves permitted the return of a spatialized sophistic outlook which Socrates might appear to have banished forever. Only by isolating this historical moment can we grasp how the modern secular order mimics the liturgical, and also rid ourselves of the theological legacy of this corruption which prevents us from envisioning the liturgical in its genuine character.

1 DUNS SCOTUS AND THE PRIORITY OF THE POSSIBLE

The theology of Duns Scotus (c. 1265–1308) is perhaps the first definite theoretical symptom of the destruction from within of the liturgical city. After receiving the Franciscan habit in 1281, and being ordained priest in 1291, Duns Scotus studied alternately in Oxford and Paris, and returned later to teach in both places. In England he wrote his commentaries on Aristotle, his *Opus oxoniense*, and his *Questions on the Sentences of Peter Lombard*; and in Paris, the *Reportata parisiensia* and the *Collationes*.[1] His most celebrated

---

[1] David Knowles, *The Evolution of Medieval Thought*, Second Edition, ed. D. E. Luscombe and C. N. L. Brooke, (London and New York: Longman Group, 1988), 276; Emile

doctrines – univocity of being and the "formal distinction" – are deliberately and consciously opposed to those of Aquinas, and spawn further anti-Thomistic ideas, such as the actual existence of matter, individuation through form (*haecceitas*), a new leaning towards voluntarism, and the priority of the possible over existential actuality.[2]

Univocity of Being

In his *Opus oxoniense*, reacting against the Thomistic framework of *analogia entis*, (as it has later but not inaccurately been named), according to which the ontological difference permits participation in the divine,[3] Duns Scotus asserted the metaphysical priority of Being over both the infinite and the finite alike. Thus God is deemed "to be" in the same univocal manner as creatures, and although God is distinguished by an "intensity of being," He nonetheless remains within, or subordinate to the category of Being (which now becomes the sole object of metaphysics).[4]

This indifferent Being, shared between the infinite and the finite, might seem to confer a degree of proximal relation between the two realms. For, surely, metaphysics itself might bring us near to the subject of theology, since a fundamental Being unites us with God. But Scotist univocity unmediably separates the creation from God, precisely because the infinity of that distance can be the object of no concept other than Being, the most formal of all essences, independent of all further determinations. One cannot peer through such an interminable *quantity* of sameness, for God's infinite

Bréhier, *The History of Philosophy: The Middle Ages and the Renaissance*, tr. Wade Baskin, (Chicago and London: University of Chicago Press, 1931/1965), 183.
[2] Bréhier, *ibid.*, 183–90; Eric Alliez, "1300: The Capture of Being," *Capital Times*, tr. Georges Van Den Abbeele, (Minneapolis and London: University of Minnesota Press, 1996), 197-239; John Milbank, *The World Made Strange: Theology, Language, Culture*, (Oxford: Blackwell Publishers, 1996), 41–5.
[3] Amos Funkenstein, *Theology and the Scientific Imagination from the Middle Ages to the Seventeenth Century*, (Princeton, N.J.: Princeton University Press, 1986), 50.
[4] "*Cette «infinitas intensiva» n'est pas un attribut extrinsèque de l'être . . . mais un mode si intrinsèque,*" Etienne Gilson, *Jean Duns Scot: Introduction à ses Positions Fondamentales*, (Paris: Librairie Philosophique J. Vrin, 1952), 209 n. 1; Alliez, *op. cit.*, "1300: The Capture of Being," 199; on Being and God, see Duns Scotus, *Opus oxoniense*, I, dist. III, q. iii; and I, dist. III, q. i [*Philosophical Writings*, ed. and tr. Allan Wolter, O.F.M., (Edinburgh: Nelson, 1962), 4-8, 19-33 respectively]; *idem*, *Reportata parisiensia*, prol. q. iii, art. i [*Philosophical Writings*, 9-12]; John F. Wippel, "Essence and Existence," in ed. Norman Kretzman *et al.*, *The Cambridge History of Later Medieval Philosophy*, (Cambridge: Cambridge University Press, 1982), 385–410, 388–9; Jean-François Courtine, *Suarez et le Système de la Métaphysique*, (Paris: P.U.F., 1990), 137-57.

intensity of Being exceeds every measure. He is *"ultra omnem proportionem assignabilem."*[5] The difference of intensity is continuous with an individuating modality which radically distinguishes the finite from the infinite, but without in any way modifying the common essence of Being. Thus, the univocity of Being between God and creature paradoxically gives rise to a kind of equivocity, for the difference of degree or amount of Being disallows any specific resemblance between them, and excludes the possibility of figural or analogical determinations of God that give us any degree of substantive knowledge of His character. By withdrawing the means through which creatures might distinguish themselves ontologically from God through figuring or analogically drawing near Him, the distance between the infinite and the finite becomes an undifferentiated and *quantified* (although unquantifiable) abyss.[6] Thus, the "same" becomes the radically disparate and unknowable.

This unbridgeable relation precipitated several epistemological and theological manoeuvres. The abandonment of participation in Being encouraged the establishment of *contractual* relations between the creature and God. For despite an apparently pious humility, which stressed one's radical distance from God, a secret proximity to, or "covenantal bond" with the Creator, was nevertheless smuggled in.[7] This was combined with an increased emphasis upon the sovereignty of God's will, which, because the universe had now been desymbolized, becomes the only explanation for the way things are.[8]

The formal distinction

In the same way that univocity of Being paradoxically distances the creature from God, it also distances creatures from each other, and each creature from itself. How does this happen? It emerges as a consequence of the Scotist "formal distinction" which follows from univocity of Being, and which itself enables the thinking of univocity.

What is the Scotist "formal distinction"? It is the name given to a kind of differentiation which relates indifferent, neutral Being to difference. Hovering halfway between the Thomist categories of "real distinction" and

[5] "beyond every assignable proportion"; cited in Alliez, *op. cit.*, "1300: The Capture of Being," 200; Duns Scotus, *Tractatus de primo principio*, tr. into French by Ruedi Imbach *et al.*, (Geneva: Cahiers de la Revue de Théologie et de Philosophie, 1983), 4. 78; "*Une contingence ontologique aussi absolue interdit toute déduction qui prétendrait lier le monde fini des être à la transcendance absolue de l'être*," Gilson, *op. cit.*, *Jean Duns Scot*, 629–30.

[6] Duns Scotus, *op. cit.*, *Tractatus de primo principio*, 4. 86.

[7] John Milbank, *Theology and Social Theory: Beyond Secular Reason*, (Oxford: Blackwell Publishers, 1990), 15.

[8] Funkenstein, *op. cit.*, *Theology and the Scientific Imagination*, 57–9.

"intellectual distinction,"[9] the "formal distinction" is at once both real and logical, and neither real nor logical.[10] For Scotus, Being (the object of metaphysics) cannot be solely the *real* Being of singular phenomena because this would reduce metaphysics to physics, and there is, in any case, no *material* essence common to everything, since everything exists in different ways. And yet the formal distinction of existence and essence *is* real to the extent that each instantiated essence must occupy the neutral empty site of "what is" if it is to establish itself at all.[11] And as well as being in this fashion both *not real* and *real*, the object of metaphysics both is not and is a Being of *reason*. It is not, however, *exclusively* a being of reason, because this would reduce metaphysics to logic, that discipline for which there can be no concept whose definition is common to every being. And yet it must also be to a certain degree an intellectual distinction because univocity is neutral, empty, and abstract: to think any essence we must first think that it "can be," in a manner quite unlike the construal of an always specific actuality of content in the case of the Thomistic *analogia entis*. Because neither real nor intellectual distinction can finally satisfy this new object of metaphysics – univocal Being – an intermediary distinction is invoked to situate that which is neither a singular and unified existing being nor a universal and logically distinct intellectual being of reason. This in-between being is neither being nor Being, neither particular nor universal, neither wholly real nor wholly thought; it is a *formality*.[12]

Because Scotist univocity is itself situated within the formal distinction, disclosing neither an empirical quality in common between things, nor any logical necessity for things "to be" in a particular way, univocity abstracts actuality from itself. For whilst the Being which is univocal is deemed by

[9] Wippel, *op. cit.*, "Essence and Existence," 39–6.
[10] Duns Scotus, *op. cit.*, *Opus oxoniense*, I, d. 2, q. 4, a. 5, n. 41–5; q. 7, n. 44; d. 8, q. 4, a, n. 17; IV, d. 11, q. 3, n. 46; d. 13, q. 1, n. 38; d. 16, q. 1, n. 10; *idem, Tractatus de primo principio*, 4. 51; Gilson, *op. cit., Jean Duns Scot*, 244–6; *idem, History of Christian Philosophy in the Middle Ages*, 765 n. 63; Wippel, *ibid.*, 406–7.
[11] Duns Scotus, *op. cit.*, *Opus oxoniense*, III, d. 6, q. 1; IV, d. 11, q. 3, n. 46; Gilson, *op. cit., Jean Duns Scot*, 245; Gilles Deleuze, *Difference and Repetition*, tr. Paul Patton, (London: The Athlone Press, 1994), 39; Marilyn McCord Adams, "Universals in the Early Fourteenth Century," in ed. Kretzman, *op. cit., The Cambridge History of Later Medieval Philosophy*, 411–39, 415.
[12] Alliez, *op. cit.*, "1300: The Capture of Being," 202–3; "*Considérée à titre d'être, la «nature» n'est pas «un être» existant à part, comme le singulier, mais elle n'est pas non plus un simple «être de raison», comme l'universel logique; elle est, non un* esse *singulier au sens plein du terme, mais une «entité», une «réalité» ou encore, et il y aura lieu de s'en souvenir, une «formalité»*," Gilson, *op. cit., Jean Duns Scot*, 110.

Scotus to be *actual,* this actuality is instantaneously *rationalized* in and through its univocity. Thus actuality becomes a *virtual reality,* or the "real-possible."[13]

The actual-possible

It was seen that the varying intensity, or distinct *modality* of Being which differentiated God from creatures did not in any way modify or compromise the commonality or univocity of their essence insofar as this is Being.[14] This same priority of essence over varying intensities of existence (or modalities of Being) not only characterizes, for Duns Scotus, the distinction between creatures and God, but also distinctions within God (for example, between the one essence and the Trinitarian relations),[15] between one creature and another, and between one creature and itself. In the case of God, univocity of Being and the formal distinction apply also to His attributes, in such a way that God can possess formally distinct – rather than really identical (and distinguished only from our perspective) – attributes without losing anything of His simplicity, which is grounded in the indeterminacy of Being and the supremacy of divine will which unites the attributes as its own virtual powers. Likewise, in the case of creatures, the real unity of a substantial whole is regarded by Duns Scotus as the essential unity of nonetheless virtually distinct

---

[13] See Alliez, *ibid.*, 287 n. 208; also 207, 288 n. 231.

[14] Deleuze, *op. cit.*, *Difference and Repetition*, 39.

[15] "Here an objection is raised: if a thing can be a necessary being only by reason of one, but not the other of two realities in it (for otherwise it would be necessary twice over), then it follows that in a necessary being one can never assume the existence of any realities that are formally distinct. Therefore one could never postulate such a distinction between the essence and relation in a Divine person. The consequent is false, therefore the first proof is invalid. A similar objection can be raised against the second argument that each will be the ultimate actuality or else one is unnecessary. To this I reply: wherever we have two formally distinct entities, if they are compatible like act and potency or as two realities fit by nature to actuate the same thing, then if one is infinite, not only can, but does indeed include the other by identity, for otherwise the infinite would be composed . . . But if it be finite it does not include by identity anything which according to its formal meaning is primarily diverse. For such finite realities are mutually perfectible and can serve as component parts. Consequently, from the assumption that a necessary being consists of two realities neither of which contains the other through identity – the condition required for composition – it follows that one of the two will not be necessary either formally or by identity, or else the whole will be twice necessary. Consequently, both proofs hold. The counter instances about the Divine Person are irrelevant, since the two realities involved are not component parts, but one is the other by identity since one is infinite." Duns Scotus, *op. cit.*, *Tractatus de primo principio*, 4. 51.

forms. This unity hovers halfway between the logical and the actual, for it refers to the way in which the substantive properties of a thing subsist in exactly the same manner as the totality of the thing since, at the level of ontology, they all equally "are" in the same fashion. So although these constituents, or lesser existences, do not exist separately insofar as they are virtually contained within the totality, a residual logical possibility that they could do so is now introduced.[16] This "unity" is completely unlike that of Aquinas, for whom the constituent parts of a substance (including accidents) only "are" through the whole substantive form in which they inhere, in such a way that the being of a thing is continuous with its unbreakable unity. The Scotist unity is already reducible to the unity of method or formality, since consideration of how things might be redistributed within a neutral logical space, is now taken to define the unity they actually possess.

In this way, Scotus achieves a priority of essence over existence which tends in effect to instantiate a logical order preceding actuality, although he concedes a certain inseparability, since essence obligates existence in varying degrees of intensity. This anterior logical order produces the equalization of the necessity of the actual and the possible. For the necessity of existence attached to any essence now applies as much to *possible* essences (which continuously urge towards Being) as to *actual* essences, since, according to the Scotist priority of the essential over the existential, all essences, even actualized ones, were themselves at some stage only potential or possible essences. This priority of the possible effectively detaches or at least loosens the bond between essence and existence, since for Scotus the necessity of every realized essence becomes dislodged or qualified by the lurking possibility of alternative essences. That is to say, by formally distinguishing essence and existence, despite the fact that this would seem to tie existence more firmly to essence than the Thomist real distinction of the two, Scotus opens the possibility for a thing to be radically transposed into another thing, thereby relativizing a thing in favour of all that it *could be*, rather than affirming the actuality of all that it *is*. Because of the potential independence of matter from form, and because of the evacuation of

[16] For Duns Scotus, the more a creature tends towards perfection, the more it comprises composite organs within it, and the more these organs themselves acquire distinct substantive forms. A corpse which decays is for Duns an example of the partial actuality of the possible because, although the corpse cannot survive without the soul (and so it is not *really distinct* from the soul), the fact that it survives at all, albeit impermanently, indicates its formal distinction. See *Opus oxoniense*, l. IV, d. 11, q. 3, n. 47; Gilson, *op. cit., Jean Duns Scot*, 495–6. This composite unity applies to all creatures, including animals: "*Les formes spécifiques distinctes qui entrent dans la composition de l'animal n'y sont pas amassées en tas; elles ne sont pas nonplus absorbées en une seule; elles restent formellement distinctes dans l'inclusion unifiante du tout,*" ibid., 494 n. 1.

all resemblances, being becomes unhinged from itself, destabilized by its own inherent and yet strangely extrinsic possibilities, or indifferently stable and yet discontinuous potentiality. And, since the "possible," as distinct from the "actual," is by definition realized only in *thought*, or in some prior or virtual realm, the place given to the "possible" by Scotus inaugurates the logical basis for privileging epistemology over ontology and the rational over the actual, thereby opening the way for modern metaphysics.[17]

This is, in effect and in the long run, a substitution of the transcendental for the transcendent, since, according to the traditional view, the "actual" has no hidden *mathēsis* but arrives from God. For Aquinas, there is no prior essence legislating the intensity or modality of existence appropriate to any pre-given position.[18] And there is no necessity other than the logical exigencies of non-contradiction (which presume no actuality), existing before any actual arrangement. It is for this reason that existence in the Thomist perspective has to be *added* to essence.[19] But this does not mean that, as if by reverse procedure, existence is a necessary "given" which *already is*. Rather, it arrives from an unknown and plenitudinous source. It follows that the in-between region where essence and existence, possibility and actuality, contingency and divine "actual necessity" unite, cannot be explicated in purely analytic terms which deal only in necessities, nor in purely existential terms, which deal only with contingencies. Nor do Scotist quasi-logical terms sufficiently describe this event of being on the Thomist account. For here the structures of the way things are derive from God, and are to be characterized as exhibiting neither a pure necessity nor an arbitrary arrangement, but rather an "actual necessity" into which we can have no complete insight. It might seem that in this respect there is a similarity between the mysterious unrepresentability of the structures of Thomistic actual necessity (the genuine transcendent) and the Scotist formal distinction (the proto-transcendental) which is perforce never fully understood (by virtue of its in-betweenness). But there is a difference. For Scotus, the "mysterious" is relegated to a flattened-out realm of virtual possibility, or partial actuality, which threatens perpetually to undermine the necessity of all realized possibilities. Actuality thus becomes divided from itself, paradoxically in and through its own potentiality. For actuality now *testifies* that its specific arrangement is one of an apparently endless arraignment of equally viable

---

[17] See Alliez, *op. cit.*, "1300: The Capture of Being," 207.

[18] Funkenstein here seems to attribute to Aquinas a more Scotist position, suggesting that "essence demands . . . actual existence," in *op. cit.*, *Theology and the Scientific Imagination*, 52; see also 51. On Scotus as anticipating the Kantian transcendental with his doctrine of *passiones entis*, see Courtine, *op. cit.*, *Suarez et le Système de la Métaphysique*, 366–76.

[19] See Gilson, *op. cit.*, *Jean Duns Scot*, 493.

alternatives. Even though these possibilities might never be actuated, they remain "virtually present" in order to qualify the necessity of all realized possibilities. Thus, for example, Duns Scotus now thinks of the internal organs of an animal as having relatively independent subordinate forms; of prime matter as having in a sense its own independent form; and of the substantive form itself as having its own non-material individuating principle: *haecceitas*.[20] Later, this segmenting process was taken even further by William of Ockham, who, acknowledging only *real distinctions* between singulars, regarded both subjects and predicates (unlike Aristotle) as equally logically graspable as "Names." In this way, an ontological path was opened to the dominance of modern language by "nominalization" as described in chapter 2.[21]

In contrast to Scotus, the "mysterious" is more positively construed by Aquinas. For it is not that which belies actuality, but that from which actuality derives its fulfillment. Moreover, actuality is not here *opposed* to mystery or possibility, since being is not idolized as inert by Aquinas. Rather, being is aporetically suspended between its nothingness outside God and its optimum realization in God. Thus creatures have no ground in themselves, but perpetually receive themselves from the infinity of God.[22] It follows that, for Aquinas, necessity cannot be fully scrutinized by us, for, at the divine level, there is no unrealized possibility, nothing prior to actuality. All possibilities are infinitely actualized in God and the unrealized possibilities for creation (recognized by Aquinas) do not yet usurp this more fundamental sense in which there is no prior possibility (as they will, following Duns Scotus). In consequence, necessity must simply be received in and through its coincidence with mysterious actuality.[23]

In consequence the Thomist "real distinction" does not allow us to understand creaturely existence as either a simple or a rational phenomenon. It stresses that creatures exist in a determinate *fashion*, which is in one sense more

---

[20] Duns Scotus, *Opus oxoniense*, II, q. 1, n. 11; *Reportata parisiensia*, l. II, d. 12, q. 6, n. 13; John F. Boler, "Intuitive and Abstractive Cognition," in ed. Kretzman, *op. cit.*, *The Cambridge History of Later Medieval Philosophy*, 460–78, 46–4.

[21] See Arthur Gibson, "Ockham's World and Future," in ed. John Marenbon, *History of Medieval Philosophy*, (London: Routledge, forthcoming in 1997), chapter 14.

[22] On this Christian intelligence, see Milbank, *op. cit.*, *The Word Made Strange*, 44–5: "Between one unknown and the other there is here no representational knowledge, no 'metaphysics,' but only a mode of ascent which receives something of the infinite source so long as it goes on receiving it."

[23] It therefore seems that there is something like Scotus' metaphysical opposition of the actual and the possible in the postmodern insistence upon the supremacy of the *nihil*, which, as I showed in the previous chapter, is equivalent to a duality of known and unknown.

inscrutable than the Scotist intensity or modality of Being, but in another sense more meaningful as it leads us into greater and greater insight into the beauty of the world, or its actual necessity. This assumption of a particular character of existence, rather than a stress on "possibility," might seem to foreclose the potential of a creature's essence. But this is not the case. Rather, the creature constantly becomes more itself precisely because of its contemporaneity with existence, since it is really distinct from its own being, which is not fully its own but is always re-arriving, always being regiven. Thus Saint Thomas stresses that a creature more fully participates in Being by growing towards God, without ever departing from its own specific creaturehood. Such an ecstatic actuality, whilst it might seem to deny a creature's own essence, in fact holds open a horizon of the ever fuller realization of that essence. It is an irony that for Duns Scotus, the very mark of actuality itself betokens further or alternative possibility (in the form of alteration), so that the discrete autonomy of essence remains radically "open," whilst the Thomist construal of essence as open to analogically delimited development disallows both such extreme alteration and such endless atomizing and fixing of identity. By refusing both these aspects, which together amount to a vision of discontinuous futurity, the Thomist essence remains more fully other from itself, and thereby more fully itself. The real distinction between existence and essence is therefore the inner kernel of both *analogia entis* and participation because it permits essence to be realized as essence only through the Being from which it always remains distinct: essence forever simply participates in that which alone realizes and fully determines it. Thus, ontological difference invites the possibility of likeness and proximity, whereas univocity of Being produces unmediable difference and distance.

The thinkable

We have seen how the possible, for Duns Scotus, subsists in a realm of partial actuality, and qualifies the necessity of the realization of all actualized possibilities. Nothing real is regarded as necessary, whilst nothing unreal (i.e. the essential) is regarded as unnecessary. This gives rise to a tendency in Scotus to assume that the possible, if it can be thought at all, requires formalization. Moreover, the thinking of something in this fashion now becomes the criterion for existence, given that existence now includes possible or virtual existence. Thus, the mathematization of reality described above in chapter 2 finds its roots in Scotus' assertion of the univocity of Being, which, as we have seen, turns actuality into a kind of logicalized matter.[24] The formal distinction

---

[24] Alliez, *op. cit.*, "1300: The Capture of Being," 210.

leads to the scientific ideal of a new mode of knowledge which proceeds from an *a priori* analysis of clear and distinct concepts formed by the understanding, combined with the idea that for every distinct idea or possibility, there really corresponds something distinct. Thus it is as if the work of the actual physical object in understanding merely occasions our understanding, but makes no further contribution within the supra-reality of human reason. This follows directly as a consequence of the tendency in Duns Scotus to put possibility before act, or the knowable before the known.

Insofar as the "real" is now determined by the intellect, and the first object of the intellect is now Being, it seems that Scotus anticipates the modern invention of the object and its distinction from the subject.[25] This distinction apparently becomes more fundamental than any theological consideration, since cognitive possibilities assert themselves over any less explicable mysteries. An object can now be defined independently of a material thing, and in indifference to materiality or spirituality, whereas for Aquinas our mode of grasping any being is always conditioned by our grasp of the material thing. In consequence, the object is now defined on the basis of the concept, as *representation*.[26] This departs from Aquinas' Aristotelian theory of knowledge, whereby the form of a thing disengages itself from its matter and becomes a thought or "species" in our mind.[27] For Scotus, by contrast, the possibility of divine intervention, compatible with his notion that actuality can always and unpredictably be superseded by any imaginable possibility, forces him to distrust the traditional more ontological account of truth. In theory, Scotus imagines, God might bypass the role of the thing altogether, and imprint directly upon our intellect an apparent species, even though the object and its form do not actually exist.[28] It would in that case be impossible to distinguish between the species of an actual form and a miraculously imprinted one. Thus Scotus' apparently pious scepticism of the need for a formal causality of all species ironically operates according to an artificial *mathēsis*, or system of knowledge which does not depend upon material actuality for cognition as such, but uses it to supply information to the senses, and then applies the mind to translate that information into its own *a priori* categories. The reverse side of this intellectualism also opens up the possibility of an empiricism which

[25] *Ibid.*, 201–3; Courtine, *op. cit.*, 157ff.

[26] *Ibid.*, 209.

[27] *"forma autem intellectus est res intellecta,"* Saint Thomas, *De Potentia*, q. 8, a. 1, cited in Alliez, *ibid.*, 208. See also *Summa Theologiæ*, I. qq. 85–86; I–II, q. 12, a. 4; q. 85, a. 2. Courtine, *op. cit.*, 170.

[28] Duns Scotus, *In. Metaphysics*, VIII, q. 18, n. 11; Alliez, *op. cit.*, "1300: The Capture of Being," 288, n. 236; Courtine, *ibid.*, 159.

thinks of material reality in terms of isolated atoms of information streaming in from the outside world, which the mind must then synthesize, since they act upon the mind in the mode of merely *efficient* causality. This involves a departure from the traditional hylomorphic view that the form of a thing is already synthesized before it "informs" the mind (even though the active intellect must bring out its full coherence), and that the thing fulfills itself in and through its comprehensibility. Such a view regards the knowing of a thing as commensurate with the known thing's own constitutive repetition. For when the species is formed in our mind, the thing perceived happens again (since being is an event), or repeats itself, though in a different mode. Knowledge, for Aquinas, is therefore akin to an ontological event. In contrast to this, post-Scotist representation is equivalent to a de-ontological process, for the perceived object is reduced to an empirical exigency which simply happens to facilitate or occasion an act of cognition.[29]

The Eucharist and other possible miracles

All the theological shifts detailed above have implications for Duns Scotus' construal of what occurs at the Eucharist. As I shall show in the remaining sections of this chapter, it is precisely here that the most abstruse theory coalesces with social practice and assists in its transformation, since the event of transubstantiation in the mediaeval epoch was the ever repeated miracle of the emergence of the "social body", as such.

I have mentioned above how, for Duns Scotus, the physical order as it is governed under normal circumstances, is regarded as no more necessary than any imaginable or possible alternative configurations, and that there are many logically possible universes.[30] The actualization of such possibilities is determined, in the last instance, by the sovereign will of God.[31] Scotus' departure from *analogia entis*, which distances God from the world, precipitates a necessary preparedness to undergo at any moment a radically discontinuous

---

[29] "It (the *ens*) becomes a *veritable* object to the extent that it is an object of cognition, to the extent that *it is within cognition that the true constitutes itself. Within* representation – a not «*as* a repetition of what 'is found in things,' *as if* the judicatory relation too existed with an ontological status.»" *Ibid.*, 209, quoting Martin Heidegger, *Traité des catégories de la signification chez Duns Scot*, (Paris: Gallimard, 1970), 99 [emphasis added by Alliez].

[30] Funkenstein, *op. cit.*, *Theology and the Scientific Imagination*, 57–8.

[31] Duns Scotus, *Ordinatio*, I, dist. 44 [*Duns Scotus on the Will and Morality*, ed. and tr. Allan B. Wolter, O.F.M., (Washington, D.C.: The Catholic University of America Press, 1986) 255ff]; J. B. Korolec, "Free Will and free choice," in ed. Kretzman, *op. cit.*, *The Cambridge History of Later Medieval Philosophy*, 629–41, 638–40.

and arbitrary alteration caused by God, whose presence in the world is now viewed more ontically, in terms of a willingness to intervene. The miraculous is no longer to be found in the analogical resemblances of the physical order, but in the possible radical discontinuities of that order. Later, with William of Ockham, even the inner determinations of God came to be regarded as arbitrary arrangements; Ockham (and Luther after him) construed the coincidence of the persons of the Trinity with pure substantive relations as merely a revealed *datum* – three persons distinct apart from the relations would have been equally possible, whereas for earlier theology this would have violated divine simplicity.[32]

Such an emphasis on the supremacy of the divine will might seem to conflict with Duns Scotus' prioritization of the possible and his inauguration of knowledge as representation. For, surely, these are predicated upon the sovereignty of human intellection? However, it is only his stress on possibilities *de potentia absoluta Dei* which permits the establishment of cognition absolutely independent of its object, and so it is by no means the case that Duns Scotus wishes to attribute to the intellect alone the production of cognition. It is true that his crucial move, which substituted an *a priori* order of knowledge on the basis of cognition, for the traditional formal causality of Saint Thomas, inaugurated a new tradition which could now imagine the migration of all knowledge to the intellect alone. However for Duns Scotus himself, and his paradoxically revolutionary ultra-pietism, it is enough that the prescience of possibility realized in the physical order, whilst it confirms logic's incipient hold on the world, is nonetheless still determined solely by the will of God.[33]

The supremacy of God's will, according to Duns Scotus, is such that it can realize all possibilities, even those which contradict the actual necessities of the particular created order in which we live. Thus divine will can enact the seeming contradiction that a body can be in two different places at once.[34] It

---

[32] "Luther's position was more liberal, and this liberalism seems to derive from Ockham. Ockham certainly held that, *as it happens*, the persons of the Trinity are distinguished from one another by the relations: that is, that the persons are each constituted by the essence and the appropriate relation; they are, furthermore, only three relations (fatherhood, sonship, and passive spiration). However, he claims, this is by no means obvious, and is only to be accepted on authority – the position that the persons are distinguished and constituted by *absolute* properties is just as easy, if not easier, to argue for, even though it is false," Graham White, *Luther as Nominalist: A Study of the Logical Methods used in Martin Luther's disputations in the Light of their Medieval Background*, (Helsinki: Luther-Agricola-Society, 1994), 201, citing William of Ockham, I *Sent.*, d. 1, q. 2 and d. 26, q. 1. See Franz Wieacker, *A History of Private Law in Europe*, (Oxford: Clarendon Press, 1995), 208–9.

[33] Alliez, *op. cit.*, "1300: The Capture of Being," 208–9, 288 n. 229.

[34] Duns Scotus, *op. cit.*, *Ordinatio*, I, dist. 44.

is for this reason that the new Scotist emphasis on absolute divine power has a bearing on his understanding of the way in which Christ's body is present in the Eucharist. Christ's body is in the Host *not* because the latter is joined to the divine person of the Logos, as for Saint Thomas, for whom Christ is not an individual but only hypostatic as coincident with Being as such, and therefore ubiquitous. Instead for Duns Scotus, Christ's body can be ontically in two or more places simultaneously, in heaven or on earth, simply because God wills in this case to allow Christ's Body to have extension in the sense of containing different parts in a whole without those parts occupying different spaces.[35] His body is therefore present in a locative dimensional sense.[36] The change which takes place, therefore, in transubstantiation, is seen as specifically a change in dimensional reality, according to what one might call a proto-Cartesian determination of "body" as exhaustively extensional in character.

Although for Saint Thomas, Christ's body is really extended in the Sacrament, it is present "by way of substance, and not by way of quantity."[37] It is not that the dimensions of the bread and wine are changed into the dimensions of the Body and Blood, in such a way as to suggest that the whole is in the whole, and individual parts in individual parts. Rather, the *substance* of one is changed into the substance of the other. Thus, the whole is as much present in individual parts as it is in the whole.[38]

It is such holism which is threatened by Duns Scotus' theory of the potential autonomy of virtual existences. This does not, under normal conditions, actually mean that a human being can be radically separated from its soul, even though, for him, there is a virtual form of the body distinct from the soul. Even Scotus would concede that such a separation would result in mere

---

[35] Marilyn McCord Adams, *William Ockham*, (Notre Dame, Indiana: University of Notre Dame Press, 1987), Volume I, 188.

[36] Duns Scotus, *Reportata parisiensia*, 4, d. 10 q. 3; q. 6; cited by Funkenstein, *op. cit.*, *Theology and the Scientific Imagination*, 59.

[37] Saint Thomas, *Summa Theologiæ*, III. q. 76. a. 1, ad. 3.

[38] "Christ's body is in this Sacrament substantively, that is, in the way in which substance is under dimensions, but not after the manner of dimensions, which means, not in the way in which the dimensive quantity of a body is under the dimensive quantity of place," *ibid.*, III, q. 76. a. 3; "[T]he whole dimensive quantity of Christ's body and all its other accidents are in this Sacrament," although this does not displace the dimensions of bread and wine, III, q. 76. a. 4. But in reply to Objection One, Aquinas argues that whilst it is the substance of Christ's body which is present in the Sacrament, its dimensive quantity "is there concomitantly and as it were accidentally," though "not according to its proper manner (namely, that the whole is in the whole, and the individual parts in individual parts), but after the manner of substance, whose nature is for the whole to be in the whole, and the whole in every part."

quasi-existence, in the form of a corpse.[39] He does maintain, however, that this usually residual logical possibility is realized in the extraordinary and miraculous moment of transubstantiation, when the Body of Christ is given without His Soul being made fully present. This contrasts with the Thomist view, according to which, in any human being, the soul and the body are not *really* distinct (since there can be no animal body uninformed by soul), but are differentiated by an operation of the mind (in the same way that it is only the *modus* of the human mind which distinguishes between the divine attributes). Such real unity means that wherever one "component" is, the other is also. So, although for Aquinas, the bread and wine "terminate" in Christ's Body, this perforce includes His Soul, in the manner of an unbreakable unity. St Thomas uses the phrase "real concomitance" to describe this inclusion.[40] But for Duns Scotus, soul and body are configured as parts of a whole,[41] as formally, rather than either really or intellectually distinct.[42] Thus, in the Eucharist, Christ's Soul is invoked as only partially present. Moreover, it follows that the fact that it is the Body of Christ whose presence in the Eucharist is more fully actualized, and not His Soul, is no more than an arbitrary decision on God's part. In this way, the absolute potential of God is invoked not only to explain why the Body is caused to be present in more than one place, but also why the Body is more intensely present than the soul in the Sacrament.[43] The implication is that Christ's Body is present in the Sacrament in a most unusual way. Because, in the case of transubstantiation, Body and Soul are disjoined, His Body is here effectively presented in the manner of a corpse. Here, therefore, in the very heart of piety, the cult of necrophilia is begun.

The haunted middle

In the previous subsections of this chapter, we have seen that it was Duns Scotus' extreme *pietism*, his too purist theology, which dissolved the mysterious necessities of the world as encountered, and permitted the emergence

[39] Duns Scotus, *op. cit., Opus oxoniense*, l. IV, d. 11, q. 3, n. 54; Gilson *op. cit., Jean Duns Scot*, 496.
[40] Saint Thomas, *Summa Theologiæ*, III, q. 76. a. 1 (and ad. 1).
[41] "*comme le quadrangle contient le triangle*," Gilson, *op. cit., Jean Duns Scot*, 491; Duns Scotus, *op. cit., Opus oxoniense*, l. IV, d. 11, q. 3, n. 25–7.
[42] Duns Scotus, *op. cit., Opus oxoniense*, IV, d. 43, q. 2 [Reply Arg. I]; Z. Kuksewicz, "Criticisms of Aristotelian Psychology and the Augustinian-Aristotelian Synthesis," in ed. Kretzman, *op. cit., The Cambridge History of Later Medieval Philosophy*, 623–8, 626–8; S. J. Curtis, *A Short History of Western Philosophy in the Middle Ages*, (London: Macdonald and Co., Ltd, 1950), 222.
[43] Gilson, *op. cit., Jean Duns Scot*, 491–2.

of a secular and autonomous logicism and a secular and autonomous empiricism working either in rivalry or in uneasy harmony. But always, henceforth, in the middle of this alternative, the secular realm finds the "in-between" or the co-ordination of logic and fact problematic, as first witnessed by Scotus' "formal distinction." This in-between (which eventually becomes Kant's "transcendental") remains as a kind of ghost of actual necessity, which construed the interval as a real distinction, the trace of transcendence. By disallowing theological mystery, secularity remains haunted by a mystery all the more mysterious, since there is no longer any ground for its presence.

2 THE DECLINE OF LITURGICAL ORDER

Excursus on Scotist politics

The Scotist transformations of theoretical reason described above have parallels in the realm of practical reason. In the same way that the act of understanding, for Duns Scotus, becomes separated from the informing species, so the "will" becomes a self-propelling power, detached from the lure of teleology. Whereas for the tradition, the "voluntary act" was defined by the compulsion of the good, Scotus effectively definalized and de-eroticized the will by asserting the excess of its autonomy over the attraction of a particular goal.[44] Recognition of the good becomes a purely "ostensive," rather than "directional" matter.[45] And although it is by no means the case that Scotus abandons teleology to the degree of Cartesian voluntarism which comprehensively compares the free will of God with that of human beings,[46] nonetheless Scotus' assertion of the supremacy of the will ruptured the necessity of the good's sway over voluntary acts. It is precisely this doctrine of the autonomy of the will which permits Scotus to question the natural necessity of the Commandments of the Second Table of

[44] "From the fact that the will is perfectly free, it does not result that it throws itself with all its forces into its object; on the contrary, with whatever force it tends towards its object, it has still more for the purpose of dominating itself, so that toward whatever object it may tend, it tends toward it freely, and by virtue of its absolute freedom, it could not tend in this way toward it": Duns Scotus, op. cit., Opus oxoniense, II, d. 7, q. 1, a. 1, n. 9, cited by Alliez, op. cit., "1300: The Capture of Being," 212–13. Saint Thomas, op. cit., Summa Theologiæ, I, q. 82, a. 1, responsio. See also, Gilson, op. cit., Jean Duns Scot, 603–24.

[45] Duns Scotus, op. cit., Opus oxoniense, Prologue IV; see Alliez, op. cit., "1300: The Capture of Being"; "La Bonitas moralis s'ajoute à la substance de l'acte volontaire comme la beauté s'ajoute à la substance du corps." Gilson, op. cit., Jean Duns Scot, 606.

[46] See Descartes, Meditations on First Philosophy, in eds John Cottingham, Robert Stoohoff, Dugald Murdoch, The Philosophical Writings of Descartes, (Cambridge: Cambridge University Press, 1985), VII. 57–60.

the Decalogue (concerning one's duties toward fellow human beings). These, he argues, are valid only insofar as they comprise positive legal propositions determined by the will of God and insofar as God has not yet revoked them. For if it were the case that the Second Table expressed the character of natural law, how could one account for the occasions in the Old Testament when God Himself seems to have dispensed with their precepts?[47]

By detaching the will from the lure of the good, and subsuming it within the dominant *fiat* of divine volition, the principle directing practical reason is transposed from the ambiguous and medial synthesis of divine will and human freedom, whereby to tend *away* from God's will paradoxically denies the full potential of human freedom, to a dialectic of active and passive. This new ontological grammar could not fail to resound upon broader, societal practice. By unleashing the will from teleological determination, the political order must instead presume the imposed structures of a formalized and legalized practical reason. Thus, at the same moment that the will is asserted as paramount, it is foreclosed by an arbitrary but necessary imposition of a new juridical authority to prevent a dissolution of order. Indifferent to the goodness of any particular political arrangement, the Scotist will becomes de-politicized, no longer subordinated to the good embodied in the city,[48] but to the radical indetermination which represents the new ontological reality for Scotus. This arbitrary assertion of the will presupposes the rise of the nation-state. For no longer is the social realm intentionally subordinate to the ancient order of nature, but to the decrees of the single legislator which alienate the supposedly "free" subjects: "Led to its full political explicitation, the reversal of Thomism is contemporaneous with the transition from a *feudal* to a *national* king."[49] Only through the will of the legislator can the state now exceed the merely artificial: the mere fact of that will's expression is now justification enough of its divine sanction. The basic source of power, therefore, is transferred from the natural community to the sovereign will, whilst the de-politicized individual exercises a parallel but domesticated potency within the familial unit.[50] Both private actions within the conjugal and domestic realm

---

[47] Duns Scotus, *Ordinatio* III, suppl. dist. 37 in ed.Wolter, *op. cit.*, *Duns Scotus on the Will and Morality*, 268–87; see Aquinas, *Summa Theologiæ*, I–II, q. 100, a. 1; a. 8; Alliez, *op. cit.*, "1300: The Capture of Being," 213. Only the First Table of the Decalogue represented the laws of natural necessity: *Reportata parisiensia*, l, IV, d. 28, n. 6; see Gilson, *op. cit., Jean Duns Scot*, 623–4.

[48] Aquinas, *Summa Theologiæ*, I–II, q. 1.

[49] Alliez, *op. cit.*, "1300: The Capture of Being," 215. See Wieacker, *op. cit.*, *A History of Private Law*, 8, 14 n. 4, 283 n. 15, 284. I am grateful to Professor J. H. Baker for drawing attention to Wieacker's contribution to this topic.

[50] Duns Scotus, *op. cit.*, *Reportata parisiensia*, IV, d. 26, q. 1, n. 8; Alliez, *ibid.*, 215.

and those performed over against the collective now consummated as the *nation*, are no longer situated within the eschatological dimension of time, but within an open-ended but empty and indifferent order of temporal successive-ness. A fundamental indifference, therefore, now orders or constitutes civil society. This social order oscillates between the immanent universal and the individual, each repeating the circuit of active and passive operation.[51] Such a political configuration anticipates the Kantian conception of the State as the condition of possibility of morality in history, since it is the guarantor of the protection of individual freedom of will against infringement by the free will of others.[52] Paradoxically, in protecting the freedom of the will, Kant forbade any type of rebellion or resistance to the legislative authority of the State, since to oppose the State is now to contradict one's own will.[53]

These historical transformations of civil structure, therefore, repeat and extend the equivalent theoretical structures of Scotist theology. The consum-mation of the political community in the nominal unit of nationhood is the political counterpart of the reification of being in, and virtual actuality of the object; the novel assertion of miraculous possibility and the supremacy of divine will corresponds to the political assertion of the divine right of the absolutist monarch; the priority of the act of cognition for representation, where the object merely "occasions" the content of intellection, mimics the new order of nominal political representation of a flattened-out or decom-posed civic realm held together by the forces of contract. This new order of political representation replaces a structure in which the monarch's power could be based on popular assent since both people and monarch assumed a shared horizon concerning the agreed common good.[54] In the new order, by constrast, the possibility arises of conceiving the fact of the exercise of power

---

[51] "The arbitrariness and radical discontinuity which Duns Scotus introduced into even the divine reality dominated his conception of politics. A fusion of social atomism and unbridled authoritarianism, this conception was the reflection in society of the vision of the universe that we have been examining: men were at first equal, but they willingly sacrificed their independence to an authority established by them in order to limit the dangers to which they subjected each other on account of their egoism; since that time the authority that they set up has become omnipotent and absolute, the chief establishing, distributing, and revoking properties as he sees fit; there are no laws other than the positive laws instituted by him," Bréhier, *op. cit.*, *The History of Philosophy*, 189.

[52] Immanuel Kant, *The Metaphysics of Morals*, tr. Mary Gregor, (Cambridge: Cambridge University Press, 1991), 123–6.

[53] *Ibid.*, 131; William T. Cavanaugh, "A Fire Strong Enough to Consume the House: The Wars of Religion and the Rise of the State," *Modern Theology*, 11.4, (October 1995), 377–420, 408–9.

[54] Alliez, *op. cit.*, "1300: The Capture of Being," 290 n. 271.

in isolation from the reasons *why* it is exercised. Power itself acquires an independent reality which corresponds to the arbitrary Scotist will detached from teleological determination.

How does this new Scotist politics effect the dimension of inhabited social being? Because the goal of human operation is now exhaustively terrestrial (albeit modelled upon a transcendent potency) the supremacy of the sovereign *fiat*, anchored immanently in a contractual will, derives its transcendence from a quasi-eternal permanence.[55] The secular authorities thus erect a rival sacrality. This parodic theological politics necessitates its own rival eschatology which substitutes an uncertain dependence upon a futurity of accumulation and possible discontinuity for Christian teleology. The discipline of this new social practice, not fully developed perhaps until the eighteenth century, becomes orientated towards a reflexive speculation upon an immanent future of increase and change. This accompanies an economy of representation in its first emergence, with the transition from merchant to finance capital,[56] and the rise of bankers and money changers who quantify and commodify time by offering interest over its defined interval. A fulfillment of this secular postponement was reached in the bill of exchange, a "draft drawn on time,"[57] which encouraged confidence that a mere sign of something would in the future generate a present reality. Such a parrying of promised possibility and its deferred realization corresponds to the Scotist virtual reality of essence, priority of the possible, and epistemological order of representation, for which the purely willed (arbitrary) convention of the play of writing is fundamental.[58]

Duns Scotus' own metaphysical speculations on time and space resound with a corresponding abstraction of these variables, or substitution of a virtual or written realm for their inhabited counterparts. Whereas for the traditional Augustinian and Thomist view, time was inseparable from the movement of

---

[55] "The autonomy of the political bond takes the time of history away from the gaze of eternity *as* from the destructive flow of becoming . . . (A)nchored in a consensual will that founds it forever from within, the fact of collectivity is rooted via its representatives in an indivisiable perpetuity, endowed with a subjective, immanent, and nonetheless transcendent permanence. An unalterable identity, for which eviternity (*sic*) (*aevum*), situated between the eternity of the Creator and the distended time of creatures, offers the obligatory model." *Ibid.*, 217.

[56] *Ibid.*, 197.

[57] *Ibid.*, 218.

[58] Alliez notes the association of *credit* with *credence*, *confiance* with *croyance*, the *fiduciary* with *fideism*. *Ibid.* Regarding the usurious "sale of time," Alliez notes that although Duns Scotus was explicitly opposed to usury (*Opus oxoniense*, IV, d. 15, q. 2, n. 17), he permits the possibility of *reward* for risks incurred in commerce which implicitly includes the practice of usury. *Ibid.*, 219, 290 n. 280.

memory and desire, that is, from a tracing of deferral, Scotus detaches time from motion of every kind, even psychic motion. For in the same way that matter and form were taken as formally distinct, so time and motion were now conceived separately, so as to produce a possible time cognized distinctly in the absence of any body's movement.[59] Although this abstracted time is separated from motion, it is transposed into a time of absolute measure which permits all motion to be taken as of one and the same kind.[60]

This order of uniform time later culminates in the mathematical physics of Galileo, with its protocol of the substitution of acceleration for motion, the production of novelty in terms of growth, and the optimum goal of absolute motion in a void.[61] Here the Scotist legacy is palpable:[62] the independent variable of time operates upon a reality univocally governed by a numerical and linear, rather than differential and cyclical, order. In the same fashion, the practices of social being become lateralized, with no perpetual return of the soul to its meditation upon God. Where traditionally the order of linearity and temporal homogeneity were restricted by the liturgical order, subduing the rise of the State with its economy of liturgical return, there now reigns the "production at every moment of the new," "(a)n order with no Sunday."[63]

These transformations of theoretical and practical reason correspond to the tenor of actual events at the time of Duns Scotus and beyond. To say whether these events were precipitated by new theological developments (supremely, Scotism), or whether those theological shifts were themselves occasioned by historical events, is impossible. The best one can do is suggest the operation of a reciprocal causality. At the very deepest level, it seems that an alteration of ritual pattern took place, in the inseparable domains of thought and practice. Indeed, in every cultural realm in the late Middle Ages, a liturgical ordering of society was giving way to an organization in terms of the exercise of pure will and power divorced from love, combined with a formalized logic and an

---

[59] Duns Scotus, *op. cit.*, *Opus oxoniense*, II, d. 2, q. 11; Alliez, *ibid.*, 223–4.

[60] Pierre Duhem, *Medieval Cosmology*, ed. and tr. Roger Ariew, (Chicago: Chicago University Press, 1987), 400–4.

[61] Duhem, *ibid.*, 369–414, 377; Alliez, *op. cit*, "1300: The Capture of Being," 226, 291 n. 294; Henri Lefebvre, *The Production of Space*, tr. Donald Nicholson-Smith, (Oxford: Blackwell Publishers, 1991), 272; Alexandre Koyré, *From the Closed World to the Infinite Universe*, (Baltimore and London: The Johns Hopkins University Press, 1952/1970), 2–3; Edward Grant, *The Foundations of Modern Science in the Middle Ages: Their Religious, Institutional, and Intellectual Contexts*, (Cambridge: Cambridge University Press, 1996), 92, 100–4, 122–6.

[62] Edith Dudley Sylla, "The Oxford Calculators," in ed. Kretzman, *op. cit.*, *The Cambridge History of Later Medieval Philosophy*, 541.

[63] Alliez, *op. cit.*, "1300: The Capture of Being," 226.

increased enforcement of positive law. Through a consideration of various orders of social bonding, I shall now investigate the historical decline of the liturgical order.

Kinship

In the high Middle Ages, there was no abrupt gulf between the familial on the one hand, and the social on the other. Indeed, in a sense, the social was only realized through kinship relations. Following John Bossy, one can best illustrate this by considering two institutions: those of godparenthood and marriage. Godparenthood, in the high Middle Ages, was more than a metaphor; it was one of the most immediate forms of kinship. Although the parenting was spiritual, it was no less a *real* parenting, so real, in fact, that marriage between godparent and godchild was forbidden by the barrier of incest.[64] Its principle was that of *compaternitas*, which affirmed that a godparent was kin not only to the child, but to his natural family as well.[65] It represented the creation of a formal ritual friendship, symbolized by gifts and festivals, to which natural kinship could only aspire. And such psuchic parenting, or care for the soul, was the very thing which mediated between blood relations and the wider community. The principle of *compaternitas*, or development of a society structured upon kinship bonds, qualified any tendency to proffer the alternative societal structure based upon contractual "bonds."

The same principle of alliance and social bonding governed the idea of marriage. The law of charity obliged Christians to seek a relationship with those to whom the natural tie of consanguinity did not belong, in such a way that the bonds of relationship and alliance might extend throughout the community of Christians. This creation of an actual social relation, at least in theory, came before considerations of particularity and sexual relation, for the marriage alliance was above all a method of conferring peace and reconciliation between feuding families and groups.[66]

However, transformations of political structure in the later mediaeval and early modern periods altered the traditional priority of bonding with the wider community. The importance of the spiritual compaternity of godparenthood,

---

[64] John Bossy, *Christianity in the West 1400–1700*, (Oxford: Oxford University Press, 1985), 18. Henri Bresc, "Europe: Town and Country (Thirteenth–Fifteenth Century)," in eds A. Burguière *et al.*, tr. S. H. Tenison *et al.*, *A History of the Family*, Volume 1 (Cambridge: Polity Press, 1996), 430–66, 437–8; R. A. Houlbrooke, *The English Family 1450–1700*, (London: Longman, 1984), 39, 45–50, 73, 78–9.

[65] *Ibid.*, 15.

[66] *Ibid.*, 19–26; Pierre Toubert, "The Carolingian Moment (Eighth–Tenth Century)," in *op. cit.*, Burguière, *A History of the Family*, Volume 1, 379–406, 396–7, 399, 405.

with its plurality, bilaterality of gender, and disparities of age, was gradually displaced by the singular authority of blood paternity, and the structure of the enclosed family supplanted the wider collective. With Jean Bodin, paternity came to be conceived in terms of an absolute sovereign power of life and death, rather than as the mediation of a tradition, or the teleology of traditional natural politics, thereby consummating the Scotist instigation of the autonomy of the will.[67] This elevation of literal paternity, which reached its fulfillment in the promotion by Luther of the Fourth Commandment, "Honour thy father and thy mother," as the model of all social and political obligation,[68] over against the seemingly atavistic and mythic persuasions of ritual kinship, affected the meaning and practice of the sacraments of baptism and marriage. Although the institution of godparenthood was not altogether abolished, Luther lifted the taboo of marriage between godparent and child, while the general tendency of Calvin's teaching was to reverse the former exclusion of the role of natural parents in baptism, so that it was they, and not a child's spiritual parents, who presented and received a child at this occasion.[69] The ritual stress on symbolic initiation and alliance became gradually displaced by disciplines of instruction in the faith, a task which was now assumed by the *paterfamilias*.[70] Although the Reformation sought to stress the priesthood of all believers, by thus subordinating the ritual role of godparenthood, a central quasi-priestly lay role was lost. And throughout this development, one notes a strange double drift which nonetheless is entirely coherent: on the one hand, family authority ceases to be embedded in a wider network of custom and becomes a simple *de jure* power which the State can codify and regulate; on the other hand, the locus of this *de jure* power is simply *de facto* the most powerful parent, the father, so that a return is half-effected to the most primitive, even most animal kind of control.

Parallel to the decline of the extended Christian family was the transformation of the sacrament of marriage. Whereas it had traditionally been the case that the bond of marriage was sacramental even without the presence of a priest, and took place significantly not within, but at the threshold of the Church,[71] in the later period, parental consent was required to validate the

---

[67] *Ibid.*, 156. See Robert Fossier, "The Feudal Era (Eleventh–Thirteenth Century)," in *ibid.*, *A History of the Family*, 407–29, 412ff.

[68] *Ibid.*, 116.

[69] *Ibid.*, 116–17; Bossy notes that after the Council of Trent, the former plurality and disparity of the godparents was reduced to a pair of symbolic parents, one of either sex. *Ibid.*, 118; J. D. C. Fisher, *Christian Initiation: The Reformed Period*, (London: S.P.C.K., 1970), 3–16, 112–17.

[70] Bossy, *ibid.*, 118–21.

[71] *Ibid.*, 21. Jean-Baptiste Molin and Protais Mutembe, *Le Rituel du Mariage en France du XII⁰ au XVI⁰ Siècle*, (Paris: Beauchesne, 1974), 32ff. See also Augustine, *City of God*, XV.16.

marriage, in both Protestant and Catholic weddings, even though the Catholics, unlike Luther, continued to believe marriage to be a sacrament and not simply a contract.[72] But in either case, marriages could now only be contracted in the face of the Church before the parish priest and witnesses, after the publication of the banns. All other marriages, whether clandestine, public, sacred or secular, were declared void. In the Protestant case, this helped to elevate the authority of parenthood over the contract of marriage, while in the Catholic case, it reinforced a sense that sacramentality was coterminous with the decree of hierarchical authority. For whilst this emphasis upon the ecclesial context of marriage might seem to lay stress upon its liturgical nature, to the contrary, it suggested that there *could be* a sexual union that was secular and not sacramental. The sexual union itself was now effectively reduced to the equivalent of a civil contract permitted by the consent of the father (who held dominion over the "small commonwealth" or "little church"),[73] whilst the ecclesial contribution was reduced to an extrinsic miracle simply authorizing the legitimacy of the bond. As such, marriage was detached from the order of charity whereby the family opened out to wider collective bonds, and became equivalent to a contractualized exchange of commodities in which a transfer of private property secured a legalized alliance. This is of course not to deny that Protestant theology eventually permitted a new recognition of the natural goodness of sexual relations *within* marriage, and even, as in the case of John Milton, of a kind of sacramentality of sex. But the point remains that if such relations were newly considered "good," they were also, on the whole, desacramentalized by no longer being regarded as cementing wider social bonds. One might say that as the social and objective character of friendship declined, so also, in a compensatory move, married love came to be seen as more of a haven of *erōs* and *philia*.[74]

The economic realm

In the Middle Ages, the role of the lay fraternities and craft guilds ensured an active connection between the liturgical and the economic. These associations, formed under the patronage of a particular saint, the Trinity, Blessed

---

[72] Bossy, *ibid.*, 24.

[73] Patrick Collinson, *The Birthpangs of Protestant England: Religious and Cultural Change in the Sixteenth and Seventeenth Centuries*, (London: Macmillan Press, Ltd., 1988), 60. See Houlbrooke, *op. cit.*, *The English Family*, 68–9, 79–80. John Calvin, *The Adultero-Germanic Interim Declaration of Religion*, in *idem.*, *Tracts and Treatises of the Reformed Faith*, tr. Henry Beveridge, (Edinburgh and London: Oliver & Boyd, 1958), Volume 3, XXI.10–11.

[74] *Ibid.*, 62–77. André Burguière and François Lebrun, "Priest, Prince and Family," in *op. cit.*, Burguière, *A History of the Family*, Volume 2, 95–158, 97–102, 104, 108–10. Jean-

Virgin Mary, or Corpus Christi, incorporated the individual within a ritualized social collective whose principle end was the attainment of a state of charity, through establishment of a confraternal kinship (which included women), and through the practice of certain rituals which stressed the bonds of love, charity, and peace.[75] Central to these rituals of association, apart from election of new officers, admission of new members (with the token of a kiss), and worship, were participation in many forms of salutation and celebration. The statutes of many guilds contained exhortations to members to greet one another peacefully and in fraternal fashion; this mode of behaviour included the discipline of settling disputes between members through internal arbitration, and not via external juridical intervention.[76]

The bond of friendship was not limited to the membership of the fraternity, but was actively extended to the wider community in the form of charitable acts. These were not extrinsicist deeds towards strangers, but were part of the essential extension of the social bond of exchange. As well as admitting new members to "intercommune" at their annual feasts and festivals, the fraternities and trades guilds provided for the poor and founded hospitals, schools, and almshouses; they looked after certain liturgical feasts, theatrical performances, and other societal tasks such as rebuilding churches, bridges, and highways, and maintaining seabanks and sluices.[77] And these provisions for the community were complemented by even more immediate and personal acts of giving, so fulfilling the view expressed in mediaeval theology and canon law that charity was better directed to those with whom one was in some actual kinship or neighbourly relation than to strangers. Charity, as Bossy notes, was at this time construed more as a state of being than a deed, just as giving took place within a presupposed framework of reciprocity without setting precise bounds of content, time, and place as to what was expected in return. Giving was never regarded as a utility, nor as measuredly meritorious, but rather as further opportunity for making alliance, without precluding the obligation to extend charity by *extending* kinship and friendship.[78]

Louis Flandrin, *Le sexe et l'Occident: Evolution des attitudes et des comportements*, (Paris: Editions du Seuil, 1981), 64–5.

[75] J. J. Scarisbrick, *The Reformation and the English People*, (Oxford: Blackwell Publishers, 1984), 19-20; Bossy, *op. cit.*, *Christianity in the West*, 57–9; R. N. Swanson, *Religion and Devotion in Europe c. 1215–c. 1515*, (Cambridge: Cambridge University Press, 1995), 206–34.

[76] Scarisbrick, *ibid.*, 21.

[77] *Ibid.*; Bossy, *op. cit.*, *Christianity in the West*, 62–3; J. J. Jusserand, *English Wayfaring Life in the Middle Ages*, (London: Methuen, 1889/1961), 20–3.

[78] Bossy, *ibid.*, 143–52. See W. K. Jordan, *Philanthropy in England, 1480–1660*, (London: George Allen & Unwin Ltd, 1959), 54.

This reciprocal framework for the activities of the fraternities ensured that charity remained a liturgical discipline. Giving to the poor was neither a legal obligation, nor a matter of personal whim, but a sacramental entering-into a mysterious cycle of outgoing and returning love whose widest sphere was the divine charity itself.[79] It was the liturgical cycle of feasts and festivals which freed charitable donation from the anxiety of private choice, and qualified any attempt to transpose such giving into an impersonal and formalized tax where no bond is created between the donor and donee. Conversely, the practice of charity in the fraternities and guilds constantly ensured that surplus wealth was perpetually returned to the order of the liturgical cycle through the support of churches, monastic houses, hospitals, hospices, and annual festivals. In this way, the economic was subordinated to the liturgical order, into whose cyclical repetitions, a potentially abstract capital was expended. Thus, liturgy prevented the tendency of capital to displace the eschatological reserve in favour of an immanent teleology of accumulation.

By contrast, the decline of the fraternities in the decades prior to the early 1530s,[80] due to religious, political, and economic uncertainties, had implications not only for the various charitable and educational foundations which they had maintained, but also transformed the notion of charity itself. The centrality of kinship and the expansion of sociability lost persuasiveness as a principle of Christian action. As early as 1400, a new idea of charity had arisen in Florence whereby it was "transvalued into a generalized concept of philanthropy."[81] An actual connection between benefactor and recipient was no longer valued as central to the act of donation, which meant that giving was now deemed a one-way and impersonal phenomenon, no longer limited to the extension of friendship and kinship. In the Middle Ages, as Swanson says, the function of *caritas* was "the establishment of a state of reconciliation between individuals, to ensure an integrated social body,"[82] but now it was transposed from an active and personal alliance to a *private feeling* of abstract beneficence, closer to a customary tax or duty on the part of a citizen. Such "philanthropy" was

---

[79] See further Antony Black, *Guilds and Civil Society in European Thought from the Twelfth Century to the Present*, (London: Methuen, 1984); Eamon Duffy, *The Stripping of the Altars: Traditional Religion in England 1400-1580*, (New Haven: Yale University Press, 1992), 141–54.

[80] See Greg Walker, *Persuasive Fictions: Faction, Faith, and Political Culture in the Reign of Henry VIII*, (Aldershot: Scolar Press, 1996), 127.

[81] Marvin B. Becker, "Aspects of Lay Piety in Early Renaissance Florence," in eds C. Trinkaus and H. A. Oberman, *The Pursuit of Holiness in Late Medieval and Renaissance Religion*, Studies in Medieval and Reformation Thought, Volume 10, (Leiden, 1974), 185–6. Jordan, *op. cit., Philanthropy in England*, 83–108, 156ff, 240ff, 297ff.

[82] Swanson, *op. cit., Religion and Devotion in Europe*, 207.

accompanied by an apparently paradoxical distancing from social relations, symbolized by a discouragement of giving to beggars and a concentration on less specific, grander projects such as providing for "durable" works like schools and hospitals.[83] By 1500, this new idea of charity affected the reconstruction of the fraternities in which charity came to comprise less a state of being achieved through ritualized disciplines of friendship, and more a distinct operation of benefaction towards an anonymous body of needy outsiders which could take place without the presence of a state of love.[84]

The decline of fraternities also resulted in a transferral of power from the laity to an aggrandized priesthood. This might superficially seem to suggest a transfer to a more intensely liturgical focus, but in fact it lost the lay sustaining of a link between charitable association and the liturgical cycle. Moreover, whilst the theology of the confraternities, which presupposed belief in Purgatory, the sacrificial efficacy of the Mass, and veneration of the saints, all dependent upon priestly mediation, might seem in some ways to have excluded the active role of the laity,[85] and although the new order in its Protestant variant seemed to correct this imbalance by denying the sacrificial role of the Protestant minister in favour of the communication of the word (and the assumption of the task of preaching and disciplining), nevertheless, Protestantism, in abandoning the "middle voiced" role of a mediating priesthood, abandoned *also* the mediating functions of a laity in practices of social intercession. Since the new role of the minister was not to mediate but to announce an all-powerful sovereign word, the Reformation cast the laity as listeners to that word and recipients of the ministerial discipline. Here, the new modern active-passive framework without a true "middle" was not a less but a *more* clericalized framework than before. One may note, with Bossy, as an example of this tendency, that the disappearance of the confraternities removed also the guild clergy who had been largely under lay control.[86]

---

[83] "The prohibition of begging, and discouragement of giving to beggars, signified (the arrival of a dichotomy between public and private) because it symbolized the decay of the notion that reciprocity and some kind of personal relation (on the beggar's part, praying for the soul of his benefactor) were necessary characteristics of an act of charity. It intimated that there was such a thing as an act of charity which did not need a state of charity to take place in." Bossy, *op. cit.*, *Christianity in the West*, 146; also, 146–50. Bossy notes that in *A Christian Directory; or a Summ of Practical Theologie and Cases of Conscience* (1673), Richard Baxter, although dedicated to the task of concord and peace, viewed kinship and the cultivation of friendship (beyond the edification of the domestic family) as a hindrance to God's work, *ibid.*, 150–1.

[84] Bossy, *ibid.*, 145.

[85] But see Bossy, "The Mass as a Social Institution 1200–1700," *Past and Present*, 100 (August 1983), 29–61, 33–5.

[86] Scarisbrick, *op. cit.*, *The Reformation and the English People*, 24–5, 38–9.

The civic realm

The sacraments of baptism and marriage, together with such institutions as godparenthood and the confraternities, were viewed by mediaeval society as providing opportunities for social integration, the forging of alliances, and the attainment of a state of peace. These sacramental and liturgical practices were so central to mediaeval culture that one can view them as in some sense constitutive of the social realm. It might seem that the specifically *ritual* performance of peace and alliance in some sense belied its genuine attainment, but this would be to presuppose a duality of ritual and non-ritual modes of practice, and thence mistakenly to correlate ritualized with artificial actions and to segregate such forms of action from the "real" or "everyday." But mediaeval social practice was definitively ritual or liturgical in character. There simply was no duality of the liturgical and the mundane, just as the dichotomy of public and private was foreign to the mediaeval mind. Such specifically ecclesial occasions as the celebration of the Mass, processions, festivals, and pilgrimages,[87] extended beyond themselves. For all forms of social interaction were themselves embedded in a structure of worship, ritual, and charity. As Talal Asad declares, in the Middle Ages, *all* inculcation of virtue was a ritual matter, because it was instituted through disciplinary (and, one might add, festive) practices which were physical and external rhythms, rather than through a supposed direct working on the "inner" mind alone.[88] At this stage, virtue, including peaceableness and the exercise of charity, was regarded as something visible and apparent in outward and public signs which could not dissemble: there was as yet no "ironic" space. (Such "liturgical" order in which one cannot distinguish ritual from "everyday" was of course most perfectly realized in the monasteries; yet it was approximated to in lay life.)

Within the social realm, therefore, peace, like charity, was characterized as a state of being attained through repeated affirmations of ecstatic collectivity. It was an ontological condition which, although *actively* forged, was nevertheless also *received* (though not passively, since it was genuinely welcomed and by definition actively passed on to others in the bonds of kinship) from the altar. Indeed, at the Mass, the reception of the Host was accompanied by the choir's singing of the words "*Dona nobis pacem*" and was followed by the exchange of the ancient kiss of peace or the kissing of the *Pax*.[89] It

---

[87]   *Ibid.*, 42.
[88]   Talal Asad, *Genealogies of Religion: Discipline and Reasons of Power in Christianity and Islam*, (Baltimore: The Johns Hopkins University Press, 1993), 55–79, especially 77.
[89]   Bossy, *op. cit.*, *Christianity in the West*, 69f.

is by no means arbitrary that it was the Eucharist, rather than any other sacrament, from which all other activities flowed, because, as will be described below, for mediaeval thought, the Eucharist gives the Church, the Body of Christ, and as such, the Church alone legitimates politics, and provides the restoration of our genuine being through salvation. It was at the Mass that the social realm received itself as the union of the social limbs of the Body of Christ, a theme of reconciliation which was symbolized in the great procession at Mass of the craft guilds and fraternities leading up to the canopied Host. Precisely because of this ultimate and sacral reconciliation with Christ's Body, peace could be incarnated in all particular, even "extra-ecclesial," activities, and was not isolated or defined within any privileged or exclusive realm of sanctity.

What undermined this notion of peace and the unity of the Body of Christ was in the end the rise of a devout piety of frequent communion which focussed not upon the integration of disparate limbs into a single Body, but upon a private and interiorized devotion to Christ's miraculous presence in the Sacrament. It was this unique intensification of piety which paradoxically segregated the sacred from the secular, for by concentrating sacrality in a singular and exclusively holy event or place, any location beyond that focal intensity was effectively secularized.[90]

How did this early-modern transformation of piety affect the mediaeval notion of peace? In the early sixteenth century, Erasmus brought to fruition the de-ritualization of peace. Although he affirmed the desirability of peace, alliance, and reconciliation, he denied the traditional methods of their attainment, through sacraments and rituals. Peace was now to be achieved through rigorous discipline and moral teaching. Thus, the (newly de-vocalized and de-ritualized) Word now prevailed over all else to produce a spirit of *pietas*, meaning a civilized devotion characterized by a dominance of the spirit over the passions of the flesh.[91] This precipitated the substitution of civility, or a civic peace, for a ritual or sacral peace, to be instilled by the absorption of the proliferating manuals of manners and civil behaviour.[92] Peace was now taught rather than received. Moreover, the substitution of manners for ritual meant, as Asad has well observed, that "outward sign" was sundered from "inner meaning." The civic peace achieved through good

[90] *Ibid.*, 72.
[91] *Ibid.*, 98–9; C. S. L. Davies, *Peace, Print and Protestantism 1450–1558*, (London: Hart-Davis, MacGibbon Ltd, 1976), 148–52.
[92] "In the long run (Erasmus') deepest impact on the West was probably to supplant in daily life the rituals of Christianity by the rituals of civility." Bossy, *op. cit.*, *Christianity in the West*, 98; see also 120.

manners might be a mere *apparent* peace which cloaked insincerity, and, indeed, the disguise of one's real intentions could itself be seen as a *politique* means of sustaining civic order in the long run. Hence, as Asad shows, citing Bacon's essay "Of Simulation and Dissimulation," civility was compatible with deceit; whereas ritual behaviour simply *manifested* inward intention, (just as, for Aquinas, materialized form became knowledge, and the *telos* informed the moral will), manners now "represent" an inner state on the model of "Scotist" epistemology, and may therefore represent incorrectly. Once this cultural development has occurred, as Asad argues, ritual itself is viewed on the model of manners, and becomes a drama apart from life, a fiction, a temporary dressing up; a "mere" ritual which will soon be seen as a pointless excrescence probably concealing devious purposes.[93] Inversely, one can also say that manners are a sort of parody of ancient liturgical discipline, since they do indeed inculcate through habit, obedience, and conformity. But the fact that the only moral attitude they seek to encourage is an inner compliance with authority is mirrored by the fact that the form of manners is usually arbitrary and without symbolic signification (for example, "don't hold your knife in your left hand"). This new ritual in no way expresses anything inward and essential.[94]

The rise of the notion of civilized manners,[95] which represented a new mode of non-sacral, "rational" (as opposed to religious) civic ritual not only displaced the sacral social realm which had been ritually constituted via festive performances of peace, but also effectively distanced people from one another. John Bossy notes the significance of the fork in this transformation of peace into civic distancing, as an implement which reconfigured the communal (even familial) feast as a civilized, rational operation. Without a common cup or dish, the former continuity between rites of domestic eating and the Eucharistic meal was sundered.[96]

The new civil peace was itself regarded as sacred. Yet this did not in any sense mean that it was viewed as flowing from the Eucharist. Rather, sacral order now emanated from the sovereignty of the monarch or, later on, the State, whose realm was a space within which civility might flourish.[97] Peace was thereby transposed from the category of gift mediated through Christ, to

[93] Asad, *op. cit.*, *Genealogies of Religion*, 59, 65, 77.
[94] Pierre Bourdieu, *Outline of a Theory of Practice*, tr. Richard Nice, (Cambridge: Cambridge University Press, 1992), 94–5.
[95] See Norbert Elias, *The History of Manners*, tr. Edmund Jephcott, (New York: Pantheon Books, 1982).
[96] Bossy, *op. cit.*, *Christianity in the West*, 121–2.
[97] *Ibid.*, 155.

a given fact coincident with the being of the State, and enshrined in the duty of the citizen. As a consequence, Christ's peace was relegated to an other-worldly dimension, a detached spiritual parallel of, or model for, civil, earthly peace. This formulation of the State as peacemaker was fully realized in the political theory of Jean Bodin, for whom matters of religious disagreement were subordinated to the now innocuous realm of the "soul," whilst the State took responsibility for the maintenance of civil order.[98] Hobbes took this tendency even further, not merely subordinating the Church to civil power, but swallowing it whole into the belly of Leviathan. The members of this Church cohere, as before, as a natural body, but no longer to one another. Rather, each member of this body depends directly on the sovereign and the coherence of the body is an artificial phenomenon, merely occasioned by this diversion through the centre. The Body of Christ has now been nominalized, scattered, and absorbed into the body of the State.[99] And the peace of the body is no longer an active and noisy festival of extended kinship resulting from the sacral power of love. It has become instead an enforced and silent tranquillity imposed by the sovereign and sacralized political state. This state of political peace is held in place by the distance which subsists between the source of absolute power and individual subjects bound together into small conjugal units.

The juridical relation

Alongside the tendency to regulate social behaviour through informal codes regarding manners, shifts also occurred in the realm of strict legality itself. First of all, within the Church, historians recognize an increasing drift towards the dominance of canon law in Church procedure and episcopal operation.[100] This came about partly because of an increase in boundary disputes between different bodies within the Church, for example between the regular clergy and the religious orders;[101] because of these, formal and coercive resolution had to be substituted for genuine, spontaneous reconciliation. As a result, the Church itself became more and more a legally defined and contractual body, while the notion of the Church as formed through the Eucharist was gradually lost. Concomitantly, the bishop ceased to be regarded as primarily a eucha-

---

[98] See Cavanaugh's discussion of Bodin's "How Seditions May Be Avoided" (1576) in *op. cit.*, "A Fire Strong Enough to Consume the House," 404–5.

[99] *Ibid.*, 406–7.

[100] Scarisbrick, *op. cit.*, *The Reformation and the English People*, 40.

[101] Max Weber, *Economy and Society*, (Berkeley: University of California Press, 1978), Volume II, 828–31.

ristic president and instead came to be viewed as someone embued with juridical powers.[102]

This shift towards a Church constituted through positive legal procedure exemplifies in social actuality the same loss of the teleological which was described in the case of Duns Scotus' account of practical reason. In both cases there is a resultant evacuation of the significance of time, just as in the late Middle Ages the much-documented narrowing of salvation history to a focus upon the crucifixion and its implications for the individual, led to a loss of focus upon the temporal dimension of typology,[103] the resurrection, and the eschatological future of the whole material world. Instead of the mediation of eternity through time one therefore already had in the late Middle Ages a beginning of the spatialization I have described in chapter 2. This had two aspects. First, the public sphere was now dominated by formal structures without any teleological or eschatological reference. This had the consequence that the Church, insofar as it was becoming more "modern" and contractual, for the first time became "other-worldly" in the sense that it positioned people within a static eternal present. Secondly, in contrast to this public eternal space which became an increasingly secularized space (although instituted by a spiritual authority), the more strictly religious aspects of life became confined to the concerns of the isolated individual. Because this individual was removed from his social belonging, and because society itself had become detemporalized, the individual was now doubly removed from sacred time. Instead, the individual now stood alone before God, even if this standing was only achievable through the mediation of sacrament or scripture. The loss of emphasis on resurrection and teleology in favour of often morbid preoccupation with Christ's death meant that already late mediaeval piety imposed a division between life and death, since death and suffering were regarded as a price of exit from a sinful life to eternity. And the notion that the effective Christ is essentially the dead Christ can be seen as cognate with Scotus' reduction of Christ's Eucharistic body to a "dead body." Likewise, the Scotist paradox whereby a univocally proximal God is also the most distant God is echoed in the way in which, for much late mediaeval piety, the increasingly extra-ecclesial directness of the relation of the individual to God only confronts the individual with an inscrutable deity who looks upon him with a juridical gaze akin to that of the post-feudal sovereign or the now more disciplinarily-defined clergy.

[102] Scarisbrick, op. cit., The Reformation and the English People, 41. Brian Tierney, Religion, Law, and the Growth of Constitutional Thought, 1150–1650, (Cambridge: Cambridge University Press, 1982), 30ff.
[103] Milbank, op. cit., The Word Made Strange, 95; Henri de Lubac, Exégèse Médiévale; Les Quatres Sens de l'Ecriture, (Paris: Aubier, 1964).

The same loss of substantive reconciliation is adduced in the new use of prescribed formulae in pastoral care. The increased role of disciplinary manuals and of books of catechism (instead of oral instruction) in the late Middle Ages, and then manifest in both Reformation and Counter-Reformation practice meant, as Bossy has noted, that Christian virtue itself was being redefined as obedience to authority, just as faith itself became defined as a set of propositions.[104] As a result, the normative reference point in ethics gradually ceased to be the seven deadly sins and became instead the Decalogue.[105] The former list of vices instilled a virtue ethic, albeit in a negative mode: by implication, the list recommended certain admirable attitudes and practices, such as generosity and love, rather than proscribing specific acts – in contrast to those more negative injunctions of the ten Commandments which came to be most insisted upon. And, as Bossy notes, whereas in the earlier Middle Ages the crucial sins were those of pride and envy which severed social peace,[106] now the crucial sins were those which concerned the individual's control over his own passions.[107] For public peace, as we have already seen, was now to be guaranteed in an external manner by the operation of custom and law.

Secondly, the drift towards legal formality tended to remove law from the ecclesial sphere to the State. This is most dramatically seen in the privatization of penance,[108] and its abolition in the case of the Reformation. Here, a whole area of legality and processes of social reconciliation were desacramentalized. It was only the viewing of such processes *sub specie aeternitatis* which allowed reconciliation to complete the sacrament of penance. For when our ultimate salvation is allowed to inflect social restitution it becomes important first of all that the malefactor consents to such restitution and, secondly, that between victim and perpetrator or else between litigious civil parties a bond can be restored.[109]

Once this social function of penance starts to erode, justice becomes, like power, an altogether more abstract and autonomous phenomenon.[110] Instead of the whole point of justice being to restore actual peace between members of the community, it becomes instead a matter of marking a violation against the will of the State because this will is already in advance supposed eternally and automatically to guarantee the highest degree of peace achievable here on

---

[104] Bossy, *op. cit.*, *Christianity in the West*, 49–50, 120, and *passim*.

[105] *Ibid.*, 35–7, 116–25; see also Alasdair Macintyre, *After Virtue*, (London: Duckworth, 1981), for a general account of the shift from a virtue-based to a law and rule-based ethic.

[106] Bossy, *ibid.*, 139.

[107] *Ibid.*, 134–5.

[108] Michel Foucault, *The History of Sexuality: An Introduction*, tr. Robert Hurley, (London: Penguin, 1976), 18–19.

[109] Bossy, *op. cit.*, *Christianity in the West*, 47–8.

[110] *Ibid.*, 139. See Wieacker, *op. cit.*, *A History of Private Law*, 210.

earth. In consequence, crime is now regarded as an affair between the individual and the sovereign authority; concomitantly, enforcement of law becomes simply a matter of reasserting sovereign arbitrariness, whether or not the individual consents or the estranged are reconciled. One can see, therefore, how the same tendency to simplify reality in terms of an active-passive system which omits a difficult sacramental area of complex ambiguity between the active and the passive is here manifest. For on this model of justice, the State alone is active, and no activity on the part of the subject can ever exceed that supremacy. Thus, the subject is unqualifiedly passive, and his mediating assent, whether in the form of repentance or forgiveness of the other, is no longer required. One could even say that the middle voice of atonement is here expunged in favour of the pseudo-middle of law which only apparently mediates, but is really situated at two poles held at an absolute distance from each other, as the post-Scotist God is absolutely distant from His creation. The mediating functions are henceforward relegated to the private familial sphere. In the light of these developments, it is scarcely a surprize that eventually, and before Descartes, it is a theologian, Martin Bucer, who will uphold Sparta and its draconian and inflexible legality as a model for Christendom.[111]

The political

The foregoing considerations have shown that in the late Middle Ages the political emerges as a pseudo-liturgical power whose absolutist colonization of every realm of life parodies the traditionally sacramental structure of all forms of social interaction. Concomitantly, as we have seen, in anticipation of the baroque monarch, the sovereign power of the late mediaeval era acquires a quasi-divine status.

Given the rise of a soteriology of the State as guarantor of social peace and justice, to what dimension was the religious relegated? Although it is commonly argued that until the sixteenth and seventeenth centuries, the Church remained the supreme common power, whilst the civil authority was the "police department of the Church,"[112] and that it was the turmoil of the Wars of Religion which necessitated the inversion of this hierarchy, it is clear from the previous sections of this chapter, that the inversion of the political and the ecclesial took place a good deal earlier.[113] William Cavanaugh has noted instances as early as the fifteenth century, such as the controversy

---

[111] *Ibid.*, 129.

[112] John Neville Figgis, *From Gerson to Grotius, 1414–1625*, (New York: Harper Torchbook, 1960), 5; Cavanaugh, *op. cit.*, "A Fire Strong Enough to Consume the House," 398.

[113] See Cavanaugh, *ibid.*, *passim*.

between Papalists and Conciliarists, which gave rise to a new configuration of civil power. Marsilius of Padua (*c.* 1275–*c.* 1342), an early-fourteenth-century opponent of papal claims to comprehensive power, already argued that the natural process of earthly politics had a self-sufficiency which not only needed no completion or rectification from higher sources, but could be represented as endangered by such interference.[114]

With these and other assertions of civil dominance over the Church came a reconfiguration of the Church, as we have seen, as servant of the State, perpetuating structures to support, rather than to challenge, the latter's own sovereignty. It was a short step from the view of religion as a set of propositions of faith to the idea of religion as a set of privately held beliefs or personal convictions. Such privatization of religion is correlative to the rise of the State.

The shift in the meaning of the word "*religio*," as Cavanaugh has shown, clearly demonstrates the transfer of religion from the public to the private domain. For Saint Thomas, the word *religio*, as well as referring to the monastic orders, named a virtue which directs a person to God. *Religio* was a habit, a form of public knowledge embodied in the disciplined and ritual actions of the Christian. Such actions did not follow from a rationalized set of propositions separable from the narrative and sociability of a person's life, but were embedded in communal practices of the habituation of body and soul in the direction of the good. This definition presupposed the context of ecclesial practices, specifically Christian in character.[115]

However, just as Duns Scotus was able to conceive theology as detached from both metaphysics and physics, and the soul as formally distinct from the body,[116] by the late fifteenth century, Marsilio Ficino presented *religio*, in his *De Christiana Religione* (1474), as a universal pulsion distinct from other human activities, and variously manifested in disparate but equally valid or invalid

---

[114] Marsilius of Padua, *Defensor Pacis*, Dictio I, cc. 4, 9; A. S. McGrade, "Rights, Natural Rights, and the Philosophy of Law," in ed. Kretzman, *op. cit.*, *The Cambridge History of Later Medieval Philosophy*, 738–56, 741–2; Alan Gewirth, *Marsilius of Padua and Medieval Political Philosophy*, Volume I, *Marsilius of Padua: The Defender of Peace*, (New York: Columbia University Press, 1951). So marginal was the Church's power, as Cavanaugh notes, that in 1438, the Pragmatic Sanction of Bourges had accomplished the elimination of the papal collection of the Agnate tax, removed the Pope's right to nominate candidates for vacant Sees, and transferred to the Crown the prerogative to supplicate in favour of aspirants to most benefices. Cavanaugh, *ibid.*, 401; Tierney, *op. cit.*, *Religion, Law, and the Growth of Constitutional Thought*, 48–50; Norbert Elias, *The Civilizing Process: State Formation and Civilization*, tr. Edmund Jephcott, (Oxford: Blackwell Publishers, 1982), 91ff.

[115] Cavanaugh, *ibid.*, 403–4; Aquinas, *Summa Theologiæ*, I–II, 49–55; II–II, 81.7–8.

[116] Gilson, *op. cit.*, *History of Christian Philosophy in the Middle Ages*, 455.

practices. This idea of religion as a natural instinct or drive, privatized its relevance and segregated it from the ecclesial sphere of bodily practice. Others carried this tendency even further, until, in 1576, Jean Bodin brought it to its most explicitly realized expression: people should be free in conscience to choose whichever religion they wished. But once a form of religion has been chosen and embraced, the sovereign will forbid any public dispute over religious matters. Religion therefore no longer comprises bodily practices within the sphere of the *Corpus Mysticum*, but becomes limited to the sphere of the "soul." At the same time, the body is surreptitiously handed over to the State, now promoted as an equivalently transcendent power.[117] As Talal Asad has argued, religion as a universal essence, detachable from a specific locus in ecclesial practices, becomes compatible with any practices whatsoever.[118]

Eternal bonds

The bonds with the dead, with the saints, angels, and God are here considered last, but in fact, for a liturgical community, they came first. The fraternities, which played so many practical roles in mediaeval life, nonetheless only existed in order to provide funerals for their members and to say Masses and prayers for their souls after they were dead. The doctrine of purgatory permitted both the living and the dead both to be involved in one unfinished story of salvation and reciprocal aid. It is not to be considered an accident that these societies organized around death were nonetheless in no sense necrophiliac or other-worldly, since they also supported buildings of all kinds, hospitals, schools, festivals, and other public works for the living. Such active charity was grounded in a concern with their members beyond the point where those members could possibly be seen to confer any positive, immediate or predictable benefits back towards the fraternity in return for the liturgical offerings made on their behalf (although this is not to deny some element of gift exchange with the dead; the point is that exchange with the dead is particularly resistant to commodification of the gift). In this way, the fraternities delayed the emergence of the later modern duality of life and death as already described. They both encouraged a sense of kinship between the living and the dead, and, by making life beyond death the primary community concern, prevented an accumulation of life in defiance of death as the main aim of human existence: for economic surpluses were continuously expended on liturgical purposes connected with the care of souls now and hereafter.[119]

---

[117] Cavanaugh, *op. cit.*, "A Fire Strong Enough to Consume the House," 404–7.

[118] Asad, *op. cit.*, *Genealogies of Religion*, 27–54.

[119] "Even before the doctrine of purgatory had been fully formulated, the dead had come

Furthermore, as Scarisbrick notes, mediaeval wills often exhibited extensive public generosity.[120] Rather than being, as later was so often the case, directed mainly to securing various modes of dynastic power, they helped to institute, like Christ's initial "will" to inaugurate the Eucharist, a flourishing of community, out of the passing away of the physical body.

The fraternities were, of course, mostly dedicated to saints, and the invocation of saints was a further vital aspect of ritual kinship. This is most clearly evident from the fact that Christ's satisfaction was in every way held to be entirely adequate. For the Reformation, it only appeared that the cult of saints denied this adequacy because, as Bossy notes, by this time, the sense of ritual kinship had weakened. The saints' prayers and transferred merit, and supremely the prayers and merit of the Mother of God, were indeed superfluous and excessive, and their importance conveys not so much a primary means towards salvation, as the working out of salvation itself as a process of interpersonal support and reconciliation. In addition, the practice of regular address to absent and unknown powers (the dead, saints, and angels) tends to personify and make present the absent, whereas in modernity, as we have seen, an unknown and deathly absence finally corrodes even living presence.[121] Only in the later Middle Ages, with emerging individualism as described, and an increasingly desperate and mechanical invocation of saints no longer easily seen as friends and kin, did the cult of saints indeed effectively seem to deny the efficacy of Christ's merit, so that against this background the Protestant response was entirely comprehensible. But after the Renaissance and Reformation, and to a large degree, in the Counter-Reformation also, the saints gradually ceased to be primarily friends and benefactors of transferable merit, and became instead models of virtue to be imitated.[122] Once again, one sees here a genuinely mediating role – since the saints are at once like us and

---

to be seen as a double of the society of the living, their 'souls,' in the imagination of ordinary people, scarcely less physical than their own bodies; they formed a collectivity which had its allotted space in the territory of the community, an 'age-group' between whom and the living intricate relationships of concern, devotion and fear, and a complicated passage, obtained." Bossy, op. cit., "The Mass as a Social Institution," 37, see also 42–3; N. Z. Davis, "Ghosts, Kin and Progeny," Daedalus, 106.2 (1977), 92–6; Houlbrooke, op. cit., The English Family, 40, 204; Jean-Louis Flandrin, Families in Former Times: Kinship, Household and Sexuality, (Cambridge: Cambridge University Press, 1979).

[120] Scarisbrick, op. cit., The Reformation and the English People, 2–12.

[121] See chapter 4, The Apostrophic Voice.

[122] As Bossy notes, the Thomist sociology of salvation, whereby the satisfaction of one man is accepted for another, became gradually individualized, until Luther could say: "But as ye massmongers cannot be baptised nor believe for other, no more can ye receive the sacrament for other. As every man is baptised for himself, so must he eat and drink . . . for

not like us – collapsing in favour of a more authoritarian structure: the saints now stand austerely over against us, we have lost their sympathy.

Kinship with the other world extended in the Middle Ages beyond the dead and the saints to God Himself. As Bossy argues, the early mediaeval construal of Atonement depended upon the notion (which was indeed an entirely New Testament notion) that Christ was one of our kin and could take our debt upon Himself. Furthermore, the Atonement itself was regarded as achieving reconciliation with God, our ultimate parent.[123] In, for example, Anselm's account of the Atonement, there is no real sense that God Himself requires any compensation, or even that God has been insulted by sin, since God is perfect and replete. What has been insulted is divine justice and the bond between man and God. Only God is able to restore this bond since man has rendered himself powerless through sin, and the compensation for sin which consists in the gratuitous act of a sinless man offering His own death flows back from God towards man since God Himself, being replete, does not need to receive this gift.[124] Hence, for the Middle Ages, it was Christ's divinized humanity which was offered as a gift to humankind. However, all this became disturbed during the late-mediaeval and early-modern period. By the time of Luther and Calvin, the Atonement is no longer framed within the terms of restoring the bonds of kinship by the aid of the power of kin itself, and is instead framed in judicial terms. God's unknowable sovereign will is now regarded as what has been offended, and as requiring a sufficient punishment of humanity in compensation. His eternal decree requires that this sufficient punishment be the death of a perfect man, absolutely obedient to the divine will; such a man can only be a divine man. And there remains something inscrutable about this divine decision to offer the divine Son to God on our behalf since, for Luther, divine righteousness is utterly unknowable by analogy, and is only manifest *sub contrario* in the Cross which negates all human value, inciting simply our trusting submission to the unknown. (This consummates the late-mediaeval tendency of univocity to produce distance; now even the ultimate divine closeness of the incarnation is reduced to the

---

himself. Can my eating slake your hunger? No more can your eating of this sacrament do me good. 'The righteous man,' saith the Prophet, 'shall live by his own faith.' " *Martin Luther, Selections from his Writings*, ed. J. Dillenberger, (New York: Garden City, 1961), 283, cited by Bossy, *op. cit.*, "The Mass as a Social Institution," 44.

[123] "(The Mass) secured or re-enacted the 'paying' ['Pay'= *pacare*, 'satisfy,' 'placate'] of God, the appeasement of his anger, the restoration of diplomatic or social relations between God and man, the return of the universe to a condition of peace." Bossy, *ibid.*, "The Mass as a Social Institution," 34, (see also 34, n. 8; and *idem, op. cit., Christianity in the West*, 169).

[124] Milbank, *op. cit., The Word Made Strange*, 163–4.

distance of Christ's death).[125] In consequence, the relationship of the believer to the Atonement is no longer one of being incorporated into the Son and thereby achieving an affective state of reconciliation with the Father, but rather one of simply accepting a transaction carried out by God on our behalf. So once again, it is the active-passive schema which dominates: there is a direct relationship between the sovereign God and the individual believer omitting the roles of other Christians and even that of the Son and the Holy Spirit, since salvation is now rarely conceived as our being swept up into the reciprocal exchanges which take place within the Trinity. Above all, the sense that we are able to receive God in the middle voice, since, in Christ, God is ineffably both divine and human, active and passive, is lost.

The rupture of power and love

In all the above examples it has been seen how power and love were gradually sundered to produce a loveless power and an impotent love, which no longer had any primary role in the sacral economy. The transfer of focus from charity as the bond between us and God, whereby God *was* this very bond, to the idea of a primary submission to an inscrutable divine will, meant that an extreme, although distorted, piety which stressed God's ability to change things and work miracles itself encouraged a new cult of power in every domain of human life. Power became something increasingly "virtual" and abstractable from affectionate social bonds, from kinship and ritual action, while the public love that remained came to be regarded as a formal, abstract duty towards strangers, enshrined in the humanist protocols of civility. These constituted another layer of formality and virtuality in that they hovered uneasily between the formal injunctions of law and the genuine spontaneity of affection, and neither the formal structures of power, nor the new codes of manners were in any traditional sense liturgical; although they presupposed the sacralization of pure power in the immanent realm, they nonetheless rendered this realm ripe for secularization. By contrast, the complex rituals and institutions of charity in the early and high Middle Ages made possible a fusion of love and power upon a liturgical basis. (None of this account is supposed to imply that a liturgical order was perfectly realized in the high Middle Ages; the claim is rather that certain social and intellectual conditions of possibility for such an order were present.)

---

[125] See Alister McGrath, *Luther's Theology of the Cross*, (Oxford: Blackwell Publishers, 1985), 158–9; John Calvin, *Institutes of the Christian Religion*, tr. Henry Beveridge, (Michigan: Wm. B. Eerdmans, 1989), II, XVII, 4–5.

All these rituals and institutions were of course focussed upon the Eucharist. As we shall see below, it was the gift of Christ's Body and Blood which was seen as continuously bringing about the Church as the Body of Christ, and hence, as bringing about the Christian community. Given that this community took its power to be from the divine gift of God Himself, this rendered any abstraction of power impossible and refused any acceptance of a mere "appearance" of peace. While lay communion in the Middle Ages was infrequent, it was serious, and communion could be refused if the would-be recipient was involved in unresolved dispute.[126] One can agree with Bossy that "[t]he special virtue of the salutary Host was that it managed to offer a supreme representation of love and power at once."[127]

3 THE THEOLOGICAL BODY

It will now be shown how the drift towards spatialization described above affected the liturgy and Eucharistic theology in the course of the Middle Ages. Not only the structure and content of the liturgy and the Mass, but also their status in relation to the Church and the enactment of relational celebration, were transformed by this process. Indeed, it could be argued that these themselves in part provoked the broader movement away from a liturgical way of life.

The most fundamental shift which took place involved an alteration in the "punctuation" of the three dimensions of the theological "body" − the historical body of Jesus, the sacramental body, and the ecclesial body. In the conclusion of *Corpus Mysticum*, Henri de Lubac explains that these three foci, which had traditionally been ordered in relation to one another in such a way as to place an implicit *caesura* between the first and second foci (the historic body of Jesus and the sacramental body), later came to be organized with the *caesura* placed between the second and the third (the sacramental body and the ecclesial body).[128] The shift therefore pertains to a change in the distribution of the binary organization of ternary foci, as Michel de Certeau describes it.[129]

---

[126] Swanson notes the case of a woman seized by the devil after offering a merely feigned forgiveness before receiving the Host. Swanson, *op. cit.*, *Religion and Devotion in Europe*, 207–8.

[127] Bossy, *op. cit.*, *Christianity in the West*, 75; see *idem*, "The Mass as a Social Institution," *op. cit.*, 34.

[128] Henri de Lubac, *Corpus Mysticum: L'Eucharistie et L'Eglise au Moyen-Age*, (Paris: Aubier-Montaigne, 1949), 228.

[129] Michel de Certeau, *The Mystic Fable*, tr. Michael B. Smith, (Chicago: Chicago University Press, 1992), 82–5.

The former scansion of this distribution conjoined the sacramental and the ecclesial bodies as, together, the contemporary performance of a distinct, unique "event" designated by the historical body of Jesus, which laid stress on the contemporary continuity between the act of receiving the eucharistic Body and being received *by* and *as* the ecclesial "body."[130] This manifestation in time of the effects of the historical body of Jesus in the communion of the Church and the sacrament opened the space of liturgy as the "site" where the visible community (*laos*) and the mysterious work (*ergon*) combined, sustaining the linear series extending from the apostolic historic origins to the present ecclesial moment, and ever onwards. According to such a distribution, the mysterious work of the sacrament is a relational communication or exchange rather than an objective or visible "thing" requiring interpretation or commentary,[131] and ensures the unity between two times, overcoming the division of anteriority and futurity, by beckoning toward a journey to be taken "beyond" all present points of reference.

In addition, as de Lubac argues, this distribution of the threefold theological body, which connected the ecclesial body with the sacramental body, has implications for an understanding of reality, for it assumes the logical continuity of the categories of "mystical" and "literal" or "real," rather than their opposition. In the early Middle Ages, the term "*mysticum*" could as equally properly be applied to the Eucharistic body as to the Church (although initially it applied only to the former), for the two were mutually allied – the Church was only a unified body because of its reception of the Eucharist, and inversely, the mystical body of the Eucharist signified the Church, by synecdochal extension, as that in and by which it was received, and which attested to it through its *essential* manifestation of unity.[132] This (later) nomination of the Church as a "mystical" body did not make it any less a "real" body. Indeed, to the contrary, it is precisely *because* the Church was considered a *corpus verum*, and was efficacious in producing a unified body, that the Eucharistic body itself was considered, in the patristic and early-mediaeval period, to exceed the status of a mere symbol and to comprise the *real* Body and Blood of Christ.[133] Such unity could only be attained through reception and concomitant entry *into* the body of Christ, and so the real presence of the sacramental body is *essentially* and not merely nominally attested to by the

---

[130] Dom Gregory Dix, *The Shape of the Liturgy*, (London: Dacre Press, 1945), 15–19, 35, 251.
[131] de Certeau, *op. cit.*, *The Mystic Fable*, 79–83; de Lubac, *op. cit*, *Corpus Mysticum*, 47–66; Dix, *ibid.*, *The Shape of the Liturgy* 12–13, 247–55.
[132] de Lubac, *op. cit.*, *Corpus Mysticum*, 281.
[133] *Ibid.*, 283–4.

reality of the ecclesial communion. This mystical unity of the Church is not simply a moral designation, but physical and natural. Because the sacrament of the Eucharist is a *mysterium unitatis* or *sacramentum conjunctionis*, the "mystery" of the ecclesial body is precisely its "real" synaxis, just as we have seen in the previous sections of this chapter that the *sacraments* of baptism, marriage, and restitutive penance were only fully realized in the actuality of reconciliation.[134] By the same token, for Augustine, it is the Eucharistic body "*quo in hoc tempore consociatur Ecclesia.*"[135] The mystical is also the real because it is efficacious: "*Présence réelle, parce que réalisante.*"[136] This reciprocal continuity between the mystical and the real has further implications. First, it ensures that truth is seen as occupying a dynamic and diachronic plane, as more an event or action which constitutes the realization in time of a mystery, than a fact or thing denuded of any unknown or spiritual dimension.[137] And, secondly, it guarantees that the ecclesial community, constituted in and through its reception of the Eucharistic body, subsists within the character of gift, and in a context of sociality with the transcendent, as that which has always previously bestowed the (historical-sacramental-ecclesial) gift.

However, this configuration of the threefold relation began to alter towards the end of the Middle Ages, gradually being replaced by a formula according to which two "positivities," apostolic (historic) authority and sacramental authority, became the new binary pair, split off from the ecclesial body which concomitantly acquired the status of the mysterious (hidden) extension, a position formerly occupied by the "absent" historical body. This shift had far-reaching effects. First, the co-articulation of two "positivities," (1) historical fact, and (2) the "present" fact of the sacrament, instantiated a transposition from a *temporal* distribution (which linked sacramentally the past and present to the eschatological future), to a *spatial* one, according to which the sacramental "action" became less a non-identical repetition continuous with the "original" event and more a simple, positive, authoritative "miracle" in the present. Secondly, this new distribution had implications for the casting of both "positive" poles. The historical tradition became a code or law which required interpretation in order to disclose its authoritative "essence," and the sacramental body was concomitantly recast as a visible, objective "thing" which designated something invisible – such as grace or the effects of

---

[134] *Ibid.*, 27–8; de Lubac here notes that Greek *koinonia* , translated into Latin *communio*, first of all designated reception of the Eucharist.

[135] [*by which in this time the Church is assembled*] Augustine, *Contra Faustum*, 1. 12, c. 20 (*P.L.*, 42, 265) cited in de Lubac, *Corpus Mysticum*, 284; see also 290.

[136] *Ibid.*, 284.

[137] "*un mystère, au sens ancien du mot, est plutôt une action qu'une chose*," *ibid.*, 60.

salvation.[138] Thirdly, the visibility of that authoritative object now supplanted the communal celebration, displacing the collective operation of liturgy as the site of eschatological and historical communion between the visible and invisible. Instead, in order to fulfill its new articulation of the positive and visible, the Church must now be re-invented as the place where invisible authority is made either legible (the read historical accounts) or manifested (the totalized visibility of the sacrament), or both together. This re-invention of the ecclesial body was itself the Reformation, as de Certeau describes it, inaugurating two tendencies, one (Protestant) which privileged the historical corpus, and the other (Catholic) which privileged the sacramental body.[139] Thus, in each case, the new binary formulation prioritized the visible, and cast the ecclesial body not as the relational "moment" of theological time, and communal liturgical operation, but as the other in relation to visible positivities.

Alongside this alteration in the articulation of the three aspects of the theological body, by which the sacramental and ecclesial poles became disjoined, a change took place with regard to the traditional coincidence of the mystical and the real as reciprocally constitutive dimensions of the Eucharistic and ecclesial bodies, which had important consequences for theologies of both the Eucharist and the Church. I referred above to de Lubac's analysis of how, in the Middle Ages, it became theologically natural to describe the Church as a "mystical" body since it was so closely conjoined to the Eucharist. He goes on to narrate the subsequent semantic shift of the term *corpus mysticum*, whereby, from the late twelfth century onwards, it came to designate the ecclesial body exclusively, in contrast to the Eucharist, which, by the thirteenth century, was designated the *corpus Christi verum*.[140] Although at this time, the reciprocal link between these two bodies was still active, this semantic bifurcation betokened an incipient alteration in the relationship between the Church and the Eucharist as no longer so potently mutually confirming.[141] The traditional understanding of the real presence of the sacramental body as attested to by the real unity of the ecclesial body was gradually inverted in such a way as to prioritize the sacramental body over the

---

[138] de Certeau, *op. cit.*, *The Mystic Fable*, 83–4.
[139] *Ibid.*. In the Middle Ages, "the Bible" was not conceived as a singular entity but was dispersed into several manuscripts, often surrounded by commentaries and allegorical representations. However, printing allowed the emergence of the Bible as a discrete, written artefact, which encouraged a Protestant sense of it as an authority over-against the Church. See Bossy, *op. cit.*, *Christianity in the West*, 97, 99–101, 103.
[140] de Lubac, *op. cit.*, *Corpus Mysticum*, 120–6.
[141] "*Réalisme eucharistique, réalisme ecclésial : ces deux réalismes s'appuient l'un sur l'autre, ils sont le gage l'un de l'autre*," *ibid.*, 283.

Church, so that, as de Lubac argues, the Church was seen as the true body of Christ because it is *founded upon* the Eucharistic body, as an effect subordinate to its cause. Although this formulation was not theologically "wrong," it nonetheless announced a significant change in the nature of Eucharistic and ecclesial theology, both in relation to one another, and in themselves.

The separation of the "mystical" from the "real" caused a transformation of the *symbolic* potential of the Church as a unified structure to signify in the nature of its own body its *essential participation* in the Eucharistic body. Instead, the ecclesial body becomes the secondary, lateral arena in which the "real" sacramental body is exhibited, and its nomination as the "mystical" body of Christ no longer denotes in equal proportion its character as the "real" body, but instead acquires a less essentialist connotation. The phrase is now reduced to metaphor, and the Church is figuratively "a body" simply because Christ is its head, and has authority over it.[142] This separation of the "mystical" from the "real" in terms of the relationship between the ecclesial and sacramental bodies therefore can be seen to anticipate an absolutist structure where a single, centralized power wields dominion over a flattened-out social body, in contrast to the traditional model which preceded it, whereby the hierarchized polarization between the two elements was qualified by a genuine participation in both directions.

A second consequence of the later mediaeval semantic opposition between "mystical" and "real" pertains to the Eucharistic body itself. As we have seen, according to the patristic and early-mediaeval formulation of the Church and the Eucharist, the latter was deemed to exceed a purely symbolic status precisely because the former obtained a *real* unity. De Lubac argues that this is an inevitable outcome since, if the configuration of the Church as the body of Christ ceases to stress the coincidence of a "mystical" and a "real" status, acquiring simply a symbolic connotation, the reality of the Eucharistic presence will itself be affected. He cites the example of Calvin's theology, according to which there is only a *"présence virtuelle"* in the sacrament because an essential participation between Christ's physical body and the Eucharistic body does not occur: *"car il est au ciel et nous sommes ici-bas en terre."* The reason for this dilution can only be grasped if one realizes that the Ecclesial body *likewise* has ceased to be in any literal sense Christ's body, for just the same reason: Christ's body is locally and ontically positioned in heaven.[143] Whilst for patristic theology, the reciprocal relation

---

[142] *Ibid.*, 129–30.

[143] *Ibid.*, 284; B. A. Gerrish, *Grace and Gratitude: The Eucharistic Theology of John Calvin*, (Edinburgh: T&T Clark, 1993), 8–9, 173–90. See John Calvin, *op. cit., Institutes of the*

between the Church and the Eucharist gave rise to a notion of the *fecundity* of the sacrament, fundamentally attested to by the reality of the communion, the gradual conceptual separation of the two bodies inevitably provoked debate as to sacramental validity, and the notion of "presence" became a theological "problem" which relied solely on the effect of the words of Consecration.[144] The notion of Eucharistic *presence* was gradually substituted for that of sacred *action*, giving rise to a literalist concern as to what the Eucharist "is," as an isolated phenomenon, rather than an ecclesial event.[145] In consequence, Eucharistic theology, from around the eleventh century onwards, acquired an apologetical tone, organized in defence of the real presence.[146] Accordingly, the Eucharist itself came to be seen as a local or extrinsicist "miracle" whose demonstration alone was seen as a positive or rational verification of real presence.

This exaltation of isolated presence gave rise to a change in the role of the Church, as the arena in which the *corpus Christi verum* was exhibited. The decreased emphasis on the corporate unity of the Church as an essential component of the Eucharistic presence was inversely proportional to an increase in individualistic piety and sentimental excesses.[147] Paradoxically, however, this stress on the Eucharist as a new present fact located exclusively within the order of the "real" encouraged a tendency to think of the Eucharist as a *symbol* concealing an equally present meaning, subsisting within a synchronic register of logical demonstration. This apparent paradox is parallel with the way in which, as described above, empiricism is collusive with rationalism in producing an order whose dialectic operates between an artificial *mathēsis* on the one hand, and God's miraculous intervention to substitute an alternative and equally arbitrary *mathēsis* on the other hand. In the same way, an extrinsically miraculous interpretation of the Eucharist secretly colludes with the merely symbolic interpretation of the Eucharist. If transubstantiation is regarded as merely an inert fact, in the manner of a discontinuous miraculous "arrangement" of reality, the only way in which one can know it as a fact is to think of it as an arbitrary symbol, by-passing a

---

Christian Religion, and *idem.*, *On the True Method of Giving Peace to Christendom and Reforming the Church*, in *op. cit.*, *Tracts and Treatises in Defence of the Reformed Faith*, 279–80; and *On Shunning the Unlawful Rites of the Ungodly, and Preserving the Purity of the Christian Religion*, in *Tracts and Treatises*, 384.

[144] de Lubac, *op. cit.*, *Corpus Mysticum*, 290.

[145] *Ibid.*, 185.

[146] *Ibid.*, 240–7.

[147] *Ibid.*, 292; Dix, *op. cit.*, *The Shape of the Liturgy*, 249, 598–603.

more existential sense of the doctrine of transubstantiation as real presence because it generates the Church (in parallel with the Aristotelian and Thomist order of knowledge whereby the "form" of a thing migrates to the intellect and repeats it anew in a different but analogically recognizable form). The traditional configuration of transubstantiation, combining the "real" and the "mystical," obtained a diachronic aspect, as the signifier participated ontologically in the signified, (that is, the historical body of Christ in which the Eucharistic body really participates). Thus, to know the "real" did not here mean to eradicate the mysterious, and involved not an isolation of a given fact, but a whole bodily contact including person, desire, will, faith, and memory. But, according to the new epistemological separation of the "real" from the "mystical," the alternative readings of the Eucharist, as either purely symbolic or as an extrinsic miracle, *both* tend towards a synchronic interpretation, and can be seen therefore as dialectically identical. It is ironic that, in the eleventh century, the doctrine of Bérenger, in explicit opposition to the orthodox "realist" interpretation, argued for a symbolic reading of the Eucharist precisely because the traditional symbolic dimension of the patristic theology of the Eucharist had been left behind.[148]

This gradual drift towards a synchronic reading of the Eucharist as either a symbol or a "local" miracle occurred in parallel with an amelioration of the legible and visible, encouraged by various other changes, such as the centralization of clerical administration at the Third Lateran Council (1179), and professionalization of theology whereby the priests became the privileged operators of the visible instituting of the sacramental authority.[149] Parallel to these shifts, attempts were made to isolate rural or private deviations in devotional practices, in order to underline the singular authority of the visible institution, seen in the rise of "confessional" checks on private practice, and the explicit manifestation of sacramental authority, through the popularizing of doctrine, displaying the sacrament, unveiling the lives of the saints, and interpreting the truths of the scriptures. More and more, the emphasis was laid upon persuasive spectacle, uniformity, simplicity, and the mapping out of the lineaments of the visible, in order to secure epistemological, social, and theological *transparency*.[150] This generation of visibility can be seen to anticipate, or perhaps accelerate, the full unfolding of the process of spatialization

[148] de Lubac, *Corpus Mysticum*, 252–3. See, for example, Calvin, *op. cit.*, *Institutes of the Christian Religion*, IV. XVII.10; and *op. cit.*, *On the True Method of Giving Peace*, 277.
[149] Miri Rubin, *Corpus Christi: The Eucharist in Late Medieval Culture*, (Cambridge: Cambridge University Press, 1991), 51–3.
[150] de Certeau, *op. cit.*, *The Mystic Fable*, 85–94; see also Rubin, *Corpus Christi*, 55–63, 351.

described above in chapter 2: the early-modern movement towards a cartographic and encyclopaedic epistemology, increased emphasis upon empirical – ocular – verification in the scientific production of knowledge, priority of form and order over content, and of epistemology over ontology. It seems also to prefigure the Cartesian dualism of the body as purely sensual extension, and the spiritual as purely ideal, rather than the two as reciprocally and essentially real.[151]

How did these changes in the status of the Church and the liturgy in the overall distribution of the components of the theological body affect the structure of the liturgy? Above all, the shift towards visibility led to the centralization of liturgical form, dispelling the varieties of local difference, which took place most markedly at the Council of Trent.[152] Any drift towards a static centre must automatically involve a movement away from liturgy embedded within an ecstatic temporality, and as reciprocally and substantially situated within the Church, towards a liturgy of spectacle. In accordance with this, the *satura* (gift of varied fruits, or gift of difference) which characterized the early Offertories was disconnected from the produce of everyday life, as a simplification and abstraction of the notion of gift causally linked to the process of centralization, and concomitant separation of life and liturgy.[153] Rather than being cast as the mysterious work which united the historic-apostolic origins, the present ecclesial body, and the eschatological consum-mation of these through the Eucharistic sacrament, the liturgy became a means by which the invisible was made visible, in the local, authoritative – and authorizing – moment of spectacle arrangement. This development was part of a twofold loss of narrative; first, a static focus on the spectacle of the Passion in abstraction from the whole drama of salvation; and, secondly, a loss of the sense of the Eucharist as an event within the narrative action of the ecclesial liturgy as a whole – defined broadly, as a mode of life, as well as a particular

---

[151] de Lubac, *op. cit.*, *Corpus Mysticum*, 253–4.

[152] This is not to deny that this same drift towards standardization was in part a pragmatic response to the superstitious excesses of "arithmetical piety" characteristic of popular piety at the end of the middle ages. See Johan Huizinga, *The Waning of the Middle Ages: A Study of the Forms of Life, Thought and Art in France and the Netherlands in the XIVth and XVth Centuries*, (London: Edward Arnold and Co., 1924/1952), 124–81; E. Delaruelle, E.-R. Labande, and P. Ourliac, *L'Eglise au temps du Grand Schisme et de la crise conciliare: 1379–1449*, 2 volumes, (Paris: Bloud & Gay, 1962–4), Volume Two, 775–6; E. Delaruelle, *La piété populaire*, (Torino: Bottega d'Erasmo, 1975); K. L. Wood-Legh, *Perpetual Chantries in Britain*, (Cambridge: Cambridge University Press, 1965), 312; Jacques Toussaert, *Le Sentiment religieux en Flandre à la fin du Moyen Age*, (Paris: Librairie Plon, 1963), 361–71.

[153] Bossy, *op. cit.*, "The Mass as a Social Institution," 33.

celebration. For example, in the early-modern period, a trend arose whereby the laity would attend Church only to see the elevation of the Host.[154] This reduction of narrative gave rise to an impoverishment of liturgical temporality, for the event of transubstantiation came to be seen as occupying a single moment, rather than as being embedded within the prefatory and distended chronotope which I shall describe in the next two chapters.[155]

---

[154] Eamon Duffy, *op. cit.*, *The Stripping of the Altars*, 95–107.

[155] A corollary to this rise in spectacle was an increase in inward devotion in contrast to an ecclesial mode of worship involving oral participation, dialogue, and enacted narrative. De Lubac refers to "a general development of individualism" which "appears to coincide with the gradual dissolution of mediaeval Christianity." De Lubac, *Catholicism*, tr. Lancelot Sheppard, (London: Burns & Oates, 1950/1962), 163–4.

PART TWO

THE SACRED POLIS

These then, though unbeheld in deep of night,
Shine not in vain, nor think, though men were none,
That heav'n would want spectators, God want praise;
Millions of spiritual creatures walk the earth
Unseen, both when we wake, and when we sleep:
All these with ceaseless praise his works behold
Both day and night: how often from the steep
Of echoing hill or thicket have we heard
Celestial voices to the midnight air,
Sole, or responsive each to other's note
Singing their great Creator: oft in bands
While they keep watch, or nightly rounding walk,
With heav'nly touch of instrumental sounds
In full harmonic number joined, their songs
Divide the night, and lift our thoughts to heaven.

John Milton, *Paradise Lost*, IV, 674-88

Chapter Four

I WILL GO UNTO THE ALTAR OF GOD: THE IMPOSSIBLE LITURGY

1 INTRODUCTION

In the second half of this essay, I shall counterpose to the polity of death described in Part I, the liturgical lineaments of the sacred polis. In the next three chapters, I show, by means of a linguistic, theological, and philosophical interpretation of the mediaeval Roman Rite, how a liturgical philosophy is expressed, and more consistently realized than with Plato, in the central liturgical text of mediaeval Christendom. The Roman Rite, which dominated the Latin western tradition up until the changes wrought by the Second Vatican Council in 1962,[1] provides a model for a genuine consummation of language and subjectivity in and through a radical transformation of space and time. It will be argued that in the Roman Rite, the configuration of language as simultaneously "gift" and "sacrifice" exalts a different and salvific formulation of the various dichotomies which have been seen to reside at the heart of immanentism: orality and writing, time and space, gift and given, subject and object, active and passive, life and death.

In contrast to the immanentist manipulation of signs (described in Part I), which is reliant upon a construal of language as innocuous decoration, or mere "adornment" of a prior frame of "the real," so that its true signs arrive invisibly, "over against" the subject, the liturgical city, as we shall see, is *avowedly* semiotic. Its lineaments, temporal duration, and spatial extension are entirely and constitutively articulated through the signs of speech, gesture, art, music, figures, vestment, colour, fire, water, smoke, bread, wine, and relationality.

---

[1] Louis Bouyer, *Eucharist: Theology and Spirituality of the Eucharistic Prayer*, tr. Charles Underhill Quinn, (Notre Dame, Indiana: University of Notre Dame Press, 1968), 243.

both/and...

These "signs" are both things (*res*) and figures or signs – of one another and of that which exceeds appearance. Such a language of signs is received openly, willingly, and repeatedly, in and through its being passed on to others, and itself constitutes the offering and consummation of the citizens' subjectivity as a "living sacrifice." This sacrifice through the *communication-as-offering* of signs stresses, therefore, the superlatively articulate *relationality* of subjectivity. In addition, I will argue that genuine subjectivity is to be attained through the redemptive return of doxological dispossession, thus ensuring that the subject is neither autonomously self-present, nor passively controlled from without (the pendulum of "choices" available to the citizen of the immanentist city).

2 SPATIALIZATION AND THE LITURGY

I have chosen as my paradigm of genuine liturgy the mediaeval Roman Rite rather than more recent revised liturgies of the Anglican and Roman Church because the latter, although ostensibly the result of an attempt to interrupt the drift towards decadence characteristic of the liturgical practice of the seventeenth century, and to recover a purer and more ancient liturgical structure, nevertheless can be seen to have (unwittingly) incorporated the linguistic and epistemological structures of a modern secular order as described in Part I. The Vatican II reformers of the 1960s tended to assume that the text of the Roman Rite, which reached more or less its mature form in the Italian Mass Books of the eleventh and twelfth centuries, represents a corruption of an "original liturgy," a debasement of what went before. They often alluded rather mysteriously to earlier times when things were different, when there apparently was no intrusive *Kyrie*, no Preface, no *Hanc igitur*, not even a *Pater Noster*,[2] and they would then invoke such supposedly pure liturgies as Hippolytus' *Apostolic Tradition* and Justin Martyr's *Apology*, texts which are now almost universally regarded as treatises *on* liturgy, rather than actual liturgical traditions. It is because of this dominant view of the mediaeval liturgy that in order to study the Latin Mass, one has sometimes instead to turn to other disciplines in order to derive some adequate understanding of these early times, of the nature of ritual in antiquity and the Middle Ages, and of the character of early theological reflection. We have seen in the previous chapter, for example, that the liturgy of the Middle Ages was embedded in a culture which was ritual in character. This was a time when the Offertory gifts were

"older" = "better"

---

[2] See Josef A. Jungmann, S.J., *The Early Liturgy To the Time of Gregory the Great*, (Notre Dame, Indiana: University of Notre Dame Press, 1959).

not disconnected from the produce of everyday life; indeed, the category itself of "everyday life" was perforce a thoroughly *liturgical* category. For the community was not something which existed prior to, or in separation from, the Eucharist as a *given* which simply met at regular intervals to receive the Sacrament. Rather, the community as such was seen as flowing from eternity through the sacraments.

Because of this reciprocal link between life and liturgy, any liturgical reform must take into account the fact that the liturgy which it seeks to revise was as much, or more a cultural and ethical phenomenon, as a textual one. Now, criticisms of liturgical reform, such as those implicit in what I have just said, are often dismissed as conservative or nostalgic. But because the Vatican II reforms of the mediaeval Roman Rite failed to take into account the cultural assumptions which lay implicit within the text, their reforms participated in an entirely more sinister conservatism. For they failed to challenge those structures of the modern secular world which are wholly inimical to liturgical purpose: those structures, indeed, which perpetuate a separation of everyday life from liturgical enactment. So, the criticisms of the Vatican II revisions of the mediaeval Roman Rite contained within this section, far from enlisting a conservative horror at change, issue from a belief that the revisions were simply *not radical enough*. A successful liturgical revision would have to involve a revolutionary re-invention of language and practice which would challenge the structures of our modern world, and only thereby restore real language and action as liturgy.

What were the criticisms levelled by Jungmann and others against the Roman liturgy of the Middle Ages?

In an attempt to interrupt the drift towards decadence characteristic of the liturgical practice of the seventeenth century, the Vatican II reformers extolled the spare forms of the so-called "simple eucharistic rite" of the primitive Church. Jungmann wrote that "In contrast to the smooth-flowing eucharistic prayer recorded by Hippolytus, the Roman canon, with its separate members and steps, and its broken-up lists of saints, presents a picture of great complexity."[3] Echoing these sentiments, Louis Bouyer spoke of the "retinue of prefaces" and "incongruous veneer" of which the ancient Eucharist needed to be "divested."[4] In contrast to the Hippolytan ideal which for the reformers most embodied the antique structure of the "simple primitive meal," they complained that the Roman Rite of the Middle Ages was overburdened by an

[3] Joseph A. Jungmann, *The Mass of the Roman Rite: Its Origins and Development*, tr. Francis A. Brunner, (London: Burns and Oates, 1959), 37.
[4] Louis Bouyer, *op. cit.*, *Eucharist*, 443.

empty secular rhetoric of repetitions; its "loosely arranged" succession of oblations, prayers of intercession, petitions, and citation of apostles and martyrs, plus its random and ceaseless recommencements testified to its contamination by haphazard and decadent accretions. The mediaeval Latin liturgy seemed to consist in disorientating ambiguous overlappings between the stages of advance towards the altar of God, and a lack of clarity in the identification of the worshipper and the priest. Its repeated rites of purification and pitiful requests for mercy and assistance apparently laid a morbid and all too Augustinian emphasis on the worshipper's guilt, whereas the reformers favoured a recovery of the Greek Fathers' stress on deification and the glorification of the *cosmos*. The Roman humiliation of the worshipper before God, together with the inclusion of various ceremonial accretions, confirmed their suspicion that the Rite contained interpolation from secular court ceremonial and emperor worship, betokening a dubious politicization of the Eucharist.[5]

However, it is possible to argue that the Vatican II reformers overstated the case against the Roman Rite. This is not to deny, however, most of their case against later-mediaeval and early-modern liturgical practice and theology. One must, indeed, fervently join forces with scholars like Henri de Lubac, Michel de Certeau, John Bossy and others who critically identify the drift towards individualistic devotional practices, and the rise in liturgical spectacle – such as the displaying of the Sacraments and the decrease in the practice of lay communication.[6] Perhaps the most crucial theological alteration which precipitated a significant impoverishment of liturgical theology, as well as encouraging the centralization of clerical administration and aggrandizement of the role of the priest over against the laity, was, as we have seen, the gradual loss of the ancient three-fold understanding of the theological "body" documented in de Lubac's book, *Corpus Mysticum*.[7] However, the increasing over-emphasis on the visible and legible, on the role of priests as privileged operators of sacramental authority, and the rise of uniformity in liturgical practice, though *inaugurated* in the later-mediaeval period, are as much, or

---

[5] See Aidan Nichols, O.P., *Looking at the Liturgy*, (San Francisco: Ignatius Press, 1996), 84 n. 44.

[6] Eamon Duffy, *The Stripping of the Altars: Traditional Religion in England 1400–1580*, (New Haven: Yale University Press, 1992), 95–107; Miri Rubin, *Corpus Christi: The Eucharist in Late Medieval Culture*, (Cambridge: Cambridge University Press, 1991), 51–65.

[7] Henri de Lubac, *Corpus Mysticum: L'Eucharistie et L'Eglise au Moyen-Age*, (Paris: Aubier-Montaigne, 1949); Michel de Certeau, *The Mystic Fable*, tr. Michael B. Smith, (Chicago: Chicago University Press, 1992), 82–5; Otto Gierke, *Political Theories of the Middle Age*, (Cambridge: Cambridge University Press, 1900), 30–4.

more appropriately attributable to the early-modern period, not just to the
formalizations which took place at the Council of Trent, but other cultural
changes, such as the invention of the printing press,[8] and the concomitant
spatialization of European thought in the early Renaissance.[9]

It is therefore arguable that the Vatican II reformers were reading back into
the Middle Ages developments which, although incipiently present from
around the tenth century, primarily belonged to a later period. Moreover,
those impugned features of the liturgy which *were* indigenous to the Roman
Rite can themselves be defended.

First, as I shall argue below, the many repetitions and recommencements
in the mediaeval Roman Rite can be situated not within a context of secular
interpolation, but rather of oral provenance conjoined with an apophatic
reserve which betokens our constitutive, positive, and analogical distance
from God, rather than our sinfulness and humiliation. According to such a
perspective, the haphazard structure of the Rite can be seen as predicated upon
a need for a constant re-beginning of liturgy because the true eschatological
liturgy is in time endlessly postponed.

Other criticisms of the Roman Rite can be addressed by a deeper attention
to social and political history than was undertaken by Klauser, Jungmann, and
the others. For example, the accusation of politicization through incorporation of aspects of court ceremonial might perhaps be modified, given a re-
examination of the historical understanding of such courtly ceremonial, of the
precise understanding of the role of the emperor, and of the structure of
society implied by it. It is certainly true that mediaeval Popes and Bishops
adopted elements of court ceremonial and vestments, but if such aspects of the
ritual are examined within a larger context, it can be seen that the argument
that the liturgy was contaminated by politics is misleading. In the Middle Ages,
the monarchs were not *absolute* monarchs and were themselves included
within the liturgical congregation. Because they too had to obey divine
justice, any borrowing of court ceremonial by the ritual cannot be seen as an
unambiguous manifestation of secularization or centralization.[10] Indeed, mir-
roring the monarch's own deferral to God, the Celebrant's position was an
ambiguous one, shifting between being on the side of the congregation to
being on the side of God. He was not simply "above" the congregation, but
had to request the *assistance* of the bystanders, and was subject to a permutation

[8] See Elizabeth L. Eisenstein, *The Printing Press as an Agent of Change, Communications and
Cultural Transformations in Early-Modern Europe*, (Cambridge: Cambridge University Press,
1979).

[9] See chapter 2 above.

[10] Gierke, *op. cit.*, *Political Theories*, 30–4, 63.

of identity which, as I will argue below, is integral to a liturgical characterization of the worshipping self. Moreover, God Himself, far from being "over against" the congregation in the Rite, is represented as ambiguously "positioned" in relation both to humanity and within the Trinity.

This ambiguity of structure seems to mirror the decentred ordering of mediaeval society, for in that period there was no absolute centre of sovereignty on an immanent level. According to a model in which there is only one centre of sovereignty (a model which could be used to describe the absolutist political structure of the later-mediaeval, early-modern and baroque periods),[11] there can only be a connection with the transcendent at that central point, so that everything beneath that point is effectively secularized. However, according to the decentred and organic structure of mediaeval society, every social group was, as we have seen, formed by worship. Whilst one might at first suppose that a sacred society would have only one invested sacred centre or "site," it is to the contrary clear that a Christian society has many centres because, as manifest in the theology of the Roman Rite, the true sacred centre is unplaceable and lies beyond place itself, in God. Thus, any drift to one centre on earth causes a concomitant loss of focus on God, and whilst it is *not* clear that such a drift can be seen in the liturgy of the mediaeval Roman Rite, nor in much of what we know about mediaeval liturgical practice, it is certainly evident in the development of liturgical practice in subsequent times, from the late middle ages onwards.

A further perspective must be adopted when considering the criticism that the "simple primitive meal" of antiquity had been overburdened, and ultimately lost, by the Roman Rite. A more historico-anthropological perspective would find much that is questionable in the assumptions which provoke this criticism. The revisers' notion that the primitive eucharistic rite was originally a simple *agape* meal which served as a pre-linguistic frame for the eucharistic ritual was interpreted by the reformers in such a way as to lay stress on the link between the Eucharist and everyday life as an ordinary feast shared in common. This was an important correcting of an imbalance; however, it failed to realize that this original context can also be read the opposite way round. That is to say, this context implies that every meal should only occur *as* a ritual feast, thus drawing everyday life towards a ritual mode just as much as vice-versa. The community which prepared and enjoyed the feast was itself only bestowed in and through the liturgical celebration. Thus,

[11] Sir Robert Filmer, *Patriarcha*, ed. Johann P. Sommerville, (Cambridge: Cambridge University Press, 1991); Ernst Kantorowicz, "Mysteries of State: An Absolutist Concept and Its Late Mediaeval Origins," in *Harvard Theological Review*, 48 (1955), 65–91.

the meal could be seen as a communal activity which took place only because it was embedded in liturgical life, rather than as a liturgical form additional or subordinate to the meal, in the form of a linguistic elaboration.

Finally, I would like to suggest that the reform of the liturgy instigated by Vatican II was itself not adequate to its theology, for example, the work of de Lubac, Hans Urs von Balthasar, Yves Congar, and the influence of the restored Thomism of Etienne Gilson. In being too eager to find secularization in any forms of repetition or apophatic re-beginnings which it associated with a decadent epoch, the liturgical revisers of Vatican II chose as a liturgical paradigm a text which, as being more of a treatise *on* liturgy than a liturgy as such, would in the end prove misleading for the programme of liturgical recovery.[12] Moreover, in rejecting the features of multiple repetition, complexity of genre, instability of the worshipping subject, and continued interruption of progress by renewed prayers of penitence, under the assumption that these were secular interpolations, they ironically perpetuated certain features of the truly secularizing modern epoch.[13] For example, they imposed such anachronistic structural concepts as "argument," "linear order," "segmentation," "discrete stages," and the notion of "new information" outside "linguistic redundancy" or repetition, on a text whose provenance and theological context is wholly oral and apophatic, set within a passionate order of language which calls in order to be calling, or in hope of further calling (and not for any instrumental purpose).[14] They reacted to such complexity by

---

[12] Aidan Nichols, O.P., following Waldemar Trapp, discusses the way in which the Vatican II reformers uncritically adopted assumptions originating in the eighteenth-century Enlightenment: "Its keynotes were: a utilitarian or pragmatist philosophical infrastructure for which happiness or usefulness is the key to truth; anthropocentrism; a predominance of ethical values over strictly religious ones; a downplaying of the notion of special revelation in favour wherever possible of religion within the limits of reason; and in aesthetics an ideal of noble simplicity, *edle Einfalt,*" *op. cit., Looking at the Liturgy,* 21; see also 21–4.

[13] I have examined these themes in more detail elsewhere: "Asyndeton: Syntax and Insanity; A Study of the Revision of the Nicene Creed," *Modern Theology,* 10.4 (October, 1994), 321–40; "The Confession," *Theology,* XCIX.793 (January/February, 1997), 25–34.

[14] On attempts to disentangle the Roman Rite, see Ralph A. Keifer, "The Unity of the Roman Canon: An examination of its unique structure," *Studia Liturgica,* 11 .1 (1976), 39–58; Theodor Klauser, *A Short History of the Western Liturgy: An Account and Some Reflections;* tr. John Halliburton, (Oxford: Oxford University Press, 1969/1979); M. J. Connolly, "The Tridentine *Canon Missæ* as Framework for a Liturgical Narrative," in ed. Andrej Kodjak *et al., The Structural Analysis of Narrative Texts,* (Columbus, Ohio: Slavika Publications, 1980), 24–30. But see Jungmann, *op. cit., The Mass,* 368, and Geoffrey G. Willis, "Some Problems in the Early History of the Roman Canon Missæ," in eds

simplifying the advance towards the altar of God to a defined structure, of which J. D. Chrichton boasts: "Nothing could be simpler, nothing nearer to the eucharist of the primitive Church";[15] they ironed-out the liturgical stammer and constant re-beginning; they simplified the narrative and generic strategy of the liturgy in conformity with recognisably secular structures, and rendered simple, constant and self-present the identity of the worshipper. There are other implications which I could add to this list, but, above all, the liturgical reformers of Vatican II failed to realize that one cannot simply "return" to an earlier form, because the earlier liturgies only existed as part of a culture which was itself ritual (ecclesial-sacramental-historical) in character.

A genuine liturgical reform, therefore, would either have to overthrow our anti-ritual modernity, or, that being impossible, devise a liturgy that *refused* to be enculturated in our modern habits of thought and speech. Such enculturation, one would have to realise, can only be appropriate for a society that is itself, as a whole, subordinate to liturgical offering. But in *our* society, any "equivalent" of the liturgies before the period of baroque decadence, correctly refused by Vatican II, would have to create a liturgy which not only internally registered the need "to pray that there might be prayer" – by restoring an apophatic liturgical "stammer," and oral spontaneity and "confusion" – but also the need to pray that we again begin to live, to speak, to associate, in a liturgical, which is to say truly human and creaturely fashion. It would have more actively to challenge us through the shock of a *defamiliarizing* language, to live only to worship, and to be in community only as recipients of the gift of the body of Christ.

3 THE IMPOSSIBILITY OF LITURGY

In contrast to the "urge" of Derridean *différance*, liturgical language is neither autonomously in command of itself, nor an instrument controlled invisibly by a lurking and manipulative power.[16] Rather, its language is in several ways "impossible." For liturgy is at once a gift *from* God and a sacrifice *to* God, a reciprocal exchange which shatters all ordinary positions of agency and

C. Francis and M. Lynch, *A Voice For All Time: Essays on the Liturgy of the Catholic Church since the Second Vatican Council*, (Bristol: Association for Latin Liturgy, 1994), 157–67, on the typographical intensification of the Canon.

[15] J. D. Crichton, *Christian Celebration: The Mass, The Sacraments, The Prayer of the Church*, (London: Geoffrey Chapman, 1971/1979), I. 68.

[16] See chapters 2 and 3 above.

reception, especially as these have been conceived in the west since Scotus. Moreover, liturgical expression is made "impossible" by the breach which occurred at the Fall. This breach is the site of an apparent *aporia*, for it renders the human subject incapable of doxology, and yet, as I have suggested above in my analysis of the *Phaedrus*, the human subject is constituted (or fully central to itself) only in the dispossessing act of praise. However, the *aporia* is resolved in the person of Christ, whose resurrection ensures that our difficult liturgy is not hopeless, and enables us to rejoin the angelic liturgy taking place in an ambiguous and shifting space beyond our own. Later in this section, I will show how the Roman Rite makes manifest and surmounts the difficulty of liturgy, and discuss the peculiarly *oral* dimension of this struggle, and its implications for a negotiation of human subjectivity, space, time, and an understanding of the "name" of God. In particular, I will consider the preparatory passages of the Rite, its inaugural phrase, "*In nomine Patris et Filii et Spiritus Sancti. Amen,*" Psalm 42, the subsequent Antiphon, and the *Confiteor.*

Many liturgiologists have attempted to discern the structure of the Roman Rite, especially the Canon. Some have debated where particular sections begin and end, whilst others have complained that the apparent repetitive and haphazard structures of the Rite bear witness to the decadent impurity of subsequent interpolations, and that it is contaminated by its complicated use of Roman rhetoric. Others have sought to discern symmetry within the Rite by enumerating segments and dividing them so as to flank the centrally posited "*Qui pridie.*"[17] It is no accident that these attempts to delineate the "shape," "cohesion," or "unity" of the Rite always conclude by conceding "exceptions" to their construal, for their exercises impose the ordered precepts of spatial thinking: of category, segment, method, "unities" of place and time, beginning and end, "argument," and diagrammatical balance, upon a text which bears all the traces of an *oral* provenance, and whose shape emerges from its theological struggle to articulate itself. This struggle is embarrassing from an immanentist perspective for which language is fundamentally written and issues from a permanent, enclosed, and powerful stronghold. But it is precisely this admission of the crisis of articulation by which liturgical expression can be seen as a critique of secular modes of language and knowledge. Whilst the apparently arbitrary and repetitive structures of the Roman Rite have been criticised for being corruptions of "pure" liturgy, it is implicit in my analysis of this liturgical text that nothing is more arbitrary than the spatial suppositions as to the consummate "possibility" of human action, as expressed in such

---

[17] See section 2, and n. 14 above.

liturgy meanders toward God, stammering its praise...

complacent structures, mentioned above, as "argument," "order," "discrete stages." Indeed, unlike the view of reality implicit within immanentist language and the power of its textual permanence, the recommencements and stammer of the liturgical text are supremely but ineffably "ordered" through genuine mystery and transcendent "distance," and are by no means devoid of cohesion, purpose, or genuine surprise. In contrast to the purified asyndetic "advance" of secular discourse structure and its claim to apprehend the "real" without encumbrance, the liturgical stammer bespeaks its admission of distance between itself and the transcendent "real." It is this very admission of distance which permits a genuine proximity with God.

In the present chapter, I will begin by invoking the apparent similarity of liturgical structures to those invoked by Derrida as undergirding all language: the Roman Rite turns out to be riven with supplementations and deferrals which constitute the possibility of liturgy as simultaneously "impossible." However, I will show how this impossibility does not, as with postmodernism, indicate a suspension over the abyss, but rather, the *occurrence* of the impossible through Christological mediation, which reveals the void as a plenitude, impossibly manifest in the very course of deferral and substitution. The character of this mediation is then further described via a demonstration that the subjectivity established through worship is neither a foreclosed nor ironic – the characteristics, as we have seen, of the subject of civic ritual or "manners," but rather achieves an "analogical" identity. This will finally be shown to be possible through a liturgical balancing of writing with orality. Having thus dealt with two of my crucial dichotomies in this chapter – the ironic secular subject versus the identified liturgical subject, and secular writing versus liturgical orality, I will then deal in chapter five with liturgical time versus secular space and liturgical gift versus the secular given, before concluding, in chapter six, with a contrast of the Eucharistic reconciling of life and death, as against their secular rupture.

A summary of the mediaeval Roman Rite

Briefly, the structure of the Rite is as follows. The Fore-Mass or Entrance-Rite comprises, first of all, prayers at the foot of the altar, including a recitation of Psalm 42 on the way to the altar, and two orations added in conclusion, followed by various *apologiæ*. Amongst these were numbered the *Confiteor*, and attendant *Misereatur*, the absolution, and the Versicles. Following on were the greetings, and the reverential kissing, first of the Altar, and then the Gospel book and Crucifix. Because, from the beginning of the Middle Ages, the Altar doubled as a sepulchre or reliquary, the Kissing of the Altar was combined with a private prayer, said by the Priest, in memory of the martyrs, together with a prayer in longing for purification from sin, reminiscent of the prayers said at the foot of the altar. After the incensing of the altar came an *Introit* chant, followed by the *Kyrie* and *Gloria*. Next, in an oration by the Priest in which he "collects" the preceding prayers of the people and presents them to God, the priest addresses the congregation with a *Dominus Vobiscum* and a summons to prayer.

The second main movement of the Rite, still within the Fore-Mass, and with the Catechumens still present, was the Service of Readings. This comprised the Epistle (followed by the *Deo Gratias*, and intervenient Chants and responses), the Gradual sequence, and then the Gospel reading, including its stately escort and responses. Finally, the Sermon, the *Credo*, and the dismissal of the Catechumenate concluded the Fore-Mass.

The Offertory or oblation-rite commenced with the procession of the people, accompanied by chants, echoing the entrance procession of the clergy, and foreshadowing that of the communion. The action of laying upon the altar the Offerings of bread and wine was accompanied by a notoriously complex succession (or what Jungmann calls a "veritable jungle")[18] of prayers. These included prayers for God's acceptance of our oblation, prayers for our worthiness both to make and to receive such an offering, a list of the redemptive mysteries commemorated, the mention of saints, and the blessing and incensing of the elements. One of the few fixed points which recur unchanged in all the mediaeval oblation rites is a petition by the Priest for the prayer of the bystanders, the *Orate Fratres*, just at the moment when the presentation and arrangement of the gifts is completed. After this came the so-called Secret, a prayer concluding the rite of oblation.

The Canon, or Eucharistic Prayer, came next, opening with the introductory dialogue and an invitation to a prayer of thanks, and concluding with the acclamation, *Dignum et iustum est*. This is taken up again at the beginning of the Preface, as a declaration of the propriety of giving thanks. The prayer is one of gratitude, which must be paid always and everywhere. And our praise is finally joined with that of the heavenly choirs, so that the Preface then spills over into the *Sanctus* and *Benedictus*. Next, the *Te igitur*, or plea for acceptance, is followed by the general intercessory prayers, the very thorough *Memento* of the Living, and then the complementary *Communicantes*, or invocation of the kinship of the Saints. The *Hanc igitur*, yet another prayer for acceptance, culminates in a final doxological swell, in the form of a plea for the ultimate hallowing of the earthly gift, before the account of the Institution.

---

[18] Jungmann, *op. cit.*, *The Mass*, 335.

Technically, therefore, this prayer, *Quam oblationem*, is the *epiklesis*, or plea for consecration. This plea is then instantly granted in the Institution Narrative, whose accompanying gestures and the veneration of the *anamnesis* and sacrificial prayer, the *Unde et memores*, which follow, make it clear that this simple account *is* the consecration or re-enactment. Two further prayers, asking that God look favourably upon our offerings – invoking the sacrificial precedents of Abel, Abraham, and Melchisedech – and that He bid our sacrifice to be borne to the Heavenly Altar, trace exhaustively each step of the sacrifice just performed, and further confound Josef Jungmann who imagines that after the gifts have been consecrated and changed, it would not be unreasonable to assume their acceptance by God.[19] After we have prayed for the dead, we then pray for ourselves (*Nobis quoque*), that we may obtain a part with the Saints of heaven. The Canon then closes with two doxologies, both of which give the impression of summary and conclusion.

Next, the *Pater Noster* (with its final embolism or interpolation) served as a preparation for the assembled people for the reception of Holy Communion. It was followed by the Fraction of the Host, and its commingling with the wine in the Chalice. This was succeeded by the kiss of peace, after which began at once the singing of the *Agnus Dei*. Next came the Communion of the Priest, and then of the Faithful, together with certain preparatory prayers. This was often accompanied by a chant. After the post-reception prayers, and ablution-rite, came a general prayer of thanksgiving, blessing, and then the formal Dismissal. Aside from various remaining ritual and prayers for the clergy, including the Last Gospel and Recession, that was the end of the mass.

In what follows, I shall attempt to fuse a continuous line of argument with a comprehensive line by line (but not entirely consecutive) reading of the text of the mediaeval Roman Rite.

The journey's name

In chapter 1, I discussed the establishment of a link between *topos* and *genus*, place and lineage, in the opening question of Plato's *Phaedrus*, "*poi dē kai pothen?*" This question is posed at the mid-point of a journey, reversing the chronological order of origin and destination, to suggest that the place of origin which constitutes a person's identity is a supplementary place characterized by its open-endedness and recursive structure. Implicit within this question, therefore, is a critique of any claim to a singular, unaltering, anterior origin. For the journey subsequent to the origin is as much constitutive of that

---

[19]   *Ibid.*, 434–41.

origin as it is dependent upon it. And here the "second" is not merely that which arrives too late to be first, but is that which permits the "first" its priority, in such a way that its constitutive force of delay prevents the origin's primitive autonomy. Thus, Socrates' opening question suggests not only that the origin cannot be seen as a tranquil, unambiguous, and interior identity, but also, that human subjectivity is not a self-contained "given" anterior to its performance, but that its subsequent performances are just as much involved in the constitution of its identity.

There is a similar coincidence of identity and journey in the opening words of the Roman Rite, "*In nomine Patris et Filii et Spiritus Sancti. Amen,*" which communicate a particular liturgical construal of the subject, and the difficulty of its passage.[20] These words constitute an ambiguous beginning in several ways. Despite being words by which the liturgy is "begun," they are themselves testimony to the supplement at the origin, for they are spoken by the Priest even *before* the liturgy proper.[21] Moreover, they enact an affirmation whose content is unspecific, lacking both verbal temporality and agency. This beginning invokes two contradictory journeys: a sending out of God and a going into God. It instantiates both a commission bearing divine authority, and an unmoving invocation of divine protection and subsumption within the name of the Father, Son, and Holy Spirit. This hierarchical confusion is also a spatial confusion, for there is ambiguity as to whether the speaker is inside or outside the name he at once boasts and invokes. Furthermore, this doubly-dislodged "outset," devoid of specific temporality, is to become a *repeated outset* throughout the Rite.

This "name" is itself a very uncertain place, for how can one be situated inside a name unless it is a name one carries about wherever one goes? And in order to be inside a name, it must be an unusual name which opens up. The name in which the speaker is situated is that of the Father, Son, and Holy Spirit. This is a difficult name. Whilst ordinary names are often multiple, they refer unambiguously to a particular person, and are extrinsically affixed after the event of birth. And although such nominations are constitutive of social being, they are not emergent or epiphanic names contemporaneous with being itself. However, this name is a triple name, three different names which do not exactly name three differently named beings. The liturgical proceedings are not enacted "In the names," for the three names are really only one name

---

[20] Bernard Botte and Christine Mohrmann, *L'Ordinaire de la Messe*, (Paris: Editions du Cerf, 1953), 58.

[21] I am grateful to Dr Eamon Duffy for drawing attention to this point. Jungmann, *op. cit.*, *The Mass*, 202.

which is non-identically repeated, a name which is also a journey, for the Father is the journey of the generation of the Son from which the Spirit proceeds. This name is therefore not a static name affixed outside being, but is an essential name commensurate with the existential space of the Trinitarian journey. In contrast to the nominalizations of immanentist language which disallow or eventually cancel alteration, multiplicity, and temporality, this name understands and inaugurates the *journey* of lineage, and the *narrativity* of naming. And unlike the "powerful" wielding of totalizing names, this liturgical language of naming bespeaks the impossibility of immediacy, recognizing through its complex protocols of address that to name is already to distance oneself.

The impossible name then passes or journeys forth in the word *"Amen."*[22] This word is not merely a statement of veracity, but Truth's own performance, which accounts for the inadequacy and subsequent rejection of the Septuagint's translation of the Hebrew root, 'MN, ("steadfast," "true") as *genoito* ("would that it were so") and *alēthinos* ("it is not false") which were seen as too negative. The word *"Amen"* is continuous with the *event* of truth: "Thus saith the Amen."[23] It is also testament to the ambiguity of origination, for the Amen is "the faithful and true witness, the source of the creation of God,"[24] simultaneously witness and source, both outside and inside, the manifestation of the beginning within the conclusion, the commencement which perpetually returns anew. This Amen is the language in common between God and worshipper, for it is at once the incarnational bodying forth of God and the true human response to God: "In [Jesus] is the Amen by us to the glory of God."[25] In both respects, it is also eschatological, for Amen is the site of the dawning of the Messianic age, the presence of the Kingdom, constantly on Jesus' lips: "Amen, Amen, I say unto you."[26]

Within the opening doxology, therefore, there are two different attempts to begin, both of which, although uttered privately by the priest, are not unambiguously human in perspective, for God is both the name in which the unnamed speaker travels, and the Amen. The Priest and Ministers then repeat the outset in a dialogic form, *"Introibo ad altare Dei. / Ad Deum qui lætificat iuventutem meam"*[27] (a versicle which is to be taken up again and again, with difference), and although they are specific speakers, they are not specifically

22 Botte and Mohrmann, *op. cit.*, *L'Ordinaire*, 58.
23 Revelation 3:14.
24 Botte and Mohrmann, *op. cit.*, *L'Ordinaire*, 58; cf *idem.*, *L'Excursus I: Amen*, 97f.
25 II Corinthians 1:20.
26 Dom Gregory Dix, *The Shape of the Liturgy*, (London: Dacre Press, 1045),129–30.
27 [*I will go unto the altar of God/ Unto the Lord who giveth joy to my youth.*]

named. They all undertake the same journey together, and are named by the name of their journey, which is none other than a difficult journeying name.

The deictic ambiguity of these assertions gives rise to a radicalization of space, not only manifested in the identity of the speaking "I" as he who travels *within* (the name of) that which he travels *towards*, but also, in and through the nature of the journey's destination, and its constitutive relation with the speaker.

The problematic altar

What is the nature of the journey's destination, the *"altare Dei"*? Unlike ordinary geographical destinations, the altar of God is an infinitely receding place, always vertically beyond, in the sense of *altaria*, a raised place where offerings were upwardly burnt, possibly linked in Latin to *adolēre* ("to burn in sacrifice"), *adolēscere* ("to burn") and the concomitant sensual diffusion of *olēre* ("odour").[28] This raised place of sacrificial burning is the site where offerings are altered and transubstantiated. Indeed, the place of the *altaria* itself undergoes alteration for it continually borrows from itself. At first the word referred to a receptacle placed *upon* the altar to hold the offerings before a sacrifice, but it was later synecdochally transferred to the whole place of alteration. Thus, the altar cannot be conceived as the fixed launching pad for vertical apotheoses, but is itself always already an apotheosis, already upwardly transfiguring before we could even have instigated such a movement. Hence, the site itself has always gone before us, has always, in anticipating our offerings, moved beyond our steps and above the level of our gaze. The altar is therefore a supplementary, and, in worldly terms, superfluous destination which is also a beginning, the place towards which we must travel in order to be able to offer our sacrifice of praise. It follows that the liturgy of our text is always about to begin, not in a "hollowed out" sense, but as a necessarily deferred anticipation of the heavenly worship towards which we strive. Our liturgy in time can only be the liturgy we render in order to be able to render liturgy.

But within this context of "impossibility," how is the worshipping "I" identified? We have already seen that the "I," impersonated by both the Priest and the Ministers, identifies himself by means of his situation in a particular

---

[28] *Oxford Latin Dictionary*, eds A. Souter *et al.*, (Oxford: Clarendon Press, 1968); *Dictionary of Medieval Latin from British Sources*, ed. R. E. Latham, (Oxford: Oxford University Press, 1975); *A Greek-English Lexicon*, eds H. G. Liddell and R. Scott, (Oxford: Clarendon Press, 1871/1990); G. W. H. Lampe, *A Patristic Greek Lexicon*, (Oxford: Clarendon Press, 1961).

(mobile) place, within and towards the Trinitarian name; a place itself identified as that which travels towards the altar of God. Thus the question "where am I?" precedes "who am I?" underlining the embodied nature of the worshipper, and the importance of place and physicality.[29] But its constitutive location in space is by no means a totalizing occupation. For this space, neither static nor abstract, is mobile, ensuring that the identity of the "I" is *in medias res*, not established prior to the journey but contemporaneously with its pilgrimage. Ahead of identification, therefore, is the journey whose apparent assertion of power "*In nomine Patris et Filii et Spiritus Sancti*" is self-erasing by virtue of its act of borrowing: the distancing effect of impersonation at once confirms the provisionality of power and the surmounting of weakness.

If the identity of the worshipper is radically affected by the ever-receding altar which requires perpetual recommencement of the journey, it is equally affected by the fact that the journey towards the altar instantiates, and is made possible by, a movement of God towards the worshipper.

The complexity of this relation can be seen in the double framing of the repetition of the versicle, "*Introibo ad altare Dei./ Ad Deum qui lætificat iuventutem meam.*" The initial assertion of the journey is framed, as we have seen, by the Trinitarian Name, which dislodges our deictic security: are we inside or outside? What is our place? The first re-assertion of the Antiphon occurs only shortly afterwards in the recitation by the Priest and Ministers of Psalm 42,[30] but in an entirely different context. For whilst the journey began in an exalted locus ("*In nomine. . .*"), the opening of the psalm suggests a far greater distance from God: "*Iudica me, Deus.*" This "judge me" opens a threefold distance. First, God is now summoned as a distinct subject, a "Thou," rather than as that within which the "I" travels. Secondly, this distance is not only that between two interlocutors, an "I" and a "Thou," but is of an hierarchical cast, for the distance is that which obtains between the judge and the judged. And, thirdly, it constitutes an apostrophic beckoning, a plea for proximity, which is at first apparently unsuccessful: "*Quare me repulsti?*"[31]

These qualifications of the traveller's strength and security are supplemented by the following lines of the psalm which communicate the complexity of the journey: "*Emitte lucem tuam et veritatem tuam : ipsa me deduxerunt et adduxerunt in montem sanctum tuum. . . .*"[32] Here, in asking God to send His

---

[29] Jean-Yves Lacoste, *Expérience et Absolu*, (Paris: P.U.F., 1994), 7–49.

[30] Psalm 43, according to the Book of Common Prayer.

[31] [*Why do you cast me off?*]

[32] [*O send out Thy light and Thy truth : let them lead me and let them bring me unto Thy holy hill.*]

light and truth in order to lead the worshipper to God, the "I" vocalizes more precisely the aporetic impossibility of liturgy: our journey towards God cannot begin before its ending, before God Himself has journeyed towards us. Hence, the reason why the altar perpetually recedes is that to arrive at the place of worship, of divine presence, we must *already be in that place*. Yet it is as if this more precise expression of impossibility constitutes its partial surmounting, for the journey then begins again but with all the difference of a repetition: "*Et introibo ad altare Dei : ad Deum qui lætificat iuventutem meam.*" Thus it becomes difficult to accord priority either to our journey towards God or His movement towards us, an ambiguity which precipitates a reappraisal of the nature of "arrival," both insofar as we must now comprehend "arrival" as that which is perpetually repeated, and the beginning of a journey as in some sense contemporaneous with arrival at its destination. For "*introibo*" is an announcement of intention, an arrival *at*, and an entering *into*.[33]

But despite this new confidence, the text re-issues the distension of space, and the impossibility of our commission, for after the completion of the psalm, the Priest again repeats the Antiphon, "*Introibo ad altare Dei.*"[34] This inverts both previous beginnings, since despite the fact that the psalm concludes with the secure locus of the rendering of glory, it seems that we are still only *on the way* to the place where glory can be offered. This third repetition is made different by virtue of its increased Christological emphasis: "*Adiutorium nostrum in nomine Domini*,"[35] which links the Lord's "name" to God's journey towards us, and offers a typological reading of Psalm 42, according to which the "*Adiutorium*" retrospectively consummates our "*Spera in Deo.*"[36] Thus, this last reference to God's name brings about a new perspective, for, on the one hand, Christ enables us to journey towards the altar of God, and, on the other hand, this true "way" which He opens for us is itself the altar of God, since Christ only mediates God by being fully God. Whereas previously in the text, liturgical impossibility seemed to betoken a bad infinite according to which sinful man in time could never arrive because he could never start out, now it seems that to be in the time of sin is nonetheless to dwell in a kenotic space in which we have always already unknowingly arrived. Thus, the prior inversions – arriving is beginning, the goal is the journey – are now themselves inverted: to begin is to arrive, the way is the goal. And one can only ever have begun; there is no other way to be than to be on the way.

---

[33] "Arrival" is not a static attainment: "*et circumdabo altare tuum, Domine*" [*I will compass Thine altar, O Lord*], Botte and Mohrmann, *op. cit., L'Ordinaire*, 70.

[34] *Ibid.*, 60.

[35] [*Our help standeth in the name of the Lord.*]

[36] [*Hope in God.*]

The time of purification

So far, I have illustrated the impossibility of liturgy by concentrating on the inceptive repetitions of particular lines at the opening of the Rite. But these are balanced by larger, structural re-beginnings which recur throughout. Naturally, in accordance with the terms of most sacrificial cultures, the prelude to arriving at an altar is not simply a temporo-spatial journey, but also a *preparation of the self*, a putting-on or putting-off to render oneself fit for, or partially protected from the divine presence; in other words, a process of purification. Thus, in the Roman Rite, this process is also continuously re-enacted.

The first explicit request for purification is the "*Confiteor*" which, following the invocation of the power of God's name, "*Adiutorium nostrum in nomine Domini./ Qui fecit cœlum et terram,*"[37] assimilates purification with recreation. After the Confession and Absolution, we ask twice to be recreated, first, in "*perducat te ad vitam æternam*"[38] and then in the versicle address to God, "*Deus tu conversus vivificabis nos.*"[39] This short antiphonal section concludes with a dialogic exchange of the Spirit between the Priest and Ministers: "*Dominus vobiscum./ Et cum spiritu tuo*"[40] which would suggest an attainment of purification. But as soon as we arrive at this state of purity, sufficient to bless one another in this way, we must again repeat our request for purification, in an oration which recommences our journey to God: "*Aufer a nobis, quæsumus Domine, iniquitates nostras : ut ad Sancta sanctorum puris mereamur mentibus introire.*"[41] This particular incantation reveals that the distended place towards which we travel is so pure that our travelling towards it becomes continuous with an act of purifying divestment. Does this suggest that in order to obtain our goal, we must find an entrance within ourselves? In that case, one would be confronted with an ambiguity of within and without which problematizes once again the possibility of prayer, for in requiring purification in order to enter the inner sanctuary – which, it seems, is the only place where prayer can be offered felicitously – one must already be within that inner sanctuary in a state of impossible purity. The prayer just cited, therefore, is a prayer that we might be able to pray. Thus, liturgy is not only a difficult language, but it is an expectant work, the hope that there might be a liturgy. Indeed, it seems that up until now, our liturgical text has consisted in prayers for the removal

---

[37] [*Our help is in the name of the Lord. / Who hath made heaven and earth.*]
[38] [*bring thee to everlasting life.*]
[39] [*Wilt Thou not turn and quicken us*]; Botte and Mohrmann, *op. cit.*, *L'Ordinaire*, 60–2.
[40] [*The Lord be with you. / And with thy spirit.*]
[41] [*Take away from us, we beseech Thee O Lord, our iniquities : that we may be worthy to enter the Holy of Holies with pure minds*]; *ibid.*, 62.

of hindrances to prayer: the removal of enemies impeding the pilgrim's path, the sending of light and truth, a request that God heed our prayer to be able to pray, and a request for purification to be able to enter the locus of prayer. Furthermore, this request is followed by an invocation not only of Christ, but of many other helpers, "*per merita Sanctorum tuorum*,"[42] appealing for the Saints' contagion of merit to effect further purging. Thus, no sooner have we been offered Christological solace for the impossibility of the journeying, by invoking Christ who has made our sinful condition itself a place of arrival, than a new obstacle appears to be placed in our path. Christ, within the time of sin, could travel and arrive, because in the midst of sin He was pure. To travel with Him, then, we must ourselves be pure as He was, and yet, it seems, we are never pure enough. Indeed, there are no real degrees of purity; purity is absolute, and it seems that to have lost purity, will be forever to have lost the secret of knowing how to regain it. We can only cry for it, in a futile gesture.

However, if ritual purification is divestment of impurities, it is also revestment in a borrowed, glorious outer covering fit for divine presence. Hence, to the requests for purgation, succeeds the blessing of the incense, which, before we can offer it to God as smoke, must descend upon us as a heavenly cloud, echoing all the Biblical instances of transfiguration. But just as purification cannot be undertaken once and for all, and becomes, like the journey, an infinitely receding task, so also, incense is forever destined to vanish. The incense and thurible are indeed objects "at hand," and the Celebrant addresses them as such: "*Ab illo benedicaris, in cuius honore cremaberis*,"[43] yet they are there to enact the displacement of solid matter into ascending smoke.[44] Here again, however, we have a repetition with difference. For this temporalization through burning of the object does not take place through divestment towards an abstract or ideal interior "life," but first through a revesting of us by the cloud of divine glory, and then through the inevitable ascent of this cloud which unites life and death as resurrection. The invocation of resurrection is then echoed by the ninefold turns of the *Kyrie* which follow the order of salvation history, first invoking the mercy of the Lord of creation, then of Christ, the saving Messiah, and finally, the ascended Lord.[45] This entire sequence, from incense to *Kyrie*, ensures a Christological resumption of the theme of purification, just as earlier there was a Christological resumption of the theme of liturgical journey. And again, the "bad infinite" is overcome: we *can* enter into purification because we are not

[42] [*through the merits of Thy saints.*]
[43] [*By Him be thou blessed/ in whose honour thou shalt be burned.*]
[44] *Ibid.* 62.
[45] *Ibid.*, 62; Jungmann, *op. cit.*, *The Mass*, 223–31, especially 227.

simply purified *like* Christ, but, through the gift of the Spirit, invoked by the incense, we *put on* Christ's own purity. The cloud of divine embodiment descends upon us, revesting us in a holy garment. But to be clothed with this cloud is also to be consumed: here, to live is equally to die, and without conflict between the two, because it is no longer merely to decay in time, but to leave time as resurrected and ascended.

Thus the repetition of Christ's saving action seems at first to have consummated all preceding requests for purification, for at the beginning of the *Gloria*, with the words "*GLORIA in excelsis Deo*," we *seem* finally to have reached the beginning of doxology and to have attained angelic status, through our upward ascent.[46] Yet by means of a scarcely perceptible transition between two clauses, which hinges upon the double signification of the word "*Domine*," our exaltation slips from doxology ("*Domine Deus, rex cælestis, Deus Pater omnipotens*")[47] to abasement before Christ ("*Domine Fili unigenite, Iesu Christe. Domine Deus, Agnus Dei, Filius Patris. Qui tollis peccata mundi, miserere nobis.*")[48] This slippage reminds us of two related aspects of the nature of doxology. First, it recalls our lapsed condition which persists, despite the incarnation. Accordingly, we can only *impersonate* angelic voices and must continuously ask to be purified through Christ, since our purification is not yet complete, and, therefore, in some sense not yet genuine at all.

However, the requests for purification embedded in the *Gloria* represent a subtly communicated advance in our difficult journey. The twice repeated request "*miserere nobis*" in the *Gloria* occurs quite suddenly, mid-sentence, after a cumulative chain of apostrophic identifications. In contrast to these modes of petition and apostrophe, Christ is identified in a constative mode, "*Qui tollis peccata mundi*," which implies that, in the eternal present, his taking away of our sins has "already" been accomplished, that purification is now

---

[46] Botte and Mohrmann, *op. cit.*, *L'Ordinaire*, 62–4. Luke 2:14. Although in mediaeval liturgical practice, at High Mass it was the Priest (*in medio altaris* just as the angel at Bethlehem stood *in medio eorum*: Jungmann, *The Mass*, 239 n. 3) who intoned the *Gloria* (VOCE SUBMISSA: loud enough to be heard by those around, but not so loud as to disturb the singing), it was said on *behalf* of the congregation, and so I include the latter in its semiotic effects, as also for the other prayers in which the congregation was not a direct participant. For how can one assign a limit to the reach of liturgical expression? Adrian Fortesque and J. B. O'Connell, *The Ceremonies of the Roman Rite Described*, (London: Burns Oates and Washbourne Ltd, 1932), 127–9. See also, Jungmann, *The Mass*, 278 on the participation of the people in Responses.

[47] [*O Lord God, heavenly King, God the Father almighty.*]

[48] [*O Lord, the only-begotten Son, Jesus Christ. O Lord God, Lamb of God, Son of the Father, That takest away the sins of the world, have mercy upon us.*]

possible. The appeals of the *Kyrie*, therefore, are now transposed into a more affirmative context, (since in the *Kyrie*, the context of salvation history was only implicit), for each appeal for mercy in the *Gloria* is issued in the context of the various (explicit) stages of salvation. First, we appeal to the Lamb of God, Son of the Father, as he who takes away the sins of the world, and, secondly, to the risen, ascended, and glorified Christ ("*Qui sedes ad dexteram Patris. . . .*")[49] By tracing these stages, we are again within the perspective of eternity, for at the end of the *Gloria*, our voices re-enter angelic worship: "*Tu solus Altissimus . . . ,*"[50] praising that which is most high, the altar of God, the only place where worship can be given, the only "true" place there is. The world itself seems to have become displaced by this doxological accumulation, for in the following prayer, after the Epistle, the Deacon prays for purification of his heart and lips, with the words "*Munda cor meum. . . .*"[51] This word *Munda* implies a request not only for purification (*mundus*), but also a request to be *worlded*, to be offered as a citizen of the world (*mundanus, municeps*), as a gift (*munerari*), and as a liturgy (*muneris*), offered to the world as a figure of the gift of purification. And so our momentary attainment of exaltation is indistinguishable from a moment of supposedly "preparatory" purification, since the condition for admission into the divine presence is to ad-mit that we require purging. This admission being made, we discover that we are already within the place of purity, and that our travelling through time is already the offering of ourselves to God. After Christological resolution of the bad infinite of purification, whereby we are "already" purified, we nonetheless admit the infinite task of fully appropriating that new garment which we already possess. Our retracing of the way of Christ is the work of the Holy Spirit and, in this new "spiritual" time, glorification and renewed abasement and purification ceaselessly oscillate, and yet ineffably coincide.

The same dialectic of exaltation and subsidence or self-abasement occurs throughout the Rite, illustrating not only the difficulty of worship, but also the ambiguous nature of its various "stages."[52] In this case, as with that of the

---

[49] [*Who sittest at the right hand of the Father.*]

[50] [*You alone are the most high.*]

[51] [*Cleanse (world) my heart*]; Botte and Mohrmann, *op. cit.*, *L'Ordinaire*, 64.

[52] This ambiguity is clearly indicated by early manuscripts of the Rite, in which there were no separate paragraphs and what we now discern as "sections" were at one time indistinguishable from one another. See Keifer, *op. cit.*, "The Unity of the Roman Canon." The fact that the liturgical journey was unsegmented explains why nearly every paragraph of the Canon begins with a subordinating or co-ordinating conjunction: "*Te igitur,*" "*Quam oblationem,*" "*Qui pridie,*" by a deictic marker of familiarity, "*Hanc igitur oblationem,*" or by proximous repetitions, such as the Celebrant's doubling of "*Vere dignum et iustum est.*"

liturgical journey, the passage of the worshipper's advance is not construed as unicursally progressive, nor as undertaken by one worshipping voice alone, but as stuttering, constantly retracing its syllables, and calling for aid by means of many voices.

The other offering

Here we can invoke once again the general pattern of ritual sacrifice common to many different cultures, in order to underline the *strangeness* of this Christian ritual, and the way it violates this pattern's linearity. In terms of such a pattern, after the supplicant has advanced towards the altar and undergone purification, he then *offers* that which is to be sacrificed on behalf of others. Before it is offered, the offering must itself undergo purification, or consecration. According to liturgiological scholarship, this conventional ritual pattern is echoed in the Christian mass. Thus, the Consecration of the elements is supposed to follow *after* the Offertory. However, an examination of the lineaments of these episodes in the Roman Rite, reveals that the movement of Offertory of bread and wine continues *through* the Consecration, and is then reasserted, in intensified form, in the Memorial, as now the offering of the Body and Blood.[53] This single movement of offering first the "symbolic" and then the "real" is fully in accord with the mediaeval non-separation of the two, as described by de Lubac.[54] At the same time, what seems to be a "second offering" is but the consummation of the action of Consecration which, by definition, does not occur outside the effects of repetition. Any alternative account which, encouraged by the spatial segmentation of the text, treats these movements as discrete sections, necessarily falls into a debased theology according to which it appears as if, in response to a divine miracle, the priest makes again to God a sacrifice of his Son.

The diverse and reciprocal movements of offering *within* the Consecration suggest a liturgical radicalization of subjectivity (as that which is "completed" only by means of a perpetual re-entering of God); of what constitutes an "action"; and of a certain negotiation of movement through space and time. The "first" movement of the Consecration proper, linked causally by the "*TE igitur*" to the preceding Offertory, constitutes a request that God accept and bless the offerings of bread and wine. This inaugurates a double movement of reception and giving, for God's benediction of the bread and wine constitutes a giving of the elements *to themselves*, by enabling them to enter further into God's presence.

[53] Botte and Mohrmann, *op. cit.*, *L'Ordinaire*, 72–6.
[54] See previous chapter.

This is the case because that which is offered *to* God must, by virtue of the contagion of transcendence, become one *with* God, and so the request that God bless that which is offered to Him as gift is tantamount to a request that God bless Himself. At the same time, that which enters into the presence of God to the point of becoming one with Him, also becomes more fully itself.

This extreme movement into God is itself cast as ambiguous, for it is balanced, in the following commemoration of the living, "*Memento Domine,*" by a more this-worldly emphasis, in the offering of the "*sacrificium laudis*" on behalf of the earthly Church, which involves specific mention of particular people.[55] However, this shift towards proximity involves a further inversion, for in returning to our lateral reality, by offering on behalf of others ("*vel qui tibi offerunt hoc sacrificium laudis*")[56] – a wholly gratuitous gift since the offering we offer on their behalf is offered by them as well – we enter further into God, into the kenotic path of Christological presence (which constitutes the Church). With each offering of gift, a further connection is established between donor, donation, and donee, who, as transcendent, is the condition of possibility for all acts of donation. Thus, the complexity of offering as it occurs in the liturgy ensures that our doxological journey is not undertaken solely in an other-worldly or ideal direction, but is concerned with real individuals, both living and dead, and the earthly Church as a whole.

Furthermore, the apparent other-worldly direction is *constitutive* of our lateral proximity, and of genuine human action. For, by offering praise on behalf of other members of the Church, we bring them into being, give them to themselves by giving voice to the distant. And yet, this offering by proxy is entirely superfluous, for God already knows of their faith and devotion: "*quorum tibi fides cognita est et nota devotio.*"[57] Just as the Christian supplicant

---

[55] Botte and Mohrmann, *op. cit.*, *L'Ordinaire*, 76.

[56] [*or who themselves offer unto Thee this sacrifice of praise.*]

[57] [*whose faith is approved and devotion is known unto Thee.*] On liturgical offering as beyond utility, see Jean-Yves Lacoste, "*De la Technique à la Liturgie: un pas ou deux hors de la Modernité,*" *Communio* 11.2 (1984), 26–37: "Man has something better to do than *to do*"; "The unusable is perhaps the only condition under which work can be fundamentally non-alienatory." (Lacoste offers a somewhat ambivalent reading of gift, however, in which he seems to suggest that the subject has an identity prior to his liturgical self-offering, and insists upon something contemplatively given, rather than on God arriving to us in our activity of giving rise to words in praise of God. If such praise opens up the world as creation, as Lacoste suggests, then *all* work, to be non-alienatory, must be liturgical. Otherwise, we would be alienated whilst we "worked" and then re-united with ourselves in subsequent acts of liturgy. Furthermore, it is not clear whether Lacoste holds that all liturgical "making" is simultaneously a giving and a receiving, or whether, for him, one first makes and then gives.)

must, uniquely, arrive before he can travel, by being arrived at, and be purified in advance of purification, so also his offering is only made by the one to whom he offers and who includes his own self, as constituted only through offering. Therefore, in the Christian liturgy, we are only enabled to give, or to pay what is our sacrificial due, when this gift is superfluous, no longer due, but coterminous with the given excess which we already are.

4 THE APOSTROPHIC VOICE

For a secular critique, the perpetual renewal of commencement, the unfulfilled imperative of purification, and now the superfluity of gift which is never enough and always too much, might appear to dissolve the subject, and render meaningful human action impossible. However, an alternative, specifically *liturgical* construal of these circumstances is possible, because liturgy transfigures our notions of genuine human action. More specifically, it refuses altogether the post-Cartesian understanding of action, which assumes that a self-present and yet punctual and empty, undefined subject acts by mastering a clearly grasped but inert object. This Cartesian picture is not refused by "postmodern" thought, but both deconstructed and intensified; deconstructed, because the lack of presence-to-self and unambiguous presence of the object means that human action is dissolved into the flux of "partial objects" or of signs and non-independent events. It thereby becomes a pre-constituted, deferred, and excessive subject of just the kind which liturgy *seems* to invoke. However, the Cartesian subject is also, in consequence of this deconstruction, intensified in its punctual emptiness, that nullity which turns out to be its most enduring characteristic. And, equally, as was seen in chapter 3, the void undergirding the flux is a perfect reduction, in its clear nullity and spatial emptiness, of the Cartesian object. In knowing this nullity, the postmodern subject still acts, if he does authentically act at all, by commanding the object.

By contrast, I will show how the liturgical subject avoids this postmodern lack of identity. It will be seen that he does so because the liturgical understanding of action, unlike that of postmodernity, is genuinely non-Cartesian. The subject is not, for this vision, empty, but does indeed have a substantive, though not completed identity. However, if it has such an identity, it can only be achieved and manifest in action (since there is no "private" sphere other than action), and this action cannot be the manipulation of represented objects – "modern" action – for the correlative of such action is emptiness. Liturgical action, in consequence, must concern something *other than objects*, and it follows that if we are to understand how a liturgical subject can have an identity, we must first understand "the liturgical object," though, to be sure, that is the wrong term.[58]

At the end of chapter 2, I showed how the Cartesian dichotomy of subject and object eventually penetrates everyday language and practice in the form of the ever-increased prevalence of the trope of nominalization in a linguistic system whose syntax is dominated by asyndetic forms. It has already been seen how liturgical use of repetition refuses any discrete procedure from point to point, and hence stands in total contrast to the modern preference for asyndeton. Now it will be shown how liturgical discourse substitutes for nominalization, the figure of *apostrophe*.

What is the figure of apostrophe, and what are the implications of its use in the Roman Rite for a theory of liturgy? Apostrophe, which in Greek means "turning away," is a rhetorical figure used to signify vocative address to an absent, dead, or wholly other person, idea, or object. It is characteristic of dramatic and exclamatory styles of discourse, and is supremely vocal and emotive.[59] And whilst it constitutes a calling to be heard by that which is absent, it is also, in the context of liturgical enactment, a *communal* figure: it is both heard and overheard.

In the Roman Rite there are two main types of apostrophe. First, there are invocations which seek assistance for projects related to the vocation of the liturgical journey. These tend to occur within petitional prayers, requesting purification, assistance, or acceptance of an offering: "*Iudica me, Deus, et discerne causam meam . . .*"; "*Emitte lucem tuam. . . .*"[60] Secondly, there are functionally gratuitous apostrophic identifications. Because this latter type is removed from the economy of utility, it is more readily assimilable to the character of language as gift, or *sacrificium laudis*, and takes the form not of a petition but a calling which, like music, both *invokes* and *attracts*. It instantiates a sensual calling which, without instrumental purpose, represents the dislodging of language from diurnal orders of reasoning. The apostrophic voice calls in order to be calling, or in the hope of a further calling, and is thus situated within an expectant and passionate order of language: "*Confiteor tibi in cithara, Deus Deus meus,*" "*Domine Fili unigenite, Iesu Christe. Domine Deus, Agnus Dei, Filius Patris.*"[61]

---

[58] This priority of the question of the object acknowledges the priority of Cartesian ontology over the Cartesian *Cogito* described in chapter 2.

[59] Katie Wales, *Dictionary of Stylistics*, (London: Longman, 1989), 32; James Paxson, *The Poetics of Personification*, (Cambridge: Cambridge University Press, 1994), *passim*; J. A. Cuddon, *A Dictionary of Literary Terms*, (London: André Deutsch, 1977), 51–2.

[60] [*Judge me, O God, and plead my cause*]; [*O send your light*]; Botte and Mohrmann, *op. cit.*, *L'Ordinaire*, 58.

[61] [*On the harp will I praise Thee, O God my God*]; [*O Lord, the only begotten Son, Jesus Christ. O Lord God, Lamb of God, Son of the Father*]; *ibid.*, 58, 64.

The gift-character of the second type of apostrophic address is very similar to the structure of liturgy itself, in its perpetual acts of postponement, and casting as the hope that there might be a liturgy. In the same way, apostrophe is an invocation of invocation, a sacrifice which hopes for a repetition, as a various, conscious, always-differing animal cry. The apostrophic voice does not convince by arguments, for one cannot verify the felicity of an invocation by empirical investigation. Devoid of mundane reference to an object, the cry of invocation is a physical event, a desire for proximity, in the pure "O!" of undifferentiated voicing.[62] In thus dispossessing himself, the worshipper calls upon God to enter him, in a double movement of ecstasy and attraction which is a supreme expression of desire.

But this passionate cry of invocation is not simply or hopelessly directed towards that which is wholly absent, and therefore is in some sense concerned with "objectivity." Because that which is invoked is transcendent, the utterance of apostrophe is, by definition, contemporaneous with God's entry, not simply as a subsequent response, but as that which enables the worshipper to call out in the first place. Thus, it is impossible to desire God emptily, without that desire provoking and constituting its own consummation. And although the object of invocation is not ordinarily present in the manner of an empirical "thing," so lending apostrophic address the appearance of a *monologic* figure, apostrophe has a fundamentally *dialogic* aspect, as the "mutual confrontation of two realities,"[63] and the personification and temporalizing of that which is physically absent.[64]

This latter aspect reveals the figure of apostrophe to be the obverse of nominalization, for it transcends the ideal spatiality of immanentism by "temporalizing" and restoring personhood to the abstrusely "absent." And whereas spatialization is predicated not only upon the elision of personhood and time from space – thus disallowing the object's potential to exceed its physical appearance – but also upon the reduction of the "unknown" or "absent" to objective nothingness (a predication fully articulated by Derrida), the figure of apostrophe offers the reverse movement. Where spatialization, in its postmodern consummation, renders absent every present, apostrophe renders present every absent, yet denies

[62] See Umberto Eco, "On Animal Language in the Mediaeval Classification of Signs," in eds Eco *et al.*, *On the Mediaeval Theory of Signs*, (Philadelphia: John Benjamins Press, 1989), 3–41.
[63] P. B. Shelley "A Defence of Poetry," in ed. D. L. Clark, *Shelley's Prose*, (Albuquerque: University of New Mexico Press, 1954), 281.
[64] The absent is therefore not reduced to the "nothing" of objectivity, as for a Derridean or Heideggerian reading. See chapter 3 above.

that objective presence reduces to clarity without depth and independent initiative.

How does apostrophe achieve this within the Roman Rite? First, its reconstrual of presence. Before he reads the *Introit*, the Celebrant blesses the incense, addressing it as though it were another subject, saying *"Ab illo benedicaris, in cuius honore cremaberis. Amen."*[65] This release of the object from its mundane apprehension is figured in its physical displacement. When the object is addressed by apostrophe, it is treated as "at hand," or dialogically proximal, but at the same time, this proximity is seen to be unlike that of an enclosed object, for the incense is immediately displaced, in all its otherness, as the vaporizing sacrifice of smoke. The figure of apostrophe used in this context can be seen, therefore, to provoke a problematizing of the category of the "real" as no longer referring to that which is purely physical and graspable as such. Instead, it is now granted a constitutively spiritual component. Furthermore, instead of condemning the object in its scalar manifestation to be its own final and impeccable reality, apostrophic address reveals the object's character as "sign," as pointing away from itself towards its mysterious aspect, thus suggesting that those dimensions of an object's physicality which do not "appear" have no less a part in the object's being. This liturgical problematizing of the "real" does not thereby deprioritize the "physical," but rather intensifies its force and potential, and ability to signify its own invisible magnitude.[66] Furthermore, the invocation of that which is absent – either physically or subjectively – constitutes an attraction *towards* the physical and the temporal, for apostrophe restores to time and physicality that which cannot be seen, and exteriorizes that which is contained within ideality.

In addition, it is possible to discern a structural parallel between the incense's own self-consummating evaporation and the utterance of an apostrophic invocation, for both enact a self-dissolution in and through the attainment of their purpose, which, in both cases, forms the reciprocal movement of an *ekstasis* which sensuously *attracts*. At the same time that they call attention to another, they draw attention to themselves, in and through their act of displacement. The apostrophic address of the incense, and the incense's subsequent ecstasy, therefore, form together a chain of out-breathing invocations which occupy the expectant and supplementary space of liturgy, sacrificing themselves in the time of their own constitution, in order to provoke further sacrifices.

[65] [*Be thou blessed, in whose honour thou shalt be burned. Amen*]; Botte and Mohrmann, *op. cit.*, *L'Ordinaire*, 62.
[66] See chapter 6 below, where I discuss the Eucharistic signs as paramount.

The figure of apostrophe not only permits the "present" object to exceed its scalar appearance, but also, in the second phase, allows the object which is physically absent to exceed its "disappearance," in contrast to the way in which the immanentist order reduces the unknown to indicative nothingness and therefore objectivity.[67] The repeated vocative address of God in the Roman Rite lays stress on this problematizing of what constitutes the "real," inverting the immanentist epistemology according to which reality is that which "appears" and is appropriable by the subject. Indeed, this inversion is intensified by the way in which the invoking subject is ontologically dependent upon that which he invokes. For the apostrophic voice does not merely invoke an absent "Thou," but in the process of invocation is itself dramatized or enacted. This is paradoxical since the figure of apostrophe points away from the worshipper in a gesture of humility. Yet the paradox is clarified if one realizes that this is not the false humility of secular reasoning which pretends to extirpate subjectivity by abasing itself before the supposedly underived object in any act of empirical representation, or else by cancelling its desires turns the subject into an object, but instead a humility which fully admits its dependence upon that which is invoked for it to be a subject at all. Thus, there can be no attempted denials or rubbings-out of the subject in the course of liturgical expression, for without the liturgy, there *is* no subject, and the ultimate and holy expression of humility is that which voices its desire to *be* a subject, which is to be one with God. In addition, it can be seen that this doxological humility is the obverse of that immanentist and absolutist manipulation of the subject (the postmodern guise) which invisibly ensures that the subject is disempowered when he assumes his apparent height of autonomy, in his linguistic acts of "creativity."

The figure of apostrophe is thus predicated upon a dialogic dynamic. It is not voiced into the void, but towards the ultimate source of the invoker's desires. The object or absent thing which is addressed by apostrophe and thus becomes a "subject" implies in return that the "I" becomes a "you." In this way, one who calls upon God is one to whom God in turn speaks, thereby situating the unidentified worshipping "I" with which the Rite opens, not only within a shifting place, but also within a relational place, in an I–Thou relationship with the ultimate Thou. In the case of apostrophic address to God, the calling "I" does not occupy a prior or more primitive subject-position, because God alone makes the cry both possible and audible,[68] such that to call

[67] See chapter 3 above, "*The Abyssal Gesture.*"
[68] "*Domine exaudi orationem meam. / Et clamor meus ad te veniat,*" [*O Lord, hear my prayer. / And let my cry come unto Thee*]; Botte and Mohrmann, *op. cit., L'Ordinaire*, 62.

upon God is always already to have entered into Him. Thus, the apostrophic figure repeats the Amen, simultaneously spoken and speaking, without and within, as an epiphany which carries the "I" towards that which it addresses, and thereby more utterly towards itself. This supreme dialogic relationship shatters the protocols of all other relationships by taking place between the visible and invisible, the present and the absent, and at the same time reveals the merely (or empirically) "present" to be that which, without this relation with the apparently "absent," constitutes the ultimate absence. And yet this radical and impossible relationship is nonetheless the condition of possibility for all other relationships, for without its self-dispossessing apostrophic abasement before the ultimate absence, there can be no subject at all (only a self-presence dialectically identical with the *nihil*), and, concomitantly, no relationship either. In this way, we can see how the redefined, apostrophized "object" renders possible a non-ironic, non-indeterminate subjectivity. The primacy of the subject-object relationship for knowledge, a relationship always fully-realized and transparent to the light of day, has been displaced by the priority of the inter-subjective, on condition of allowing that ultimate transcendent subjectivity remains nocturnally absent even in and through its flashes of illuminated presence. And one may note that however much a particular finite relationship might seem to have a quality of destiny, it ultimately remains fortuitous and is at most transitory, since one I–Thou relationship can be followed by a second and a third, and in each case, the new "Thou" will be endowed with a new and different name.[69] By comparison, it is only this "absent" Thou which does not allow dialogue to be broken off, even though this means for us a dialogue of perpetual striving. For this reason, the acquisition of this I–Thou relationship does not end with the first utterance of an invocation, since the divine "Thou" is not an object which our voice can stop at or appropriate. Rather, our utterance must give rise to further speaking.

The agony of apostrophic striving is evident in the Roman Rite, in its repeated attempts to be heard, and frequent withdrawals and interruptions. Its voice bespeaks its own appalling distance from God, in a stammer which abruptly shifts from a mode of passionate doxology to melancholia, in the space of two lines: "*Confiteor tibi in cithara, Deus Deus meus : quare tristis es anima mea et quare conturbas me?*"[70] The liturgical I–Thou relationship involves a

---

[69] Martin Buber, *I and Thou*, tr. Ronald Gregor Smith, (Edinburgh: T&T Clark, 1937/ 1994).

[70] [*Upon the harp will I praise Thee, O God my God : Why art thou cast down, O my soul and why art thou disquieted within me?*]; Botte and Mohrmann, *op. cit., L'Ordinaire*, 58.

ceaseless struggle for the worshipper, for whom the secular assumptions of empirical priority and instrumentality, as well as the immanentist import of spatialized structures, inimical to voice, gift, and redemptive sacrifice, perpetually threaten to suspend the ontologically necessary liturgical dispossession of the "I." Can his voice be heard by that which is absent? Will God respond? The words "*Domine exaudi orationem meam. / Et clamor meus ad te veniat*"[71] express the fear that the worshipping voice will not be heard, that the silence of the text will triumph, and neither voice nor vocation will remain.[72] The voice seems in danger of becoming less than nothing, since its striving language – as calling, welcoming, praising – casts speaking as continuous with being. This urgent cry of "O!" is issued by that which seeks proximity with absence, not as a nihilism which desires death above all else, but as part of a desire to release itself from the nihilism of immanent presence. Thus, the apostrophic voice desires the ultimate and elusive boundary of being which surrounds emptiness, and yet, by opening nothing onto itself, is fuller than fullness.

In this section it has been seen how the substitution for nominalization by apostrophe in liturgical forms redefines objectivity as holding a depth of absence and spontaneous initiative. In this way, objectivity is grounded in transcendent subjectivity, and liturgical truth is understood not to involve primarily the clear apprehension of a mastered object, but rather a prior seizure of the subject by an overwhelming subjectivity. But since even absence can be addressed and itself makes an address, however obscurely, the flow of signifying and unmasterable objects is articulate and meaningful, and permits us a specific place or identity within that flow. The liturgical use of apostrophe insinuates, against the modern and postmodern, a non-ironic, identifiable subject. However, I shall now show how the liturgical subject also avoids the other (post)modern danger, namely, that of slipping into absolute self-identity.

5 THE PERMUTABILITY OF IDENTITY

In Part I of this essay, I showed how from an immanentist perspective, it becomes necessary to perform a gesture of security against the void, in an attempt to avoid a slippage of the ironic self into nothingness. I showed also how this gesture has many different forms, that *even nihilism itself* is situated

---

[71] [*O Lord, hear my prayer. / And let my cry come unto Thee.*]
[72] *Ibid.*, 62.

within its act of resistance, and concomitantly, that any mobilizing or totalitarian attempts to deny the void are themselves ultimately nihilistic. In the various negotiations of subjectivity which I have discussed, from the examples of Lysias and Phaedrus, to those implicit within Scotist theology, baroque modes of government, scientific protocols, modernist poetics, and contemporary linguistic practices, this gesture of security is evident, and despite the manifold approaches to the problem, there is a recurrent and inevitable dimension: the immanentist subject – whether autonomously in command of the object, or passively controlled from without – is ultimately seen as *self-identical*, and therefore as objectified and erased. Even the postmodern subject, ostensibly denied all continuity through the ravages of radically non-identical flows and ruptures, is nonetheless reducible to the self-identity of indifference, and the supreme objectivity and continuity of the *nihil*. Hence, the emptiness of the modern and postmodern subject has a dialectically-opposite and yet identical other face: the insistence of autonomy and self-identity.

In contrast to this inevitable erasure of the subject through its very over-assertion, I shall now show how a liturgical negotiation of identity genuinely restores the subject, by casting its endless permutations and borrowings as redemptively and analogously different. I argue that this is in part achieved by employing the device of epithetic identification characteristic of ancient modes of oral diction, but that the Christian liturgical casting of oral modes differs necessarily from its pagan counterparts. Whilst in sections 6 and 7 of this chapter, I shall consider the diversity of genres in the liturgy, and the effect of the *text* of the liturgy upon its casting of orality, in this section, I will argue that the liturgical portrayal of the subject's and God's identity or character involves a divergence from characterizations in a pagan setting. In treating of the liturgical permutations of identity, I shall consider both God and the worshipper, and show how permutation and permeation occur not only *within* both realms, but also *between* them, and argue that this openness of "identity" is crucial to a restoration of the subject.

The Roman Rite contains many features characteristic of oral modes of discourse. As well as the multicursal "plot" structure already discussed, one can mention, first, the complicated use of *anaphorae*, whereby phrases and themes are constantly repeated, sometimes with variation, in different contexts. Secondly, there is the related device of *supplementation*, or long enumeration of "authorities" or precedents, used to intensify a certain petition or prayer. For example, at the "*Confiteor*," "*Suscipe, sancta Trinitas*" and "*Communicantes*," comprehensive enumerations of specific names of saints are invoked in support of respective requests for purification, the reception of our offering, and for

protection.[73] This oral listing, which specifies particular names carefully selected
to suit the requirements of a particular context, testifies to the liturgical stress on
the restoration of individuality and personhood discussed in the previous section
of this chapter, in contrast to the de-personified generalizations and totalizations
of spatialized structures. Thirdly, the liturgical text also deploys another
characteristically oral type of supplementation, namely, the bardic tradition of
narration, according to which, there can be no definitive account of a particular
story, but each performance of a tale constitutes a supplemented "origin" in its
own right.[74] Thus, the liturgy reflects the oral character of the New Testament
itself, for the Institution Narrative in particular is perforce derived from three
gospel and one Pauline accounts: none of these is more original or authentic, and
therefore from the beginning, this tale – which is the tale of the Mass itself – is
told necessarily in many versions, to whose number, every celebration of
the Mass adds, with equal "originality."[75] From the outset, even the Body and
Blood are still to be, in the final eschatological resurrection of the whole body
of Christ, (the Church), and hence the story must be told in endlessly new
first versions, just as the liturgy is always recommenced, in the hope that there
might be worship.

However, although it can be demonstrated that the Roman Rite contains
many structural features which point to an oral provenance, a divergence
between the Christian casting of orality and its pagan epic counterparts can be
shown. First, in contrast to the heroes of Greek epics, the worshipper – like
the characters in biblical, especially Mosaic, narratives – undergoes develop-
mental alteration: "While the Homeric heroes have many adventures, they
remain essentially the same people, distinguishable by certain marks of body
and temperament. They do not become but are heroes. . . . The characters of
the Mosaic authorship, on the other hand, carry the trace of their past and the

[73] *Ibid.*, 60, 72, 76 respectively.
[74] On the theory that the Homeric epics and other oral poetry are combinations of earlier
fragments and that there is no definitive "original," see Milman Parry, *The Making of
Homeric Verse*, ed. Adam Parry, (Oxford: Clarendon Press, 1971); Alfred B. Lord, *The Singer
of Tales*, (Cambridge, Mass.: Harvard University Press, 1960); Eric A. Havelock, *Preface to
Plato*, (Cambridge, Mass.: Belknap Press of Harvard University Press, 1963); Berkley
Peabody, *The Winged Word: A Study in the Technique of Ancient Greek Oral Composition as
Seen Principally through Hesiod's Works and Days*, (Albany, New York: State University of
New York Press, 1975); David E. Bynum, *The Daemon in the Wood: A Study of Oral
Narrative Patterns*, (Cambridge, Mass.: Harvard University Press, 1978).
[75] Matthew 26:26–9; Mark 14:22–5; Luke 22:18–20; I Corinthians 11:23–9.
[76] Gerard Loughlin, *Telling God's Story: Bible, Church and Narrative Theology*, (Cambridge:
Cambridge University Press, 1995), 70–3, 71, with reference to Erich Auerbach, *Mimesis:*

expectation of their future."[76] Furthermore, in contrast to the essentialization and generalization of Homeric heroes, the characters of biblical – and especially Christian – stories are particular and uniquely "unsubstitutable" persons.[77]

However, a qualification of this trait of unsubstitutability is necessary, namely, that of the many *permutations* of character which occur in the liturgy. I have already discussed, for example, the borrowed identity of the worshipping "I" with which the Roman Rite opens, whose decentred nature distends through earthly and transcendent regions. This permutability contrasts markedly with the clarity and simplicity of identification character-istic of Homeric heroes who are delimited by condensed and standardized epithets, which, although varying in accordance with the hexameter rhythm, are nonetheless unavailable to substitution between individual characters.[78] Thus, Achilles is swift-footed, Hector has a shining helmet, Diomedes is good at the war cry, and Odysseus is both cunning and much-enduring, but Achilles is never much-enduring, nor Odysseus swift-footed, and so on.[79] It therefore seems that Homeric epithetic identification is designed to differentiate characters rather than to communicate ambiguities of nature, either through time, or between individuals, and is more concerned to depict them as fixed entities than subject to unspoken qualification or alteration. Thus, the Homeric hero does not *exceed* his generalized and immanent identification: a character's swift-footedness, bronze-claddedness, or plume-crestedness does not so much illumine, as envelop him.

Homeric heroes are also identified as uniform and discrete by the consist-ency of their actions and reactions within the plot, and although a character may be to a certain degree subject to circumstantial alteration – such as when possessed by a god or goddess – he is, nonetheless, never "out of character."

The Representation of Reality in Western Literature, tr. William R. Trask, (Princeton: Prince-ton University Press, 1953), 1–20, and Georg Lukács, *The Theory of the Novel: A Historico-Philosophical Essay on the Forms of Great Epic Literature*, tr. Anna Bostock, (London: Merlin Press, 1971), 35–6.

[77] Loughlin, *op. cit.*, *Telling God's Story*, 73–7.

[78] On "the dependence of the choice of words and word-forms on the shape of the hexameter line" in the Homeric poems, see Milman Parry, *op. cit.*, *The Making of Homeric Verse*, 1–190, xix ; Marcel Jousse, *Le style oral rhythmique et mnémonotechnique chez les Verbo-moteurs*, (Paris: Beauchesne, 1925); Jack Goody, *The Domestication of the Savage Mind*, (Cambridge: Cambridge University Press, 1977), 115.

[79] D. H. F. Gray, "Homeric Epithets for Things," in *idem*, *The Language and Background of Homer: Some Recent Studies*, (Cambridge: Heffers, 1964), 55–67.

Indeed, when Athene turns her attention to Diomedes in the *Iliad*, she does not so much alter his characteristics, as *intensify* their sameness.[80] Moreover, divine intervention in the Homeric poems does not contribute any "otherness" to the proceedings or characters because the gods are not genuinely other-worldly. The world of the gods is a social world with its own accepted and recalled history of thefts, deceits, cuckoldries, murders, and whimsical interventions, in which only Zeus seems to occupy a position without earthly parallel. But even his considerable mystery and withdrawal do not contribute a genuine, contagious transcendence, for, from within his Olympian enclo-sure, his interventions can be immanently rationalized in the form of messages conveyed by Iris, Dream, and Rumour, or else by the articulate or legible communications of thunder-claps, animal entrails, or the flight-path of a bird.

In accordance with such an anthropomorphic world view, all events, including divine, are explicitly described, accounted for, and given precise temporal boundaries.[81] And in keeping with this immanence, the attributes allocated to the different heroes are various manifestations of the implicit cultural aspiration of *aretē* (excellence), a supremely this-worldly qualification which received its acclaim in terms appropriate to the city. Similarly, all characters, things, and events are represented in palpable and fully externalized form, and despite the various manipulations of linear emplotment,[82] nothing takes place worldlessly or ambiguously, even to the extent that direct and fully recorded conversational exchanges take place between the heroes and gods.

From the various features of liturgical structure and modes of identification discussed in the previous two sections of this chapter, it can already be seen that the secure *loci* of the Homeric universe differ markedly from those of the liturgy. In the Roman Rite, there are no easily located places or place names, and no physical descriptions to delimit the characters or places involved in the events which occur. Similarly, there is no singular thread of plot, but instead a series of recommencements which casts the Rite in the mode of a radicalized *propemptikon*,

---

[80] Homer, *Iliad*, V.1–8.

[81] Auerbach, *op. cit.*, *Mimesis*, 13. See also, Loughlin, *op. cit.*, *Telling God's Story*, 36–42. In keeping with its this-worldly and non-developmental perspective, the Homeric poems make no ethical claim to alter the reader, except on an earthly and more especially urban or agorean scale, insofar as they might (or might not) disseminate the various manifestations of *aretē*.

[82] In Homer's *Iliad* and *Odyssey*, his narrative ordering is not iconic with the "fabula" [or series of chronologically experienced events: see Mieke Bal, *Narratology: Introduction to the Theory of Narrative*, (Toronto: University of Toronto Press, 1985), 5], and makes use of the devices of flashbacks, recapitulations, repetitions, and narratological prolepses. In spite of this, his plots remain rooted in linear temporality and the certainty of place.

a song for the occasion of a journey, but one which is itself a journey in preparation for the song of the angels, a song that there might be a song. Indeed, even this lyrical destination is not a final closure, but only the threshold of a destination, which itself recedes, for the "place" of angelic worship is a *subliminal* place. The manner in which the worshipper's journey is undertaken, and the details of God's reciprocal movement toward him are not physically described, and remain only implicit within the prayers and petitions of the Rite. And when God "appears," his physically penetrative proximity shatters spatial etiquette: he nonetheless does not vacate his heavenly "place." We hear his voice, but not in a straightforwardly empirical way, and even His name is not a "rigid designator," but is both non-identically repeated and ambiguous.[83]

Divine identifications

Given these general differences between Homeric and liturgical characterization, I shall now consider the identification of God in the Roman Rite in greater detail, with particular reference to the *Gloria* and *Credo*.

Throughout the Rite, God is assigned various recurrent epithets, such as "*Deum qui lætificat iuventutem meam,*" "*qui fecit cælum et terram,*" "*omnipotens Deus,*" "*Rex cælestis,*" "*sancte Pater*" etc.,[84] and is addressed variously as "*Deus,*" "*Pater,*" "*Domine,*" and although it was not uncommon for Homer to assign multiple epithets to one character, there is an important difference with regard to these liturgical nominations. The identifications of God (and the worshipper) are subject to *ambiguity* and *distension*. For example, the opening phrase of the *Gloria*, "GLORIA *in excelsis Deo,*" which is non-identically repeated in the concluding ("little") doxologies of many of the Rite's prayers,[85] is highly ambiguous. Is it a constative statement to the effect that glory is *being given* to God in the highest places? Or an optative wish to offer God glory? It could alternatively be interpreted as a performative utterance, instantiating an actual offering of God's glory, or else, as an *impersonation* by the Celebrant (on our behalf) of the angelic worship of God. Not only is the whole utterance ambiguous, but also its various parts. For example, does "*in excelsis*" refer qualitatively to the intensity of the glory offered to God, or alternatively by God? Or does it stress the situatedness of God in high places? The word

---

[83] Saul Kripke, *Naming and Necessity*, (Oxford: Blackwell Publishers, 1972/1980), 3–15, 48–9.

[84] [*God of my youth and gladness*]; [*who has made heaven and earth*]; [*almighty God*]; [*heavenly King*]; [*holy Father*]; Botte and Mohrmann, *op. cit., L'Ordinaire*, 58–60, 60, 60, 64, 68 respectively.

[85] Jungmann, *op. cit., The Mass*, 218–19.

"*excelsus*" means lofty, elevated, and glorious, and is related to the qualitative "*excello*"; so we can interpret "*in excelsis*" as both a matter of deictic location and qualitative identification. This ambiguity underlines an important difference between the divine nature and our finite identities, for whereas God's quality and "place" are contemporaneous with, and not additional to His being, human qualities and positionings always remain somewhat contingent and accidental, rather than thoroughly substantive.

The uncertainty as to whether the opening phrase of the *Gloria* refers to the glory which God receives from human worshippers or angels, or to that which He possesses and which radiates from Him, is itself crucial to His identification, for there is nothing which can be offered to God which is not already continuous with His being. Accordingly, the series of doxological offerings rendered to God in the *Gloria* culminate in this ambiguous glory: "*Laudamus te. Benedicimus te. Adoramus te. Glorificamus te.*"[86] How can our doxological offerings not spill over into that very glory which God Himself radiates? This overflow of praise into that which is praised reminds us that, throughout all our acts of giving, He is the real donor: "*Gratias agimus tibi propter magnam gloriam tuam.*"[87] Moreover, the ambiguous lineaments of glory underline the theological nature of donation, for although we offer the gifts of praise, blessing, adoration, and glory to God, He is not a discrete donee who merely "receives," but radiates outwards in glory which overtakes and makes possible our offerings even before they are offered. Thus, our doxological expressions are not distinct from God's epiphany. This can be seen in the phrase which expresses our passionate gratitude: "*Domine Deus, Rex Cælestis, Deus Pater omnipotens.*"[88] The triple apostrophe – beyond the distinction of performative and constative utterance – coincides with the continuation of God's ecstatic manifestations. This is the first occasion in the Rite when God is emphatically and repeatedly *named*. Unlike the frozen nominations of Greek heroes and deities, God is both praised and made manifest, freely and gratuitously, through this naming for the sake of naming. And such epiphanic naming also reveals the Trinitarian identification of God, for, as I have mentioned, the word "*Domine*" is taken up in the next apostrophic phrase, this time assuming the identification of the Son: "*Domine Fili unigenite, Iesu Christe.*" It is almost as if the persons of the Trinity borrow or swap nominations in order to fulfill their identifications.[89]

---

[86] [*We praise Thee. We bless Thee. We adore Thee. We glorify Thee*]; Botte and Mohrmann, *op. cit., L'Ordinaire*, 62–4.

[87] [*We give thanks to Thee for Thy great glory.*]

[88] [*O Lord God, heavenly King, God the Father almighty.*]

[89] See section 4 above, "*The Apostrophic Voice.*"

Finally, in the concluding phrases of the *Gloria*, addressed to the Son, the question of "*in excelsis*" is simultaneously resumed, problematized, and resolved by the Trinitarian non-identical repetition of unity: "*Quoniam tu solus sanctus, Tu solus Dominus. Tu solus Altissimus, Iesu Christe. Cum Sancto Spiritu in gloria Dei Patris. Amen.*"[90] Given that at the opening of this hymn, God was established as "*in excelsis*," how can we now say that Jesus Christ *alone* is the most high? According to mundane reason, this necessarily excludes shared occupancy, and yet the Father has already been situated in the same exalted places. He is alone (*solus*), and yet not alone, but both "with" the Holy Spirit (*cum Sancto Spiritu*) and "in" the glory of God the Father.

Accordingly, I shall now discuss the ambiguity of the boundaries between the persons of the Trinity, as both depicted and enacted in the *Credo*. Whilst there is no explicit elucidation of the doctrine of three-in-one, and the word "Trinity" is not used, the reciprocally constitutive relations between the Father, Son, and Holy Spirit are performed syntactically, and analogously repeated with every enunciation of belief.

The Trinitarian relations of three-in-one are performed by means of a combination of two syntactic extremes, co-ordination and subordination, resulting in a highly complex textual structure. At the most general level, the Credal text is divided into three main sections of continuous prose, each ostensibly concerned with a respective hypostasis. Yet these sections are by no means discretely separated, but are continuous with one another by means of the text's syntactic organicity. This organicity can be divided into two interacting types. The first concerns the linear development of successive clauses from their immediate precursors. For example, the phrase "*visibilium omnium et invisibilium*"[91] modifies the preceding clause which supplies the basis of its ellipsis, "*factorem.*"[92] This preceding clause is in turn a modification of its own precursor, "*Patrem omnipotentem,*" and so on. The movement of linear modification is combined with the second syntactic dynamic, which involves more complex anaphoric relations, whereby a clause reaches further behind its immediate precursor to find its semantic satisfaction. Accordingly, whilst "*per quem omnia facta sunt,*"[93] which occurs in the section pertaining to the Son, refers to its precursive clause, "*consubstantialem Patri,*"[94] this preceding clause refers back to the first section, pertaining to the Father (ie. "*factorem cœli et*

---

[90] [*For Thou only art holy, Thou only art the Lord. Thou only art the most High, O Jesus Christ. With the Holy Spirit in the glory of God the Father. Amen.*]
[91] [*all things visible and invisible.*]
[92] Botte and Mohrmann, *op. cit., L'Ordinaire,* 66.
[93] [*by whom all things were made.*]
[94] [*consubstantial with the Father.*]

terræ"). Similarly, the relative pronoun in the clause, "*Qui propter nos homines et propter nostram salutem*"[95] bypasses its immediate precursor (pertaining to the Son) to resolve itself in the opening clauses of both the first and second sections ("*CREDO in unum Deum . . . Et in unum Dominum Iesum Christum*").

These are just a few examples of the complex, embedded syntax of the *Credo*, but they are sufficient to express the zig-zagging of anaphoric references, entwining these two persons of the Trinity in complex co-ordination and reciprocal subordination. Each clause engages in a reaching back to the opening clause, "*CREDO in unum Deum . . .*," which straddles the entire text in unimpeded lineage, and finds in this opening clause its semantic consummation, even as it proceeds onwards to its successor, in the lived time of proclamative narration.[96]

This dual movement of linear and anaphoric modification performs both the unity of the Trinity and the analogous difference of its persons. The anaphorae provoke a recalling of a previous instant of the enunciation, and engage the worshipper in a complex activity, simultaneously anamnetic and anticipatory. For in recollecting a fragment, one at once attains the ability to proceed onwards, and acquires a consciousness of the remainder of the whole, as well as anterior parts. In this way, each subsequent appearing (upon familiarity with the procession) will perforce result from the immediate antecedent, its future arisings, and the text as a whole. No clause stands in isolation, but traces its lineage to the first and every other clause, and is contingent upon the whole for its meaning. The figural dynamic of the anaphorae is balanced with the linear movement of free modifiers and co-ordinating conjunctions ("*et . . .et . . .et . . .*") which abound, and function to carry forward the narrative of salvation history, neutralizing any disjunctive

---

[95] [*Who for us men and for our salvation*]

[96] The replacement of complex by asyndetic syntax in the *Roman Missal* (1975), *Alternative Service Book* (1980), the Episcopal *Book of Common Prayer* (1979), and British Reformed liturgies, inevitably results in some alteration to the felicity of this Trinitarian performance. The Credal text of these liturgies (ratified in common by the International Consultation on English Texts) is divided into five paragraphs of thirty-five lines of undiffused (discrete) sentences, thus textually disjoining the Trinitarian persons, which are now perforce considered *serially*. The only cohesion obtained for the persons and the events of Salvation History with our own "event" of proclamation now relies upon pre-established knowledge and the implicature of temporal iconicity whereby one infers the unified chronicity of the fabula from the sequential position of events in the text. This strategy does not perform the cyclicity of eternal relationships portrayed in the former version. For a delineation of the catechetical, performative, and epistemological implications of this, see Pickstock, *op. cit.*, "Asyndeton: Syntax and Insanity."

effects of full-stops, or other pauses in the punctuation. This story and its three persons override all interruption.

The implication for a performance of Trinitarian relations of this syntactic complexity is that one cannot confess belief in "*unum Dominum Iesum Christum*" except by means of belief in God "*Patrem omnipotentem*," because belief in one or belief in the other is belief in one and the same thing. The third section, concerning the Holy Spirit, is structured almost entirely by means of an aggregation of "*qui*" clauses, each referring back to "*Et in Spiritum Sanctum*," which itself recalls the openings of the first and second sections. Thus, all three persons, as well as the Church and its rites, and the anticipation of the life of the world to come, are bound into the same act of belief, in such a way that one cannot isolate one part without summoning the whole. Moreover, this "whole" contains also our own Credal and liturgical enactment, and the continuing action of God in our daily lives.

The co-dependence of the persons of the Trinity is further demonstrated by the position of the *Credo* in the liturgical narrative itself, following the enunciation of the Gospel. For the latter concerns the history of Christ's incarnation which was the condition of possibility for the revelation of the Trinitarian God. Thus, just as our faith in and confession of the Trinity follows on from the manifestation of God in the incarnation, so the *Credo* is a continuation of the Gospel narrative, not only as a summary of salvation history, but also because every act of faith is implicated in that narrative. Similarly, the story of salvation tells of, and is continuous with, the bestowal of life, in a tangle of report and event, in such a way that the enunciation of the Credal narration of that story is at once a part of the events recorded in the Gospel story, and contemporaneous with their salvific effects. It is a story we have heard before and which we know. Even within its tale, nothing "new" happens, for its narrative turnings fold endlessly in upon one another in its ceaseless permeations of continuous lineage, its "*lumen de lumine*," "*Deum verum de Deo vero*," "*Genitum, non factum*," and "*consubstantialem Patri*."[97] But whilst this story is unfinished, its lack of conclusion does not compromise the value of its telling, but intensifies its unsettling familiarity: this performance provokes the perpetual anticipation and postponement of its own dénouement.

Thus, in conclusion to this section on the permutations of divine identification, it can be seen that the *Credo* fulfills its ancient catechetical function not as an exposition apart from faith, but as a performative *act* of faith – a "confession" in its truest sense – which perforce *disseminates* its components: this doxological expression of the doctrinal boundaries of belief radiates

[97] [*light of light*]; [*very God of very God*]; [*Begotten, not made*]; [*consubstantial with the Father.*]

outwards in a contagion of definitive boundlessness. Liturgical doxology, therefore, is many things: thanksgiving, confession, dissemination, invocation, theophany, anticipation, repetition.[98] But this performance of faith, which does not operate according to the worshipping subject's full command of his action, but, rather, his submission to a *narrative* mode of knowledge which disallows the isolation of empirical or intellectual essences,[99] subordinates that which the worshipper knows and does to that which passes through him, beyond his analytic grasp. This *willing* subordination to the surprise of what arrives *alone* genuinely liberates him from the de-constitutive assumptions of autonomy, epistemological certainty, and self-presence of secular existence. By committing himself actively to becoming the conduit of the event of the Trinity, that is, by confessing his faith, the worshipper's subjectivity is enacted and fulfilled.

Borrowed names

In the Roman Rite, as we have just seen, the worshipping "I" is both designated and realized by self-dispossessing acts of doxological impersonation which displace any sense of enclosed autonomy in the subject in favour of that which is impersonated. However, this does not result in a radically discontinuous subject, but rather intensifies his continuity, by revealing the zenith of differential continuity to reside in God. Thus liturgical impersonation is not a matter of *arbitrary mimicry* across a lateral plain of ultimately interchangeable identities, but an altogether more radical and redemptive mimesis which transgresses the hierarchical boundaries between the worldly and the other-worldly. Unlike the random mimetic arts which Socrates expels from the city, the transcendence of that which is imitated in the Roman Rite ensures that mimesis does not remain a purely extrinsic act. By impersonating angelic voices or the Trinitarian persons, the worshipping impersonator cannot but participate in that which he emulates, and so, to travel in another's name becomes the nomination of the traveller himself. In consequence, he does not ashamedly conceal his inadequate and stammering voice by assuming divine voices, in the covert manner of ventriloquist substitution, but boldly asserts that he acts "*In nomine Patris et Filii et Spiritus Sancti.*" He borrows this name

---

[98] The Credal confession of faith locates its genesis in the summary passages of *proclamation* and *acclamation* of God and his saving action found in the Jewish scriptures (e.g. Deuteronomy 5:4, 26:5). Frances Young, *The Making of the Creeds*, (London: SCM Press Ltd, 1991), 3ff.

[99] Jean-François Lyotard, *The Postmodern Condition: A Report on Knowledge*, tr. Geoff Bennington and Brian Massumi, (Manchester: Manchester University Press, 1984), 18–27.

not in order to deny its own speaking, or to silence its declaration, but in order to disseminate it still further. For, the borrower of the name is also that name's ambassador.

Just how is the nomadic naming of the traveller indissociable from his acts of impersonation? At the opening of the *Gloria*, I mentioned above that one possible interpretation of the attribution of glory is that the Celebrant enacts on our behalf an impersonation of the angels in their perpetual hymn of praise.[100] This would suggest a protean ontology whereby impersonation precedes our "authentic" voice, thus disallowing any construal of the subject as autonomous or self-present. By being *figured as* angels, we become one with their worldlessness and unfallenness, and are displaced from the earthly congregation to a position where we can momentarily participate in the economy of salvation, turning back to the world so as to confer upon it peace and good will: "*Et in terra pax hominibus bonæ voluntatis.*"[101] The acquisition of this newly borrowed angelic status paradoxically qualifies us to *become ourselves*, in the instant of mimicry. For at this moment we overflow into doxological enactment: "*Laudamus te.*" Such laudation seems to exalt us still further, until we seem almost to overstep God Himself, turning back in order to bless or consecrate Him: "*Benedicimus te,*" but in this we also overstep *ourselves*, and so resume our subordination to God in the mode of adoration: "*Adoramus te.*" The summit of "*Glorificamus te,*" which invokes the equal offering of glory between the persons of the Trinity, resolves this doxological crisis of identification through a peculiarly Christian synthesis of equality and hierarchy,[102] with all the ambiguity of agency described above.

Thus, the cumulative glorification of God in this doxological series communicates a link not only between the worshipper's name and his acts of mimicry, but also with that which, through impersonation, he praises. By means of a consideration of the various alterations in the Celebrant's and Ministers' statuses during the turns of the Antiphon shortly before the *Gloria*, it can be seen that this Trinitarian exchange is already anticipated. In the successive turns of these exchanges, the worshipper enters into those which take place between the persons of the Trinity, in such a way that he perpetually *becomes* what he praises.[103] In the first antiphonal turn, the petition, "*Deus tu conversus vivificabis nos,*"[104] is instantly fulfilled, for before we can be provoked

---

[100] "The definition, aim and purpose of ecclesiastical liturgy is to imitate the gestures, dances, music, songs, words and actions of angels, in the presence of God," Michel Serres, *Angels: A Modern Myth,* tr. Francis Cowper, (Paris: Flammarion, 1993/1995), 94.

[101] [*And in earth peace, good will to men*]; Botte and Mohrmann, *op. cit., L'Ordinaire,* 62.

[102] For example, see John 7:16–18, 33, 39.

[103] Botte and Mohrmann, *op. cit., L'Ordinaire,* 62.

[104] [*Wilt Thou turn and quicken us, O God?*]

into worship, God must already have turned towards us. And, indeed, no sooner have we requested God's turning, then we begin to express doxological desire: "*Et plebs tua lætabitur in te.*"[105] These two movements, the request for God to turn towards us, and the desire to rejoice in God, cannot be differentiated: they remain components of the same petitional clause. The second antiphonal turn is addressed to the Son, and requests a manifestation of His mercy: "*Ostende nobis, Domine, misericordiam tuam/ Et salutare tuum da nobis,*"[106] and this petition is then non-identically repeated: "*Domine exaudi orationem meam./ Et clamor meus ad te veniat.*"[107]

These three antiphonal turns in combination can be seen to supply the co-ordinates of salvation itself, since God's turning towards us and our journey towards God are pre-enabled by the eternal journey of the Logos to the Father, which, by our invocation of the Son's mercy and salvation, includes our own liturgical journey. Our concomitant and immediate reception of the Son's salvific effects is implicit within the Antiphon's conclusory dialogue, for at this point it is as if the Celebrant and Ministers accomplish an entire Trinitarian exchange: "*Dominus vobiscum./ Et cum spiritu tuo.*" Humanity opens up so as to confer peace upon itself, through its incorporation into that divine economy. And this earthly gift-exchange seems consequently to displace the earth, for in bestowing the Lord upon the Ministers (and implicitly, the Church) in the words "*Dominus vobiscum,*" the recipients are ordained as spiritual or other-worldly, to such a degree that they are thus empowered to bestow the Lord in return, to the Celebrant who is now also spiritualized: "*Et cum spiritu tuo.*" Having received the Spirit, they become one with the Spirit, and as the spiritual condition is by definition ecstatic and mobile, this reception cannot be distinguished from subsequent acts of bestowal. The Trinitarian exchange in which we participate at this point emphasizes that for human beings, a gift is something which is not given simply once, but is defined by subsequent and repeated offerings (every gift being a promise to give again and more). Moreover, the gift and counter-gifts of the Spirit do not here betoken a turn away from the world, but rather, through these lateral enactments of exchange, stress the centrality of corporate life. Indeed, whilst the "*Dominus vobiscum*" occurs on several occasions throughout the Rite, its "final" occurrence takes place at the Rite's conclusion, which implies that the liturgical bestowal of the divine nature is but a prologue to the wider liturgy which the participants will offer continually in their daily lives.

---

[105] [*That Thy people may rejoice in Thee.*]

[106] [*Show us Thy mercy, O Lord, have mercy upon us/ And grant us Thy salvation.*]

[107] [*O Lord hear my prayer/ And let my cry come unto Thee.*]

This exaltation of the worldly in the Roman Rite suggests a displacement of the hitherto quarantined realms of the earthly and transcendent. It is a paradox that the strict delimitation of these two orders in the Homeric universe should result in such this-worldly deities, whereas the genuinely transcendent nature of God is to be discerned in his ability to overflow into immanence. The figure of the worshipper as metamorphosed into the object of his praise underlines a further difference. Even for Plato, the redemptive significance of *eros* ultimately involves the recollection of a timeless moment whose constitutive *worldlessness* alone sustains its capacity to fulfill the philosophic life.[108] The embodiment of the Good remains for Plato an ideal – even though the guardian must finally return to the city – which is to be acquired not through contagious impersonation, but by means of a programme of educative stages lasting many years, available only to an élite section of society. Moreover, it can be argued that this attainment was not intended as a *realizable model*.[109] And, beyond this, *eros* ultimately leaves the beloved person behind for a condition which errs towards self-presence, for however much the Platonic good is manifested in physicality, the Forms transcend time.[110] This contrasts with the superlatively and demonstrably realizable transformation of the Forms into the Ideas of God in Christianity, where God's Ideas "eminently" *include* everything specifically manifest in the world, including time. Whereas the self-identity of the Homeric characters suggests a construal of subjectivity as an anterior "given" essence which must be re-claimed, the worshipper's protean assimilations reveal subjectivity as that which is open to potential. Thus, the alterations which the worshipper undergoes are not to be seen as a dissipation of character into a nihilistic explosion of differences, nor as a separation of the subject from his position

---

[108] However, in the *Phaedrus*, Platonic recollection approaches something not unlike the forward-moving dynamic of repetition. See Jean-Louis Chrétien, *L'Inoubliable et L'Inespéré*. (Paris: Desclée de Brouwer, 1991), 9–56, and the "*Conclusion*" below.

[109] On the ideal city of the *Republic* and *Laws* as not intended as a political blueprint but as a *paradeigma* "in speech of a good city" which does not exist except in heaven or within the self (*Republic*, 592 a–b, 472 d–e) see Zdravko Planinc, *Plato's Political Philosophy: Prudence in the* Republic *and the* Laws, (London: Gerald Duckworth, 1991), 1–27 and *passim*; Gadamer, "Plato's Educational State," in *idem, Dialogue and Dialectic: Eight Hermeneutic Studies on Plato*, tr. P. Christopher Smith, (New Haven: Yale University Press, 1980), 73–92; and *idem, The Idea of the Good*, 71–2; and Drew Hyland, "Plato's 'Three Waves,' and the Question of Utopia," in *idem, Finitude and Transcendence in the Platonic Dialogues*, (Albany: State University of New York Press, 1995), 59–86.

[110] See further Christopher Gill, *Personality in Greek Epic, Tragedy, and Philosophy: The Self in Dialogue*, (Oxford: Clarendon Press, 1996), 386–8.

in the world, but rather as a perpetual fulfilling of the very possibility of character in and through a transfiguration and intensification of the world as such.

In the above, I have described the way in which the worshipping "I" is dislodged from his mundane priority, and subject to the permutability of identity, becoming other from himself as a kind of "third" or un-numberable person. This re-ordering of subjectivity can be seen in other aspects of the Rite, where otherwise inanimate or physically absent creatures assume a redemptive priority over the subject. In the *Communicantes* – the enumeration of the saints, who might perhaps be proximal in the form of statues, effigies, or relics – the Celebrant invokes real, historical human beings who have become other-worldly, either through canoniza-tion, or else through committal to stone or inscription. Thus, appeal is made to these various other-worldly saints for their merit to defend and protect the living worshippers: "*quorum meritis precibuscue concedas, ut in omnibus protectionis tuæ muniamur auxilio.*"[111] These mute, lifeless, possibly sculpted beings are invoked as spokesmen and makers by the speaking worshippers who pray to be thus remade by their defence and protection. The sculptors are sculpted, and the made things become vital makers, via a chiasmus which ironizes the priority of subject over object, and of identity as such.

This *chiasmus* is repeated with every utterance of apostrophe, when that which is spoken about suddenly speaks, and one enters a different realm where it is the normative trope to address that which is not empirically present. To enter this realm is to become like or be figured as that which one addresses, in a crossing-over which erases the ordinary diegetic proprieties which quarantine the divine and worldly.[112] This transgression of domains is sublimated in the upward movement of incense which ascends towards the heavenly altar, and concomitant movements from God to us: "*Incensum istud a te benedictum ascendat ad te, Domine : et descendat super nos misericordia tua.*"[113] Here, the ascent of our offering of incense occurs in between two descending movements from God, in the form of blessing and mercy. The censing of the

---

[111] [*by whose merits and intercessions do Thou grant, that in all things we may be defended by the help of Thy protection*]; Botte and Mohrmann, *op. cit.*, *L'Ordinaire*, 78.

[112] On the establishment of a dialogic relationship with mute works of art, see Walter Benjamin, "On Some Motifs in Baudelaire," in ed. Hannah Arendt, *Illuminations*, (New York: Schocken Books, 1968), 155–200; on the narrative device of crossing-over between two realms, see Genette's discussion of "transdiegetic metalepsis" in his *Narrative Discourse*, tr. Jane Lewin, (Oxford: Blackwell Publishers, 1980), 51f.

[113] [*May this incense which Thou hast blessed, O Lord, ascend unto Thee: and may Thy mercy descend upon us*]; Botte and Mohrmann, *op. cit.*, *L'Ordinaire*, 70.

Oblation and altar by the Celebrant at this point superimposes a further *chiasmus*, for this implicitly horizontal act is fulfilled vertically, in the inevitable ascent of smoke, which rebinds the earthly Church with its heavenly setting.

6 LITURGICAL SATIRE

In the previous section, I described the metamorphic condition of the worshipping "I" and protean reversibility of the seer and the seen, the speaker and the spoken. I intimated that within this representation of both the subject and God, one can discern two apparently contradictory movements: first, the decentring of a strategic vocal *locus*; and secondly, an attempt to constitute a continuous subject. However, it was implicit within my delineation of characterization in the liturgy, that this is only an apparent contradiction, that in fact, genuine subjectivity is only attained *through* such divine permutations, and that any subject which appears self-identical and strategic is reducible to a subject under erasure, an ironic void.

A further poetic manifestation of this striving for a genuine consummation of subjectivity can be found in the liturgy's manipulation of genres. It is noticeable that the Roman Rite deploys a polyphonic texture of voices and poetic positions. Its constant play of differences modulate through narrative, dialogue, antiphon, monologue, apostrophe, doxology, oration, invocation, citation, supplementation, and entreaty. This manifold genre disarms in advance any assumption of an authoritarian or strategic voice of command, for as we have seen, even God Himself, whose Word is the optimum *fiat* which gives rise to our very being, speaks in many guises, and cannot be isolated as a singular deictic origin.

The multiplicity of voice and genre in the Roman Rite can be described as *satiric*, as a gift of difference, whose complexity sets it apart from earlier manipulations of genre. Whereas the term "satire" nowadays denotes a particular *tone* of prose, it referred originally to a textual form which consisted in a diversity of genres whose multiplicity had possible magical or incantatory functions.[114] A *satura* was a verse composition, or "medley," which treated of a variety of subjects in a variety of voices, and is supposed to have had a culinary etymological origin in the term *lanx satura*, a dish of various fruits offered to

---

[114] Cuddon, *op. cit.*, *A Dictionary of Literary Terms*, 584–9; Robert C. Elliott, *The Power of Satire: Magic, Ritual, Art*, (Princeton: Princeton University Press, 1960); Lyotard, "Philosophy and Painting in the Age of Experimentation: Contribution to an Idea of Postmodernity," in *The Lyotard Reader*, ed. Andrew Benjamin, (Oxford: Blackwell Publishers, 1989), 181–95.

the gods. Early satires combined ritual, poetic, prophetic, and celebrative functions, and were characterized by sudden changes in mood, from joyous invocation to misery or aggressive invective. The Homeric hymns can be placed within the satiric genre, for they employed diverse modes of invocation, description, genealogical narrative, devotions, and lamentations. They were thought to have had a prefatory function, in anticipation of the recitation of an epic poem, usually concluding with a salutation and a formula of transition, in expectation of further song.

The Roman Rite's textual and vocal multiplicity shares this diversity of genre and mood, as well as its overall prefatory tone, but while the Homeric Hymns led conclusively to the recitation of an epic (whose purpose is to glorify the deeds of men), liturgical performance anticipates a supplementary chain of further such prefatory paths in the hope that there might be a song. And the "epic" which liturgy anticipates is more our own current inhabiting of the Christian narrative, lived out or emplotted not in a glorious past, but towards a future eschaton.

Besides the decentring of a strategic voice, the adoption of the satiric poetic genre in the liturgy involves a further possible motivation, which pertains to the liturgical restoration of the subject. The constant play of poetic difference and alteration of vocal positions can be situated within the overall casting of liturgy as the *hope* that there might be a liturgy, within which one can isolate the worshipper's manifold attempt to be heard by God, or fear of his own vocal and doxological inadequacy. Thus, the play of satire is a mode of "defamiliarization," a means of sustaining the worshipper's effort to prevent the descent of language into mere mechanical "babble" or recitation by rote.[115] This attempt at textual renewal is not merely aimed to prevent loss of concentration, but is part of a perpetual attempt to stave off the intrusion of language in its humiliated or spatialized form, inimical to liturgical purpose, which threatens also the dissolution of the subject. If this is successful, then the utterance of the hope that there might be liturgy itself turns into a present, partial arrival of liturgy (which is one and the same with the attainment of a definite but open identity by the subject).

Yet, for all this essential, Christological achievement of the impossible, and hence of a Christological continuity of the subject, the liturgical event can only be genuine if it retains always an eschatological reserve, or continuing

[115] The term "defamiliarization" was coined by Russian Formalists to describe the textual strategy of "renewal" which I am attributing to the liturgical genre of satire. See Tony Bennett, *Formalism and Marxism*, (London: Routledge and Kegan Paul, 1979), 32.

acknowledgement of the impossible and need for repeated divine arrival. And so a further contrast to the Homeric use of satire pertains to the worshipper's "mood." Its fear of the monotony of language, of becoming *"blasé par l'habitude,"*[116] gives rise to an altogether more uncertain voice, an uninsured locus which repeatedly sinks into despondency: *"quare me repulsti?,"* *". . . quare tristis incedo dum affligit me inimicus?"* *"Quare tristis es anima mea et quare conturbas me?"* *"Domine exaudi orationem meam. / Et clamor meus ad te veniat"* *"redime me et miserere mei."*[117] Such expressions of ontological and vocal crisis can be situated within a traditional mediaeval poetic commonplace known as *dorveille*, a psychological term describing the peculiar psycho-physical and spiritual depression suffered by bardic narrators, who typically complain of bodily exhaustion, restlessness, social withdrawal, or hypnotic suspension, an ontological diminution linked with the sin of *acedia* – a psychic deterioration or apathy which fears its own vocal erasure into silence.[118]

This narratorial dereliction is a symptom of the continued "impossibility" of the liturgical task, and is manifested in its own vocal stammer. The obscuration of repeated beginnings, shifting personae, oblique calls, cries to be heard, recommenced purifications, and apostrophic petitions for assistance reflect the same "slow tongue" of Moses, the "unclean lips" of Isaiah, the demur of Jeremiah, and the mutism of Ezekiel.[119] Thus, we can situate the liturgical poetics of satire, verbal "blockage," obscuration, supplementation, and preface, within an overall response to, and expression of the crisis of liturgical expression, the transgression of the mundane order of language, and the magnitude of its task: to mingle its voice with that of the supernumerary seraphim.

---

[116] Marcel Proust, *Le Temps Retrouvé*, (Paris: Gallimard, 1927), I. 916.

[117] [*why do you cast me off?*] [*. . . why go I mourning because of the affliction of my enemy?*] [*Why art thou cast down, O my soul, and why art thou disquieted within me?*] [*O Lord, hear my prayer/ And let my cry come unto Thee*] [*redeem me and be merciful unto me*]; Botte and Mohrmann, *op. cit.*, *L'Ordinaire*, see 58, 62, 70.

[118] *Dorveille* is suffered by the narrators of Dante's *Inferno*, Boethius' *Consolatio Philosophiæ*, and Chaucer's *House of Fame* and Prologue to *The Legend of Good Women*. See Michel Zink, "The Allegorical Poem as Interior Memoire," in eds Kevin Brownley and Stephen Nicholls, *Images of Power: Mediaeval History/Discourse Literature*, (Yale: Yale University Press, 1986), 100–26; Siegfried Wenzel, *The Sin of Sloth: Acedia in Mediaeval Thought and Literature*, (Chapel Hill: North Carolina University Press, 1960).

[119] Herbert Marks, "On Prophetic Stammering," in ed. Regina Schwartz, *The Book and the Text*, (Oxford: Blackwell Publishers, 1990), 60–80.

7 LITURGY AS BOTH TEXT AND VOICE

It has been seen how the multiple satiric genre of the Roman Rite performs an important liturgical function in resisting the linguistic structures of immanentism. In addition, its restless movement from one mode to another, together with the many structural and verbal aspects which imply an oral provenance, dislodge a metaphysics of the liturgical "book" as a static presence or pure origin. I shall now briefly discuss three ways in which the combination of these oral features with the fact that the liturgy is a written text gives rise to a peculiarly Christian negotiation of the "duality" of orality and writing itself, considering especially the significance of the Gospel and its enunciation. It will be realized that this is precisely the linguistic and structural precondition for the liturgical achievement of an open and yet continuous subjectivity.

First, the liturgical text as a whole is not *in excess* of its vocal performances, which suggests that, rather than obtaining a universalized presence, it is continuous with its repeated oralizations through time. It is neither prior to, nor other from its lived and variant enactments. And many of the features of the linguistic structure of the liturgy already discussed are not merely enunciated or read aloud, but draw attention to their supreme vocality, and thus serve doubly to qualify the nature of the book as an enclosed artefact. In particular, one can mention the figure of apostrophe, whose exclamatory invocations underline the contagious vocality of the text, for they are, as I described above, a calling in the hope of further calling. In this way, the liturgical text, as a physical phenomenon, leans away from itself towards further constitutive performances. Moreover, the vocative nature of apostrophe has implications for the book construed as a passive object, for its second person invocations of an ("absent") third person draw all potential absent addressees, including the worshipper himself, into the realm of possible dialogic relation with the text.[120] Thus, the book returns our gaze, and includes within its return a proclivity for all that is absent. In this way, there can be nothing off-stage, or too distant from its reach.

The second implication of the liturgy's textuality concerns a radicalization of notions of purification and the dichotomy of interior and exterior, which can be used to qualify Derrida's characterization of orality as predicated upon a metaphysical prioritization of the interior as spiritual and pure.[121] This

---

[120] Walter Benjamin *op. cit.*, "On Some Motifs in Baudelaire."
[121] See chapter 1 for a discussion of Derrida's deconstruction of Plato, and chapter 3, where I discuss his deconstruction of Husserl.

outwitting of the metaphysical interior-exterior duality can be seen in the deacon's prayer for purification, prior to his enunciation of the Gospel: "*Munda cor meum ac labia mea, omnipotens Deus, qui labia Isaiæ Prophetæ calculo mundasti ignito. . . .*"[122] The implication of his prayer for an account of the process of purification is that the outward enunciation itself is that which effects the purification of the interior heart. The heart and lips of the Deacon are worlded (*munditia*) and cleansed in the same action of verbal exteriorization. Thus, in its drawing attention to the heart as that which must be cleansed, and the Deacon's mouth as the ecstatic locus of purification, the prayer underlines that it is not that which *enters* the body which causes contamination, but one's own "ecstasizing" language, inverting the metaphysical account of pollution as that which comes from without.[123]

This prayer constitutes a petition for release from a "sophistic" separation of language from desire, and for a worthy enunciation of the Gospel. ". . .*Ut sanctum Evangelium tuum digne valeam nuntiare,*"[124] requires the uniting of both heart and lips. This prayer for purity, therefore, not only communicates the "site" of purity as that which issues from within language itself, which first of all arrives from without, but more particularly a linguistic issue which is combined with *erōs*, as that which emerges from the heart and only exists *as* outgoing. Such language therefore arises from both without *and* within. One can conclude that the significant distinction is not that which obtains between orality and writing, but rather, between liturgical and non-liturgical language, that is to say, erotic and *an*erotic expression. For that which is not "worthily" enunciated is language which has become monotonous, divorced from right desire. Such language is either taken to arrive purely from without, as if it reflected a set of given objects or (in the postmodern variant) as if it impersonally controlled the subject, or else it is taken to manifest merely the arbitrary whim of an essentially empty, interior subjective space.

The third implication of the textual nature of the liturgy pertains to its negotiation of time. Unlike the negative temporality of Lysian textuality, which views time's passage as synonymous with personal dissolution, the temporality of the book in the Roman Rite is more complex. Significantly, the verb used by the Celebrant to describe the Deacon's proclamation of the Gospel is "*nuntiare*," "to make now," which reminds us of the genuine

---

[122] [*Cleanse my heart and lips, O almighty God, who didst cleanse the lips of the Prophet Isaiah with a burning coal . . .*]; Botte and Mohrmann, *op. cit.*, *L'Ordinaire*, 64.

[123] "What goes into a man's mouth does not make him 'unclean,' but what comes out of his mouth, that is what makes him 'unclean,'" Matthew 15:11.

[124] [. . . *that I may worthily proclaim Thy holy gospel.*]

contingency and openness of the events narrated, despite their condition of writtenness, which, in other circumstances, would communicate those events as enclosed and anterior. The Deacon's request for purification is, therefore, the same as that which is made in advance of a sacrifice, for although the Gospel is written down in a book, its proclamation is continuous with the sacrifice it narrates. Its enunciation "makes now" a total sacrifice which is not a prior, closed-off event, but enters the interstices of our present, in contrast to the non-sacrificial silence of the unspoken text. Like Isaiah, whose request for purification is invoked, the Deacon stands in a position anterior to the purificatory sacrifice of the Gospel events. His prayer, therefore, is an analeptic repetition of Isaiah's own proleptic purification, figured through the burning coals. Like Isaiah, we stand in need of those events, which, although "historical," *exceed* our present. The Deacon's prayer concludes with a Christological doxology, "*Per Christum Dominum nostrum*," requesting purification through Christ, even though we stand *expectantly*, in a position *prior* to the "making now" of what mundanely lies *behind* us. Despite our "anteriority," like Isaiah, we are purified through Christ, in advance of Him, in order to be purified by Him. For the Deacon prays for purification so as to be worthy of enunciating the Gospel, which itself reaches both forwards and backwards as the condition of possibility for our purification. Here the liturgical work of the Holy Spirit is to put the Christological attainment of the "impossible" – that humans, with angels, may worship – back into the eschatological reserve of future anteriority.

It is just this entanglement of anteriority and posteriority which is redemptive; for Christ, who contains all our true identities, is eternally present in God's decrees, a presence which is to be correlated with that of the *written* word. As such, he is able to purify that which lies both "ahead" and "behind." Since writing here represents eternity, it is not spatialized, but becomes a bodily event, not "left behind" in historical anteriority, but perpetually realized in the Eucharistic-Ecclesial action: *Sanguis Christi, novum testamentum.*[125] Thus we are purified by the Gospel even though we are historically "subsequent" to its events, and liturgically prior to their repetition, and despite the Gospel's "givenness" as a text, and our perpetual need of purification in order to read it. In a sense, the combining of the written text – whose words are always already "given," and therefore obtain a double "writtenness" as the

---

[125] Florus, *Expositio missæ*, c.61, cited in de Lubac, *op. cit., Corpus Mysticum*, 217. De Lubac notes that in patristic times, the body of the Scriptures was thought of as "un véritable *corpus Christi*," 103; for a discussion of the interweaving of the scriptural and sacramental in the patristic and early Middle Ages, see de Lubac, 57–60.

trace of memory – with its "enunciation," permits a performance in liturgical time of eternity.

This combination of salvific narration and purificatory reading makes of the book a sacrificial altar, which is censed in preparation for the sacrifice, so that its words appear to ascend as an offering to God. But the text thus burns upwards to join the eternal divine text of the Logos which is nonetheless a book perpetually *uttered* by the Father, uttered as writing, only to re-expire in the out-breathing of the Spirit.

Chapter Five

SERAPHIC VOICES:
THE SPACE OF DOXOLOGY

1 INTRODUCTION

In Part I of this essay, it was explained how the modern colonization of time by a lateral and abstract space is predicated on a violence which promotes the divisions of inside and outside, subject and object, active and passive. And it was demonstrated that its probity of permanence and security is nonetheless reducible to nihilism, both in terms of objectivity as fulfilled in the *nihil*, and in its secret (or not so secret) disempowerment of the subject.

However, my discussion, in the previous chapter, of the lineaments of liturgical impossibility as linking the distinctive temporality of the liturgy with its character as both oral and written, began to suggest an alternative negotiation of time and space, which offers a radicalization of such dichotomies as inside and outside, before and after, and proposes the possibility of a redemptive restoration of genuine subjectivity, and a dismantling of the "object" as that which does not exceed its physical extension. I shall now delineate the co-ordinates of liturgical time and space, arguing that far from being opposed, they are only fully realized in their combination and resolution in the relational, ecclesial gift of peace. Following from this, I shall conclude this chapter with a discussion of the centrality of gift in the Roman Rite, as a consequence of the non-violent resolution of space and time, its characteristics, and implications for a restoration of genuine subjectivity in God.

2 "VESPER IN AMBIGUO EST": THE TIME OF LITURGY

In this section, I shall discuss the time of liturgy, with particular reference to the Institution Narrative, and shall characterize it as, first, prefatory, and secondly, "uncovered." I shall also show how, by contrasting this temporality with that of the spatialized order, the liturgy offers a redemptive critique of secular time, and its concomitant epistemological assumptions.

In contrast to pagan temporality, which, as we have seen, is subject to a kind of "closure" derived both from its definition of time as that which occupies an epilogic space "after" the origins and its concomitant recollective epistemology, the time of liturgy is more intensely open. This "openness" is not that of nihilism, which reduces time to a non-teleological "passing," but rather is predicated upon a protocol of redemptive return, not of an anterior "essence," but of that which is both before and after, and repeated with difference. This non-identical "return," which places time within the category of anticipatory *prelude* of a post-temporal fulfillment, is enacted by the spoken word itself, whose ultimate reconciliation to the passage of each syllable is the condition of possibility for there to be a word at all. The word arrives both from the past – the remembered tradition of language – and from the future – as that which can only arrive because of the futurity of each subsequent syllable, and which ultimately betokens the futurity of resurrection. This verbal foreshadowing of redemptive return is repeated by the self-consuming figure of incense, whose disappearance, like that of the apostrophic call, is paradoxically necessary for the fulfillment of its sensuous message.[1]

From the examples of speech and incense, it can be seen that the time of liturgy is not that of a measurable "advance" away from a magnificent past which it nonetheless yearns to reclaim identically, nor does it offer the satisfaction of a spatial accomplishment, which, in the case of immanentism, mimics a pagan attempt to return to an anteriority prior to time. Rather, liturgical time is tilted away from any delimited or inscribed attainment, and, in its prefatory casting, implicitly offers a critique of the violence of an immanentist construal of time which claims to obtain an "arrival," and perforce closes off the *potential* of human action. For although the time of liturgy is forever "before," this does not humiliate the possibility of human action, but rather exposes the dishonesty of any claim that ethical action consists in discrete accomplishments, or that action stands on its own, outside an anticipation of its ultimate eschatological consummation. The liturgy reminds us that all our actions, even those of our past, do not exceed the status of that which is going-to-happen, although this *establishes* rather than erases the possibility of action. In the same way, our liturgical

[1] See Augustine, *Confessions*, Book XI Sections 26–7; Søren Kierkegaard, *op. cit.*, *Repetition: An Essay in Experimenting Psychology* by Constantin Constantius, tr. Howard V. Hong and Edna H. Hong, (New Jersey: Princeton University Press, 1983), 131; see above, chapter 4, section 4, "*The Apostrophic Voice.*"

offering is still no more than a *propemptikon*, sung on the evening before a journey.

The recurrent theme of the time of evening can be situated within this prefatory dimension of time. At the recitation of Psalm 140, when the Celebrant censes the altar, he prays that the lifting up of his hands will be an evening sacrifice: "*Dirigatur, Domine, oratio mea, sicut incensum, in conspectu tuo : elevatio manuum mearum sacrificium vespertinum.*"[2] Why especially is it to be an evening sacrifice? First, according to the Jewish and Christian lectionaries, the evening is cast as the beginning of the ensuing day, and so obtains the status of that which is just-before-itself.[3] Secondly, in Apocalyptic literature, the evening is the in-between time of angelic visitation, and the descent of God's heavenly fire. The eschatological Day of the Lord is a day of evening, for when the light diminishes, the final light, which shows our mundane "day" to be only before-itself, descends as fire from heaven. The evening is therefore the time when diurnal human action and grids of reason are made redundant by the diminution of daylight, yielding place to the vulnerable time of maximum exchange between heaven and earth,[4] a time ensuring that prayer – as that which introduces the ensuing "day" – becomes the gateway to time itself.[5] In this way, the liturgy poses a critique of mundane time, inverting the quotidian construal of evening as the time when we cease productivity and put aside activity in order to augment our productiveness the following day, by presenting the sacrificial evening as the beginning of the "real," authentic (liturgical) work from which all our diurnal activities are suspended.

The critique of mundane time implicit within this inversion of the notion of "evening" is continued in the transgression of historical time which takes place in the Institution Narrative. For this time of in-between when God descends is also that of the ultimate sacrifice instituted in the evening *in advance of itself* ("QUI *pridie quam pateretur*")[6] at the Last Supper. The blood which we are commanded

[2] [*Let my prayer, O Lord, be set forth in Thy sight as the incense : and let the lifting up of my hands be an evening sacrifice*]; Bernard Botte and Christine Mohrmann, *L'Ordinaire de la Messe*, (Paris: Editions du Cerf, 1953), 70.

[3] Roland de Vaux, *Studies in Old Testament Practice*, (Cardiff: Cardiff University Press, 1964), 47.

[4] "The man Gabriel . . . being caused to fly swiftly, touched me about the time of the evening oblation," Daniel 9:21; "I saw in the night visions, and, behold, one like the Son of man came with the clouds of heaven," Daniel 7:13; see also I Kings 18:38; Zechariah 14:6.

[5] "Yet the Lord will command his loving kindness in the daytime, and in the night his song shall be with me, and my prayer unto the God of my life," Psalm 42.8; see further, Lacoste, *op. cit.*, *Expérience et Absolu*, 93–7, on evening as the time of vigil.

[6] [*WHO the day before he suffered*]; Botte and Mohrmann, *op. cit.*, *L'Ordinaire*, 80.

to drink is the blood which has yet to be shed ("*effundetur*," future passive), and thus, by participating in the event of the Last Supper, we occupy the sacrificial moment *before* the Passion, the moment anterior to itself, which we both anticipate and remember. The command to repeat, "*in mei memoriam facietis*,"[7] is a present imperative, a recall that is anticipated, a detour not by the past but by the future, when after is before, and before is after, and where isolating an homogeneous thread of time becomes a delicate task, and disturbs our ordinary understanding of memory and expectation.[8] Furthermore, this confounding of memory as that which extrinsically recollects is intensified by Christ's own remembering of Himself even whilst He is still empirically present. Memory is here cast not as that which is subsequent to an initial loss, but as an excessive memorial which remembers that which still remains.[9]

These transgressions of mundane chronologies and proprieties of time suggest that whatever the literal clock-time at which a Mass is celebrated, it occupies the prefatory time of evening, but not in the sense of a moment before the next moment, but of the distended moment before the eschaton. Here, protocols of seriality and repetition are defamiliarized, for in addition to the entanglement of remembering and anticipating, our own celebration of the Mass is neither a "new" sacrifice, nor "extra," but the same, always already repeated sacrifice which we remember even before it occurs. The "original" action is continuous with its subsequent repetitions: "*Haec quotiescumque feceritis, in mei memoriam facietis*,"[10] in such a way that Christ's own historical institution of the Eucharist cannot be fetishized as the ultimate node of the repeated event, or a more privileged instance of it, for even within the repeated "origin" of the Eucharist, its own completion is postponed: it only *becomes* an event by virtue of its subsequent repetitions. In the words "*Haec quotiescumque feceritis*," this event looks forward to itself, towards its own future as an event.

3 CHRISTIC ASYNDETON

A consideration of the Institution Narrative as it is situated within the liturgical journey as a whole shows a gradual temporal transposition from "aesthetic" time

---

[7] [*do this in memory of me.*]
[8] On "achrony" see further Genette, *Narrative Discourse*, tr. Jane Lewin, (Oxford: Blackwell Publishers, 1980), 79–85.
[9] "What the church 'remembers' in the eucharist is partly *beyond* history," Dom Gregory Dix, *The Shape of the Liturgy*, (London: Dacre Press, 1945), 264.
[10] [*As often as you do these things, you shall do them in remembrance of me.*]

(to use the Kierkegaardian classification), understood as an act of remembering which is external and subsequent to that which is recalled, towards "uncovered" or dislocationary time. The Service of Readings and the narration of salvation history recited in the *Credo*, can be categorized as "summary" or "accelerated" narratives, which recount in a few paragraphs the events of several days, months, or years of existence, omitting close attention to particular details.[11] These larger narrative strokes can be seen to occupy a preparatory space in the movement of the overall liturgical text, in which the participants still occupy an "aesthetic" position, external and subsequent to the events related.

However, this externality becomes increasingly ambiguous, even during the preliminary stages. For example, the introductory sentence which the Deacon pronounces before enunciating the Gospel, "*SEQUENTIA sancti Evangelii secundum,*" reminds the participants that their own lives are implicated in the events that are narrated, and that an aesthetic stance in relation to its events cannot be sustained.[12] The *Credo* immediately follows this intimation of inclusion, itself repeating the same transition from aesthetic narration to contingent performance, for although its account of salvation history remains an "accelerated" and aesthetic narrative, its diegetic speed is gradually attenuated as it approaches its final phrases: "*Et exspecto resurrectionem mortuorum. Et vitam venturi sæculi,*"[13] phrases which explicitly implicate the present and future life of the Church.

These gradual inclusions of the worshipper into the liturgical events signify a shift towards "uncovered" time. There are several other poetic alterations which herald this transition. For example, there is an increase in direct address to God, dialogic exchanges between Celebrant and Deacon, and the direct and physical participation which occurs at the Offertory. These stress, through the use of direct speech and action, an assimilation of "lived" time in the Rite, and a concomitantly *decelerated* narrative speed. In addition, the syntax of the prayers becomes increasingly complex, signalled by the use of subordinated conjunctions: "*Te igitur,*" "*Hanc igitur,*" "*Quam oblationem,*" "*Qui pridie.*"[14]

This intensified complication of language in the Canon plays an important

[11] Genette, *op. cit.*, *Narrative Discourse*, 95.
[12] [*THE CONTINUATION of the Holy Gospel*]; Botte and Mohrmann, *op. cit.*, *L'Ordinaire*, 64. This notion of the inhabited contingency of what is nonetheless "historical" is transformed by the rendering of the introduction to the Gospel in the *Roman Missal*, "A reading from the holy gospel according to N." This stresses first the exclusively textual status of the Gospel, and the anterior position occupied by the events narrated by the Deacon. There is no explicit sense of ecstatic contingency or "making now."
[13] [*And I look for the resurrection of the dead. And the life of the world to come*]; *ibid.*, 66.
[14] [*Thee therefore*]; [*This therefore*]; [*Which oblation*]; [*Who the day*]; *ibid.*, 74, 78, 80.

role in anticipating the complete attenuation of mundane time at the Institution Narrative, which marks the transition from mundane to sacral time, paralleled by that from "summary" narrative to what Genette would classify as a "scene" (or from nondramatic to dramatic narrative). Indeed, the almost obsessively detailed attention in the narrative account of Christ's actions at the Last Supper does not merely coincide with the events of the fabula in terms of duration and speed, but *outlasts* them.

The narrative attenuation and obsessiveness serve to accentuate the radical difference between human and divine language, for the words which Christ now utters are expressed elliptically, in syntax which omits all explanatory conjunctions and subordinations:

> *Accipite, et manducate ex hoc omnes.*
> HOC EST ENIM CORPUS MEUM.
> *Accipite, et bibite ex eo omnes.*
> HIC EST CALIX SANGUINIS MEI, NOVI ET ÆTERNI TESTAMENTI :
> MYSTERIUM FIDEI :
> QUI PRO VOBIS ET PRO MUTIS EFFUNDETUR IN REMISSIONEM PECCATORUM.
> *Hæc quotiescumque feceritis, in mei memoriam facietis.*[15]

Christ's ineffable dicta are constructed by means of asyndetic syntax to which, in chapter 2, I attributed a nihilistic and spatialized drift. However, it can be shown that his use of this syntactic category obtains a sacral resonance.

As well as the explicit omission of conjunctions between each clause, the manner of institution is itself supremely segmented. Christ's divided actions, first the dividing of the bread, and secondly, the lifting of the cup, give rise to more divisions, as His Body and Blood are divided again and again and distributed many times over. The only rational cohesion in these utterances is that of the chronicity of their segments, for the co-ordinating conjunction, "*et*," connecting the commands to take and eat, and take and drink, the subordinating conjunction providing purposive information, and the temporal adverbial "*quotiescumque*," do not diffuse the overall asyndetic ellipsis, but *add* to it. The linguistic claim to reason to which these conjunctions contribute provides an *appearance* of explanation which dissolves senselessly into the dislocationary reason of God.

---

[15] [*Take, and eat ye all of this.* FOR THIS IS BODY. *Take, and drink ye all of this.* FOR THIS IS THE CUP OF MY BLOOD OF THE NEW AND ETERNAL TESTAMENT : THE MYSTERY OF FAITH : WHICH FOR YOU AND FOR MANY SHALL BE SHED FOR THE REMISSION OF SINS. *As often as you do these things, ye shall do them in remembrance of me];* ibid., 80.

Christ's use of a syntactic form which is usually reserved for secular inventories, or monitored control of random data, betokens a dissolution of that very order in which it seems to be composed, for the apparently serial components of this event exceed their context, demanding subsequent repetition and re-division, not in such a way as to signify an inadequacy in the "original" event, but because of that event's excess. Christic asyndeton is not monitored or confined, for His words leap beyond such controlled arbitrariness into the region of the eternal Logos, exploding in gestures, paradigms, and words, the distinction between time and eternity, reason and insanity. His locutions do not "refer" in the manner of ordinary taxonomies, but are universals which insist on the readjustment of all representation to configure his optimum signs. Thus, the naming of the bread and the cup as Body and Blood has no chronological confinement: it is achronic, affording each nominating tableau a climactic rather than chronicle identity. Similarly, the actions of breaking the bread and lifting the cup are not connected serially, but are interrupted by the communion of supper: "*Simili modo postquam cœnatum est.*"[16] Thus, the beginning and ending of the human meal, like all beginnings and endings, take place in God, as a transposition of the morning and evening sacrifices of cereal and blood which all meals, as figures of the Eucharist, repeat.

Christ's use of asyndetic syntax has implications for a liturgical critique of modern, secular modes of epistemology. In my description of the complex, anaphoric structures of the prayers – especially manifested in the *Credo* – of the Roman Rite in the previous chapter, it was seen that pre-modern language readily reflects a sacral universe in which all elements form a constitutive part of the greater whole, and one element recalls another. This was expressed by means of a synthesis of hypotaxis (syntax with subordinating conjunctions) and parataxis (syntax with co-ordinating conjunctions) which I described in the previous chapter as "organic" syntax. The use of this complex and figural structure in the liturgical text shows it to be an essentially *open* configuration which allows itself to be subverted by an order which exceeds its own reason. Although its complexity is hierarchically disposed, and contains explicit expressions of human rationality ("*Te igitur,*" "*Hanc igitur,*" "*Quam oblationem,*" "*Qui pridie*"), it does not thereby preclude the possibility of difference or change, and can be seen to follow a narrative openness which looks forward in faith towards the potential of its own future. It is in this context that Christ's use of asyndetic syntax at the Last Supper is a reminder in every liturgical performance that human reason is incomplete, and that the work of praise is

16 [*Likewise after supper.*]

never finished.[17] By contrast, contemporary spatial language, which claims absolute openness and spontaneity as its probity, bespeaks falsely the ultimacy of human reason, and so operates according to a closed system which admits of no difference, and yet seeks to mimic this eucharistic ultimacy.

Thus, by situating our narrative of things into the explicitly and humanly "rational" form of complex syntax, and Christ's ineffable dicta in asyndeton, we pay homage to the never-ending work of Eucharist. It is a syntactic expression of the relationship between the worshipper and God, through the human use and concomitant derision of mundane reason in the face of the incomprehensible wisdom which can only be expressed in the silences between words. By deliberately exposing the mechanisms of our "reason" – as in our syntactic performances in the *Credo* and *Gloria* – of that which we "understand" of the Trinitarian relations and the economy of salvation, our apparent human pride is grounded in a supreme and doxological humility which wishes to experience the contrast between its own cumbersome reasons and the eternal and inscrutable wisdom of God, thus expressing its agonizing desire to witness the nullification of the false fullness of its own reason by that which it tries hard not to see as madness.[18]

Christ's omission of rational conjunctions in his words of Institution is not, therefore, a deliberate, monitored removal or obscuration of explication, but an expression of that supra-reason which mundane epistemologies condemn as insanity. The insanity of the Cross, the non-sense of sacrifice, gift, and excess, express a wisdom which is obscured in the rationalized exchanges of instrumentalized transactions of the mundane world. By the asyndetic silence

---

[17] My interpretation of the liturgical implications of the asyndetic "difference" of Christ's speech at the Last Supper applies also to His characterization in the Gospel narratives. I am grateful to Dr Janet Martin Soskice for this observation.

[18] The substitution of complex by asyndetic syntax in the revised liturgies results in an elimination of this distinction between the deliberately and constitutively self-humiliating "rational" syntax of the earlier version, and the sacral asyndeton of Christ's words of consecration. Unlike the absence of conjunctions in Christic asyndeton, their elision in the remainder of the text has sinister implications for (1) an understanding of subjective desire, now monitored and provoked in terms of lack; (2) the overall temporal structure of the liturgical journey which I have shown to be in part dependent upon syntactic differentiation and variation; (3) a theory of liturgy: the resultant simplification of the overall narrative strategy means that our liturgical journey no longer comprises ceaseless stammering recommencements, thus implicitly assuming the unicursality of our route, and straightforward appropriability of its destination. See further Catherine Pickstock, "Asyndeton: Syntax and Insanity: A Study of the Revision of the Nicene Creed," *Modern Theology*, 10.4 (October, 1994), 321–40.

which binds his anamnetic utterances, Christ's speech opens a genuine and salvific void (in contrast to the enforced and studied nihilism of immanence) which no words can "explain," and which commands a mystery which can only be received and repeated. This language of *lacunae*, which provokes a breach between human rationality and divine wisdom, is that before which the world – compelled to position itself in relation to such strange "reason" – becomes culpable.[19] Thus, in the liturgical (syntactic) differentiation of two types of reason, the worshipper – who once had measured his own command of reason by an announcement of subordinations and co-ordinations, and insanity by its refusal to articulate such hierarchies – now abases himself before that very insanity.

4 LITURGICAL SPACE

In Part I of this essay, I argued against the process of spatialization which I characterized as an attempt to substitute a unicursal, abstract, and purely immanent ordering of reality for both eternity and time. I also described the concomitant illusory assumptions which a spatialized reality encourages, and how these assumptions, in the interests of secular and absolutist power, conspire to erase the possibility of genuine subjectivity. In this section, I shall contrast these uniform and lateral lineaments of immanentism with their liturgical counterparts, arguing, first, that in the Roman Rite, space is not identified as opposite to time; and secondly, that it shatters the various proprieties of mundane topology. In the next section, I will argue that in the liturgy, time and space are only fully realized when they coincide in the liturgical and overtly ecclesial bestowal of peace.

The two main characteristics of liturgical space which were indicated in chapter four were its importance for the identification of the worshipping subject, and its distended nature. In the first section, I described the way in which the worshipper is identified by his location "*in nomine Patris*," and by the journeying character of this location, "*Introibo ad altare Dei*." It was seen that the geographical destination of this journey was unlike that of mundane journeys, for it perpetually recedes and becomes other from itself. The journey towards the "*sublime altare*" is towards that which is definitively neither here nor there, but is "almost" (*sublime*: the just-below which implies the beyond) that which is itself a matter of "not quite" betokening a rising and an alteration (*altare*: the place of sacrificial burning). Thus, it can be seen that the

[19] On the superlative "reason" of Christ's madness, see Michel Foucault, *Madness and Civilization: A History of Insanity in the Age of Reason*, (London: Routledge, 1989), 78–81.

worshipping "I," identified by its journey, will perforce never attain its
identity in the sense of a stable totality, but must, like the nature of its journey
and destination, be always only prefatory. Moreover, before it becomes
anything it all, it must first become that which it is not: an impersonation and
dispossession.

However, in the Roman Rite, spatial location is a means by which we
identify and characterize not only the worshipper, but also both God and the
angels. For example, Archangel Michael is identified as "*a dextris altaris
incensi*"; Jesus Christ "*sedet ad dexteram Patris*"; and the Holy Spirit "*ex Patre
Filioque procedit.*"[20] The liturgical text thus enables the worshipper to identify
angelic and divine characters by means of spatial locations, but not in such a
way as to indicate their occupation of a representable or delimited place. This
qualification can be seen in several ways. First, God is located within the
Trinity, which is a *relational* rather than geographical place.[21] Secondly,
because of the divine nature, the place where God is located is not a place in
addition to His being, nor could it be said, in contrast to the spatial
identifications of the worshipper, that God is defined by His situation. To the
contrary, place itself is defined by God: "*Domine, dilexi decorem domus tuæ et
locum habitationis gloriæ tuæ.*"[22] The place where God is, which is the place of
glory, is a place defined in relation to God, for He is the ultimate place which
defines even the "Where am I?" of place itself. And the beauty of the place
of God is the beauty of God, whose radiance defines the place as beautiful, and
as more than itself. In this way, one understands that whilst one might speak
of one's own occupation of space, one can only speak in terms of God's
preoccupation of space, for He occupies space even before there is a space, and
occupies it more than it occupies itself. God is also preoccupied in relation
to space because He is displaced: He is permanently concerned with the
Other. In Himself, He is ecstatically preoccupied. So although God is not in
a place for He is infinite, He is not non-spatial, for He situates sites themselves.
And therefore He is the eminent (or pre-eminent) space of preoccupation,
which gives space its job in advance of itself, which is to make space for
worship.

This radiant and excessive structure of divine space overflows into that of
our liturgical journey, in such a way as to defamiliarize mundane topologies

---

[20] [*on the right hand of the altar of incense*]; [*sitteth at the right hand of the Father*]; [*who proceedeth
from the Father and the Son*]; Botte and Mohrmann, *op. cit.*, *L'Ordinaire*, 70, 67.

[21] "*Iesu Christe. Cum Sancto Spiritu in gloria Dei Patris,*" *ibid.*, 64.

[22] [*Lord, I have loved the habitation of Thy house : and the place where Thine honour dwelleth*];
ibid., 70. See Jean-Yves Lacoste, "En marge du monde et de la terre: l'aisle," *Revue de
metaphysique et de morale*, no. 2 (1985), 185–200.

which, by defining space as pure extension, stipulate that the goal of a journey
cannot be simultaneously attained and postponed, before and after, within
and without, "to hand" and distant. These apparently oxymoronic combinations are definitive of liturgical space. For, as I described in the
second section of chapter four, the traveller asserts his direction "*ad altare Dei*,"
which communicates a deictic exteriority from its destination, but despite
this, appears to expect God's proximity: "*Quare me repulsti?*" The complexity
of liturgical space derives from this ambiguous relation with God Himself,
the pre-positioner. For the worshipper is never outside God, for any place
which claims to be extra to God is a disappearing place. And yet, we are fallen
away from God, which means that, although we are never without God, we
must nonetheless travel towards Him. And again this journey appears
impossible, since in order to journey towards God, we must already have
reached Him. As we saw in the previous chapter, this impossibility is only
realized through God's kenotic journey towards us. Since God is the God who
pre-occupies, He redeems as the God who precedes us.

This preceding, however, does not render the liturgical effect automatic.
On the contrary, the need for a prayer that our earthly incense will reach, and
be received by God, reveals the liturgical journey through space to be subject
to deferral and distension. Its journey is not from A to B, as for ordinary lateral
journeys, but more a matter of A sending itself again and again from A to A to
A: "*PER intercessionem beati Michaëlis Archangeli, stantis a dextris altaris incensi, et
omnium electorum suorum, incensum istud dignetur Dominus benedicere et in odorem
suavitatis accipere.*"[23] Our own earthly offering of incense, which configures our
sacrifice of praise,[24] is itself only a preface to the angelic incense which rises
from the altar of incense.

The repeated returning to itself of the incense's attempt to travel to God
signifies a second characteristic of liturgical space and the nature of the
worshipper's journey "*ad altare Dei*," which is that an "outward" journey
towards God is not an unicursal route, but involves a concomitant journey *into
ourselves*, though not at the expense of our proximal and communal physicality:
to the contrary, our physicality is intensified. This inward aspect of our
outward journey is figured variously throughout the Rite. Most obviously,
our physical journey towards an actual altar is balanced by a movement of God
into our own, physical bodies. At the Commingling, when the Celebrant

---

[23] [*THROUGH the intercession of blessed Michael the Archangel, who standeth at the right hand of
the altar of incense, and of all his elect, may the Lord vouchsafe to bless this incense, and receive it in
an odour of sweetness*]; *ibid.*; Apocalypse 8:3-4, (Luke 11:18f).
[24] "*Dirigatur, Domine, oratio mea, sicut incensum, in conspectu tuo,*" *ibid.*

repeats three times the words of the Centurion, "*Domine non sum dignus, ut intres sub tectum meum : sed tantum dic verbo et sanabitur anima mea,*"[25] it is made explicit that the worshipper's journey does not consist in a movement towards an outer place, but towards God's journey into us, where our living bodies are exalted as God's temple. At this point, therefore, we assume the prefatory stance of the Centurion – like the prophetic figures of Abraham and John the Baptist, prior to the Passion – but with a difference, for we occupy an already realized eschaton, and so do not remain "aesthetically" exterior to God, but receive Him physically into our bodies.

This inward journey therefore is not to be interpreted as a crudely metaphysical escape from our embodied character towards a spiritual interior, for it serves to intensify the physicality of our bodies, reminding us that we eat and drink, and are situated within a community. However, because liturgical space, by its recognition of the transcendent, is not purely scalar, physicality is intensified as much or more by its continuity with a spiritual – indeed metaphysical – dimension as by its reception of God as food. Since our outward journey towards the Holy of Holies is identified as a journey for which we must find an inner entrance, our interior minds must be purified: "*Aufer a nobis, quæsamus Domine, iniquitates nostras : ut ad Sancta sanctorum puris mereamur mentibus introire.*"[26] But this consciousness of the need for interior purification is not an ascetic denial of the self, nor an erasure of any possibility of being a subject. On the contrary, our outward and inward journey towards the reception of God into our bodies is concomitantly a journey towards our own constitution as a subject.

So far, I have identified liturgical space as a journey which is continuous with time, and as a forward-moving space which, whilst striving towards the receding and heavenly distance, also involves a journey into ourselves for which we must find an inner entrance. But perhaps we must look in another place for this inner entrance? The worshipper is not only identified by his situation within the space of journey and desire, but also another kind of space which is *retrospective*. I speak of the space of memory, which is a temporal and perpetually supplemented space. But the two types of space I have isolated, prospective and retrospective, are not really to be distinguished from one another, for the worshipper's forward journey is precisely its journey *towards memory*: the occasion of our meeting God is our remembering of Him

---

[25] [*Lord I am not worthy that Thou shouldst come under my roof : but speak the word only and my soul shall be healed*]; *ibid.*, 90; Matthew 8:8.

[26] [*Take away from us, we beseech Thee O Lord, our iniquities : that we may be worthy to enter the Holy of Holies with pure minds*]; *ibid.*, 62.

(although this anamnetic epiphany is not simply retrospectively experienced, as I described in the previous section).

What is specific to liturgical space, therefore, is that within it a journey does not proceed from one situation (or circum-stance) to another, but instead travels always further into its own real situation within God – for this reason, it is a journey both without and within, and at once backwards (in memory) and forwards (in desire). Such a journey is not therefore *through* space, but is rather the journey *of* space, of a space which can only abide (ontologically) in its return to its real situation. Liturgical space, therefore, instead of obliterating time in the manner of secular space, becomes coterminous with a sacred time by bringing its own situation along with it, and yet continuously transforming that very situation in its quest to situate its situation as not its own at all. In a sense, like the elusive "present moment," this space is nowhere, since it is perpetually suspended between a bounded but never autonomous, never finitely definable space, and an infinite "space" which is a strange, situating metaspace, without any bounds or even areas.

Thus the supreme characteristic of liturgical space is that it exceeds the distinction between worldly and other-worldly. In this regard, it contrasts to the immanent space of paganism, according to whose topological protocols, both human beings and gods are subordinate to the contrast between earth and world, familiar and distant. In his book on liturgical experience, *Expérience et Absolu*, Jean-Yves Lacoste argues against Heidegger's acceptance of this pagan limitation of space as a fundamental given, showing that liturgy transgresses the distinction between the local and familiar "earth" and the totality of alien space, or "world," because the event of the incarnation marks the end of purely human history.[27] By invoking the vision of St Benedict, a dream in which the saint finds himself looking down upon the world as a global totality, Lacoste shows how liturgy enables the worshipper to exceed the distinction between the familiarity of one's proximal home and the anxiety of being in the world.[28] The apparently impossible non-place in which the worshipper is thus situated reveals his true, exalted nature which, as always already located in God, is that which exceeds even the world – or the totality of all possible spaces – itself. And because the worshipper has a definitive – if ineffable and other-worldly – direction, he is figured as a pilgrim, in contrast both to the devotee of purely chthonic, local gods, and to the cosmopolitan cosmic sage, an unhomed nomad who refuses the specificity of place, at home everywhere and so nowhere (invoked by Lacoste).[29]

[27] Jean-Yves Lacoste, *Expérience et Absolu*, (Paris: P.U.F., 1994), 7–25.
[28] *Ibid.*, 28–48.
[29] *Ibid.*, 30f.

Like the sacrifice which the pilgrim offers, he is himself *adscriptor*, travelling "*in nomine Patris*," and *adscriptio*, supplementary. The citizens of the heavenly space are neither autochthonous nor homeless, but belong in a place which is always elsewhere, and must become naturalized by being redeemed.[30] In this way, liturgical space is given as an alternative to the all-conquering space of the secular, in either its modern or postmodern versions, which are dialectically at one. Its character as both mobile and yet infinitely situated precludes, on the one hand, any absolutist mobilization or strategic emplotment of space, and, on the other, the displaced speculative abstraction of the void which negates physical existence. Thus, the liturgical raising of space to be a partner of time puts an end to secular spatiality's paradoxical *humiliation of space* which mistakes permanence and accumulation in space for the ultimacy of transcendence, and so robs space of itself.

5 'DONA NOBIS PACEM': THE LITURGICAL CHRONOTOPE

In this section, I will qualify Lacoste's configuration of the pilgrim according to the lonely vision of St Benedict by arguing that it too much emphasizes the liturgical journey as solitary and unicursal. Instead, this journey must be more fully situated within the proximal, communal, and temporal ecclesial space.

At the moment when the presentation and arrangement of the gifts is completed, and the Celebrant at the head of the congregation and in its name is about to draw near to God with those gifts, he kisses the altar and then turns to face the congregation. In a highly personal address, which petitions the congregation for a mobilization of all the forces of prayer to assist his own sacrifice – which is likewise theirs – so that it might be acceptable, he implicitly shows that such an entrance into God – concomitant upon the offering of a sacrifice – does not involve a disappearance from proximity, but requires it all the more intensely: "*Orate, fratres : ut meum ac vestrum sacrificium acceptabile fiat apud Deum Patrem omnipotentem.*"[31] The Ministers then respond by asking that God receive his sacrifice to the benefit of those present, explicitly including the proximity of the community and the whole Church: "*Suscipiat Dominus*

---

[30] "We are, as Christians, priests; but we are not so by natural right. It is by grace that we are given a sacrifice . . . and accounted worthy to 'stand and serve as priests' in the presence of God," Rowan Williams, *Eucharistic Sacrifice – The Roots of a Metaphor*, (Grove Liturgical Study no.31, Grove Books, 1982), 8–9 (citing Hippolytus' *Apostolic Tradition*, IV.11).

[31] [*Pray, brethren : that my sacrifice and yours may be acceptable to God the Father almighty*]; Botte and Mohrmann, *op. cit.*, *L'Ordinaire*, 72; Jungmann, *op. cit.*, *The Mass*, 352–5.

sacrificium de manibus tuis ad laudem et gloriam nominis sui, ad utilitatem quoque nostram, totiusque Ecclesiæ suæ sanctæ."[32]

This request is self-fulfilling, for the subsequent doxological exchange between Celebrant and Ministers is as much constitutive of community as it is doxological: *"Dominus vobiscum. / Et cum spiritu tuo. / Sursum corda. / Habemus ad Dominum. / Gratias agamus Domino Deo nostro. / Dignum et iustum est."*[33] The performance of community in the offering of gift characterizes liturgical space as both relational and temporal. In addition, its space contrasts with that of the pagan *polis*, in which only a full citizen could offer a liturgy: only a citizen could be a citizen. In Christian liturgical space, there are no prior determining criteria for both the subject and the community, outside the offering of gift which *all* may offer. This priority of gift, which (as we shall see) is a category which integrates spontaneous initiative with a constitutive exchange, results in an *equivalence* of individual and community. It follows that while we exceed the world through our liturgical transgression of lateral limits, the world – as a now non-totalized community – continues to exceed *us*. We remain with the other in praise. This modification of Lacoste's account also has implications for the liturgical co-ordination of space and time. It has been seen how liturgy *temporalizes* space, ensuring that it is mobile, supplemented, and deferred. However, if time were simply all-conquering in this fashion, then it would be assimilable to a pure flux whose "presences" are mere illusions, like the postmodern void. And it was shown in Part I how such a flux-as-void is really the *consummation* of spatialization, since the void is the perfect object. Hence the absolute reduction of space to time would paradoxically achieve spatialization after all. If the journey of the worshipper moves in a sphere-towards-God which is contextually more fundamental than the polyphonic simultaneity of "world" (understood not as a totalized nowhere, but as the open sequence of created relations), then this would seem dangerously close to a flux without measure. But, to the contrary, because the worshipper only offers his gifts along with others, and also with and through an exchange of giving with these created others, it is also the world itself, and not just the lone worshipper, which outflanks the world. This means that while liturgical space is mobile, supplemented, and deferred, it is also true that liturgical time is both *articulated* and *polyphonous*. Articulation involves ceaseless segmentation and sub-segmentation to produce phrases divided by *intervals*. In these pauses, the

---

[32] [*May the Lord receive the sacrifice at thy hands, to the praise and glory of His name, to our benefit, and that of all His holy Church.*]

[33] [*The Lord be with you. / And with thy spirit. / Lift up your hearts. / We lift them up unto the Lord. / Let us give thanks unto our Lord God. / It is meet and just.*]

memory is able to recollect and order the phrases – otherwise time would be an unconscious, seamless flow. Thus, memory, as has been said, is indeed a space: to be recognized as a phrase, words that passed successively must be recollected simultaneously. In consequence, in liturgical time the narrated past and the desired future coincide, yet not entirely, and not once and for all. Moreover, and just as importantly, it is the articulation of liturgy as a pattern of ordered phrases and pauses which permits the co-ordination of different but structurally compatible words and actions at the same time: for example, the different motions of Priest and Deacon, Ministers and congregation. But, again, this compatibility is not like a static chord, but more like the interweaving of polyphony: while time moves only collectively forward, the structural coincidence is forever shifting. Or, one might say, the gift is offered to God through an inter-human exchange of gifts and gestures, but since this exchange is itself offered, it is ceaselessly renewed and varied.

Following from this assimilation of space and time in the offering of the all-inclusive gift, I shall now argue that the communal liturgical act confers space and time upon themselves, at the very moment when the proximal community joins the angelic congregation. At the Preface to the Canon, which begins with the Celebrant's solemn repetition of the Ministers' antiphonal response that it is meet and right to give thanks to God, the words: "*Vere dignum et iustum est, æquum et salutare, nos tibi semper et ubique gratias agere,*"[34] declare that what the congregation offers up to God is a service of gratitude, due always and everywhere.

The spatio-temporal co-ordinates, "*semper et ubique,*" suggest a priority of gift over both time and space. The place and time in which it is right to offer praise are transgressive and eschatological: all places and all times, a location which shatters the priority of any particular place or time, so as to suggest that the liturgical act itself is that which confers the specificity of both time and space upon themselves, since they are here measured by the act of giving praise. Thus, the identificatory question, "Where am I?," asks not for geographical or historical details, but for a position in relation to the gift of liturgy: the "*semper et ubique*" tells us that wherever or whenever the worshipper is situated, he is in a position where grace is received.

This prayer, which bespeaks the chronotopic status of all prayer, "*Vere dignum et iustum est, æquum et salutare, nos tibi semper et ubique gratias agere,*" repositions everything according to gift. Its opening is a constative utterance about the universal necessity of performativity – of language as doxological

---

[34] [*It is meet* and right, our duty and our salvation, that we should at all times and in all places give thanks unto Thee]; Botte and Mohrmann, op. cit., L'Ordinaire, 74.

gift – which, if it were not itself embedded in the performance of prayer, would negate its own imperative. The prayer, which heralds the full unfolding of the sacred polis, implies a final critique of mundane assumptions as to the priority of objectivity, and the subordination of doxology to the instruments of state. It thus establishes "objectively" a priority of subjectivity over objectivity, or of perspectival space combined with desire over abstract spatiality, of the gift over the given.

It is in this eschatological chronotope that the worshipper is reminded of his communality. The service of praise is not rendered in an autonomous manner, but through Christ, our Lord, and in both proximal and angelic congregation. We offer praise in the first person plural, "*nos tibi semper et ubique gratias agere*," and in unison with the praise of the heavenly choirs, who also sing through Christ ("*Per quem maiestatem tuam laudant Angeli*"),[35] in the city of the living God, where thousands upon thousands of angels are gathered,[36] concelebrating in one society of exultation. This is a polity whose lateral and historical limits are opened so as to enter the transcendent city of Jerusalem: "*Cæli cælorum Virtutes ac beata Seraphim socia exsultatione concelebrant. Cum quibus et nostras voces ut admitti iubeas, deprecamur, supplici confessione dicentes.*"[37]

At this moment of angelic communion, the lateral, proximal, and historical community transgresses, in the manner indicated by Lacoste, but in its full and excessive communality, the limits of the world, so as to look back upon it: "*Pleni sunt cæli et terra gloria tua.*"[38] In saying that heaven and earth are full of God's glory, these words bespeak the moment of spatio-temporal transfiguration: heaven and earth are full of that which contains them.

If it is collective offering to eternity or "gift" which defines the liturgical chronotope, then one might still ask, what is the content of this gift? The Roman Rite answers this question by indicating, at the end of the Canon, that the liturgical chronotope is optimally realized in the relational reception and bestowal of *peace*.

In the final phrases of the *Pater Noster*, we pray to be delivered from evil: "*Sed libera nos a malo.*"[39] This evil is identified, in the subsequent prayer (addressed to the Paten, which the Celebrant holds before him), as time

---

[35] [*Through whom angels praise your majesty*]; "All the angels and powers and princedoms [are] made subject under His feet" I Peter 3:22; Jungmann, op. cit., *The Mass*, 378–9.

[36] Hebrews 12:22ff.

[37] [*The heavens and the heavenly hosts and the blessed seraphim, joining together in exultant celebration. We pray you, bid our voices also to be admitted with theirs, beseeching you, confessing, and saying.*]

[38] [*Heaven and earth are full of your glory.*]

[39] [*Deliver us from evil*]; Botte and Mohrmann, *op. cit., L'Ordinaire*, 86.

construed as spatial and linear, for immanentist time is perforce a sequence of evils: "*LIBERA nos, quæsamus, Domine, ab omnibus malis, præteritis, præsentibus et futuris.*"[40] The prayer is self-fulfilling for it presupposes an ecstatic temporality: we pray for deliverance from future sins, and from those already-committed sins of the past. We ask, therefore, to be released from the enduring and violent closure of secular time, which regrets the past and despairs of the future.

This negative time is contrasted to its resolution in peace: "*da propitius pacem in diebus nostris.*"[41] This does not refer to peace in the local present moment (as Chamberlain interpreted it), for such a time only exists in the violence of immanentism. Rather, "*in diebus nostris*" situates our desired peace "in our days" or "in our temporalities," in the time which belongs to us. This prayer, therefore, "*da propitius pacem in diebus nostris,*" says "make time peace."

In the exchange of peace which follows this prayer, "*PAX Domini sit semper vobiscum. / Et cum spiritu tuo,*"[42] the gift of the Body and Blood of Christ are identified as turning time *into* peace, or as transposing time into the gift of peace seen as the redemptive exchange between past, present, and future within the new transfigured spatiality of memory already described. In this dialogic turn, peace is both something we have received and are bestowing upon one another. Having, in the previous prayer, asked to receive peace as something temporal, coming towards us, out of God's "future," we now perform peace spatially, as something we exchange proximally, in relational, collective space. But this is not a space outside time, nor a space with parts, for we exchange a temporal peace: "*PAX Domini sit semper vobiscum*" – not simply peace now, but in all times.

This exchange, which occurs as one of a series of non-identically repeated antiphons throughout the Rite, extends into the final words of the *Agnus Dei*: "*dona nobis pacem,*"[43] where the gift is now identified as peace. The nature of God's gift to us is peace amongst us: this is the (always arriving through time) gift of (spatial) community. The vision of sacral community as consummating space and time contrasts with the more distant and solitary position of the worshipper at the beginning of the *Gloria*, when it is only by means of impersonating the other-worldly angels that the worshipper is able to confer peace upon the world: "*Et in terra pax.*"[44] For now, in a further moment (not discussed by Lacoste) the chronotope of the world has itself been transformed into peace. Indeed, this does not deny Lacoste's point that the peace of the

[40] [*DELIVER us, we beseech Thee, O Lord, from all evils, past, present, and future.*]
[41] [*give us peace in our days.*]
[42] [*THE PEACE of the Lord be always with you / And with thy spirit.*]
[43] [*grant us peace*]; Botte and Mohrmann, *op. cit., L'Ordinaire*, 88.
[44] *Ibid.*, 62.

world is never merely *inside* the world, for the world as purely human can only be expressed violently in the struggle to secure a stronghold. But at the *Agnus Dei*, true humanity has been bestowed upon us from without the world, for we have now joined the angelic voices, and stand on the brink of God's entry into our bodies. This incarnating, transubstantiating event will ensure that the worshipper *no longer* looks back on the world with an angelic gaze, but has now brought the world with him, since God's kenosis has shattered forever the pagan nomadic totality of "world," exposing it as a fiction, along with every fetishized local site (whereas Lacoste's position might seem to imply the necessity of a *reactive* relation to paganism in constituting the liturgical). The gift of peace which follows the *Agnus Dei* is the gift of humanity which places the "world" amongst the angels, and it is a gift which in turn enables us to *ask for peace*: "*dona nobis pacem*," and not merely impersonate its angelic bestowal. Indeed, the request for peace can only be made authentically from within peace, from within the heavenly realm which we now do not merely impersonate, and yet the request for peace must still be made because its attainment is not a static arrival at, but a perpetual asking for peace. This is because it is neither a substance which is appropriated, nor a spatial plot we contain, but a person, Christ Himself, who must depart from us in order that we receive Him as the gift of peace "dispersed': "*Pacem relinquo vobis, pacem mean do vobis.*"[45]

6 THE GIFT OF CITIZENSHIP

The dispossession and dispersal necessary for us to receive the gift of peace introduces the salient characteristic of my final theme already emergent: the liturgical gift. Despite the fact that gift has already been identified as "peace," this definition is not wholly satisfactory. For peace is not an "object" which we offer to each other: if peace is exchanged, then this really means that peace is the true character of a genuine flow and exchange of gift. But in that case, it must hold, inversely, that peace is only secured as an *uninterrupted* flow and exchange of gift. Just how gift delivers peace still needs further elaboration. And in the course of this elaboration, it will emerge how gift is to be contrasted with the secular "given."

So far, in this and the previous chapter, I have shown how a liturgical order is able to present a redemptive critique of immanentist illusions as to what

---

[45] [*My peace I leave with you, my peace I give unto you*]; *ibid.*, 88; John 14:27; see further John Milbank, *Theology and Social Theory: Beyond Secular Reason*, (Oxford: Blackwell Publishers, 1990), 380–438.

constitutes a genuine human action, subjectivity, identity, community, and as to the character of time and space. I have also shown how a liturgical way of life presupposes a reality which exceeds appearances, and is never exhausted by its own arrival. All this, and not just the liturgical coincidence of time and space, situates reality – and the subject's relationship to reality – within the category of "gift."

This construal of reality contrasts with the substitution of spatiality for time in immanentist modernity, described in Part I, which, by extending the Cartesian prioritization of epistemology over ontology, gives rise to a sense of reality as "given." This leads to two further outcomes. First, the establishment of the "given" instantiates the possibility of an "object," as that which makes no appeal beyond itself, and is situated in an order which places a premium upon formal arrangement, consistency, and clarity. And, secondly, it denies the possibility of genuine subjectivity, for the subject is cast as that which wields panoptic sway over the "given," mistaking this for a primary relationship with the world. I also showed how this order, despite (or because of) its claim to apprehend the "real" as a totalized outcome, is reducible to nihilism. By exalting epistemology, it ensures that there can be no concealed or spontaneous forces in matter, which concomitantly denies corporeality its full potential, and, moreover, it ensures that there can be nothing in excess of the *nihil* since that alone is able perfectly to fulfill the criteria of the "real." Thus, the subject is always already delimited, for he understands his relationship with the "given" as substantial and positive, but this is an illusion: he controls nothing, but is always already controlled by the illusion of operativity.

The liturgical casting of citizenship through gift can also be set over against that of the pagan *polis* which, although ostensibly centred upon the offering of *leitourgia*, was subject to limitations which excluded women, children, slaves, and foreigners from the possibility of citizenship. The gift of citizenship, available only to an élite, was not therefore freely given, and indeed, it became increasingly less gratuitous as it gradually turned into a tax.[46] Thus, the pagan *polis* was surrounded by a city wall which was an expression of its contractual relationship with all that was excluded by it, both in terms of those who resided outside it, and those whose interiority was nominally borrowed

---

[46] Bruit Zaidman and Schmitt Pantel, *Religion in the Ancient Greek City*, (Cambridge: Cambridge University Press, 1992), 47, 95; François de Polignac, *Cults, Territory, and the Origins of the Greek City-State*, tr. Janet Lloyd (Chicago: Chicago University Press, 1995), 77–8; P. Vidal-Naquet, *The Black Hunter: Forms of Thought and Forms of Society in the Greek World*, tr. Andrew Szegedy-Maszak, (Baltimore/London: The Johns Hopkins University Press, 1986), 4–7, 216–18; Paul Millett, *Lending and Borrowing in Ancient Athens*, (Cambridge: Cambridge University Press, 1991), 85–90, 195–6.

from it. The "freely offered" gift of citizenship was in reality a contract, and ensured that subjectivity depended not upon gift, but upon the given.

By contrast, the construal of gift in the Roman liturgy is not tied to such immanentist proprieties, and can be seen not only to exceed them, but to offer a critique of them. I shall now intensify the analyses of chapter four by showing how the liturgy casts subjective being as gift, and argue that this gives rise to two implications for the subject: first, that to give, and to have an identifiable content to our action of giving, we must already have received, and so an ontology of the gift is *relational*. Secondly, this ontology is doubly relational because the subject can only receive this gift by offering it back again. However, this action of offering back is not an indifferent nihilistic disposal, but rather offers only with faith of an incalculable return with difference. By broaching this theme of sacrifice and the relation of death and life, the way is opened to an articulation of a theology of the Eucharist in the final chapter.

The character of gift

There are many different words for gift in the Roman Rite: "*donum*," "*munus*," "*oblationem*," "*sacrificium*," and "*hostia*," which refer variously to earthly offerings to God, or God's gift to humanity in the person of Christ, and communicate the dual nature of gift as both gratuitous and sacrificial. The Rite also offers a description of gift: its consecrated disposition, its mysterious nature, and the impossibility of ascribing an "original" derivation of donation. And it casts the worshipper as that which is primarily positioned by its relation to gift. Thus, we ask God to accept our gifts as offerings and immolations, to look upon them graciously, to make us worthy of offering gifts, and for the sacrifice of gift to be of correct character. Just this brief enumeration of the aspects of gift within the liturgy reveals a crucial dimension to its economy: it exceeds the purely human.

This exceeding of humanity is nonetheless *superlatively human*, for all gifts are made possible by, and are a repetition of, the incarnation. Insofar as the person of Christ is the engendering of all gifts – which are not extra to Him, but participate in His being – it can be seen that the character of gift is determined by His own nature: "*PER quem hæc omnia, Domine, semper bona creas, sanctificas, vivificas, benedicis et præstas nobis.*"[47] In this doxology which concludes the Canon, the gifts of creation are explicitly linked to the incarnation as the consecration of all created things, and are communicated

---

[47] [*By whom all things, O Lord, Thou dost create, hallow, quicken, bless and bestow upon us*]; Botte and Mohrmann, *op. cit., L'Ordinaire*, 84.

as *figurae* of the blessing He has instituted. It is through Christ that all good things are always (*semper*) created, made holy and unapproachable (*sanctificas*), and life-giving (*vivificas*). Thus, through Christ, every good thing is transposed into gift, but not in the sense that creation is first given and only afterwards animated as gift, but insofar as creation only takes place through Christ (even including His humanity, since all creation "is" as restored creation), it is created as good, and therefore perforce participates in His character as gift. The prayer has no need to specify which particular objects qualify as gift, for all creation is a non-identical instance of the supreme gift. Through Christ, all good things are blessed (*benedicis*), which is tantamount to a bestowal of gift upon gift, or donation upon giving, which thus characterizes the overflowing nature of gift. Lastly, it is through Christ that good things are distinguished as more than themselves (*præstas*). This prefix of *præ*- contributes connotations of presentiment (*præsago*), brimming-over (*præscates*), primordial supplementation (*præscabio*), open-endedness (*præseco*), and present efficacy (*præsens*). These implicit qualities of the gift explain why we cannot *finally* give, for a gift which remains without renewal is simply a handing-over, a transfer, a ransom.[48]

Giving the impossible gift

The postponement of the gift – as that which ensures that it can never finally be overtaken (except eschatologically), and is *impossible* – does not mean that giving is futile. There are two main reasons for this, which pertain to an understanding of donation as situated within an expression of subjective desire, which unites donor and donee. First, because of the kenosis of the incarnation, to give to God is to be incorporated into the perpetual bestowal of gifts which takes place within the Trinity. Thus, our entry into God in turn constitutes us as genuine subjects, defined as that which gives: giving enables us to give. And, secondly, the liturgical reappraisal of the "real" as that which exceeds mundane appearances (as we saw in the previous section) alters the scale of possibility, in such a way that what appears impossible on a purely

---

[48] In the recitation of Psalm 25 in the Offertory, there is an implicit warning against, and critique of false gifts. Whilst the doxological congregation which journeys around God's altar and narrates His deeds (*"circumdabo altare tuum, Domine . . . Ut audiam vocem laudis, et enarrem universa mirabilia tua"* [*I will compass Thine altar, O Lord . . . That I may publish with the voice of thanksgiving and tell of all Thy wondrous works*]), the evildoers are sedentary and imprisoned: "*Ne perdis cum ipsiis, Deus, animam meam*" [*O shut not up my soul with sinners.*] Because they are "put away" ("*perdo*"), the "*munera*" they offer are not freely given, but are ransoms. *Ibid.*, 70.

human level nonetheless constitutes a possibility, which is also an imperative, if there is to be a human subject at all.

First, the kenosis of the incarnation ensures our incorporation into the perpetual exchange of gift which takes place within the Trinity. The gifts we offer at the Offertory are not instances of a unilateral initiative on our part – which, as unprefigured, would constitute a spatial degeneration into bartery or bribery – but are only made possible because they non-identically repeat the always-already superlative gift of Christ. Thus, our own historical offerings of gifts are spared an humiliation in the form of a linear or spatial accumulation against the regress of time, by being folded back into the infinite return of gift within the Trinity. By offering to God, we enter that perpetual offering which takes place within God and thus enter into ourselves as genuine subjects – defined as that which offers gift.

Nevertheless, this does not happen automatically or "over against" us, but coincides with our expression of desire: "*Da nobis per huius aquæ et vini mysterium, eius divinitatis esse consortes, qui humanitatis nostræ fieri dignatus est particeps, Iesus Christus.*"[49] The desire to "consort" with the divine nature, which is not merely to partake of it, but to be in partnership or relationship with God – a complex request to be in partnership with that which already includes us – is fulfilled by the embedded design of the prayer. When we receive the gifts of bread and wine, which are the mystery of the incarnation, we receive God by receiving our *transformed humanity* in Christ, through whose divinity, we are enabled to offer our gifts to God. Thus, it is only because of, and within God's gift to us, that we are able, first, to receive our humanity, and, secondly, to offer gifts. But this means, concomitantly, that it is only by means of offering gifts that we receive our true humanity. The *aporia* whereby we can only offer gifts once we have received our humanity is only resolved by the always-already repeated offering of Christ.

The complex overlaying of repeated gifts which I have just described reveals the ambiguity of the gift-relation which exists between the worshipper and God. For it is not a matter of subsequent stages or "responses" whereby we first receive our true humanity from Christ, and then receive the gift of divinity and the gift of being able to offer. In reality, this is all one gift, forever repeated differently, whose lineaments cannot be disentangled without seeming to be laid out in stages: we receive our capacity to receive in receiving that which we are to receive; to receive our humanity, we must already receive

---

[49] [*Grant that by the mystery of this water and wine we may be made partakers of His divine nature, who vouchsafed to become partaker of our human nature, Jesus Christ*]; *ibid.*, 68.

the gratuitous excess of divinity, and to receive the gift of humanity and divinity, we must already have begun to *transmit* this gift.[50]

The concluding doxology of this prayer situates our desire to give within the whole Trinity: "*Iesus Christus, Filius tuus, Dominus noster : Qui tecum vivit et regnat in unitate Spiritus Sancti Deus : per omnia sæcula sæculorum.*"[51] At the first level, as I have described, it is by virtue of the hypostatic union of the Son with our humanity in Jesus Christ that we are given the gift to give. But this donation is, at another level, a gift of participation in the self-giving flow of life between the persons of the Trinity. As the Father gives Himself and glorifies the Son, and the Son glorifies and gives Himself to the Father, all by the Spirit, without lack, the Father "gains" something from the Son and the Son "gains" something from the Father, but the "gain" in the donee does not correspond to any diminution or loss in the donor. Indeed, the persons are precisely this relational gaining, although it is not in excess of what they already are, since all that they are is, by definition, excessive. These relations of giving which take place within the Trinity definitively *include* the worshipper, who, as part of creation, and as offering the creation in worship, is perforce implicated in the generation of the Son by the Father as the inner ground in God for His external creative action, and the procession of the Spirit as the inner ground in God for the offering of creation back to God.

Our incorporation into the relation between the persons of the Trinity in our offering of the gift through Christ is enacted in the prayer uttered by the Celebrant at the Adoration of the Host: "*Per ipsum, et cum ipso, et in ipso, est tibi Deo Patri omnipotenti, in unitate Spiritus Sancti, omnis honor, et gloria. Per omnia sæcula sæculorum. Amen.*"[52] The deictic relation, "*Per ipsum*," suggests an hierarchical distance between the worshipper and Christ, establishing our dependence upon his salvific initiative. The next relation, "*et cum ipso*" suggests an assimilation of equal relation and co-operation between the worshipper and Christ, as well as an additional suggestion of physical proximity. And the third relation, "*et in ipso*," establishes Christ as the ultimate context of giving, whereby our gift does not exceed that of the Son to the Father. Such complex deictic expression of spatial, instrumental, and contextual relationality of gift does not exhaust the situation, for honour is given to

---

[50] On the complexity of this gift-relation, see further Williams, *op. cit., Eucharistic Sacrifice*, 21–5.

[51] [*Jesus Christ, Thy Son, our Lord : who with Thee liveth and reigneth in the unity of the Holy Spirit O God : world without end.*]

[52] [*Through whom, and with whom, and in whom, be unto Thee O God the Father almighty, in the unity of the Holy Spirit, all honour and glory. World without end. Amen*]; Botte and Mohrmann, *op. cit., L'Ordinaire*, 84.

the Father also *"in unitate Spiritus Sancti."* Whilst Christ is what is given, the generated Word once and for all, the Holy Spirit is the continuous flow of that gift, the processional place of gift which is itself that gift.

The role of the Spirit in this doxology has been subject to debate. Josef Jungmann offers a Christological account, according to which we offer glory to the Father through and in Christ, and *in the presence of* the Holy Spirit in the Church, whilst Bernard Botte offers a Trinitarian reading, whereby the Father to whom we offer glory is in the unity of the Spirit with the Son, citing antecedents in St Ambrose's examples of doxology, where the Spirit is stressed in order to resist Arian subordinationism.[53] However, the doxology is manifestly ambiguous, and so one might perhaps admit both accounts: we offer *by* and *in* Christ, because He is God, and we offer *with* the Spirit in his human presence as the Church.

In the above, I have described the complex subsumption of our gift to God into that which is perpetually offered within the Trinity. It is by thus entering into Christ's action of perfect praise of the Father that we can participate in God's own worship of Himself. In receiving the Body and Blood of Christ, we receive that which has already been perfectly offered to God by Jesus. This confirms that even the receiving of gift is still an offering; that in the liturgy, there is no action outside gift, but only the repetition of the offering which has already been made by God to Himself in the person of Jesus. But this cannot happen outside the *desire* to give – which is not a desire to master the enactment of giving – but takes place according to a genuine contingency which only arrives through a spontaneous act of giving which is the act of praise. The donor's mood of genuine desire – as opposed to the indifferent gaze of mastery over the given, as that which is already appropriated – is continuous with true humility, for our subjective regard is as much a gift as that which it regards.

The second reason why our act of giving can be sustained even despite its "impossibility" relates to the liturgical radicalization of what constitutes a genuine human action. From a non-liturgical perspective, it would seem that nothing really "happens" in the liturgy. For there is no perceptible change, nothing "new" occurs, and no action is ever accomplished: there is only a series of supplements and postponements. However, to suppose that human action is humiliated because it fails to offer an "advance" or a delimited accomplishment is to subscribe to spatial criteria which, I have argued, dissimulate their perpetuation of the disempowerment of all actions by seeing

---

[53] Jungmann, *op. cit.*, *The Mass*, 457–61; Botte, "*Excursus* VII: '*In Unitate Spiritus Sancti*,'" in Botte and Mohrmann, *op. cit.*, *L'Ordinaire*, 133–9.

them as the attainment of discretely allotted projections. In the case of our liturgical action, there is no compromise caused by the perpetually receding destination of our journey: rather, that perpetual asymptotic recession realizes our action's excessive possibility.

The genuine ennoblement of human action within the liturgy is demonstrated at the Consecration where the ambiguity of offering reaches an optimum. At the "QUAM oblationem," when the Celebrant requests that our offering become for us the Body and Blood of Christ – a request that we might receive and be received by God – the effort of trying to offer, enacted in faith of the positive excess of transcendent supplementation, coincides with its *realization*, although it is by no means a "final" realization. This movement of Consecration can be seen to continue *within* that of the Offertory, in such a way that the "second" offering of the Body and Blood back to God is not a return, but a consummation – forever yet to be non-identically repeated – of the "first" offering of bread and wine. A reading of the gift according to a spatial protocol of accomplishment might easily mistake the Consecration for the moment when God, having received from us the offerings of bread and wine, now "returns" them to us as Body and Blood. Indeed, such a reading has led several liturgiologists into an attempt to disentangle the precise "direction" of the gift: is it from God to man or man to God? Which comes first?[54] These questions betray a simplification of the gift which reduces it to an exchange of the "given." In reality, the movements of Eucharistic giving and receiving are indistinguishable: just as the Consecration is not a clear-cut "return" from God to man, but an intensification of offering as that which is always already offered by God, so also *all* offering is a Consecration. Indeed, the word "Eucharist" repeats this ambiguity as an ontological coincidence of God's gift of grace and our indistinguishable gift of gratitude. But to question the priority of one movement over the other, or to attempt to isolate initiative, is to read into the gift the possibility of its being offered outside God. Any such "gift" could only be returned "identically" and could not exceed the spatial nullity of the given.

Rather, the giving back to us of the elements coincides with a more extreme realization of offering. If God fully receives our offerings, then they must be

[54] Williams suggests that the complexity of the gift-relation "is easier to bear in mind if we do not have a liturgical structure bound to 'changes of gear,' suggesting that *here* we offer bread and wine, *here* is effected the transformation of these offerings, *here* we offer them again in a fashion that is somehow more solemn or effective," *Eucharistic Sacrifice*, 25 (see also 25 n. 2). [See further Nicol Blount, *The Eucharist*, (Bristol, 1992), Chapter 2; Willis, "Some Problems in the Roman Canon Missæ," 159–60: these writers attempt to discern "stages" of offering.]

entirely conjoined to God, which concomitantly means that we have also been received by Him. Through our offering, therefore, we receive back offering: *through offering, we can offer*. This is a forward movement of perpetual worship and entry into God which ensures that liturgical gifts are not discrete items which are exchanged, bread and wine in return for Body and Blood, but rather effects the transformation of everything we offer into God. Because of God's radiant nature, we will receive these things again, but not as an equivalence. In this way, transubstantiation is not something *in addition* to praise, but its logical conclusion: the "coming back" of the gift is the "going forward" of the non-identical repetition. For the transubstantiated elements are still *our* giving, just as the Son of God was really born of Mary.

The apparent consummation of giving which occurs at the Consecration is, however, subject to liturgical postponement: "*SUPPLICES te rogamus, omnipotens Deus : iube hæc perferri per manus sancti Angeli tui in sublime altare tuum, in conspectu divinæ maiestatis tuæ.*"[55] In this request that our gifts be borne to the heavenly altar, to be within God's sight, the whole movement of offering repeats. Indeed, this further postponement – which explicitly communicates God's distance and "otherness" – occurs at the moment of His optimum physical proximity, reminding us that all offering fulfills the promise of giving not by the completion of donation, but only insofar as it prefigures the eschatological consummation of all gifts. However, the "*SUPPLICES te*" also reminds us that God's "distance" is unlike its mundane counterpart, and that the postponement of transcendent "arrival" is neither a movement away, nor a failure: there can be no gift without distance, and distance is itself a gift.[56] It is in and through this gift of distance that we receive God into our bodies, in such a way that we are given to comprehend transcendent "distance" as coinciding with the moment of optimum and penetrative relationality. Whilst an ordinary "return" leads nowhere, liturgical postponement leads forever further into God.

The impossible return

In contrast to the obligation to "return" a gift given within immanent exchanges,[57] there can be no "return" for the transcendent gift, additional to

---

[55] [*WE humbly beseech Thee, O Almighty God : command these gifts to be borne by the hands of Thy holy Angel to Thine altar on high, in the sight of Thy divine majesty*]; Botte and Mohrmann, *op. cit., L'Ordinaire*, 82.

[56] Jean-Luc Marion, *God Without Being*, tr. T. A. Carlson, (Chicago: Chicago University Press, 1991), 7–25.

[57] See John Milbank, "Can a Gift be Given? Prolegomena to a Future Trinitarian Metaphysic," *Modern Theology*, 11.1 (1995), 119–61.

the infinite rebound of that gift itself. This impossibility of return, therefore, contributes a kind of Socratic irony to the question: "*Quid retribuam Domino pro omnibus quæ retribuit mihi?*"[58] Here, the Celebrant (as he receives the Host), speaks of the impossibility of an independent return, since there is nothing outside God's gift to us. And yet, the "return" of gift is precisely *all* that happens, non-identically: for the infinite gift is that which can *only* "return," not to an anterior ideality, but ever forward, with difference. It happens in every gift we offer, completed only beyond us in the eternal and excessive Trinitarian exchange. Thus, the Celebrant answers his own question: "*Calicem salutaris accipiam, et nomen Domini invocabo.*"[59] Our return for receiving the Body is not mundanely to weigh up what we have received and count out its value in quantities of gratitude. Rather, *our return is to receive again, differently*: to receive the Blood, the cup of salvation, and to continue calling on His name. The "return" is to receive and repeat. We go on calling upon God, even when He is within us. We cannot exhaust Him, but offer a "return" by receiving Him again and again.

Our "return" therefore is not retrospective, but a prospective calling, a desire. This is a loving return which knows that it cannot surprize God with gifts: there is nothing which can be offered which does not already come from Him. Because there is no gift outside God, every gift is *more than necessary*, a repetition. The supernumerary nature of all gifts is understood in the excessive tautologies of the prayer which the Celebrant utters: "*QUAM oblationem tu, Deus, in omnibus, quæsumus, benedictam, adscriptam, ratam, rationabilem, acceptabilemque facere digneris.*"[60] To request that our gift to God be blessed is to ask that it first be given to itself as gift, that it be made superlatively bestowing. Similarly, our gift is by definition *adscriptivus*, since all gifts are beyond necessity, and so to request this quality for our gift is to repeat its superfluity. And to ask for our gift to be *ratus*, authentic and secure in God, is to ask that our gift be gift; likewise, *rationabilis*: there is nothing more reasonable and spiritual than gift. And, finally, there can be nothing more acceptable to God than a gift, since all gifts come from God. This prayer is a prayer that there might be a gift, which communicates the nature of all gifts as that which is always already divine.

---

[58] [*What return shall I make to the Lord for all He has given to me?*]; Botte and Mohrmann, *op. cit.*, *L'Ordinaire*, 90.

[59] [*I will take the cup of salvation and will call upon the name of the Lord.*]

[60] [*WHICH oblation do Thou, O Lord, vouchsafe in all things to make blessed, approved, ratified, reasonable, acceptable*]; *ibid.*, 78.

The gift of being

In the above discussion of the characteristics of liturgical gifts and protocols of donation, I have referred to a liturgical ontology of gift, and implicitly contrasted this with the immanentist substitution of epistemology for ontology, which reduces being to the given, that which is first of all indifferently *known*, thus refusing the possibility of a positive account of being as that which arrives differently from a transcendent source and is received only through its being offered up again, in faith of a non-identical return. In the Roman Rite, the worshipper receives his restored humanity by receiving God's gift in the person of Christ, and receives his being only by offering it back, in the subjective act of praise. Thus, for this ontology of gift, being is that which is always already relational – it is first of all received from the transcendent other, and it is received in a perpetuation of this relationality, in the non-equivalent doxological return of the gift of being. This "return" reveals the openness of being, which determines life as that which is lived, offered *as* life, in and through its constitutive and redemptive entry into death.

The liturgical identification of the worshipper's being with gift is implicit from the outset of the Rite, in the threefold repetition of the Antiphon, in advance of, within, and after the recitation of Psalm 42, where the gift of praise is cast as continuous with the subject's being: "*Ad Deum qui lætificat iuventutem meam.*"[61] The word "*iuventutem*," derived from the Hebrew "*gil*" ('life,' "youth") explicitly co-ordinates the "life" of the worshipping "I" with his doxological act of praise. Indeed, it is the worshipper's new life of grace which, as praise, is that in which God rejoices.[62] Therefore, gift is not incidental to our being, but arrives through our act of giving, as life, and is by nature a contagious ontology which overflows into further acts of giving: "*Confiteor tibi in cithara, Deus Deus meus.*"[63]

Now, if our genuine being and restored humanity are received in and through our reception, and concomitant praise of God, then being – as gift – is relational. Any sense of our offering of doxology as acquiring its constitutive gratuity from an unprefigured or one-sided sacrifice is to be ruled

---

[61] *Ibid.*, 58, 58, 60.

[62] Mitchell Dahood, *Psalms 1–50*, (New York: Doubleday, 1965), 262 n. 4; St Ambrose, who cites the verse for the procession of the neophytes into the Church, understands "*iuventutem*" to refer not to biological youth, but to the new baptismal life of grace: "*abluta plebs . . . renovata in aquilæ iuventute*" (*De mysteriis*, VIII. 43); "*Deposuisti peccatorum senectutem, sumpsisti gratiæ iuventutem*" (*De sacramentis*, IV. 2, 7) in *Selected Works*, (Milano: Biblioteca Ambrosiana, 1982).

[63] Botte and Mohrmann, *op. cit.*, *L'Ordinaire*, 58.

out. Our praise of God is always issued from within an already received context of sociality, not only that of the Trinity, as I have described above, but also of the Church, as that which has always received and is forever yet to receive its repeated relationality with Christ.[64]

To give, therefore, we must already have received God's gift of our humanity, through His Son. But in receiving God's gift, there must be a subjective acknowledgement of its transcendent source of donation. It is not enough indifferently to receive – indeed, to receive the gifts of Body and Blood without discerning the trace of God within them, is to condemn ourselves: "*PERCEPTIO Corporis tui, Domine Iesu Christe, quod ego indignus sumere præsumo, non mihi proveniat in iudicium et condemnationem.*"[65] This preparatory prayer, prior to the reception of God, implies a link between desire and gift, for it is the way in which we subjectively position ourselves in relation to the gift which reveals our true nature. We are hereby warned that to receive God in a mood of either reserve or indifference is to refuse Him – and where God is refused, there subsists only the given. If one discerns the gift of God, one cannot but desire to receive it fully. Moreover, the indifferent refusal of God's gift is not just a matter of continuing as before, but – since receiving God's gift is continuous with receiving our being – condemns us (to the immanentist illusion of operativity in which we inscribe our deconstitution?). It is not simply that at this moment when we declare our relation with God's gift, our sinfulness is exposed, but that it is fully *realized*: if we receive the Body and Blood of Christ without discerning it as such, we eat and drink judgement upon ourselves. Thus, God's judgement of us, and our judgement of God, coincide in the character of the gift as relational.

My characterization of the liturgy in terms of a reciprocal gift-offering between the worshipper and God as linked with our subjective expression of both judgement and desire contrasts with Lacoste's negotiation of the relationship between the worshipper and God in *Expérience et Absolu*. He argues that whereas ordinarily, for a subject to perceive an object, it is necessary for him in turn to *be seen*, in the liturgy God can see us without our seeing Him, thus reducing the worshipping subject to the status of an object.

---

[64] "Both giving and accepting gifts indicates – and sometimes creates – *participation* in a common life or common reality. Sacrifice and offering to the holy thus have to do with the maintenance of fellowship, at the simplest level," Williams, *op. cit.*, *Eucharistic Sacrifice* 28. See further David F. Ford, "What Happens in the Eucharist?"(Paper for the Society for the Study of Theology, Durham, 1995) especially 12–24.

[65] [*LET not the partaking (discernment) of Thy Body and Blood, O Lord Jesus Christ, which I, though unworthy, presume to receive, turn to my judgement and condemnation*]; Botte and Mohrmann, *op. cit.*, *L'Ordinaire*, 88–90; I Corinthians 2:27–32, 11:29.

For Lacoste, our bodiedness is a sign of our fundamental objectivity in relation to God, more important than any notion of subjective desire, which implies that *undergoing* a relationship with God is more fundamental than desiring it. Although he does attempt to balance this with the experience of God's gift as joyful, nevertheless he neglects the relational and reciprocal nature of the economy of gift, and is therefore inclined to edge the "gift" towards the status of the "given" – as that which is unilaterally transferred or arrives "over against" us, as a given which implicitly bears no trace of donation.[66]

However, the Roman Rite affirms that what is received as gift must perforce be offered up again, in a renewal of the bond of relationality we have received. Thus, the being we receive from God is not aggrandized as that which we have now attained and may retain, but is only received as such by being offered humbly back to God as a gift which perpetuates the bond. Our being, as that which we have received, is precisely what we have to give: "*IN spiritu humilitatis et in animo contrito suscipiamur a te, Domine.*"[67] The liturgical gift of being – like any gift – cannot, according to the dynamics of mundane acquisition, be simply appropriated. At the point when the gift is received, it must be handed on. This dispossessive reception of the gift is repeated on many levels of the text. For example, it is as if in mimicry of the non-appropriation of God's gift of eternal charity, that the Priest gives the thurible to the Deacon as he says: "*Accendat in nobis Dominus ignem sui amoris, et flammam æternæ caritatis. Amen.*"[68] In the same way, we receive peace only by passing it on to others. This economy of "dispossession" is ultimately figured in the "Mass" itself, which sends us out ("*Ite, Missa est*") that we might be received as gifts into the world.[69]

We can see from this just why peace and gift coincide, how giving guarantees peace. It is the wholly *uninterrupted* character of gift which provides this: as we have seen, there cannot be gift if there is ever a moment *before* gift, or ever a subject before dispossession, or ever a giving that has not already begun to receive a counter-gift in return. Since any interruption here at any point – a moment before, beyond or without gift – would cancel gift altogether, to give or to be within the gift is to inhabit an harmonic flow and interchange which knows no interruption and which would have to experience a "stopping" of the gift *as violence*. To be within the gift, to give or receive

[66] Lacoste, *op. cit.*, *Expérience et Absolu*, 176–89.
[67] [*IN the spirit of humility and with a contrite heart may we be accepted by Thee, O Lord*]; Botte and Mohrmann, *op. cit.*, *L'Ordinaire*, 68.
[68] [*May the Lord kindle within us the fire of His love and the flame of His eternal charity. Amen.*] *Ibid.*, 70.
[69] *Ibid.*, 90.

at all, is to be within peaceful perfection, to reside within the Trinity.

The configuration of the worshipper's being as that which he offers as gift, as that which is no more than gift (both received and offered), and does not persist outside this giving, underlines the ontological priority of gift – and therefore sociality – within being. It is this priority of the social which stresses that there is no closure of the gift: it persists through a series of analogical sacrifices which narrate the story of human history as that which is never purely human.

After the words of Consecration, the Celebrant offers God back to God ("*offerimus præclaræ maiestati tuæ de tuis donis ac datis*"),[70] and asks that this offering be included within the ever-supplemented chain of redemptive offerings which are figural instances of the repeated event of God's offering of Himself: "*SUPRA quæ propitio ac sereno vultu respicere digneris : et accepta habere sicuti accepta habere dignatus es munera pueri tui iusti Abel, et sacrificium Patriarchæ nostri Abrahæ : et quod tibi obtulit summus sacerdos tuus Melchisedech, sanctum sacrificium, immaculatam hostiam.*"[71] The first sacrifice which is invoked is that of Abel, who sacrificed the firstborn of his flock: a sacrifice which, because of his faith, was attested greater than Cain's offering of grain, who slew him in response: "through his faith, though he is dead, he continues to speak."[72] So, accordingly, our own gift is the "*Agnus Dei,*" the firstborn of all creation, whose death, suffered at the hands of his own people, was in turn life-giving. Secondly, Abraham is invoked as he who was willing to live as a stranger without fixed abode, in faith of a heavenly city beyond, willing, by faith, to offer his beloved son Isaac, and so received him back again.[73] In accordance with Abraham's faith, our sacrifice, by participating in Christ, is obedient to death, does not turn away from death, and so is life-giving. Finally, Melchisedech, priest of the Most High, offers a sacrifice of bread and wine, which prefigures our own oblation.[74]

Insofar as being is that which can only be received by being offered up again as sacrifice in faith of a return, it can be seen that death is not to be construed as an infringement of life. Rather, our positive, corporeal life is constituted as much by the death implicit within our own sacrificial passage as by our prior

---

[70] [*offer unto Thy excellent majesty of Thine own gifts*]; ibid., 80–2.

[71] [*UPON which vouchsafe to look with favourable and gracious countenance, and to accept them even as Thou wast pleased to accept the gifts of Thy righteous servant Abel, and the sacrifice of our patriarch Abraham, and the spotless offering which Thy High Priest Melchisedech, offered unto Thee*]; ibid., 82.

[72] Hebrew 11:4; Also Genesis 4:4.

[73] Hebrew 11:14–19.

[74] Genesis 14:18.

reception of ourselves as a gift from beyond ourselves. The offering of our life as prayer is an outgoing which nonetheless "returns" as its own repeated offering of itself – an economy of resurrection which we can see figured through the incense's odour of sweetness, which is only achieved by its self-consuming entry into death. Its sweet odour, as its own "return," is only realized through its positive upward dissolution, offered again as gift: "*incensum istud dignetur Dominus benedicere et in odorem suavitatis accipere.*"[75] Within the text, this prayer is itself a repetition of a continuous analogically different offering of ourselves through prayer. The Chalice *of* our own salvation is offered to God as a sweet savour *for* our salvation: "*OFFERIMUS tibi, Domine, calicem salutaris, tuam deprecantes clementiam : ut in conspectu divinæ maiestatis tuæ, pro nostra et totius mundi salute, cum odore suavitatis ascendat.*"[76] Thus, we offer the sweet odour of our own salvation back to God in order that we and the whole world might again receive it. The holy perfumes of incense and wine express our subjective desire to be attractive to God, as an olfactory sign of our total offering of ourselves – outer and inner : "*IN spiritu humilitatis et in animo contrito suscipiamur a te, Domine : et sic fiat sacrificium nostrum in conspectu tuo hodie, ut placeat tibi, Domine Deus.*"[77] Our language, offered as incense, is conjoined with the lifting up of our hands as an evening sacrifice, through and in which we continue to live: "*Dirigatur, Domine, oratio mea, sicut incensum, in conspectu tuo : elevatio manuum mearum sacrificium vespertinum.*"[78] This is not a sacrifice which seeks to leave materiality behind in favour of the pure *nihil*, or a pure ideal, nor does it substitute an inner for an outer, but takes both together, as an offering of our inhabited lives.

[75] [*vouchsafe to bless this incense and receive it as an odour of sweetness*]; Botte and Mohrmann, *op. cit.*, *L'Ordinaire*, 70.

[76] [*WE OFFER unto Thee, O Lord, the chalice of salvation, beseeching Thy mercy : that it may ascend before Thy divine Majesty as a sweet savour, for our salvation, and for that of the whole world*]; ibid., 68.

[77] [*IN the spirit of humility and with a contrite heart may we be accepted by Thee, O Lord : and may our sacrifice be so made in Thy sight today, that it may be pleasing unto Thee, O Lord.*] Ibid.

[78] [*Let my prayer, O Lord, be set forth in Thy sight as incense, and let the lifting up of my hands be an evening sacrifice*]; ibid., 70.

Chapter Six

THE RESURRECTION
OF THE SIGN

1 TRANSUBSTANTIATION: BEYOND PRESENCE AND ABSENCE

In chapter 3, I described how a necrophiliac theory of the sign (that is, the postmodern theory of the sign as such) is the very consummation of an immanentist ontology. By contrast, I shall now argue that where death is not held as over against life, it is possible to restore meaning to language, and that the optimum site of this restoration is the integration of word and action in the event of the Eucharist.

In my analysis of the necrophiliac sign of postmodernity, I described how the opposing of death to life and absence to presence are linked, and how it is not presence as such which is culpably "metaphysical," but the *opposition itself* between presence and absence, for, within an immanentist order, the two extremes are dialectically identical. The Eucharistic sign, by contrast, as I shall show, is able to outwit the distinction between both absence and presence, and death and life. This genuine outwitting of metaphysical dichotomies is possible because, according to a reading of the Eucharist as an essential *action*, and not as an isolated presence or merely illustrative symbol, the (mystical) unknown is not reductively confined to a negative nothing – which amounts to the known – but is traversed as a genuinely open mystery which, by being partially imparted through the sign, and therefore recognizable *as* mystery, has a positive – but not fetishizable – content.

This positive account of the mysterious – which implies also a positive account of the sign, as that which is not simply "left behind" but participates in the hidden mystery it signifies – accords with patristic negotiations of the word *mustērion* in terms of both *mysterium* and *sacramentum*. For Augustine and Isidore of Seville, these terms assimilate a variety of related meanings in the Eucharistic context, which together communicate a coincidence of presence and absence: *signum, sacrum, sacrificium, secretum.*[1] Even when the sacramental mystery is revealed, it remains obscure and hidden.[2] But the latency of mystery in the sign does not make it equal to nothing, or incompatible with human understanding: *plena mysterii, plena rationis.*[3] Thus, as regards the Eucharist, which realizes the maximum possibility of mystery, sacrality, and signification, human rationality becomes less an attempt to make logically consistent, and more a recognition of an intimation of secret intelligibility, or luminous invitation, stimulating a contact of desire, will, and memory, which casts the act of knowing as more a "traversal" than an appropriation.[4] This traversal takes place within the community in which the utterance "This is my body" is spoken, and which is founded *by* and *as* that utterance. For the Church is properly the essence and the repetition, as both sign and secret, of that body, both in its perpetual and temporally ecstatic realization of the historical sacrifice of the body of Jesus Christ, representing that "absent" body in and through its consecrating ritual, and also in its own mystical and literal synactic configuration of the Body which it both receives and disperses as gift.[5]

If this epistemological coincidence of the mystical and the real becomes fissured, the Eucharistic signs perforce become either a matter of non-essential, *illustrative* signification which relies upon a non-participatory similitude between the bread and the Body, and the wine and the Blood, or else, in dissociation from the realization of the Church, an extrinsicist miracle which stresses the alienness of bread from Body, and wine from Blood. These alternatives, in disconnecting the symbolic from the real, in an attempt to prioritize either one or the other, are both equally reducible to a synchronic mode of presence which fails to allow the sacramental mystery its full, temporally ecstatic potential within the action of the Church. Indeed, such

---

[1] Henri de Lubac, *Corpus Mysticum: L'Eucharistie et L'Eglise au Moyen-Age,* (Paris: Aubier-Montaigne, 1949).

[2] "*Corps mystique, donc, en premier lieu, parce que caché – mystice, latenter – sous les apparences matérielles ou rituelles qui le signifient mystérieusement: corpus Christi secretum,*" de Lubac, *ibid.,* 68.

[3] Florus, *Expositio missæ,* cited by de Lubac, *ibid.,* 261.

[4] "*Tout le sensible était pour elle un sacrament, il demandait moins à être organisé ou fondé qu'il ne s'offrait à être traversé,*" *ibid.,* 264.

[5] Antoine Arnauld and Pierre Nicole, *La Logique, ou l'Art de penser,* (Paris: 1683), 58; Louis Marin, *op. cit., Portrait of the King,* 3–15; de Lubac, *op. cit., Corpus Mysticum, passim;* Loughlin, *op. cit., Telling God's Story,* 244–5; Miri Rubin, *Corpus Christi: The Eucharist in Late Medieval Culture,* (Cambridge: Cambridge University Press, 1991), 306–8; see also chapter 4, section 2, above, "*Spatialization and the Liturgy.*"

localized presences are ultimately situated within the necrophiliac order of the sign, for, in being disconnected from ecstatic ecclesial action, the Eucharistic signs must implicitly separate the signifier from the signified.[6] Even in the case of miraculous presence, the exclusive prioritization of the "real" over the merely "symbolic" gives rise to a tendency to think of the Eucharist as a sign concealing an equally present meaning, (the giving of a merely extrinsic "grace") subsisting within a synchronic realm of logical demonstration.

It is therefore consistent to stress, as I have done above in chapters 4 and 5, the *ecclesial* and *relational* context of the Eucharist, and its character as linguistic and significatory *action* rather than extra-linguistic presence, and yet at the same time defend an account of transubstantiation. For it is when the Eucharist is hypostasized as either a thing or a sign in separation from ecclesial and ecstatic action, that it becomes truly decadent. Thus, Jean-Luc Marion, implicitly building upon de Lubac, convincingly argues that transubstantiation *depends* upon the idea that Christ's Body and Blood are "present" only in the sense of the ecstatic passing of time as gift, and *not* in the mode of a punctual moment abstracted from action, under the command of our gaze. And he shows furthermore that modern theories of transignification presuppose a mundane temporality in which Body reduced to meaning is fully "present" to us, rendering such theories crudely metaphysical in a way that transubstantiation avoids.[7]

However, it should be added that in defending the ecstatic temporality of Eucharistic presence, Marion denigrates the textual sign to a secondary status. He writes: "The text does not coincide with the event or permit going back to it, since it results from it . . . One can also understand this gap as from the sign to the referent"; or again, "the text carries the trace of the event but no longer opens any access to it," and also, "we cannot lead the text back as far as that at which it aims."[8] These expressions, "does not permit going back to . . . no longer opens any access to" are spoken in the language of "aesthetic" repetition, a stance which remembers an unchanging extra-linguistic origin rooted aoristically in the distant past, and seeks to recoup that origin identically.[9] It seems that for Marion, the temporal world *conceals* the origin, whereas I would argue, with Kierkegaard, that the original is established in

---

[6] de Lubac, *op. cit.*, *Corpus Mysticum*, 253–4, 266–7.
[7] Jean-Luc Marion, *God Without Being*, tr. T. A. Carlson, (Chicago: Chicago University Press, 1991), 161–83.
[8] *Ibid.*, 144–7.
[9] Søren Kierkegaard, *Repetition: A Venture in Experimenting Psychology by Constantin Constantius*, tr. Howards V. Hong and Edna H. Hong, (New Jersey: Princeton University Press, 1983), 132.

time, that the temporal world *discloses* the origin, and that it is continuous with its forward moving repetition, since the eternal "original" also exists in supplementing itself in an infinity without bounds. To make up for the apparent inadequacy of language, Marion allows for the "presence" manifest in Eucharistic transubstantiation to open access to that anterior event, and yet, at the same time that he insists on the idea of presence outside the sign, he also argues that the presence of transubstantiation is that of Heideggerian ecstatic time,[10] which would seem tantamount to arguing that the Body and Blood of Christ are in the *same* hollowed-out condition as the supplementation of signs. But to be consistent with *this* view, the transubstantiated Body of Christ must either be absent to the same degree that it is absent in words, or else, conversely, the Body of Christ must be just as much present in words as it is in the Eucharist. Ecstatic temporality must apply as much to language as to commemorative action. And in fact it is the former option, which reverts to aesthetic repetition, which ultimately seems to determine Marion's outlook, since he regards realized visibility as idolatrous and therefore reduces the Eucharistic gift, and gift in general, to the mere gift of distance as such. In this way, he perpetuates a dichotomy of absence and presence in a manner still too akin to the mode of nihilism.

2 EUCHARISTIC SCEPTICISM

Whilst it seems that Marion would wish to accord special extra-linguistic privilege to the Eucharistic event, I argue in this final chapter that a more positive account of the sign – which in the theological context includes the historical text, the sacred and ecclesial action, and the sacraments themselves – based on the structure of the *secret*, need not deny the Eucharist its centrality.[11] This account also avoids a whole series of arbitrary and peculiar denials with regard to language in Marion's account, not least the fact that the Eucharist is celebrated *in language*, that in fact nothing here occurs without or outside language. As Louis Marin explains in his essay "*La Parole Mangée*," concerning the treatment of the sign and Eucharist in the Port-Royal Logic, it is fully consistent with the notion of the mystical body of the sacrament to

---

[10] Marion, *op. cit.*, *God Without Being*, 140, 161–82.
[11] But not the Derridean secret, "the absolute structural secret, below the level of conscious agency, of knowledge and recognition." John D. Caputo, "Instants, Secrets, and Singularities: Dealing Death in Kierkegaard and Derrida," in eds Martin Matustík and Merold Westphal, *Kierkegaard in Post/Modernity*, (Indianapolis: Indiana University Press, 1995), 216–38.

connect the sign with the ambiguous notion of the secret, for there can only be a secret if to some extent it is *not* a secret, for either nobody knows about it, and so it is unrevealed, or else it is revealed and so is no longer secret.[12] Secrecy, therefore, has a particular mode of presence which is that of partial imparting, and this medial position between known and unknown, continuous and discontinuous, and present and absent, is where I should like to locate the sign in general, and the Eucharistic signs in particular.

The words of Consecration which Christ pronounces over the elements of bread and wine, "This is my body," "This is my blood," uttered in the context of the ecclesial repetition of the historical sacrifice and essential signification of its effective unity, invite us to question the distinction between absence and presence, continuous and discontinuous sign and referent, and death and life. First, for example, they reveal that it is possible for presence and absence – or the maximum of continuity and the maximum of discontinuity – to co-exist without collapsing into nihilistic nothingness.[13] One can look at the bread in a mode of equal uncertainty and certainty, an uncertainty which results from an absolute empirical discontinuity between Body and bread, Blood and wine,[14] and an absolute certainty of faith which judges that the Body of Christ is present and completely continuous with the bread and wine. This is not to suggest that faith forces an absurd conflict with the evidence of the senses which would assign the qualities of roundness and whiteness to the substance of bread, but instead that the Eucharist might lead us to assume a doxological brand of scepticism when regarding all things – so as never to assume, nor to claim to know securely, that the way a thing appears is the way it substantially and exhaustively is.[15] Does this suggest that the Eucharist genuinely stands at the extreme of Cartesianism and nihilism, deconstructing the certainty of even the most certain-looking sign? But it is not a nihilism of dereliction, which heralds a crude annihilation of bread which yet persists as illusion, whilst making way for another, but elusively absent, presence, as Derrida might think

---

[12] Louis Marin, "*La Parole Mangée ou le corps divin saisi par les signes*," in *idem, La Parole Mangée et autres essais théologico-politiques*, (Quebec: Boreal, 1986), 12–35 on the theory of the sign in general, and 19–20 on the notion of the sign as secret. The transcendent secret, as that which remains elusive and is at once genuinely mysterious and partially imparted, escapes the problematic of secrecy as a tool of manipulation as described by Michel de Certeau, *The Mystic Fable*, tr. Michael B. Smith, (Chicago: Chicago University Press, 1992), 97–101

[13] Marin, *op. cit.*, "*La Parole Mangée*," 18.

[14] Arnauld and Nicole, *op. cit.*, *La Logique*, 211; see further, Marin, *op. cit.*, "*La Parole Mangée*."

[15] Marin, *op. cit.*, "*La Parole Mangée*," 18.

of it. Rather, it is an *epistemological* nihilism which approaches everything in an *optative* stance of open expectation, and which says that any substance is what it is only through its participation in divine being.

The verb used in the Consecration of the bread and wine is an existential "is,"[16] and in a sense, this would assign a kind of spatiality to Jesus' words, a bringing-about in language that is both infinite and immediate. If it were a vulgar transition from one substance to another, Jesus might have chosen a dynamic verb, perhaps in the imperative mood – for example, *"Turn into* my body." The reason why it is a kind of blasphemy when extra-liturgical language elides temporality and agency in such forms as nominalization and asyndeton,[17] is that through imposing a spatial logic on finite things, it performs a parody of the eucharistic "is." Such language, like the signs of the baroque monarch, wishes never to utter the place where immanent power *is not,* and so bespeaks the chronotope of absolutism as everywhere and always present.[18] This parodic and blasphemous contiguity nonetheless traces an insuperable boundary between the absolutist and Eucharistic sign. For the latter, by casting all language as flowing in time from eternity, without according itself any priority over eternity, allows *all* signs to become concelebration. And unlike the idolatrous signs of absolutism, which embody (through their permanence) the exaltation of the *nihil,* the angelic signs which flow from the Eucharist efface themselves in order to signify that which is beyond them.[19]

But through this submission of time to the "presence" of eternity, the sign is after all no longer left behind, whereas every trace of secular signification vanishes into the maw of power. Thus even after the enunciation that the bread is in fact Body, the appearance of the bread still remains in all its transitivity – in fact it so much remains in the manner of bread that it can even

---

[16] *Ibid.,* 31.

[17] See chapter 2.

[18] See Ernst Kantorowicz, "Mysteries of State: An Absolutist Concept and Its Late Mediaeval Origins," in *Harvard Theological Review,* 48 (1955), 65–91; Gierke, *Political Theories of the Middle Age,* (Cambridge: Cambridge University Press), 87–8; Marin, *op. cit., Portrait of the King, passim.*

[19] All such signs are angelic: "(t)hey pass everywhere and occupy all space, they enable divinity to be seen at all points . . . one finds them everywhere, testifying to divinity"; "As the bearer of the message, the messenger appears . . . but he must also disappear . . . in order that the recipient hear the words of the person who sent the message, and not the messenger. When the messenger takes on too much importance, he ends up diverting the channel of transmission to his own ends," Michel Serres, *Angels: A Modern Myth,* tr. Francis Cowper, (Paris: Flammarion, 1993/1995), 91, 99 respectively.

be eaten.[20] And so, it is not that the bread is a Protestant substitutional sign for the body, but that the eating of the bread is the moment of sign – as essential revelation – that the Body of Christ is our nourishment and that it is a social and unified body. It is, in fact, only *after* the bread and wine have been assumed into the Body and Blood that they genuinely become signs.[21] It is necessary that their character as bounded things become dislodged, that they point away from themselves in a signifying manner, since it is as signs that they are able partially to disclose the gift-character of the Body and Blood; for as things, the bread and wine hide the Body and Blood, but as signs, they reveal it, by realizing the true character of body as gift, synaxis, and sacrifice.[22] And as only *partially* disclosed, the gift continues to arrive, excessive even as it is supplemented.

3 TRANSUBSTANTIATION IN AQUINAS: A DEFENCE

Such a view of the bread and wine as more than extrinsic signs, but as a literal participation in and essential symbolization of the Body, *including* not only the sacramental Body, but also the historical body of Jesus and the ecclesial body, means that it was not inappropriate for Aquinas to discuss the Eucharistic presence in ontological terms of substance and accident.[23] However, the way in which the bread is not physically evacuated in order to make room for the Body pushes these Aristotelian categories to breaking point.[24] And it is not the case that Aquinas simply reads the Eucharistic "conversion" as a miracle which overrides the protocols of substance and accident,[25] but rather that he implicitly calls into question the ultimacy of these metaphysical categories, for which the interplay between *prima materia* and pure actualized form was the final ontological context, thus disallowing any exceptions to their articula-

---

[20] Marin, *op. cit.*, "*La Parole Mangée*," 20.

[21] As Marin explains, the Eucharistic signs produce their sense at the frontier between the natural and the conventional sign in that they are iconically offered as gift, nourishment, and community, and yet are arbitrarily chosen as signs. *Ibid.*, 22.

[22] The transformation of bread into the Body of Jesus Christ, serves "to conceive how Jesus Christ is the food of our souls and how the faithful are united among themselves." Arnauld and Nicole, *op. cit.*, La Logique, 58. Cited in Marin, *op. cit.*, Portrait of the King, 12.

[23] See de Lubac, *op. cit.*, Corpus Mysticum, 272.

[24] Marin, *op. cit.*, "*La Parole Mangée*," 21.

[25] This is how P. J. FitzPatrick interprets Aquinas' adoption of the terms of substance and accident, in *In Breaking of Bread: The Eucharist and Ritual*, (Cambridge: Cambridge University Press, 1993), 12–13; see below.

tions. For Aquinas, by contrast, the prime structure involves a passage between the Creator (who "is" by nature) and the created (which only is in such and such a way). Whereas normally any thing that is "accidental" in one context is "substantial" in another (for example, buttons, like the "redness" of a red jumper, are accidental in relation to the jumper, but nonetheless belong to the substance of buttons, just as red, when it is the colour of blood, cannot be other than red), in the Eucharist, the appearances of bread and wine become accident without remainder, and there is no "elsewhere" or "different context" in which they are still substantive. And indeed, all bread is on its way to figuring the Body of Christ to this condition of "pure" accidental. And yet the substantiality of the bread is not so much destroyed as more utterly constituted by being taken up into God, who is more truly "substance" insofar as He is more truly self-sufficient (although Aquinas finds even the category of "substance" to be inadequate for God). The appearances of bread and wine alone remain, since they are now sustained in a pure contingency. They no longer require sustenance through a finite subject which is, after all, only *relatively* self-sufficient, and neither do they inhere, as accidents, in the Body and Blood of Christ as subject, since the latter is replete and can receive nothing accidental. Although the appearances remain of their essence accidents, they have become seemingly impossible "free-floating accidents" – a category which really exceeds the contrast between substance and accident – since they are now directly sustained by their participation as particular, contingent created things in the *esse* of the divinely transfigured human body to which they are conjoined. There is a gap here between the *essence* or definition of the appearances – they are "accidents" – and their *existence* as signifying manifestations of the substance of Christ's Body.[26]

For this reason, I would contest P. J. FitzPatrick's critique of this gap, in his book *In Breaking of Bread*. For FitzPatrick, the interval between the essence and existence of the species of bread and wine is both incoherent and inconsistent with Aquinas' overall ontology of substance and accident, for which every accident must inhere in a substance.[27] However, this is only because FitzPatrick restricts the Thomist ontology to the form/matter, substance/accident level, taking no account of the Neoplatonically-derived *esse/essentia* level which is capable of disturbing the prior categories, but, after Duns Scotus, became unavailable, thereby indeed reducing transubstantiation to an unnecessary, arbitrary, and scarcely comprehensible miracle. Within this

---

[26] *Summa Theologiæ*, III, q. 77. a. 1 especially ad 2: "(i)t is not in virtue of their essence that accidents are not in a subject, but through the divine power sustaining them."

[27] FitzPatrick, *op. cit.*, *In Breaking of Bread*, 13–17.

level of consideration, Aquinas shows that for every creature such an interval between *esse* and *essentia* exists and is constitutive of its reality. From essence, no existence follows, and existence is received from elsewhere, from God who exists of His very nature and not in this or that manner. Hence every creature is "pulled" by its participation in *esse* beyond its own peculiar essence – it exceeds itself by receiving existence – and no created "substance" is truly substantial, truly self-sufficient, absolutely stable or self-sustaining. It follows that the violation of the substance/accident contrast and the gap between *esse* and essence in the case of transubstantiation is only an extreme case of what, for Aquinas, always applies. All substances are "accidents" in contrast to divinity, and become signs which, in their essence, realize a repetition and revelation of the divine "substance."

One should note also that since the subject of the Body and Blood of Christ is the second hypostasis of the Trinity, identical with *esse*, this body and blood is *not* simply the body and blood of an "individual." Thus FitzPatrick is mistaken in his further objection that a recurrent possibility of transubstantiation violates a necessary local specificity of "body," or of the human individual. He writes: "Christ and Aquinas are determinate individuals, not kinds of thing."[28] But for Aquinas, Christ, being God, falls no more under the category of individuality than that of categorical generality.[29]

4 TRANSUBSTANTIATION AS THE CONDITION OF POSSIBILITY FOR ALL MEANING

I argued above that in the articulations of the Eucharistic body, the sign is not left behind. Indeed, this is so extremely the case that it is possible to argue that the theological body turns *everything* into sign, in such a way that the distinction itself between thing and sign can no longer be sustained.[30] This can be seen in the assimilation of sense and referent in the words "This is my body." Under ordinary circumstances, one attaches a referential anchor to the ostensive indicator "this," for whilst the word "This" is demonstratively specific, yet also it is superlatively indeterminate.[31] If Jesus had said "This is

[28] *Ibid.*, 15–16.
[29] "In God there is no universal and singular," *Summa Theologiæ*, I, q. 39 a. 7 ad 2; "Christ's body is not in this sacrament in the same way as a body is in a place," *Summa Theologiæ*, III, q. 75 a. 1 ad 3; see Dominique Dubarle, *Dieu Avec L'Etre: De Parménide à Saint Thomas, Essai D'Ontologie Théologale*, (Paris: Beauchesne, 1986), 330–6.
[30] Marin, *op. cit.*, "*La Parole Mangée*," 25, 35.
[31] *Ibid.*, 23–5.

my bread," we could have consulted the physical bread and understood the sense of the word by looking at the object. But that is impossible here, for we cannot look at the elements in order to expand the meaning of the phrase, which suggests that the levels of sense and referent are fused together, since a bare indication of sense has to do all the referential work. The words underline that things are only ever present in the mode of sign, that there is no leaping over language, for at the beginning of the phrase, the word "This" seems to indicate bread, but where bread is simply referred to, "body" is signified, or evoked as a sense, which assimilates the sense to the referent, or rather, effaces the stage of reference altogether.[32] Whilst one might otherwise consider it as a category leap, as if to say, "The bread *has become* Body," here there is no such successive alteration, and so, short of attributing meaningless-ness to Jesus' words, (or claiming, in bad faith that they are merely "symbolic," when elsewhere in the Gospels where this is the case, Jesus always says clearly "This is given to you as a sign of x" etc.) it would seem that the phrase has occluded the distinction between thing and sign. Yet this is not to accede to a nihilistic semiotic drainage, for although it implies that all claims to certainty are dishonest, it does so without concluding that therefore there is no truth. Instead, it allows there to be something hidden which we do not know about. By thus leaping over the stage of indication or reference, we allow things to exceed their appearance, for things are never here in terms of an enclosed, exhaustive arrival. The indicated is no longer that "other" of language which anchors all signs, but instead is that which folds back into language, for instead of being confirmed by our glance towards the bread, it is confirmed by Jesus' phrase itself.

So, whereas, for Marion, the Eucharist is something extra-linguistic which *makes up* or compensates for the deathliness of language, it is on the contrary the case that the Eucharist situates us more inside language than ever. So much so, in fact, that it is the Body as word which will be given to eat, since the word alone renders the given in the mode of sign, as bread and wine. Yet not only is language that which administers the sacrament to us, but conversely, the Eucharist underlies all language, since in carrying the secrecy, uncertainty, and discontinuity which characterize every sign to an extreme (no body appears in the bread), it also delivers a final disclosure, certainty, and continuity (the bread is the Body) which alone makes it possible now to trust every sign. In consequence we are no longer uncertainly distanced from "the original event" by language, but rather, we are *concelebrants of that event* in every word we speak (the event as transcendental category, whose transcendentality is

[32] *Ibid.*, 25.

now revealed to be the giving of the Body and Blood of Christ). The words of Consecration "This is my body" therefore, far from being problematic in their meaning, *are the only words which certainly have meaning, and lend this meaning to all other words.* This is because they fulfill the contradictory conditions of the beneficent secrecy of every sign (certain/uncertain, continuous/discontinuous, iconic/arbitrary, present/absent)[33] to such a degree of oppositional tension that the inhering of bread in Body is not a relation of signification (as for a Zwinglian view)[34] but more like a condition of possibility for all signification. The bread/Body amalgam is, as it were, such an extreme case of sign that it is no longer sign, but that which gives signs to be. This amalgam is a "thing" not a sign, yet becomes a sign in being given to us, given as a promise or sign of future givings, and so given as the turning of all things into gift, which means also into sign, since a gift is a gift only in its signifying promise of renewed gift to come.

The distinction between presence and absence is further confounded, because although the word "body" is a signified, yet it is specifically "my" body. The speaker is identifying with his dead body in advance of its absence or death by pointing to something outside himself, thus claiming death as an act of giving. In pointing away from himself (towards the bread) in order to point towards himself ("my body"), he disperses himself as gift. This gift is also a bequest, as written in a will, which, being instituted before a person's death, gains authority after death. But when Mass is celebrated, one carries out this will in an event which is not outside that will's living institution, for that event is continuous with its subsequent repetitions. Moreover, Christ's will is uniquely written in His own body since this will is His death. It is His Body and Blood which are bequeathed, giving His death as life; there is here no "dead" writing distributing to us inert "remains" which are but further traces. In receiving this bequest, we do not then possess it as it were a thing, but must in turn bequeath ourselves, for we are part of that body we receive.

It would seem, therefore, following Marin, that one could argue for a perfect adequation between the Catholic dogma of the real presence and the semiotic theory of signifying representation, for, in a sense, the theological body is the semiotic function itself, because it exists in and through its supplementations, is never exhausted, persists in the modes of synaxis and *ekstasis*, and offers a partial disclosure. Transubstantiation saves the meaning of the sign (and our "common-sense" that there *is* meaning) because the element

[33] *Ibid.*, 18 and *passim.*
[34] B. A. Gerrish, *Grace and Gratitude: The Eucharistic Theology of John Calvin*, (Edinburgh: T&T Clark, 1993), 105–6.

of uncertainty remains and yet this becomes identical with a corporeal presence which, as infinite, does not arrive in the manner of an object's transferral from one place to another, but rather arrives in and through its positive supplementations, which effect a return of the sign.

⅄   5 The Eucharistic Logos

If the Eucharist repeats what was in the first place a repetition, then it repeats Christ as Himself always nothing other than the gift of the Eucharist. This Christology is most fully expressed in St John's Gospel, whose prologue was often recited at the Last Gospel, by the Priest and Ministers during their recession or unvesting at the end of the Mass in the mediaeval Roman liturgy.[35]

In this Gospel, the Logos is described as *plērōma* – that is, as fullness, an inexhaustible source of life.[36] He is at once everything and more than everything, and yet, in the Johannine story, he is present through testimony and supplementation. Paradoxically, Jesus is the fulfillment of all signs, and yet is only revealed through a series of signs. Two things can be said about this paradox. First, this is not a Derridean mode of supplementation, for it involves not primarily a chain, but a circularity in which, for example, Jesus is supplemented by John the Baptist's witness, yet also, Jesus is John's supplement, arriving after him and consummating his witness. John, standing for Israel and the Church (since John is the first to baptize), thus also stands for the dissemination of the Word, as Jesus' supplement, and yet, conversely, the Church is constitutively supplemented by the signs of the Body and Blood, which it has ceaselessly to receive again. As the Church transmits, or supplements Christ, it also receives itself again from without, from the coincidence of what it supplements with that surplus which arrives as Body and Blood, the surplus which the Church itself is: the "body of Christ." Indeed, if the theological sign were not excessive in this way, our repetitions of the Mass would suggest an insufficiency of the sign, as though it needed "topping up." Instead, the event *is* its subsequent repetitions.

In the second place, the signs which occur in the Johannine Gospel are of several kinds. Some take place before Jesus' arrival, and others occur after His death, and so function in His absence. But notably, He performs signs of

---

[35] On the "Johannine pericope" or Last Gospel, see Josef A. Jungmann, *The Mass of the Roman Rite: Its Origins and Development*, tr. Francis A. Brunner, (London: Burns and Oates, 1959), 543–6.

[36] John 1:16.

Himself in His own presence which are therefore not non-essential substitutes for "the thing itself," but rather reveal His presence to be ecstatic, and show that He resides even as presence in the mode of supplementarity. The Logos is identified as life, "In Him was life, and the life was the light of men,"[37] which would confirm that supplementation of this kind is not a necrophiliac sign of absence and death, but can, by an alternative phenomenology of "self-supplemented presence," be regarded as the principle of life. But the coincidence of absence and infinite corporeal presence can only occur where that presence is genuinely infinite, and so, outside such a structure of plenitude, signs *are* empty, and everything Derrida says about the sign is profoundly right. Without faith, Derrida is correct, and yet the construal of the sign by faith remains a rational possibility, and exposes the fact that Derrida has not offered an undeniable or exhaustive transcendental account of the sign.

By turning all things into signs, the sign now becomes the goal, but not as a terminal product at which our gaze stops. Rather, the sign becomes a goal to *transmit*, or *bestow*. Such displacement of the conclusion in the direction of the sign means that there is no "foreclosed event" – in fact, there is no closure at all. In this unity of Body and sign, there is a ceaseless movement of ecstatic expectation which is constantly realized, an eternal identity which arises in its happening again differently, traced or received (as both familiar and unfamiliar) by faith in the patterns of transmission. Because there is never a total, exhaustive arrival, once and for all, there remains a mysterious unknown which is not over-against us, but which is analogously mediated by the known.

And this space between knowing and not knowing is that of the resurrected life which is characterized by the act of worship. Residing beyond both metaphysics and nihilism, it is in turn the space of story. Above all, there is only story because of the resurrection. Resurrection is the process at work in non-identical repetition by which that which is repeated is not unmediably different, but analogously the same. This redemptive return is what allows a person to tell a story, since for there to be a story, there must be "analogous" subjects and objects, persisting as same-yet-different. Is this why Derrida claims to be a poor storyteller, and why Blanchot concludes *La Folie du Jour* with the words "*Un récit? Non, pas de récit, plus jamais*"?[38] For, on the one hand, "death" construed as nihilistic dereliction might be the end of every story; on

---

[37] John 1:4.
[38] Derrida, "*Mnemosyne*," in *idem, Memoires for Paul de Man*, tr. Cecile Lindsay, (New York: Columbia University Press, 1989), 1–44, 3; Maurice Blanchot, *La Folie du Jour*, (Montpelier: Fata Morgana, 1986), 38.

the other hand, it ends the *possibility* of story. And so every story is by definition a resurrection story, and it is thus that we can read the Gospel stories as narrating the story which sets out the transcendental condition for every story. Yet, since the resurrection ensures that there is no final death to end the story, Jesus' story is at once the story which makes stories possible, and the impossible story which never ends. Even if the world were to come to an end, his story would still continue, as the last verse of John's Gospel proclaims when it declares that if all of Jesus' actions were to be written down "the world itself could not contain them."[39] Just as John's Gospel seems not to end, revealing that there is no end to the resurrection story, so also his Gospel omits to narrate the ascension, thereby assimilating the resurrected body with the Body and Blood we receive in the Eucharist.

In this light we can no longer see the resurrection as a teleology of presence, nor an economy of totality. Indeed, the resurrection is precisely that which prevents such fetishization of outcomes. For the resurrected body is a completely *imparted* body, transmuted into a series of signs. Such constant dispersal turns body into gift. And, again, fetishization is prevented because the resurrection story has neither beginning nor end. However, this "openness" of plot does not betoken a dissolution into the formless void, nor narrative nothingness, since it is precisely because death and life are here no longer held in opposition that there can be analogous repetition, which thus realizes this story as one of quintessential form, compatible with infinity and non-closure. This is a constitutive incompletion which genuinely welcomes the other in an ecstatic presence, in contrast to the postmodern void which is trapped within the illusion of the same sameness. The analogous identity is always transcendent, and so there is always more to come: "Eternity is the true repetition."[40] Such an identity, unlike that attained through backwards recollection, would always remain to be completed, but is not thereby rendered incoherent. Rather, this incompletion is precisely the ceaseless re-discovery of a positive but unanalyzable proportion between time and eternity.

---

[39] John 21:25.
[40] Kierkegaard, *op. cit.*, *Repetition*, 221, 327.

CONCLUSION

In Part II of this essay, I have demonstrated how the complexities and displacements of a theology of the Eucharist, based on a reading of the mediaeval Roman Rite, are not situated within a gesture which seeks to evade either a loss or a positivity. Rather, its recommencements, invocations, permeations, and significations are situated within a construal of language as that which both signifies and provokes a beneficent mystery which is not wholly other from the sign, although it cannot be exhausted by the sign. Instead, the theological sign *includes* and *repeats* the mystery it receives and to which it is offered, and as such, it reveals the nature of that divine mystery as gift, relationality, and perpetuity. Such a sign is not a terminal product which stops at its own signification. Instead, its signification is a redemptive sacrifice which is offered in the hope of further offerings, offered *to* and *as* the gift of repetition. This sign disseminates the tradition into which it is born, for it is configured as a history, a ritual, a liturgy, a narrative, a desire, and a community. Such a wealth of signification bespeaks the sign which is also a person, and a people, a body which is dispersed through time as gift, peace, and the possibility of a future.

I have also shown how the theological sign has been parodically appropriated by the secular state which claims for itself a simplified version of the sempiternity of the Eucharistic body. Such transpositions have taken many forms, from the mobilization of presences to the exaltation of the *nihil*. But they are alike in many ways: (1) in their recourse to ritual modes of signification; (2) their presupposition of the triumph of the dichotomies of presence and absence, life and death, active and passive; (3) in their interpretation of the "secret" of phantasmal power as occupying the extremities of *either* presence *or* absence. Such refusal of the medial resolution of this dichotomy in the form of the transcendent Eucharistic secret ensures that their negotiation of the dichotomy of presence and absence as an either/or does not offer a genuine set of alternatives, but is reducible to the same interminability of invisibility, ideality, and detemporalization. For on an immanent level there can be only a dialectic between the metaphysical and nihilistic variants of depersonalized spatiality and depersonalized nothingness, the absolute of domination and the absolute of dereliction. The permanence of their respective realms of signification – either the permanence of equivalence and objectification, or of the homogeneous continuum of the *nihil* – promises (their own demonic variants of) resurrection, but yields only the reality of termination. Thus, the gestures of modernity and postmodernity can be interpreted as the sacraments of an infinity of lack.

It is by means of the contrast between the unliturgical world and the lineaments of the sacred polis which I have traced in Parts I and II of this essay that I hope to have provided the articulations of a model of a liturgical attitude which alone offers a genuine restoration of both the subject and of language as such. In both cases, this attitude permits openness without unmediated and formless dispersal. I have suggested that the origins of such an attitude are to be found in antiquity, but implied that its full realization is only made possible by a specifically Christian construal of liturgy. What does the Christian form of liturgy which I have described in Part II add to the Platonic one?

In order to answer this question, it is necessary first to explain why the question has been asked, for this is perhaps far from obvious. The clear contrast between Platonic recollection and Christian repetition drawn by Kierkegaard would seem to render my question redundant. He described recollection as a fundamentally negative and melancholic operation of pointing backwards, predicated upon an articulation whereby the occasion of a recollection is, by definition, left behind, or separate from the original truth being recollected. By contrast, repetition points forwards, and the occasion of a repetition is a constitutive part of the truth it repeats.[1] The implications of this for liturgical enactment would seem to make clear the superiority of the latter negotiation of truth over the former.

However, as I argued in chapter 1, Plato's implicit account in the *Phaedrus* of the erotic mediation of the good in the beauty of the physical world suggests that it is possible to overstate this contrast between Platonic retrospective recollection and Kierkegaardian prospective repetition. In his essay "*L'immémorial et la réminiscence*," Jean-Louis Chrétien argues that, unlike the Kantian or neo-Kantian *a priori* which resides as a given truth in the mind, for

---

[1] Søren Kierkegaard, *Repetition: A Venture in Experimenting Psychology by Constantin Constantius*, tr. Howards V. Hong and Edna H. Hong, (New Jersey: Princeton University Press, 1983), 131.

Plato recollection is not simply a matter of introspection.[2] Rather, it is perforce preceded by forgetting, and is only triggered by the physical reality of loving something in this world. Such recollection, Chrétien argues, is for Plato neither perfect nor unambiguously total, for it is not possible to remember exactly the experience of being a soul prior to embodiment. And unlike Plotinus, Plato does not think of the soul as being an existent in the realm of the forms, parallel to but separate from embodiment. Insofar as for Plato recollection does not entail knowing identically the past as it was experienced by the pre-existent soul, but non-identically, through inspiration via *erōs*, we can infer an intimation of a gesture towards prospectivity and difference. This would seem to close the gap between recollection and repetition, and thus urge the question: why Christianity?

Both recollection and repetition, however assimilable they might or might not be, are attempts to negotiate the *aporia of learning*, whereby if one is ignorant of something and has knowledge of one's ignorance, one must already know something of that of which one has ignorance, such as the direction in which to look.[3] How do we come to penetrate the barrier of ignorance before we have even begun? Augustine attempts to resolve this *aporia* in the opening passage of the *Confessions*, by recourse to the interpersonal, ecclesial tradition in which we stand, which is an essential part of God's gift to us of faith: "You breathed it into me by the humanity of your Son, by the ministry of your preacher (*prædicatoris*)."[4] So, whereas for Plato, we first of all exist in a solitary, pre-existent relationship with the divine, and only secondarily recollect that relationship with truth through recognition of the good in physicality or in the beloved, for Augustine, our first reference is to our sociality as the recipients of God's gift, and as situated within an historical tradition which transmits the truth through time and relational space.

But does this aspect of Augustine's answer fully resolve the *aporia*? One could argue that his recourse to the believer's position within a series of narrative continuations of a tradition only pushes the problem one stage further back. For however many stages of a tradition we receive from one another, the historical series itself implies an absolute past behind which there

[2] Jean-Louis Chrétien, *L'Inoubliable et L'Inespéré*, (Paris: Desclée de Brouwer, 1991), 9–56, 22.
[3] In the *Meno* this *aporia* is explicitly resolved via recollection. Socrates demonstrates, by means of an experiment on one of Meno's slaves, that because the soul of man is immortal, he can recollect certain facts all by himself without help from anyone. Meno's slave thus manages to recollect certain features of squares and triangles, Socrates says, because truths his soul knew still existed in it and could with a great effort be recalled.
[4] Augustine, *Confessions*, I.i.(I).

is no anterior bestower of the story, except that of the divine Logos. This ultimacy of divine anteriority, it could be argued, means that the Augustinian resolution of the *aporia* of learning is after all a variant of the Platonic paradigm, for it nonetheless casts the origin of tradition as a transcendental, rather than an historical past. And as such, does it not still have final recourse to a focus on the individual as recapturing a pre-existent unmediated relationship with the divine? So again, why Christianity?

The answers to this question cannot be absolute, for however much one might know that Christianity advances further towards a resolution, Plato will already have anticipated or hinted at that advance. Nonetheless, these non-absolute answers are as follows.

First, in Christianity there is no doctrine of pre-existent souls, and so we cannot make the same claim that this transcendental past is "our" past, because it is a past which is our origin in God. If one wishes to speak of "our" past, or of our human past, all one can do is have recourse to an infinite series. Our absolute divine "past" is not mediated to humanity first of all by an act of privileged or tranquil recollection of what was glimpsed in a prior existence by an individual soul, but rather by time and by the interpersonal series of a tradition. And that is why our journey "back" to God perforce cannot reach an unmediated anterior optimum, but is *essentially* mediated by this tradition's series, both in its historical retellings, and its present and future narrations.

Secondly, following from this, the "ground" for this narrative manifestation of truth is as much constituted by the forward movement of its inhabited enactment as by its endless retrospective presuppositions. And so, it is not that one must move forwards in order to find the past hidden in the beauty of the future (as for Plato's hint of eschatology in the *Phaedrus*), but that there is neither priority of past over future, nor future over past. Rather, both past and future perform the truth in an adequation of eternity's embrace of time, which is as much eschatological as protological.

It is in keeping with this vision that, in the third place, the Trinitarian God is an *eternally* supplemented reality, always both "before" and "beyond" its *logos*. And this alone secures a divine self-sufficiency, without reduction to presence, whereas Plato could only think the "supplementation" of the Forms by their manifestation in time, in a manner which compromised the self-sufficiency of the divine, and therefore compromised in turn the pure, non-necessitated "gift" character of time and finitude.

As a free gift, time supplements itself in an infinite series, which cannot Platonically "leap out of itself" back into the memory of eternity. Participation in eternity still remains therefore, in the fourth place, a journey *through* time, within a community of people, which is as essential to our being as our createdness. This identification of the human subject via the performance of a journey has already been anticipated by Plato, but only consummated as Christianity's equal embrace of past and future, and genuine priority of human mediation. For, as I have argued, the present performance in time of the divine truth is as essential a manifestation of its magnificence as any anterior moments.

Fifthly, although the emphasis upon the mediation of a tradition instantiated by our position within time and community can perhaps be seen to be hinted at in Plato's account of the interpersonal mode of dialectic appropriation of the truth and the publicness of education in the *Republic*, nonetheless, there are differences. Christianity more radically casts truth as an event in time, realized in one man's life, whose subsequent biographies coincide with that life's living, which is thus lived again differently in our own lives. Such truth looks forward to its own event as a repetition. By contrast, the stories which narrate the events of Socrates' life, although they participate in the mode of the truth which he taught, nonetheless cannot be identified as *commensurate* with the truth they narrate.

But is this difference substantial enough to be counted? For although in *Philosophical Fragments*, Johannes Climacus contrasts Christ's essential manifestation in and through his message to Socrates' effacement before the forms, in other passages, he discusses our relationship with Christ as within a model not unlike that of Platonic recollection. He suggests that the witness of an apostle is as nothing to the immediacy of truth itself: "when it comes down to it I (am) just as contemporary with (the god) as anyone."[5] And he describes this immediacy as an essentially private phenomenon which reduces the mediation of tradition to the level of mere chatter.[6] Apostolic testimony, like that of the Socratic pedagogue, dissolves before the glory seen with the eyes of faith, with which it is unsurpassably contemporary.[7] And so, from certain passages in the *Philosophical Fragments* and *Concluding Unscientific Postscript*, it

[5] Kierkegaard, *Philosophical Fragments / Johannes Climacus*, tr. Howard V. Hong and Edna H. Hong, (New Jersey: Princeton University Press, 1985), 67.

[6] "Only in one respect could I be tempted to regard the contemporary (in the sense of immediacy) as more fortunate than someone who comes later. If we assume that centuries elapsed between that event and the life of the one who comes later, then there presumably will have been a great deal of chatter among men about this thing . . . all the more so because in all human probability the centuries-old echo, like the echo in some of our churches, would not have riddled faith with chatter but would have eliminated it in chatter, which could not happen in the first generation, where faith must have appeared in all its originality," *ibid.*, 71.

[7] *Ibid.*, 70; See also *idem*, *Concluding Unscientific Postscript*, tr. David F. Swenson and Walter Lowrie, (New Jersey: Princeton University Press, 1968), 247.

would seem that this immediacy is something other from the sign, operating according to a private, maieutic divine intimacy with the individual: "God, . . . the eternal spirit from whom all spirits are derived, might in communicating the truth, seem to be justified in sustaining a direct relationship to the derivative spirits, in quite a different sense from that in which the relationship is one between derived spirits, who having a common derivation from God, are *essentially* equal."[8] He describes the apprehension of this immediacy as the "*autopsy* of faith," a personal act of seeing which is the private privilege of the individual.[9]

There is thus a tension in Kierkegaard between Christ's essential coincidence with signs and intersubjective communication, and an individualism prompted by Christ's withdrawal from direct presence: "(God) is in the creation, and present everywhere in it, but directly He is not there; and only when the individual turns to his inner self, and hence only in the inwardness of self-activity, does he have his attention aroused, and is enabled to see God."[10] Indeed, at the end of the Preface to *Philosophical Fragments*, Climacus explicitly abdicates his place within intersubjective community: "Every human being is too heavy for me, and therefore I plead, *per deos obsecro* (I swear by the gods): Let no one invite me, for I do not dance."[11]

Kierkegaard's covert individualism seems to omit the fact that Christ is always already repeated, even in his Eucharistic "immediacy," by which there is perforce a continuation of the incarnation in the sacraments, and the Church, and in every sign, as I have argued above in Part II. Thus, Kierkegaard's stress on the prospectivity of repetition is only *sustainable* as such in combination with an account of the Church and sociality. This very combination of prospectivity and relationality is anticipated by Plato, in his implicit suggestion of the participation of the occasion of recollection in the truth, and in the *Phaedrus*, this participation approaches an interpersonal dimension. In Socrates' second speech, he describes the lover and beloved as obtaining a future of amorous encounter which is presented as eschatological: "and when this life is ended they are light and winged, for they have conquered in one of the three truly Olympian contests. Neither human wisdom nor divine inspiration can confer upon man any greater blessing than

---

[8] Kierkegaard, *op. cit.*, *Concluding Unscientific Postscript*, 218; see also John Milbank, "The Sublime in Kierkegaard," in *The Heythrop Journal*, 37.3 (July 1996), 298–321, 319, n. 34.
[9] Kierkegaard, *op. cit.*, *Philosophical Fragments*, 70.
[10] Kierkegaard, *op. cit.*, *Concluding Unscientific Postscript*, 218. Even if, as Milbank argues (*op. cit.*, "The Sublime in Kierkegaard,") inwardness in Kierkegaard does not generally imply a solipsistic space, there are times, as in the quotation above, when it does appear to do so.
[11] Kierkegaard, *op. cit.*, *Philosophical Fragments*, 8.

this" (256b).[12] However, in this intimation of eschatological intersubjectivity, there is no fully realized community which combines relational space with the time of past, present, and future. The lover and beloved still appear isolated from a whole community. There is no suggestion here of their subsisting laterally in space, and historically through time, nor of a fully realized coincidence of prospective movement through time as an *embodied* event which itself constitutes the repeated actuality of an eternal mystery.

So, whilst Plato intimates that the lover and beloved will be together in eternity, there persists an element of sacrifice of the body for a greater spiritual gain. There is here no resurrection of the body, but instead a becoming "light and winged." The Eucharistic difference is therefore more radical. Since every Eucharist is an essential repetition of the incarnation – as the full unfolding of time, as community, as gift – our attempt to "return" to our divine origin is not so much a journey towards God, as a journey towards God's entry into our body – both physical and relational – which *really happens*. Thus, with Christianity, the optimum of meaningfulness and the optimum of living subjectivity coincide *within* the world – with all its temporality, space, and embodiment. And whereas in Plato, the body is ultimately left behind, in Christianity, the spirit and the body are sacrificed together in order that the spirit and the body together might be received back again on the eschatological morning.

---

[12] "*Dans le Phèdre, la rencontre amoureuse, pour être le lieu de la réminiscence, ne conduit rien pour autant à se reproduire ni à se répéter, elle est gage au contraire de l'avenir à l'amour ouvert, avenir de vérité et d'épreuve, joute olympique, relevant des seuls vrais jeux olympiques, ceux de la vie elle-même*," Chrétien, *op. cit.*, 29.

ANALYTICAL INDEX

Ab illo benedicaris, 187, 195
Abel, 180, 251
Abraham, 180, 231, 251
absolutism: and absence, 86, 101, 117;
    and baroque excess, 83–4; and civic
    ritual, 148–9; and the Derridean
    sign, 117; and Descartes, 82, 87–8;
    and desire as lack, 101; as dispersed,
    84–7, 103; and immanent
    transcendent, 82, 84, 86–7, 138,
    152, 257, 267; and justice, 151–2;
    and secularized teleology, 138
Accendat in nobis, 250
acedia, 215
actual, the: and Aquinas, 126–7; and
    discontinuity, 126–7; and Duns
    Scotus, 126; and *ekstasis*, 129; as gift
    from God, 127–8; as ineffable,
    127–9; as logicalized matter (Duns
    Scotus), 129, 130; and
    meaningfulness, 129; as never not
    realised, 128; as self-divided (Duns
    Scotus), 217; versus the possible,
    126–30 *see also* Aquinas, possible
Adamson, Sylvia, 89
Adiutorium nostrum, 185–6
Adonis, festival of, 29; and festival of
    Demeter, 29; gardens of, 29
Agamben, Georgio, 54, 115
Agnus Dei, 180, 237–8
Agricola, Rudolph, 50; and "place
    logics," 50, 55
akoē, 9, 22, 24, 31

Alliez, Eric, 84, 122–39
altaria, 183, 228–9
Ambrose of Milan, 244, 248
Amen, 182
Ammon-Ra, 24, 26–7, 34, 35
analogia entis, 122–4, 127, 129, 131–2
anamorphosis, 83, 85
Anderson, Perry, 88
Anselm of Canterbury, 156
apophaticism, 62, 173, 197; and liturgical
    impossibility, 176ff
apostrophe, 188; and absence, 195–8,
    212, 216; agony of, 197–8;
    ambiguous direction of, 193–5, 204;
    and animal language, 194; as beyond
    verification, 194; and *chiasmus*,
    212–3; as communal figure, 193;
    definition of, 193; and deferral, 194;
    and desire, 194–5; and dialogue,
    194, 196–7; as expectant work,
    194–5, 197; gratuity of, 193–4; and
    melancholia, 197; and monologue,
    194; versus nominalization, 194,
    198; and passionate order of
    language, 193–4; as petitional, 193,
    199–200; and stammer, 198; and the
    subject, 196; as vocal trope, 193
Aquinas, St Thomas, 122, 138, 148; and
    actuality, 126–7; and *analogia entis*,
    122, 124, 127, 129; and Aristotelian
    theory of knowledge, 130–2, 163;
    and the Eucharist, 133, 259–61; and
    existence/essence dichotomy, 127,

260–1; and "intellectual distinction," 124; and metaphysical categories, 259; and the "mysterious," 128; and "real distinction," 123, 126, 128, 129; and *religio*, 153; and substance/accident dichotomy, 259–60, 261; *De Potentia*, 130; *Summa Theologiæ*, 130, 133–6, 153, 260–1

Archangel Michael, 229

Ariès, Philippe, 101–2

Aristotle, 49, 128–9; logic of, 54; and *metabasis*, 55–6; and theory of knowledge, 130, 163; *topoi* of, 53–5; *De Interpretatione*, 94; *Posterior Analytics*, 49

Arnauld, Antoine, 254, 257

Asad, Talal, 146–8, 154

asyndeton, 95–8;
Christic: 225–8; and humiliation of mundane "reason," 225–8; and insanity, 227–8
spatial: apparent spontaneity of, 96; definition of, 95–6; disorder of, 97; economy of, 96; and grammatical voice, 97; and nominalization, 96; order of, 97; and scientific discourse, 96

atopōtatos, 44–5

Attic dramatists, 38

Auerbach, Erich, 200–2

Aufer a nobis, 186, 231

Augustine of Hippo, 62, 71, 115, 139, 141, 160, 221, 253, 269

Austin, J. L., 98

autochthony, 33, 43–4, 234, 238–40; and the gift, 46, 234; and the good, 45–6; as liturgical, 46, 57; and naturalization, 233–4; as pilgrimic, 45ff; as psuchic, 44; Socratic, 45; as textual, 45, 57 see also Boreas, Lysias

Bacon, Francis, 148

Bacon, Roger, 62

Baker, John Hamilton, 136

Bal, Mieke, 202

Balthasar, Hans Urs von, 114, 175

Bann, Stephen, 89

baroque, the: apparent deliquescence of, 82, 85; architecture of, 84, 86; as Cartesian, 84–8, 117; excess of, 82–4; fiestas of, 83; and figure of "the fold," 83, 85; and monarchical display, 83–4, 86–7, 117; poetry of, 83; as readable, 85, 117; spatiality of, 83–6, 117

Barthes, Roland, 90

Bataille, Georges, 117–18

Baudrillard, Jean, 84–5, 94–5, 99, 102, 105

Baxter, Richard, 145

Beck, Ulrich, 94

Becker, M. B., 144

Being: and analogical resemblance, 122, 129, 132; and "formal distinction," 123; as formal essence, 123; as gift from God, 128–9, 248; indeterminacy of, 125; modalities of (Duns Scotus), 123, 125–7, 129; as nothingness, 113, 128; ontic construal of, 132–3; as plenitude, 113, 128–9; as relational, 248; as sole object of metaphysics, 122, 124, 130; as time, 113–4 see also ontology, univocity

Benedict, St, 232–3

Benjamin, Walter, 212, 216

Bennett, Tony, 214

Bergson, Henri, 90–1

Biber, Douglas, 93

Black, Antony, 144

Blair, A. M., 88

Blanchot, Maurice, 106, 108, 117, 265

Blount, Nicol, 245

Bodin, Jean, 141, 149, 153

Boethius, Anicius, 49; *Consolatio Philosophiæ*, 215; *On the Different Kinds of Topics*, 49

Boler, John F., 128

Boreas, 15–16, 28, 43–4

Borgeaud, Pierre, 30–1, 44–6

Bossy, John, 140–72

Botte, Bernard, 181–252, 244

Bourdieu, Pierre, 148
Bouyer, Louis, 104, 169, 171
Boylan, Patrick, 26–30, 35
Boyle, Robert, 74–5; and contingency,
    79; and divine voluntarism, 78–80;
    and "event," 78–9; and *machina
    Boyleana*, 79–80; and Nature, 78;
    and the vacuum, 78
Brague, Rémi, 8
Bréhier, Emile, 121–2, 137
Bremond, Henri, 101
Bresc, Henri, 140
Bronfen, Elisabeth, 102–3
Buber, Martin, 197
Bucer, Martin, 152
Budge, E. A. W., 26–7
Burger, R., 7, 9
Burguière, André, 142
Burnyeat, M. P., 14
Bynum, David E., 200

Cæli cælorum Virtutes, 236
Calicem salutaris accipiam, 247
Calvin, John, 141–2, 157, 162, 164
capital: as afraid of itself, 10, 92; and
    order of charity, 144; and immanent
    teleology, 144; and Socrates, 7, 11,
    12, 33; and the sophists, 7–10; and
    syntax, 97–8; and *tokos/tokous*, 36–7;
    and writing, 7–10
Caputo, John D., 256
carnivalesque, the: and the baroque, 82;
    dubiety of, 82–6; and syntax, 97
Cavanaugh, W. T., 137, 149, 152–4
Celebrant, the: ambiguous position of,
    173; and impersonation, 183, 203,
    209ff
Certeau, Michel de, xii, 95, 158–61, 164,
    172, 257
Chafe, Wallace L., 93
charity: as abstract beneficence, 144–5;
    anxiety of, 144; and kinship, 143; as
    personal, 143–4; and reconciliation
    with God, 157; as sacramental, 143;
    as state of being, 143–6;
    transformation of, 144

Chaunu, Pierre, 101
Chrétien, Jean-Louis, 211, 268–9, 273
Chrichton, J. D., 176
Church, the: as artificial body, 149; and
    Eucharist, 147, 159, 249, 254, 264;
    as legally defined, 149; and politics,
    152–3; and positive
    supplementation, 264, 272; role in
    marriage of, 142; as secondary to
    sacramental body, 161–2; and
    spatialization, 158; symbolic
    dimension of, 162. *See also* ecclesial
    body
City, the:
    absolutist, 82–7: as Cartesian, 82–5;
        interiority of, 84–5; order of, 85;
        outsidelessness of, 84–5, 87
    and single legislator, 87 as universal,
        84, 87; violence of, 85–7
    Boylean, 74–5; and assent/dissent, 76,
        79; and capital, 77; as contractual,
        77; and exteriority, 75–7; and
        interiority, 75, 77; legislature of, 76;
        as pseudo-transcendent, 80; and
        Restoration, 76; as spatial, 81
    Cartesian, 57–61; as contractual, 70; as
        immanent, 58; and interiority, 59–
        60, 67, 69; as military, 59; and
        provisional structures, 59–60; as
        purely spatial, 57, 60; and single
        legislator, 58, 60, 73; and Sparta, 58,
        152; as universal, 60, 84, 86; as
        within the individual, 57–8, 60–1,
        67, 73, 84, 86; as written, 57–8, 70,
        73
    Liturgical: and autochthony, 233; as
        decentred, 174; as semiotic, 169
    modern: assumptions of, 94; and the
        dead, 102–5; language of, 98; as
        necropolis, 99, 118; and violence, 97
    Scotist: and dialectic of individual and
        universal, 137; and the family,
        141–2; and indifference, 136–7; and
        nation–state, 136, 149; and
        voluntarist legislator, 136
    Socratic, as constituted by liturgical

paidia, 41–2; as not "containable," 44–6, 57; as doxological, 39, 45; as favoured by Socrates, 44, 46; and the good, 40, 57; and heavenly model, 57; as in the path of the good, 44–5; and the poets, 37–9, 40, 42; as the true drama, 40, 57, 214; as within the soul, 44, 45, 57

civility: as abstract protocol, 157; and arbitrary rules, 148; and the Decalogue, 151; and dissimulation, 148; dubiety of, 148; and the fork, 148; and manners, 147; as secular liturgy, 147–8, 157

Cogito: 57, 60–2, 71, 80, 193; sceptical structure of, 65–7; and nihilism, 67

Collinson, Patrick, 142

Communicantes, 179, 199, 212

Confiteor, 186, 193, 197, 199, 148

Congar, Yves, 175

confraternities: and arbitration, 143; and charity, 143; and the dead, 154ff; decline of, 144; and the Eucharist, 147; and kinship, 143; and the laity, 145; as liturgical, 142–5; and the living, 154; operations of, 143; and saints, 142

Conley, Tom, 99

Connelly, M. J., 175

Connerton, Paul, 89, 98

Consecration, the: and ambiguity of the "gift," 190, 245–6; and realization of offering, 245; as "second offering," 190, 245–6; and sequential relation to Offertory, 190, 245

constativity, 98–100; and asyndeton, 98; and nominalization, 98

Corpus Mysticum: as *corpus verum*, 159–61; as ecclesial body (late twelfth century), 160; as ineffable event, 160; as metaphor, 162; and the nation-state, 145, 154 *see also* Church, sacramental body, theological body

Courtine, Jean-François, 61–2, 122, 127, 130

Credo in unum Deum, 179, 205, 226, 227; and accelerated narrative, 224; and doctrine of three-in-one, 205–7; and doxology, 207; and Gospel, 207; and position in Mass, 224; and salvation history, 206–7; structure of, 205–8

Croll, Morris W., 96

Cuddon, J. A., 193, 213

Curtis, S. J., 134

Cubism, 90

Dahood, Mitchell, 248

Da nobis per huius, 242–3

Dasein, 112

Davies, C. S. L., 147

Davis, N. Z., 155

death: ambiguity towards, 101–2; and capitalism, 101, 104–5; as constitutive of life, xiv, 107, 114–15, 178, 248, 251, 263, 265; definition of, 103; as deletion, 104, 117; denial of, 101–6, 111; domestication of, 102, 109; as equivalence, 104–6; and Eucharist, xiv, 253; fetishization of, 102, 107, 109, 116, 150; mastery over, 102, 111; mystification of, 101; and identical repetition, 107–8; non-appearance of, 108–9; pagan view of, 112–13; political economy of, 104–5; production of, 104–5; representation of, 102–3; scandal of, 101–2, 104–5; as separated from life, xiii, xiv, 103–113, 154, 257; and state socialism, 105; as superlative object, 108–9, 113; as universalized, 106, 116

Christ's: 155; as gift, 263

and Derrida, chapter three; as guarantee of singularity, 111; and Levinas; as pure gift, 111

and Eucharistic signs, 257; and dichotomy of presence and absence, 253; and kinship, 154; and late-mediaeval piety, 150

and Heidegger, 110ff, 112, 116; and disclosure of Being, 113; ownership of, 111; as transcendental condition, 112

Delaruelle, E., 165

Deleuze, Gilles, 83–5, 98, 124–5

Derrida, Jacques, xiii-xiv, 4, 59, 69, 257; and death, 103, 106; and Heidegger, 108ff, 110ff; and Husserl, 106ff, 109; and Levinas, 110ff; and Plato, 1–46; and the "secret," 256; and the sign, 114ff, 265; on Socrates' critique of writing, 6–7; as "sophistic," 8, 11, 20–1, 46–7; *Aporias*, 108ff; *Dissemination*, 35–6, 117; *Mnemosyne*, 265; "Plato's Pharmacy," 1–46; *Speech and Phenomena*, xiii, 47, 106ff, 114ff; "Tympan," 8; *Writing and Difference*, 69

Descartes, René, 52, 57–74, 81–2, 135, 152; and *aporia* of the *punctum*, 66, 68–9; and architectural metaphors, 58, 70; and deduction, 65; and emulation of artisans, 68; and *extensio*, 61; as favouring the homogeneous, 58–9, 63–4; and indictment of resemblance, 59; and intuition, 65, 68–9, 70–2; and language, 68; and memory, 69–71; and nihilism, 64; ontology of, 61ff; and presence of the infinite in the finite realm, 66; and rejection of philosophical inheritance, 58–60, 63, 66–7; as Scotist, 61; and time, 59, 68; and violence, 59; *Meditations on First Philosophy*, 57–74; *Rules for the Direction of the Mind*, 57–74 see also epistemology, ontology

desire: agony of, 98, 101; cancellation of, 101; and Eucharist, 254; of God, 193–4; as lack, 82, 84–5, 97–9, 101–5; and liturgical language, 194, 217, 244; as proper "gift," 247

Detienne, Marcel, 29

Deus tu conversus, 209

dialectic:
Ramist, 54ff
Socratic: as angelic mediation, 20; and dialogic genre, 20; and differentiation, 17–8, 23, 41; as doxological, 39; and metaphysics of presence, 19; as not opposed to exteriority, 28; as opposed to indifferent saturation, 22; as *pharmakos*, 28; as psuchical and erotic, 17, 20–1; and recollection, 17; as steadfastness, 46; subtlety of, 6; and supplementation, 19; as uniting time and eternity, 17; as way of life, 39

différance: 4, 176; false intransitivity of, 117; as indifference, 22–3, 34–7, 108; as metaphysical, 107–8; and middle voice, 35, 117–8; and *mouvance/resonance*, 117; as postponed value, 12, 107; and presence, 107; and the sign, 107–8; as undecideable, 117; violence of, 34–7

difference: Socratic appreciation of, 16; sophistic denial of, 15–7; and violence, 31

Dignum et iustum est, 179

Dirigatur, Domine, 222, 252

distance:
and Christ's death, 156; doxological, 7, 173; as gift, 246
Scotist, 122–3, 131, 152; and apophaticism, 173, 178, 197; and apostrophe, 197; and contractualism, 123; and decline of charity, 144; as "high piety," 123, 156; and impersonation, 184; and liturgical "names," 182, 184; and ontological difference, 129; as proximity, 178, 191, 202, 229; and rise of civic ritual, 148–9; and univocity, 122–3, 129, 131

Dix, Dom Gregory, 159, 163, 182, 223

Domine exaudi, 196, 198, 210, 215

Domine, dilexi decorem, 229

Domine non sum dignus, 231
Dominus vobiscum, 179, 186, 210, 234
dorveille, 215
doxology: ability to offer, 188; angelic, 236; as communal, 236; as condition of possibility for subjectivity, 204, 248; and difference, 16; and dissemination, 207–8; as ethical practice, 40, 45, 49, 207; and the good, 14; and humility, 196, 208, 227, 244; language as, xii, xiv, 37; nature of, 188, 208; as ontologically constitutive, 40, 45, 196, 204, 209, 248; and participation, 204; and Platonic dialogues, 42–3; and space/time, 235–6; and theological interim, 42–3; within the Trinity, 210, 236
Dubarle, Dominique, 104, 261
Duffy, Eamon, 144, 165, 172, 181
Duhem, Pierre, 139
dunamis, 15, 20
Duns Scotus, Joannes, 61–2, 121–40; and empiricism, 130–1, 134; and the Eucharist, 133, 260; "high piety" of, 123, 130, 132, 134; and practical reason, 135ff; and reaction against Aquinas, 122–3, 126, 131; and representation, 130; *In. Metaph.*, 130; *Opus oxoniense*, 121–2, 124, 126, 128, 133–5, 138–9; *Ordinatio*, 131–2, 136; *Reportata parisiensia*, 122, 128, 133, 136; *Tractatus de primo principio*, 123–5 *see also* Being, formal distinction, ontology, voluntarism

Ecclesial body, the, 158–9; and authority, 161; and continuity of "mystical" and "real," 159–64; as *corpus verum*, 159; as gift, 160; as "hidden extension," 160; and late mediaeval separation from historical body, 160; and reception of Eucharistic body, 159–61; and sacramental body, 159–60; as secondary to Sacramental body, 162; and unity, 159–63

Eco, Umberto, 62, 194
economics: and charity, 143; and craft guilds, 142; and the dead, 154; and lay participation, 142; as subordinate to liturgical offering, 142–4, 154
Eisenstein, E., 50, 173
ekgonos, 7
Elias, Norbert, 148, 153
Elliot, R. C., 213
embodiment: xii, xiii, 25; denial of, xiv, 15, 21–4, 114; and signs, xiv, 22–4, 116
Emitte lucem tuam, 184, 193
epistemology: and deduction, 65; as doomed by the *Cogito*, 65; and intuition of simple natures, 62–5; as limited to the "available," 63, 79; and knowledge as ontological event, 131; liturgical critique of, 226–7, 254; and nihilism, 64; primacy of, disguised, 80–1, 109; as prior to ontology, 61–5, 70, 109, 127–9, 132, 239; and representation, 63; Scotist, 130ff, 132 *see also mathēsis*, *Cogito*, Duns Scotus, given
Erasmus, Desiderius, 147
erōs: 5; and active/passive dichotomy, 36; and capital, 33; commodification of, 6, 9–10, 18; contrasted to desire as lack, 98, 101; defended against charge of interiority, 28–9; and *ekstasis*, 28–9; as interpersonal, 21, 29, 33; and knowledge, 13; and self-forgetfulness, 31; and supplementation, 20, 28; termination of, 101; and the unknown, 109
esse, 57
essentia, 126, 129
Eucharist, the: alleged politicization of, 172–3; as appropriated by immanentism, 87, 258; and Aquinas, 133; as central to polity, 147, 157; and Christ's soul, 134; as *corpus Christi verum* (thirteenth century), 161; and dichotomies, 257; as

extrinsicist miracle, 160; and fusion of power and love, 157–8; and holy scepticism, 257; as mere symbol, 163; as *mysticum* and *verum* 190; and necrophilia, 103; and the ordinary "meal," 148, 174–5, 226; and Scotist voluntarism, 132–3; and signification of the Church, 159; and spatialization, 160; as traversed event, 253, 255 *see also* transubstantiation

evening, the: and angels, 222; and Apocalyptic literature, 222; and eschatological day, 222–3; and Last Supper, 223; and prefatory time, 221–3; sacrifice of, 222

eternity: and desire, 223; and memory, 223; spatial reading of, 113, 228; as suppressed, 118; and time, 116, 221, 223, 225–6, 258, 266, 270–1; versus permanence, 104; versus the void, 107; and writing, 218

Experimental philosophers, 74, 103; as priests of Nature, 78

experimental philosophy: and aggregation of witnesses, 74–7; and alchemy, 78; and matters of fact, 75–9; and replication, 76–7; and spatialization, 78; and "spring" in the air, 78; and "virtual witness," 76–9, 89

extensio, 52–3, 61–3, 65–7, 69, 79, 81, 91; and Scotist transubstantiation, 133

exteriority: and death, 107; Derrida's view of, 28–35; and *ekstasis*, 28–9; and harmony, 30; and Husserl, 106ff; and indication, 106–7; liturgical, 186, 216, 231; and Pan, 30; as primordial, 107; and purification, 216ff; as viewed positively by Socrates, 28–31; and violence, 31

Fairclough, Norman, 93

family, the: and Fourth Commandment, 141; and Luther, 141; and

paterfamilias, 141–2; rise of, 141; as "small commonwealth," 142

Ferrari, G. R. F., 7–10, 15–18, 24, 30–3, 41, 44

Ficino, Marsilio, 153

Figgis, John Neville, 152

Filmer, Sir Robert, 88, 174

Fisher, J. D. C., 141

FitzPatrick, P. J., 259–61

Flandrin, Jean-Louis, 143, 155

Florus, 218, 254

flux, the: xi, xiii, 110, 116, 117, 234

Ford, David F., 249

formal distinction, the, 64, 122; and attributes of God, 125; definition of, 123; of existence and essence, 124, 126; as never fully understood, 127; and "real" versus "logical" distinction, 124, 126; and univocity of being, 123

Fortesque, Adrian, 188

Fossier, Robert, 141

Foucault, Michel, xiii-xiv, 104, 151, 228

Fowler, Norman, 93

Franklin, J. H., 88

Funkenstein, Amos, 56, 62, 122–3, 127, 131, 133

Futurism, 90; and accelerated apprehension, 91; and the adjective, 92; and the noun, 92; and presence, 91–2

Gadamer, Hans-Georg, 12, 15, 37–8, 211

Galileo, Galilei: and acceleration, 139; and "motion in a void," 139

Genette, Gérard, 82–3, 212, 223–5

Gerrish, B. A., 162, 263

Gewirth, Alan, 153

Gibson, A., 128

Gierke, Otto, 172–3, 258

gift, the, xiv, 64; and ability to give, 112, 191, 204, 240–2, 244, 246, 249; ambiguous lineaments of, 190–1, 242–5, 254, 269; as beyond calculation, 112, 247; and charity, 143–4; and Consecration, 245; and the creation, 241; and death, 111, 154, 263; Derrida on, 111–2; and desire, 244, 249, 252; and dispossession, 238, 250; and eschatological postponement, 241, 245–6; as good, 241; gratuity of, 191, 247; of humanity, 242–3; and the incarnation, 240–4; as more than human, 204, 210, 240, 247; and middle voice, 112, 190–1, 242, 249; nature of, 240–249; as ontologically constitutive, 192, 235, 240–1, 243, 248–9; of the other, 113–4; and participation, 191, 204, 241–50; as passed on to others, 112, 143, 210, 238, 250; and peace, 143, 238; perception of, 149; as received, 112; and relationality, 240, 243, 248–51, 254, 269; simplification of, 165, 245; and sinfulness, 249; and space/time, 235, 251; supremacy of, 112, 247, 251; types of, 240–1; as uninterrupted, 250; versus the given, 238, 250; within the Trinity, 241–9 and counter-gift, 112, 210; impossibility of, 246–7; and "return," 246–7

Gill, Christopher, 211

Gilson, Etienne, 50, 62, 122–4, 126–7, 133–5, 153, 175

given, the, xiv, 53, 62, 239; and Boylean "facts," 74; as corporeal, 65, 80; as epistemological projection, 65, 76, 79; and experimental philosophy, 76; as incorporeal, 65, 67, 69, 79–80; and indifference, 244, 249; as limited, 79; and mathematics, 67; and questionability, 80; as "read," 53, 67; as reducible to the *nihil*, 64–7, 70, 79; and repetition, 77, 79; and representation, 89; as universal, 77; as virtual, 64–5 *see also* object, *extensio*

Gloria in excelsis Deo: 179, 188–9, 193, 203–5, 209, 227, 237

godparenthood: and *compaternitas*, 140–1, 160; and the "family," 141; and Luther, 141; and plurality, 141; as real, 140; as spiritual, 140; and taboo of marriage, 140–1

Good, the: and autochthony, 33, 43–5; and the beautiful, 14–15, 44; and capital, 7, 12; contagion of, 11–12, 15–16, 22; and contingency, 45; Derrida's misunderstanding of, 7, 21–2; Descartes and, 58–60, 72, 74; and dissemination, 23; and *dunamis*, 15; Duns Scotus and, 135–6; *epekeina tēs ousias*, 11, 12, 20; and eternity, 13, 17; as ground of being, 11–12, 15; as inaccessible to a *mathēma*, 12, 21; and *methexis*, 12–16, 20, 25; and presence/absence, 7, 12, 17, 20, 22; speaking directly of, 7, 12, 19; and supplementation, 21; and time, 13, 45, 211; transcendence of, 13, 16

Gonda, Jan, 36, 105

Goody, Jack, 201

Görer, G., 102

Görlach, Manfred, 56

Gottfried, B., 9

Gospel, the: 207, 217–19, 224

Grant, Edward, 139

Gray, D. H. F., 201

Grice, H. P., 98

Hacking, Ian, 74

haecceitas, 122, 128

Hanc igitur, 179, 224, 226

Havelock, Eric A., 200

Hayman, David, 91, 97

Heidegger, Martin, 95, 108, 117, 232, 256; and *Dasein*, 111; and Levinas, 111; and "mineness" of death, 110; and *mitsein*, 111; and necrophilia, 111; and necrophobia, 111; and representation in Duns Scotus, 111

Hewitt, Andrew, 91–2

Hippolytus, 170–1, 233

historical body, the, 158; as "absent," 160; and late mediaeval conjunction with spiritual body, 160; as separated from ecclesial body, 160; and spatialization, 160; as authoritative essence, 160; Protestant privileging of, 161

Hobsbawm, Eric, 98

Hobbes, Thomas: plenistic philosophy of, 78; and religion, 149

Homer, 38, 200–3, 214

Houlbrooke, R. A., 140, 142, 155

Hughes, Glenn, 91

Huizinga, Johan, 165

Hulme, T. E., 91

Husserl, Edmund, 106, 114

Hyland, D. H., 15, 211

hylomorphism, 131

identity: ambiguity of, 203; and Archangel Michael, 229; borrowing of, 184, 201, 208–9; divine, 204f; and epic heroes, 200–4, 211; and epithetic identification, 199–203; finite, 204; and impersonation, 183, 203, 208f; as *in medias res*, 180f; permutations of, 173–4, 199f, 201, 204, 208–15; and place, 184, 204, 209, 229; as radiant, 204

Imagism, 90–1

impersonation: angelic, 188, 208, 209, 237; redemptive, 208–9; distance of, 184, 237; liturgical, 183, 188, 208; as ontologically constitutive, 109, 229; and participation, 208–10; and substitution, 201, 204, 208; Trinitarian, 204–8, 210

incense, 187, 221, 252; blessing of, 187; displacement of, 195, 212, 230

Incensum istud a te, 212, 252

indication: Husserl and Derrida on, 106–9; and indicative mood, 98–100, 108, 113; and non-being, 108–9, 113; triumph of, 110f, 113; and unknown, 109; versus expression, 107 *see also* epistemology

individual, the: and community, 234; as de-politicized, 136; as preferable to

the multiple, 57–8, 60; as spatial, 103; as universal, 61, 69, 72, 73 *see also* subject, subjectivity

In nomine Patris . . . , 181, 184, 208, 228

In spiritu humilitatis, 250, 252

interiority, 28, Cartesian, 72; liturgical, 186, 216, 231; and purification, 216ff; and writing, 72 *see also* exteriority

Introibo ad altare Dei, 182–3, 184–5, 203, 228, 230

Irigaray, Luce, 116

Isaiah, 215, 218

Isidore of Seville, 253

Iudica me, Deus, 184, 193

Jackson, B. D., 42

Jaeger, Werner, 42

Jameson, Frederic, 91

Jardine, Lisa, 49

Johnson, Mark, 95

Jones, R. F., 96

Jordan, W. K., 143–4

Jousse, Marcel, 201

Judovitz, Dalia, 69, 71

Jungmann, Josef, 170–5, 179, 180, 187–8, 203, 233, 236, 244, 264

Jusserand, J. J., 143

Justin Martyr, 170

Kant, Immanuel, 118, 137, 268

Kantorowicz, Ernst, 174, 258

Keifer, Ralph A., 175, 189

Kenner, Hugh, 91

Kierkegaard, Søren, 221, 255, 266, 268, 271–2

kinship: and angels, 154; and the atonement, 156–7; and *compaternitas*, 140; and contractualism, 140; and the dead, 154; decline of, 144, 155; and economic realm, 142f, 154; and the family, 140–1; and God, 154–7; and godparenthood, 140; and lay participation, 141–2, 145; and marriage, 140, 142; and reconciliation, 144, 150–1, 154f,

156–60; and saints, 154–5
Klauser, Theodor, 173, 175
Knowles, David, 121
Korolec, J. B., 131
Koyré, Alexandre, 62, 66, 139
Kripke, Saul, 203
Kristeva, Julia, 96
Kuksewicz, Z., 134
Kyrie, 179, 187, 189

Labande, E.-R., 165
Lacoste, Jean-Yves, 184, 191, 222,
    232–4, 236–8, 249–50
Lakoff, George, 95
Lanzone, R. V., 27
Larousse, P., 27
Last Gospel, 180, 264
learning: *aporia* of, 269; Augustine on,
    269–70; Plato on, 269–70
Lebrun, F., 102, 142
Lees, Robert B., 93
Lefebvre, Henri, 84–5, 90, 139
legal positivism: and arbitrariness, 148,
    152; and atonement, 156; and the
    Decalogue, 135, 151; and demise of
    teleology, 150; and Erasmus, 147;
    and juridical God, 150–1; and moral
    teaching, 147, 157; and the nation-
    state, 151–2; and privatization of
    penance, 151; and religious
    instruction, 141, 151; and rise of
    canon law, 149; and saintly
    mediation, 156; Scotist voluntarism
    and, 135–40
leitourgia, 43, 159, 222, 234, 238
Levinas, Emmanuel, 110; and Heidegger,
    111; and "mineness" of death, 111;
    and the other, 110, 113–4
Libera nos, quæsumus, 237
liturgical language: and defamiliarization,
    214ff; and dichotomy of orality and
    writing, 216–9; as ethical, 39, 45;
    and *erōs*, 217; as "impossible,"
    176–7, 198; and interiority/
    exteriority, 185–216ff; invented by
    Theuth, 27; and irony, 44–5, 197;

and *methexis*, 39; as passionate, 175,
    193–4, 197; as permitted in the
    Socratic city, 39, 45; and
    purification, 216–19; and refusal of
    discrete procedure, 193; and
    repetition, 181–2; as sacrifice, 252;
    and satiric genre, 213ff; and
    spatiality, 88–100, 177, 214, 217;
    stammer of, 178, 181, 190, 198,
    215; syntax of, 226f; textuality of,
    216; vocality of, 216 *see also* liturgy,
    Roman Rite
liturgical space: as aporetic, 185–6, 192,
    229–30; articulation of, 234–5; as
    asymptotic, 203, 230–1; and
    complexity, 213; and confused
    deixis, 181, 183, 193, 204, 209, 213,
    230–1; as defined by God, 229–32;
    and displacement, 229; as distended,
    197, 204, 228, 230–1, 233; as
    doxological, 229; and identification,
    229; and memory, 231–5; versus
    mundane topology, 228–36; and
    ontological, 184, 204, 228, 232; and
    peace, 228; as pilgrimic, 176–7,
    180–1, 192, 228–230; and
    preoccupation, 229–32; and
    prospectivity, 231–2; and
    relationality, 229, 233–7; as
    repositioned by the gift, 235–6; and
    solitude, 233; and time, 228, 231–2,
    234; within Trinity, 210, 229; as
    uncertain, 181, 183–9, 193, 197,
    202, 204, 231, 230–1
liturgy: angelic, 177; and apophaticism,
    178, 183, 190, 215; *aporias* of, 177,
    185, 197; as authentic work, 222,
    226; as beyond utility, 191, 193–4,
    222; and Christological resolution,
    177–8, 185, 187, 189, 214–15; and
    civic manners, 148; contradictory
    deixis of, 181, 183, 210;
    eschatological, 173, 183; and the
    everyday, 146–8, 165, 170–4, 207,
    210, 229, 252; as expectant work,
    183, 186, 193–5, 197, 200, 203,

214, 216; generic strategy of, 199, 213ff; as impossible, 176ff, 186, 197, 215, 226, 230; as never finished, 226–7, 246–7; as *propemptikon*, 202–3, 222; and public/private dichotomy, 146–8; reform of, 170–1; secularization of, 173; and spectacle, 164–5, 172; standardization of, 164–5, 172; and Trinitarian "name," 181; uncertain "place" of, 181, 183–6, 189, 210; and virtue, 146
Llewelyn, John, 117
Lord, Alfred B., 200
Loughlin, Gerard, 200–2, 254
Lubac, Henri de, 150, 158–65, 172, 175, 190, 218, 254–5, 259
Lukács, Georg, 90, 201
Lull, Ramon, 62
Luther, Martin, 132, 141–2, 155–6
Lyotard, Jean-François, 77, 98, 208, 213
Lysias, 5; speech of, 5–7; citizenship of, 33, 43–5, 70, 73

Macintyre, Alasdair, 151
MacPherson, C. B., 94, 104
Maravall, José Antonio, 84–7, 104
Marks, Herbert, 215
Marin, Louis, 84–7, 254–63
Marinetti, Filippo Tommaso, 91–2
Marion, Jean-Luc, 61–2, 95, 117, 246, 255, 262
marriage: Catholic view of, 142; and the Church, 142; as contract, 142; as detached from order of charity, 142; and kinship, 140–1, 146, 160; and parental consent, 141–2; and peace, 140; Protestant view of, 142; and ritual practice, 141; as sacrament, 141–2; validity of, 141–2;
Marsilius of Padua, 153
mathēsis, xii, xiii, 48, 62; as abstract, 65, 69; and acceleration, 68–9; and baroque poetry, 83; and being, 63; and Boylean protocol, 79; and the Eucharist, 163; and formal

consistency, 58, 60; and the given, 53; and geometry, 58, 63; Phaedran, 45; as political, 61, 86–8, 136ff; as private, 69, 72–3; as produced by the individual, 60, 69, 72; as pseudo-eternity, 68–9, 73; Ramist, 49–57, 60; and rational certainty, 52; and Scotist "piety," 130–2, 134; and Scotist "possibility," 127–9, 134; as secularized algebraic mathematics, 67–8, 74; and "simple natures," 65, 69; as universal, 45, 50, 54, 58, 68, 72; as virtual reality, 42, 63–5, 69; as written, 58, 60, 72
McCord Adams, Marilyn, 124, 133
McGrade, A. S., 153
McGrath, Alister, 156
McLuhan, Marshall, 50
McManners, John, 101–2
McRae, K. D., 51, 88
Melchisedech, 180, 251
Memento Domine, 179, 190
memory: Descartes on, 69–71; and the Eucharist, 254; and liturgical space, 231, 234–5, 237; and loss, 223, 232; Ramus on, 53–4, 71; and retrospection, 231–2
Mercer, Samuel, 27
Merleau-Ponty, Maurice, 107, 114, 116
middle voice, 35, 105, 112; and atonement, 152, 156–7; and gift, 244, 244–6, 249; as interpersonal, 107; and Socratic philosophy, 30, 32; and mediation of priesthood, 145; and mediation of saints, 155–6; and reconciliation, 151–2; and the Trinity, 157; and purification, 217
and pseudo-middle: and death, 109, 117; of Derrida, 35–6, 105–6, 117; and false intransitivity, 117; of Heidegger, 117; and law, 152; and nominal language, 90–3, 100; and Scotist "formal distinction," 127, 135; of sophists, 32; as violent, 85
and active/passive dichotomy: of baroque art, 85–6; and baroque

king, 86; of Boylean protocol, 81; and death, 105, 109; and *différance*, 117; and lay participation, 145; and legal positivism, 152; and liturgical gift (Lacoste), 249; as metaphysical, 105; and nouns, 98, 91–100; and Scotist voluntarism, 136–7; and spatialization, 88; and writing, 100

Milbank, John, 55, 61–2, 112, 118, 122–3, 128, 150, 156, 238, 246, 272

Millett, Paul, 239

Milton, John, 142

Mitsein, 111

Mnēmē, 7, 17, 25; as beyond banausic assessment, 7

Mohrmann, Christine, 181–252

Molin, Jean-Baptiste, 141

Morin, Edgar, 101

Munda cor meum, 189, 217

Murray, M. A., 35

Mutembe, Protais, 141

myth: as allegedly inimical to knowledge, 23; as critique of immanentism, 48; Derrida on, 23–4; Descartes' refusal of, 59–60; as inevitable, 87–8, 117; Plato on, 23–7; Socrates on, 24; structural similarity with writing, 24

names: and Amen, 182; borrowing of, 208; confusion of, 183, 204–5; contingency of, 180–1; and distance, 182; and divine epithets, 203ff; epiphanic, 181–2, 204; invoked, 181–2; liturgical, 181; non-identically repeated, 182, 203–5; Trinitarian, 181–4, 203–8, 209; Trinitarian exchange of, 204–5, 210; versus nominalization, 182

Nancy, Jean-Luc, 72

necrophilia: and Duns Scotus, 134, 150; and language of signs, 90, 114, 253; and mediaeval kinship, 154 of modernity, 101–5; as dissimulated, 101, 103; and Heidegger, 111; as inevitable, 104, 106, 107; and

nihilism, 104; and pseudo middle voice, 105

necrophobia: and early modern era, 102; and Heidegger, 111; and industrial era, 102; and necrophilia, 103ff; and Romantic era, 102; and twentieth-century historians, 101–3

Nicholas of Cusa, 66

Nichols, Aidan, 172, 175

Nicole, Pierre, 254, 257

nihil, the: 64, 67, 70, 109, 239; and the object, 64, 67; and Scotist "possibility," 128; and the subject, 70

nominalization, 92–5; and asyndetic syntax, 96; definition of, 92–3; economy of, 93; and elision of personhood, 194; and grammatical voice, 93–4; and homogeneity, 94; and modality, 93–4; versus apostrophe, 95, 155, 192ff, 194, 197; versus liturgical "names," 182; as written, 193

nouns, 89–95; brilliance of, 92; and constativity, 98; Futurism and, 92; Imagism and, 91; and lapidation, 82–3; as least conceptualized, 91; modernist poetics and, 89, 92

object, the: alleged superfluous considerations of, 64; as above alteration, 36, 62, 67, 101, 108–9, 120, 130; apostrophic invocation of, 194, 197; attempts to liberate, 90–2; as beneath the king's gaze, 86; Cartesian, 62, 64; and condition of availability, 94, 104, 109, 196; contradictions of, 67; and death, 101, 109; as exceeding scalar appearance, 194–6; existence as, 104; and false humility, 196; and ideality, 62, 65, 67–8, 91, 109, 130, 195; inauguration of, 63, 70–1, 130; as independent of corporeality, 130, 132; liturgical release of, 195, 212; as more than physical, 195; as *nihil*, 64,

67, 73, 108, 112; and
nominalizations, 94; as occasioning
cognition, 130–1, 137; ownership
of, 112; and political reification,
137; Scotist, 130; as serially
projected, 90; sophistic, 32, 57; and
termination of *erōs*, 101; versus
subject, 104, 109, 130 *see also* Being,
Cubism, death, *extensio*, Futurism,
given, Imagism
Ockham, William of, 128, 132; and
"names," 128; *Sent.*, 132
O'Connell, J. B., 188
Offerimus tibi, Domine, 252
Offertory, the, 179; and Consecration,
190, 245
Ong, Walter J., 50, 53–6
Onians, R. B., 29
ontology: Cartesian, 57, 61–2; as "clear
and distinct," 63; as "common
notion," 63; and doxology, 40, 43,
45, 197–8; as limited to the
knowable, 63; and memory, 32, 53,
71; and ontological difference,
122–3, 125, 129; as preceded by
epistemology, 61–5, 127; as
separated from theology, 62, 64, 66,
71, 122f, 130; as spatialized, 61–2,
71; traditional notion of, 63–4,
122f1f; as univocal, 62–4, 122ff *see
also* Aquinas, Being, doxology, Duns
Scotus, individual, subject,
subjectivity, univocity
orality, xii, xiv; and apostrophe, 193; as
combined with writing to
approximate to eternity, xiv, 218;
defended, 4, 24, 26, 216; and
Descartes, 69, 72; falsely accused of
structural relation with presence and
capital, 6, 7, 26, 115–6; and ideality,
115–16; and life/death dichotomy,
115; and metaphor of liquid, 29, 31;
liturgical, 177, 199; and memory,
25, 116; and myth, 24–5; and
ontological disposal, 115; and
presence, 69, 115; and repetition,

199; and supplementation, 4, 24, 25,
115–16, 199–200, 221 *see also*
Derrida, sign, time, writing
Orate fratres, 179, 233
Oreithyia, 28ff, 44
Orwell, George, 93
Ostende nobis, 210
Ourliac, P., 165

Pacem relinquo vobis, 238
paideia, 38, 41–2
paidia, 41–2
Pan, 30–1, 44, 45
Panofsky, Erwin, 84
Parry, Milman, 200–1
participation: and Aquinas, 122, 129; and
Derrida, 166; and doxology, 204,
208, 242–6; and Duns Scotus,
122–3, 127, 137
Pascal, Blaise, 66, 83–4
Pater Noster, 180, 236–7
Paxson, James, 95, 193
Peabody, Berkley, 200
peace: and charity, 143; and civility,
147–8; and the common dish, 148;
and *compaternitas*, 140; as gift, xiv;
and content of "gift," 236–8, 250;
Erasmus on, 147; and the Eucharist,
147; exchange of, 237–8; insincere,
148; as more than human, 210,
236–8; and person of Christ, 238;
and reconciliation, 151; request for,
238; and rise of private piety, 147,
149; ritual attainment of, 146–7,
171; and Seven Deadly Sins, 151;
and society, 147; as synthesis of
space and time, xiv, 220, 233,
236–7; as taught, 147, 149, 151; and
time, 237; Trinitarian conferral of,
210
pepaisthō, 42
Perceptio Corporis tui, 249
Per intercessionem beati Michaëlis Archangeli,
230
Per ipsum, 243
Per quem hæc omnia, 240

Peter of Spain, *De Locis*, 49

Pharmacea, 28ff

pharmakos, and dialectics, 28

philosophy: and doxology, 32, 40, 110; and education, 210; experimental, 76; gaze of, 7, 32–4, 107; and initiation into the Good, 13, 46, 211; and loss of self, 31; and madness, 14–16, 31, 33; and memory, 25, 32, 53; and music, 41; as nomadic, 44–5; as public, 61; and self-knowledge, 13, 30; and sophistic "glance," 7, 32–3

Planinc, Zdravko, 15, 42, 211

Plato, xii, xiii, 3–46, 62, 71; and critique in advance of modernity, 3; and critique of sophistic protocols, 3; and genre of dialogue, 20, 42; and indictment of poetry, 37; and nihilism, 27; and suspicion of writing, xiii, 19; *Crito*, 46; *Ion*, 22; *Laws*, 40–2, 57, 211; *Meno*, 269; *Phaedo*, 14; *Phaedrus*, 3–46; *Philebus*, 15; *Protagoras*, 15; *Sophist*, 20, 27; *Republic*, 11ff, 21, 32, 37, 39, 40, 44, 57, 60, 61, 73, 211, 271; *Symposium*, 15, 20, 24; *Timaeus*, 14

Polignac, François de, 239

Port-Royal Logic, 256ff; and the "secret," 256–7

possession: by beloved, 30–1; from without, 7, 22, 25, 29; and Socrates' *daimonion*, 17 *see also* exteriority

possible, the: as criterion for the actual (Duns Scotus), 126, 129, 130; and discontinuity, 127, 131–2; in Duns Scotus, 122, 128, 130–1; and finance capital, 138; formalization of, 129; as intellectual, 127, 129; and liturgical enactment, 176; potential autonomy of, 126, 133; and virtuality, 125–9; and voluntarism, 132–3 *see also*, actual

Postmodernism: as anticipated by Futurism, 91–2; and death, 106; contrasted to liturgical

"impossibility," 177f; as modern, xii, 47–8, 106, 108–9, 117

Pound, Ezra, 91

power: as abstract, 157–8; and assent, 137; of laity, 141–5; and love, 157; of nation-state, 141, 157; of *paterfamilias*, 141; and teleology, 135, 138

printing, 50, 53, 54, 68, 173

Proust, Marcel, 215

proximity: and community, 191, 210, 233–4, 237; and distance, 2–3, 229; and distension, 195; and journey into God, 230–1; liturgical radicalization of, 232; of object, 195; and peace, 210, 237–8; performance of, 234, 237 *see also* distance

punctum, the: *aporia* of, 66; Descartes on, 66–7; ideality of, 66, 68; materiality of, 66; mathematics of, 66; and Nicholas of Cusa, 66; and Pascal, 66; Plato on, 66; as secularized, 67

purification: as Christological, 187–8, 218; and exteriority, 186, 188, 216–18, 231; impossibility of, 185, 188–9; and incense, 187; as infinitely receding task, 187, 192; as interior, 186, 216ff, 231; via language, 217–19; possibility of, 189; repetition of, 185–92

Quam oblationem, 179, 224, 226, 245, 247

Quare me repulsti? 184, 215, 230

Quare tristis, 215

Quid retribuam Domino, 247

Qui pridie, 179–80, 200, 222–6; and attenuation of time, 225; and Christic asyndeton, 225; and command to repeat, 223; and decelerated narrative, 224; and evening sacrifice, 222–3; and mundane time, 223; and obsessiveness, 225; synoptic version of, 200; and uncovered time, 224

Radical Orthodoxy, xii–xiii

Ramus, Peter, 49–57; and Aristotle, 49–50; deductive reasoning of, 50; and epistemological tabulation, 50, 52, 54, 55; and reaction against Scholasticism, 50, 54, 56; and textuality, 54, 69
  method of, 49–52, 71; and dichotomization, 51; and distribution, 51; and document of wisdom, 50; and enunciation, 50, 54; and *extensio*, 52–3; and invention, 50, 54; and judgement, 50, 51, 54; and law of verity, 50; and mathematical language, 56; and memory, 53–4, 71; and mind, 53; and ocularity, 54, 56; and rhetoric, 54; and syllogism, 50; *Logike* (1574), 49–52
Ranger, T., 98
Re, *see* Ammon-Ra
religion: and Aquinas, 153; and Marsilio Ficino, 153; and the nation-state, 153; and personal freedom, 154; privatization of, 147, 149, 153; as set of propositions, 151–3; as universal "pulsion," 153; and virtue, 153
repetition: "aesthetic" (Kierkegaard), 13, 221, 223–4, 268; as aleatory, 99, 108, 123, 126; and asymmetrical reciprocity, 35, 107; and Boyle, 76, 79; as condition of possibility for knowledge, 21, 24, 77, 131; Descartes on, 61; and dialectic, 18; and Duns Scotus, 123, 126–7; and eternity, 266; and the Eucharist, 160, 223, 247–8, 265; identical, 8, 48, 50, 99, 104, 106–8; and memory, 71; non-identical, 18, 25, 35, 109, 160; and "original" event, 223, 226, 264; and Plato, 18, 25, 35, 211, 268–9; Ramus on, 56; and recollection, 13, 268, 271–2
representation, 50, 89–90; acceleration of, 91; and constativity, 98; and the daguerreotype, 89; and death, 103–4, 107–8, 131; and economics, 138; and lithography, 89; and nineteenth-century novel, 89; and object, 89; and photography, 89; political, 137; versus repetition, 131; Scotist invention of, 130; and syntax, 96–7;
Robinson, T. M., 4
Rodrigo, Pierre, 6, 16, 18, 44
Roman Rite, the: apophaticism in, 174–5; and apostrophe, 193ff; Bouyer on, 171; defence of, 173–7; history of, 170; Jungmann on, 171; and morbid emphasis on guilt, 172–3; oral devices of, 199ff, 213–16; and oral provenance of, 173, 177; and repetition, 173–7, 182; and satire, 213f; and secular interpolations, 172–7; spatialized reading of, 177–8; structure of, 171–7; summary of, 178–80; and theology of gift, 240ff; Vatican II critique of, 170–1 *see also* liturgical language, liturgy, Vatican II
Rorty, Richard, 53
Rosenmeyer, T. G., 11, 18, 30, 42
Rosenzweig, Franz, 2
Rosset, Clément, 97
Rossi, Paolo, 53
Rowe, C. J., 4
Royal Society, 74
Rubin, Miri, 164, 172, 254

sacramental body, the: display of, 164–5; entry into, 159, 163; as exhibited by the Church, 159, 162–4; as both mystical and real, 159, 161; and real presence, 159; Roman Catholic privileging of, 161; as *sacramentum conjunctionis*, 159; and unity of ecclesial body, 159, 162; as visible sign, 160, 163
sacrifice: Bataille on, 118; chain of, 251; as constitutive of life, 115; as dereliction, 105, 118; and divestment, 186; evening, 222, 226; and incense, 187–8; and Isaiah, 218;

of life, 105; madness of, 227;
morning, 226; offering of, 190; and
the Passion, 223; preparation for,
186, 190, 218; purification of, 190;
repetition of, 190, 218, 223, 226;
and revestment, 187–8; and writing,
218–19
saints: as authoritative figures, 164; and
Christ's satisfaction, 155;
enumeration of, 199, 212; kinship
with, 154–5, 187, 199; mechanical
invocation of, 155; transferred merit
of, 155, 187, 212
Sanctus, 179
satire: and absence of secure locus,
213–15; and defamiliarization, 214;
definition of, 213; as generic
strategy, 213–14; history of, 213–14;
and restoration of the subject, 214
scholē, 41
Scarisbrick, J. J., 143, 145, 149–50, 154
Schaffer, Simon, 74–80, 105
Schmidt Pantel, P., 43, 239
Schmitz, K. L., 79
Scott, Charles E., 117
Sequentia sancti Evangelii, 224
Serres, Michel, 209, 258
Shannon, C. E., 98
Shapin, Steven, 74–80, 105
Shelley, P. B., 194
sign, the:
    liturgical: 169–70; as concelebration,
    258, 262; and continuity/
    discontinuity dichotomy, 262–3;
    and death/life dichotomy, 257; and
    the Eucharist, 163, 253, 262–3; as
    excessive, 264; Kierkegaard's
    subordination of, 271; and life, 265;
    Marion's subordination of, 255–6,
    262; and metaphysical presence,
    254–5; and the secret, 254, 256–7,
    262–3; and supplementation, 264–5;
    and mystery, 253–4, 256, 262–3;
    and presence/absence dichotomy,
    253, 256–7, 262–4; self-effacement
    of, 258; and sense/referent

dichotomy, 261–2; and
transubstantiation, 259, 216ff, 263
necrophiliac: and absence, 107, 114,
117; as apparently innocuous, 86–7;
of baroque king, 86; Cartesian
object as, 62, 65, 67; Descartes on,
68; and Derrida, xiv, 106–7, 114ff,
264–5; disintegration of, 90; and
finance capital, 138; and ideality,
115; and indication (Husserl), 106ff;
and necrophilia, xiv, 90, 103–8, 114,
253; as oral, 115; and presence, 107;
Socrates' alleged hostility towards,
19, 21, 37, 40, 46; tripartite
structure of, 90; phenomenology of,
115; as written, 114–15
sophists, the: 5–7; and capital, 6–7, 16;
and consideration of the soul, 5; and
demythologizing, 5, 9, 16, 24, 53;
attitude to language of, 37; and civic
life, 40, 42; and differentiation, 18,
21, 41; and humiliation of language,
21, 40, 42, 46; and mathēsis, 19; as
mechanical technicians, 5, 18; and
physicality, 15, 17, 21, 32, 45;
subjectivity of, 45; and writing, 6
Soskice, Janet Martin, 227
soul, the, 5; Burger on, 7; care of, 140;
chariot of, 5, 14, 32; and the city,
44–5; and Duns Scotus, 133–4; and
the Eucharist, 133; and "formal
distinction," 133–4, 153;
forgetfulness of, 39, 269; hierarchy
of, 38; immortality of, 113; as
innocuous, 149; as nourished by
communion with memory, 20; ontic
consideration of (Heidegger), 113;
pre-existence of, 270; and "real
concomitance," 134; and "real
distinction," 134
Sparta: Descartes on, 58–9; as ideal city,
58–9; Bucer on, 152
spatialization: and asyndeton, 95f; and the
baroque, 83–6; and Bergson, 90–1;
and Boyle, 78; and death, 99, 103–4,
108, 118; and Descartes, 58, 60, 63;

and Genette, 82; and historical body, 160; and human action, 221; and language, 82; late mediaeval, 121ff, 160; and legibility, 164; and liturgical practice, 164ff; as normative, 48–9, 81, 88, 118; and nouns, 88, 91–2; as political, 82, 88, 93–4, 98, 105, 136ff; and printing, 50; as pseudo-eternity, 48, 50, 56, 68, 79, 82, 85, 93–4, 104, 117, 228, 257; and representation, 50, 89–90, 164; as ritual, 98–100, 158; as self-gestating, 94, 99–100

Steiner, D. T., 6, 23

Strauss, Leo, 42

subject, the:

  baroque: as fissured, 84, 86; as object, 85–6; as without memory, 87

  Cartesian, 57; as achronic, 72; as arbiter of being, 70, 80–1, 90; continuity of, 71; as dependent on politico-architectonics, 57; as disembodied, 72–3; memory of, 69–72; as nomadic, 209; as object, 71–3, 192, 199; and objectivity, 249–50; and objects, 192, 212; and ontology, 57, 73; as pure thought, 72; solipsism of, 72–3; as outsideless, 73; textualization of, 70–3

  liturgical: and *acedia*, 215; crisis of, 197–8, 214–15; as dialogic, 196–7; doxological, 170, 177–8, 192, 196, 198–9, 212, 214; as dispossessed, 194, 196, 208–11, 229; and fear of silence, 197–8, 214; and the gift, 191–2; as incapable of doxology, 177; as expectant, 194; and humility, 196, 212; as non-ironic, 44–5, 197–8, 213; as unforeclosed, 176, 178, 181–4, 192, 208–16, 229

  modern: and desire as lack, 101; as measured according to ownership of objects, 104, 192; and nominal language, 89, 92; as object, 101, 194, 199; as passive, 152; as self-identical, 199; as source of

representation, 90; and suicide, 95, 100–1

  postmodern: and death, 117; as negated, 109, 194, 199; as object, 114; as postponed, 114, 192; as punctiliar, 192; and representation, 110, 192; as self-identical, 110, 199

subjectivity: and collectivity, 170; erasure of, 86, 89. 90, 94–6; as perforce doxological, 46; and irony, 196; and place, 184

sun, icon of the: in Descartes, 71, 73; and Louis XIV, 86; in Plato, 11–12, 21, 71, 73

supplementation, 182–3, 212–13

Supplices te rogamus, 246

Suppositional logic, 49

Supra quae propitio, 251

Suscipe, sancta Trinitas, 199

Suscipiat Dominus sacrificium, 233–4

Swanson, R. N., 143–4, 158

Sylla, E. D., 139

syntax: asyndetic, 95ff; and Christ's language, 225–8; complex, 226ff; of *Credo*, 205ff; hypotactic, 226; and narrative speed, 224; paratactic, 226; transformations of, 56

Sypher, Wylie, 91

Te igitur, 179, 190, 224, 226

Theuth, Derrida on, 26, 34; as "Hermes of Egypt," 30; and Horus, 35; as inventor of liturgy, 27; and legitimate offspring, 34–5; as mediator, 35; and Osiris, 35; and Pan, 30; and Thamus, 9, 26–7; and violence, 34–5; and writing, 34–5

Tierney, Brian, 150, 153

time, 113; aesthetic (Kierkegaard), 224; and alleged humiliation of knowledge, 13; ambiguity of, 223; and apostrophe, 194; articulation of, 234–5; attenuation of, 224–5; and chronology, 226; as circumvented by sophists, 9; as deleterious, 9, 217; and desire, 139; and Eschaton, 221;

and the Eucharist, 159, 161, 165;
and experimental philosophers, 79;
and finance capital, 138; and "flux,"
116; and gift, 235–7; as
homogeneous, 139; and incense,
187; as independent variable, 139; as
linear, 98, 113, 139, 223, 237;
liturgical critique of, 221–6, 236; of
liturgical text, 217–18; measurement
of, 221; and motion, 139; and
nation-state, 126–7; and nouns, 91,
94–5; and orality, 116, 218; pagan
closure of, 221, 232; and prayer,
222; prefatory, 220–3, 231; and
"return," 221; and salvation history,
150, 206ff; as spatialized, 9, 60, 104,
109, 139, 150, 221; and
supplementation, 270; and violence,
237
theological body, the: early mediaeval
punctuation of, 158–9; reception of,
159; and time, 159; tripartite
structure of, 158–9, 172; traversal of,
159, 163, 165 see also, ecclesial body,
Eucharist, historical body,
sacramental body
theology: as necessary prelude to
doxology, 42–3; and Socratic
dialogues, 42ff
tokos, 7, 36
Toubert, Pierre, 140
Toulmin, S., 52, 73
Toussaert, Jacques, 165
transubstantiation: and Aquinas, 133,
259ff; and Calvin, 162; as condition
of possibility for meaning, 262–3;
diabolic, 110; and dimensional
reality, 133; and category of "fact,"
163, 255; as ecstatic gift, 255; and
hollowness, 256; and isolated
presence, 163, 165, 254–5, 260; and
language, 256; as logical conclusion
to doxology, 246; and mystery, 254;
as problematic, 162; and relation
between the Church and the
Eucharist, 162, 255, 259; and Scotist

voluntarism, 132–4; and separation
of "mystical" and "real," 161–4,
254–5; and social body, 131; and the
soul, 133–4; and substantial reality,
133; as symbol, 163, 254; and
synchrony, 163–4; and
transignification, 255; as verifiable,
163
Typhon, 44

Unde et memores, 180
univocity of being, 122–3; and actuality,
124–5; and analogy, 123, 126; and
attributes of God, 122–5, 132; and
contractualism, 123, 137; and
creatures, 123, 125; and distance
from God, 122–3; and equivocity,
123; and "formal distinction," 124;
and "intellectual distinction," 124;
and modalities of being, 123, 125;
and "real distinction," 124; and
virtuality, 125–6
unknown, the: and Aquinas, 128;
domestication of, 109, 113; and the
future, 113; as known, 109–10, 265;
and the mysterious, 109–14, 128,
194–6, 228; as nothingness, 109–10,
194–6; as object, 109; and
ontological distance (Scotus), 123;
and the secret, 257; as unanticipated,
(Levinas), 114; and virtual possibility
(Scotus), 127–8

Vatican II: critique of, 171–5; and failure
to challenge secularity, 171, 175;
and Greek Fathers, 172; liturgical
reforms of, 170; spatialized thinking
of, 175, 206
Vaux, Roland de, 222
Vere dignum, 235
Vidal-Naquet, P., 239
Virilio, Paul, 94
void, the: as arbitrarily primordial, 107;
gesture against, 70, 72, 99, 198–9;
gesture towards, 106ff; motion in,
139; as plenitude, 178, 228; as

superlative object, xiii, 73, 192, 234
see also nihil
voluntarism: and actualization of the
possible, 131; and baroque
absolutism, 86–7; and Bodin, 141;
and Boyle, 78; Cartesian, 135; and
the Decalogue, 135–6, 141; and
demise of charity, 156–7; and
distance, 123, 124; and Duns Scotus,
122ff; 135ff; and *erōs*, 135; and the
Eucharist, 132ff; and Kant, 137; and
knowledge, 130–2; and the nation-
state, 136; and ontic presence,
132–3; and paternity, 141; and the
soul, 134; and teleology, 135
Vovelle, Michel, 101–2

Wales, K., 93, 193
Walker, G., 144
Weaver, W., 98
Weber, Max, 149
Wells, Rulon, 93
Wenzel, Siegfried, 215
Whibley, L., 43
White, Graham, 132
Wieacker, Franz, 132, 136, 151
Williams, Rowan, 233, 243, 245, 249
Williams, Carlos Williams, 91
Willis, Geoffrey G., 175
Wippel, J. F., 122, 124
Wood-Legh, K. L., 165
world, the: and anxiety (Heidegger), 232;
fiction of, 238; and Lacoste, 232,
234, 236; liturgical displacement of,
189, 210–2, 232, 234, 236, 238;
machine of, 78; and paganism, 232;
as repository of matters of fact, 79;

and St Benedict, 232; and
worldlessness, 211
writing: and active/passive dichotomy,
21–2, 25, 36; alleged democracy of,
22–3, 26, 115; and capital, 6–10;
and liturgical contingency, 218; as
deathly, 8, 24–7, 103, 106, 115; and
Derrida, 4, 6, 20, 47, 69, 70, 103;
and Descartes, 69–72; as
disembodied, 4, 19, 22, 47, 116; and
forgetfulness, 25; hieroglyphic, 70;
as hypostasized, 8, 26, 116; and
ideality, 116; and liturgical language,
178, 199, 218–19; and the divine
Logos, 218–19; and Lysias, 44; and
memory, 19, 25, 219; as
metaphysical, 4, 8, 25, 47, 70, 115;
metaphysics of, 4, 8, 19, 19, 69;
mythic origins of, 24, 35; and
permanence, 19; and Platonic
dialogues, 43; as postponed value, 8,
115, 138; and presence, 8, 19, 69,
115–16; as sophistic, 4, 8; and the
soul, 19; and subjectivity, 72ff; and
suppression of difference, 6, 8, 26; as
transcendentally oral, 24–5; and
virtuality, 138
Wycherley, R. E., 15

Yates, F. A., 52–3, 62
Young, Frances, 208

Zaidman, L. B., 43, 239
Zilsel, Edgar, 50
Zink, Michel, 215
zōon, 26